The Tsar's Viceroys

Also by Richard G. Robbins, Jr.:

*Famine in Russia, 1891–1892: The Imperial
Government Responds to a Crisis*

THE TSAR'S VICEROYS

Russian Provincial Governors in

the Last Years of the Empire

Richard G. Robbins, Jr.

Cornell University Press

ITHACA AND LONDON

First published 1987 by Cornell University Press.

International Standard Book Number 0-8014-2046-6
Library of Congress Catalog Card Number 87–47700
Printed in the United States of America
*Librarians: Library of Congress cataloging information
appears on the last page of the book.*

*The paper in this book is acid-free and meets the guidelines for
permanence and durability of the Committee on Production Guidelines
for Book Longevity of the Council on Library Resources.*

For Carla and Nicholas

CONTENTS

European Russia in 1900: Provinces with zemstvos

PREFACE

For two centuries governors administered the provinces of the Russian Empire and thus the vast majority of the tsars' subjects. Yet these officers, the most important and powerful governmental figures outside the capitals, have been little studied. The last scholarly work about them appeared in 1905. Since then, historians either have ignored the governors or have discussed them only in the context of larger investigations of the Russian state and its institutions.

The paucity of literature about the governors seems strange at first glance, yet the reasons for scholarly neglect are not hard to understand. The subject is vast, the source materials are enormous and widely scattered. Prodigies of research would be required to produce a definitive work.

I make no such claim for this book. I have concentrated on the period 1880 to 1914, but even within this narrow time frame I do not cover many of the developments that affected the governors. Nor does this study treat all the provinces of the empire. Instead, it focuses on European Russia and on those gubernias where zemstvos and other institutions of self-government were to be found. The approach of this book is limited, too. I have attempted an exercise in description and analysis. I seek to show who the governors were, how they functioned, and why they acted as they did.

Because it is impossible to reconstruct the "typical" day of a "typical" governor in a "typical" province, I have selected and woven together a variety of incidents—some of them very petty indeed—in a way that illustrates the nature and style of gubernatorial administration. Throughout the book I try to present the governors in the light of ordinary events, to show them in the midst of their lives and work, coping with a wide range of problems, dealing with institutions, groups, and individuals at both the national and local levels. This approach gives little space to major crises or efforts at reform. What results instead, I hope, is a nuanced portrayal of the operation of provincial government which makes possible a better understanding of the way Russians ruled and were ruled in the last years of the old regime.

Work on this book began in 1974 under the auspices of a grant from the Research Allocations Committee of the University of New Mexico. The next year I continued my studies in the congenial and supportive atmosphere of the Russian Institute at Columbia University, thanks to a generous Senior Fellowship. In 1976 and again in 1981 the International Research and Exchanges Board made it possible for me to travel to the Soviet Union and to use the libraries and archives there. In 1981 my stay in Russia was financed in large part by a Fulbright-Hays Fellowship. I was able to fill many gaps in my research by participation in the University of Illinois's Summer Research Laboratory on Russia and East Europe.

I am especially grateful to the archives in which I obtained so many valuable materials: the Bakhmeteff Archive at Columbia University, the Central State Archive of the October Revolution, the Central State Archive of Literature and Art, the Central State Historical Archive, the Central State Historical Archive of Moscow, the Leningrad State Historical Archive, the Manuscript Divisions of the Lenin and Saltykov-Shchedrin libraries, and the State Archive of the Kalinin Region. The skill and courtesy of the staffs of these institutions always made my work both pleasant and profitable.

Equally profound is the debt I owe to the many people who helped me complete this study. Marc Raeff supported the project from the beginning and gave freely of his knowledge and insight. The late Petr Andreevich Zaionchkovskii permitted me to use his own unpublished research and pointed me in the direction of many valuable archival sources. W. Bruce Lincoln, Daniel Orlovsky, Samuel Ramer, and Theodore Taranovski all read and commented on the work before its publication. Words cannot express my thanks for their suggestions and encouragement. Others also read portions of the book at various stages of completion and gave me the benefit of their opinions. Boris Vasil'evich Anan'ich, Thomas Fallows, Nancy Frieden, Dominic Lieven, and William Wagner all have my deep gratitude. John Ackerman and Marilyn Sale of Cornell University Press provided much-appreciated support and encouragement. Raúl García was a diligent and sensitive copy editor.

I also thank *The Slavonic and East European Review* for permission to include in Chapter 2 material that originally appeared in my article "Choosing the Russian Governors: The Professionalization of the Gubernatorial Corps," published in volume 58, no. 4 (1980), of that journal.

I owe a special debt to my wife, Catherine, for her support, help, and patience. She put up with my long absences in the Soviet Union, endured my involvement with research and writing, read the often dreary prose that resulted, and tried, using her considerable editorial skills, to give it a proper shape. Her tolerance for the Russian governors and for their historian was far greater than either deserved.

RICHARD G. ROBBINS, JR.

Albuquerque, New Mexico

AUTHOR'S NOTES

Names and Terms

All Russian family names and, with the exception of those of the emperors, all Christian names and patronymics are transliterated according to the Library of Congress system. Place names are given as in Russian but without internal or final soft signs. Most administrative terms are provided with an English translation, but I occasionally use the Russian originals to avoid monotony. Thus *guberniia,* though translated as province, is also anglicized as gubernia. *Uezd* is translated as county and, without italics, is also treated as an English word. *Gubernator* is, of course, always translated as governor, but for stylistic reasons a much-needed synonym, *nachal'nik gubernii,* is regularly employed. A glossary of the most important Russian terms and their English equivalents can be found at the end of the book.

Archival Citations

In citing materials from Soviet archives, I have deviated somewhat from the generally accepted practice. Instead of referring to a collection (*fond*) by its number, I employ an abbreviated name. When citing a particular file (*delo),* I include, where appropriate, the title found on the folder. In addition, I have chosen to use p. and pp. instead of l. and ll. (*list* and *listy).*

The following standard abbreviations are also used:

ch.:	*chast'.*
d.:	*delo.*
f.:	*fond.*
op.:	*opis'.*

A complete list of the archives and collections consulted is included in the bibliography.

THE TSAR'S VICEROYS

— I —

Introduction

As the train pulled into the station at Bendery, Sergei Dmitrievich Urusov, the newly appointed governor of Bessarabia, gazed from the window of his special railway car with consternation. Despite his expressed wishes, a large welcoming crowd waited on the platform. The vice-governor, in full uniform, was at the head of the delegation, flanked by high-ranking members of the local police and other provincial officials. In a passageway between two sections of the crowd, Urusov saw the mayor, also in uniform, wearing the chain that was the emblem of his office and holding a platter with bread and salt. Behind the mayor stood his subordinates in city government.

Urusov had hoped to avoid this kind of display. It was not necessary, and he was certain that at least a portion of those gathered to greet him had no desire to be there and were silently cursing his name. They had turned out because of curiosity or in fear that their absence would be taken as an affront. Mostly, however, they had come because of tradition. The citizens of the province had welcomed Urusov's predecessors this way and would, no doubt, do the same for his successors.

Sergei Dmitrievich himself had a role to play in this customary drama. When the vice-governor and the police entered his car, Urusov chatted with them briefly, then stepped down from the train onto the station platform. He went over to the mayor, returned his greeting, and accepted the proffered gift of bread and salt. He then talked for a few minutes with the government officials, trying to assure them that he enjoyed at least some familiarity with their city and region. Mounting the platform of his car once more, Urusov thanked the public for coming to meet him and raised his hand to his cap in salute. The onlookers doffed their hats and replied with a loud "Hurrah!" The train started. An hour and a half later Urusov arrived in Kishinev, the provincial capital.

Driving in an open carriage down the Alexandrovskaia, the central arterial of the city, Urusov again confronted crowds. Men, women, and children stood tightly packed on the sidewalks. As Sergei Dmitrievich passed, some bowed, others waved their handkerchiefs, a few even fell to their knees. Urusov's party stopped first at the cathedral, where a brief service asked God's blessing on the work that lay ahead. This done, His Excellency rode directly to his official residence. The tsar's viceroy was ready to assume the powers of his office.[1]

The ceremonies that surrounded the installation of the new governor of a Russian province were often remarkably spare—no banners, no bugles, no public inauguration. Upon his arrival at the gubernatorial mansion, His Excellency usually spoke briefly with the major officials of the gubernia administration who had assembled to greet him. Facing a gathering of people unknown to him, the governor could voice only a few platitudes about duty, hard work, and honesty. Later, he would meet the chief representatives of the nobility, the leaders of the institutions of local self-government, and other provincial dignitaries. Everything was quite informal and on a modest scale.[2] And while His Excellency acquainted himself with the circumstances of his post, the workers of the provincial offices went about their tasks. The governor's service record was filed in its proper place, and clerks drew up the required lists of the amount of available cash and the number of papers in process on the day that command of the gubernia changed hands.

The arrival of a new governor was an important moment in the life of a Russian province, one that generated a variety of emotions: anxiety, curiosity, hope, but never indifference. A change of governors meant much more than the substitution of a different cog in the wheel of local administration. It might signify a new style of rule, new personnel. Those who had enjoyed power and influence in the gubernia

---

1. The source for this account is Serge D. Urussov [Urusov in text], *Memoirs of a Russian Governor*, trans. by Herman Rosenthal (London and New York, 1908), pp. 10–12.

2. Ibid.; I. F. Koshko, *Vospominaniia gubernatora (1905–1914): Novgorod, Samara, Penza* (Petrograd, 1916), pp. 115, 139; N. N. Kisel'-Zagorianskii, "Les Mémoires du Général Kissel-Zagorianskii," pp. 180–82, Bakhmeteff Archive, Columbia University [hereafter BAR], Kisel'-Zagorianskii papers.

Sergei D. Urusov, governor of Bessarabia and Tver

feared that they would be cast down. Their rivals savored the prospect of acquiring authority. Among the lower ranks of society, there were also rumors and expectations. Did the incoming governor carry a special commission from the tsar? Had he been sent to right some wrong, to punish some offender?

In distant St. Petersburg, too, hopes and fears focused on the new governor. His arrival signaled a fresh start in the never-ending struggle to secure the proper management of provincial affairs. Much would be asked of the man who was now *nachal'nik gubernii*. Ideally, he ought to be "a rock against which all currents break,"[3] able to contend with the needs and strivings of local people as well as the demands of the central authorities. But ministers in the capital knew that this ideal was seldom realized. The chances for error were great. Even men who had served many years in posts designed to prepare them for a governorship might stumble on the rocky ground of provincial problems and politics. Every new appointment held at least as many risks as opportunities.

Thus the lack of pomp accompanying the governor's assumption of his duties did not mean that the office he held was unimportant. Rather, it betokened the curious position that the *nachal'nik gubernii* occupied. The law stated that he was a viceroy—the personal representative of the sovereign emperor. But the development of the imperial administration in the course of the nineteenth century also made the governor the local agent of the Ministry of Internal Affairs (MVD), a fact that often put him at odds with the provincial officers of the other central ministries who looked to their own superiors in St. Petersburg for orders and guidance. Finally, the structure of gubernia politics which had emerged from the era of the Great Reforms confronted the governor with independent institutions of self-government, bodies that enjoyed considerable autonomy and authority.

From the beginning of his tenure, then, the governor was engaged in a delicate balancing act, attempting to coordinate and lead the various local forces without offending them. A low profile could be useful in this effort and, consequently, a governor often passed his first days in office with a minimum of public show. Anything else might be seen as an effort at self-glorification, something certain to provoke resentment and opposition.

The office Prince Urusov assumed with some reluctance in the early summer of 1903 had been centuries in the making. Although the basic duties and functions of the governor were not fully defined until the

3. Urussov, p. 3.

reigns of Nicholas I and Alexander II, provincial administration rested on the institutional structures Catherine II developed in the years between 1775 and 1785. Peter the Great first divided Russia into provinces and introduced the title *gubernator*. But the roots of the governorship were deeper and more ancient.

As the Muscovite state expanded in the course of the fourteenth and fifteenth centuries, her rulers sought a means of administering their new domains. They did so by appointing territorial officials to govern the subject populations. Initially called *namestniki* and *volosteli* and later *voevody*, these officers assumed two main duties: extracting revenues for the prince and maintaining law and order.[4] In fulfilling these general obligations, the local princely agents performed many ancillary functions. Beyond supervising the collection of taxes, they carried out broad peacekeeping and military operations, commanding troops against foreign enemies and those who disturbed the domestic tranquillity. They also acted as judges in criminal and civil cases, overseeing the work of local courts.

The system of provincial administration created by the Muscovite tsars was extremely rudimentary, corrupt, and weak. Governmental institutions at the local level barely existed. The *namestniki, volosteli,* and *voevody* proved difficult to control because of the great distances that separated them from the capital and the often inadequate direction provided by the central administrative departments (*prikazy*). As a result their rule was often highly exploitative, and they "fed" on the people with voracious appetites.[5]

An even greater deficiency was the limited ability of the tsars' appointed officials to make any significant contribution to the betterment of local conditions. This inadequacy stemmed from the traditional Muscovite conception of government that restricted the state to de-

---

4. Prior to the reforms of Ivan IV in the middle of the sixteenth century, *namestniki* presided over urban areas and *volosteli* governed rural districts. In the 1650s both these offices were abolished and replaced by elected officials. The social chaos of the Time of Troubles effectively destroyed local self-administration, and the *voevody*, originally military officials in frontier areas, were established to rule the major towns and districts of the Muscovite state.

5. Originally, *namestniki* and *volosteli* received no salary but were allowed to "feed" themselves at the expense of the districts they governed. Under this arrangement, known as *kormlenie*, these officials could keep certain court fees and were permitted to extract payments in kind. The amount of "food" they were entitled to was fixed by charter. *Kormlenie* was officially abolished under Ivan the Terrible, but the *voevody* of the seventeenth century continued to exploit the population. On the corruption of the *voevody* and efforts to control them, see B. N. Chicherin, *Oblastnye uchrezhdeniia Rossii v XVII veke* (Moscow, 1856), pp. 290–93, 302–5, 310–30.

fense, keeping the peace internally, and raising the men and revenues necessary for these tasks. As long as Muscovy was largely isolated, such an attitude posed few problems, but toward the end of the seventeenth century, Russia established more regular contact with European countries. In those societies new ideas about government prevailed and states assumed broad powers to regulate society and to improve human life. By the late 1600s, this new attitude toward administration began to have increasing appeal in Russia. The stage was set for Peter the Great.

Through his reforms Peter reshaped the system of provincial administration and created new offices and new territorial divisions. Moreover, the first emperor assigned to his local officials tasks that went far beyond those the Muscovite tsars had required of their territorial representatives. No longer would government officers simply engage in the passive defense of the state and the preservation of law and order. Now they would be involved actively in welfare and economic growth. They would assume responsibility for the expansion of trade and commerce, the maintenance of food supplies, the upkeep of roads, the proper ordering of factories, the education and moral development of the population. The instructions to local officials which capped Peter's provincial reforms set the imperial government on a course that would last until its demise in 1917.[6]

In the process of altering provincial administration, Peter posed many of the enduring problems of Russian local governance. How should the functions of the state be divided between the center and the gubernias? Were the men who presided over these administrative units to be given wide latitude to rule on the basis of their personal ties with the sovereign, or were they to be subordinated to bureaucratic agencies in the capital? To what degree and in what capacity could local people participate in the government of the regions where they lived?

Peter's reforms addressed all these issues, but they provided no consistent answers. Initially, the tsar appeared to favor the deconcentration of power, a strong, viceregal provincial chief, and fairly considerable public involvement in local rule. Between 1707 and 1710 Peter dismantled most of the central administration and transferred much of the machinery of government to the ten huge gubernias he had created. Next, the tsar appointed governors (*gubernatory*) to rule these territories, men who enjoyed his personal favor, and with whom he regularly

---

6. See in particular Peter's instructions (*nakazy*) to his *voevody* and local commissars (*zemskie kommisary*) issued in January 1719. *Polnoe sobranie zakonov rossiiskoi imperii* (hereafter PSZ), 1st ser., nos. 3294 and 3295.

consulted on matters of state. Finally, Peter permitted the nobility a share of power. In 1714 he issued a decree calling on the local gentry to elect councilors (*landraty*) to advise the governors on the administration of the provinces. The law stipulated that when his councilors met, the governor was to preside; but he was to function "not as a ruler, but as a president."[7]

Yet Peter was quickly disenchanted with his initial reform, and after 1719 he attempted another governmental restructuring based on different principles. A series of new measures reconstituted and strengthened the central administration. Many of the functions the tsar had earlier given to the gubernias he now transferred to the Senate and the colleges in St. Petersburg.

Peter's second reform downgraded the office of governor because the gubernia ceased to be the primary territorial unit of the state. Instead, the provintsias, created as subdivisions of the gubernias in 1712, now became the most important administrative districts. Their chief officers might be called governors-general, governors, or vice-governors; but most frequently they held the ancient title of *voevoda*. Although they were independent of the governors who ruled the gubernias in almost all matters, these new provincial chiefs did not enjoy the power or position of Peter's earlier viceroys. The 1719 reform required the men who ruled the provintsias to share authority with a variety of independent agencies, representatives of the central colleges, local military commanders, and the courts.

Peter's second provincial reform tried, as had his first, to involve the local nobility in the work of governance. The *landraty,* created earlier, had not worked as he had intended. The electoral principle had seldom been applied, and these officials, who were supposed to advise the governors, had instead quickly become their direct subordinates.[8] Now Peter introduced a new elected local officer with much more modest functions. Beginning in 1724, the nobility was permitted to choose local commissars (*zemskie komissary*) to assist in the collection of the soul tax.[9] But like the *landraty,* these officers soon lost their autonomy and were converted into agents of the state.[10] They were

7. *Ocherki istorii SSSR, period feodalizma: Rossiia v pervoi chetverti XVIII v., preobrazovaniia Petra I* (Moscow, 1954), p. 324.

8. A. A. Kizevetter, *Mestnoe samoupravlenie v Rossii, IX–XIX st.: Istoricheskii ocherk* (Moscow, 1910), pp. 100–103.

9. Another official, also called a *zemskii komissar*, was created in 1719. He was not elected, but appointed by the Kamer-Kollegiia. See M. M. Bogoslovskii, *Oblastnaia reforma Petra Velikogo: Provintsiia 1719–27 gg.* (Moscow, 1902), pp. 140–41.

10. Ibid., pp. 434–36.

abolished, along with many other aspects of Peter's provincial reform, in 1727.

The gubernia reforms of the Petrine era failed: the empire lacked the financial and human resources necessary to support the large network of offices and officials Peter had envisioned, and the underdevelopment of the nation's social classes doomed the experiments in self-government. These weaknesses, in combination with the inconsistencies of Peter's own governmental conceptions, meant that by the time of his death in 1725 Russian provincial administration was a tangled mess. Peter's successors would spend nearly half a century trying to sort things out.[11]

For all the shortcomings of his attempts to restructure the provinces, however, Peter left a significant legacy. He had established an activist style of local government, introduced the idea that the provincial chief should be an official with wide powers derived from his personal connection to the autocrat, raised the issue of decentralization, and tried to make possible public participation in gubernia administration. Although none of the rulers between 1725 and 1762 built successfully on the foundations he had laid down, his efforts were not forgotten. When Catherine II came to the throne, she drew on many of Peter's ideas. Combining these with more up-to-date theories of government and the expressed wishes of her articulate subjects, she eventually crafted a new set of institutions for the Russian provinces.

Indeed, Catherine turned her attention to the reform of provincial government immediately after seizing power. One of her first steps was to restore the viceregal status of the governor. Her instruction (*nastavlenie*) of 21 April 1764 declared the governor to be the "master of the province" (*khoziain gubernii*), a person enjoying the favor and trust of the sovereign. Catherine freed the governors from the supervision of the colleges, making them responsible only to herself and to the Senate.[12] At the same time, other reforms expanded the duties of the governors and provided them more and better paid subordinates. Through these measures, the empress hoped to revitalize the provinces and their government, but she was only partially successful. By the middle years of her reign, Catherine became convinced that a much more complete overhaul of local administration was necessary, and in

---

11. The most thorough discussion of provincial administration during the years between Peter I and Catherine II is Iu. V. Got'e's magisterial *Istoriia oblastnogo upravleniia v Rossii ot Petra I do Ekateriny II*, 2 vols. (Moscow, 1913–41). On the governors in this period, see John P. LeDonne, "The Evolution of the Governor's Office, 1727–64," *Canadian-American Slavic Studies* 12 (Spring 1978): 86–115.

12. PSZ, 1st ser., no. 12137.

the decade between 1775 and 1785, she attempted to put her ideas into practice.

Catherine's gubernia reforms sought to combine personal autocracy, regular institutions and procedures, and class self-government in a decentralized setting. The law of 1775 redrew the empire's administrative units.[13] It abolished the provintsias, leaving the gubernias and uezds as the only territorial divisions, and determined their boundaries on the basis of population. A gubernia was to have between 300,000 and 400,000 people; an uezd from 20,000 to 30,000. As a result, the twenty-five gubernias that existed in 1775 became forty-one, and later grew to fifty. The number of uezds almost tripled.[14]

In keeping with her desire for personal rule, Catherine decreed that a governor-general or *namestnik* should head the administration of a province. The governor-general was a true viceroy, representing the empress in her absence. Chosen by the sovereign, he enjoyed the right to communicate with her directly and could also sit in the Senate to voice the interests of his province. The governor-general was to be an active administrator and to make, in conjunction with various collegial bodies, the major decisions affecting local government. In addition, the *namestnik* was the supervisor of provincial institutions and acted as a guardian of legality, though he was not a judicial official.

Directly subordinate to the governor-general was the governor, who was in charge of much of the day-to-day functioning of provincial administration. His duties were not fully spelled out in the 1775 legislation, but the earlier instruction of 1764 undoubtedly served as a guide, modified by the directives of the governor-general. And indeed, in those circumstances when the *namestnik* was absent, the 1764 law was the binding regulation.[15]

The law of 1775 created a number of other institutions and offices. The most important of these was the provincial board (*gubernskoe pravlenie*). Chaired by the *namestnik,* its membership included the governor, the provincial procurator, two councilors (*sovetniki*) appointed by the Senate, and various clerks and assistants. According to the statute, the board was "to govern the entire province in the name of Her Majesty," but its powers were ill defined and its function largely consultative.[16]

13. PSZ, 1st ser., no. 14392, 7 November 1775.

14. Robert E. Jones, *The Emancipation of the Russian Nobility, 1762–1785* (Princeton, N.J., 1973), p. 222.

15. John P. LeDonne, *Ruling Russia: Politics and Administration in the Age of Absolutism* (Princeton, N.J., 1984), p. 73.

16. PSZ, 1st ser., no. 14392, art. 95.

Alongside the provincial board, there was a fiscal chamber (*kazennaia palata*), headed by the vice-governor, which oversaw gubernia finances and a welfare board (*prikaz obshchestvennogo prizreniia*), in charge of schools, hospitals, and various kinds of public assistance. The legislation of 1775 created new judicial bodies—the criminal court, the civil court, and the court of conscience—as well as special class courts for the free citizens of the province. The new gubernia structure also included the office of procurator, to which Catherine assigned great importance. Their basic duty was to see that the laws were understood and obeyed and that state agencies worked with proper dispatch and stayed within their assigned limits. Because the gubernia procurators were directly subordinate to the procurator-general in St. Petersburg and independent of the provincial administration, they served to review its decisions and the work of all local officials. They were supposed to protect citizens from the abuses of the police and the bureaucracy.

In the uezds, Catherine established a system of self-administration for the key social classes. Except for the fiscal agents and the city police, local government officials were elected. The law of 1775 and the patents (*zhalovannye gramoty*) to the nobility and the towns instituted corporate organization for the *dvorianstvo* and the inhabitants of Russian cities.[17] The nobles could assemble every three years to consider and to implement measures to meet the needs of their estate. They elected marshals (*predvoditeli*) at both the province and uezd levels and chose the chief police official of the rural areas (*kapitan ispravnik*). The towns also received extensive powers to handle their own affairs through elected city councils and mayors.

Catherine's reform of the provinces was a major turning point in the internal history of Russia. For the first time there now existed a unified territorial administration and a comprehensive network of provincial institutions. Their creation was accompanied by a significant shift of power from the center to the gubernias, though the empress maintained a direct contact with the provinces and the people through her governors-general. On paper, at least, Catherine appeared to have squared a number of circles by combining personal autocracy with decentralization and expanding bureaucracy while fostering self-government.

The gubernia statute and subsequent legislation constituted an important moment in the history of the governorship as well. In one sense, the office was downgraded by the reform, for the title *guber-*

17. PSZ, 1st ser., 21 April 1785, nos. 16187 and 16188.

nator was given to men who presided over gubernias that were not much larger than the provintsias formerly ruled by the *voevody*. Moreover, the governors were now exclusively civil officials; most of the military powers they had possessed under previous laws were taken away. The governors were also subjected to the control of governors-general, so their office was one step further removed from the source of power.

Yet Catherine's legislation and administrative practices ultimately increased the power and the status of the governors. In the first place, the men who now held the office were one or two ranks above the pre-reform *voevody;* their salaries and expense allowances were significantly greater.[18] More important, the effective subordination of the governors to the *namestniki* did not prove enduring. For reasons that remain obscure, Catherine never assigned each province a governor-general.[19] Rather, she developed the practice of combining several gubernias into a single viceroyalty (*namestnichestvo*). The governor-generalship thus became an extraordinary and, in the end, a superfluous institution. The distance of the *namestnik* from the local scene left most of provincial administration in the governor's hands. By the time of Catherine's death, the title of governor-general was largely a formal one, and several viceroyalties stood vacant. In 1797 her successor, Paul I, abolished the *namestniki* and assigned most of their powers and viceregal status to the governors.[20]

Simultaneously, the authority of the governors was also enhanced because the institutions of self-government created under the terms of the provincial reforms had not worked as Catherine had planned. Poverty and cultural limitations made it impossible for either the *dvorianstvo* or the urban dwellers to take full advantage of their rights under Catherine's legislation. The tradition of administrative dominance in local affairs was too great, the corporate organization and consciousness of the various estates too weak to sustain genuine auton-

18. LeDonne, *Ruling Russia*, pp. 71–72.

19. LeDonne argues that the governor-generalship was simply a sinecure designed by Potemkin as a way of rewarding his friends and placating leading generals whose good will he wished to obtain (ibid., p. 74). Robert E. Jones sharply questions this contention in his review of LeDonne's study (*American Historical Review* 90 [October 1985]: 981).

20. M. V. Klochkov, *Ocherki pravitel'stvennoi deiatel'nosti vremeni Pavla I* (Petrograd, 1916), pp. 428–29. The governors-general were restored during the reign of Alexander I, but they remained extraordinary officials. Nineteenth-century practice was to assign them to frontier and non-Russian territories. For a thorough discussion of the office, see K. Sokolov, "Ocherk istorii i sovremennogo znacheniia general-gubernatora," *Vestnik prava* 33 (September 1903): 110–79; (October 1903): 39–75.

omy. Moreover, those who followed Catherine on the throne, most notably Paul and Nicholas I, curtailed the powers of class institutions in favor of a more bureaucratic style of rule.

At the beginning of the nineteenth century, then, the governors presided over a more or less integrated gubernia administration, unchecked either by the intrusion of central officers or by local institutions of self-government. Moreover, Paul had eliminated the supervision of the governors-general, weakened the powers of the independent procuracy, and made the governors true viceroys.[21] Yet these halcyon days would not last long. The trend of the age was one of centralization. Paul planned to restore the central colleges and turn them into ministries with a national scope of activity.[22] After 1801 Alexander I developed and implemented his father's policy of reconcentrating power in St. Petersburg.

The creation of the ministries in 1802 was an important step both in the process of centralization and in the regularization of autocratic government. By the beginning of the nineteenth century, Russian administration had grown in size and complexity to the point where it was impossible for a single individual to control and direct all aspects of its activity. Ministries were seen as a way of bringing order to the state, rationalizing the processes of decision making and coordinating the execution of policy. They were also viewed as a means of minimizing imperial caprice, which had had such unfortunate consequences during the reign of Paul.

The ministries would have significant impact on the governors. Their introduction and subsequent growth during the reigns of Alexander I and Nicholas I destroyed the territorial administrative system Catherine had established by means of her gubernia statute. The ministries now stood as intermediary instances between the *nachal'niki gubernii* and the sovereign. Moreover these new central institutions quickly began gaining control of portions of the gubernia administration and their attendant personnel. The Ministry of Finance soon held sway over the fiscal chamber; the Ministry of Justice subordinated the provincial courts. The Ministry of Court and Appanage Lands opened its own local offices. The Ministry of Education divided the empire into six large educational districts whose borders transcended those of the gubernias; the Ministry of War set up a similar system of eight military districts for the army command.[23]

21. Klochkov, *Ocherki*, pp. 418–29.

22. Ibid., pp. 398–406; Daniel T. Orlovsky, *The Limits of Reform: The Ministry of Internal Affairs in Imperial Russia, 1802–1881* (Cambridge, Mass., 1981), p. 17.

23. N. P. Eroshkin, *Istoriia gosudarstvennykh uchrezhdenii dorevoliutsionnoi Rossii*, 2d ed. (Moscow, 1968), pp. 180–92.

The governors, too, came under the increasing control of the Ministry of Internal Affairs. The MVD assumed a major role in selecting, rewarding, and punishing these officials, and wherever possible, it sought to underline their subordination. But the MVD also tried to increase gubernatorial power to make the *nachal'niki gubernii* more effective local agents. In pursuit of this goal the ministry reduced the status of the provincial board and converted the "highest institution in the province" into little more than a second gubernatorial chancellery. The MVD also gave the governors a more effective means of maintaining law and order. In 1837 it created the district (*stan*) police, and for the first time the governors had a network of local constables who were directly under their control.

Yet ministerial authority over the governors was far from perfect, and the MVD never really succeeded in making the *nachal'niki gubernii* completely part of a bureaucratic system. Despite the ministry's best efforts, the governors remained viceroys, creatures of the emperors and linked to them directly. Their special status reflected the autocrats' own ambivalence toward their ministerial creation and their unwillingness to abandon fully the practice of personal rule.

For although the tsars sought to use the ministries in order to achieve greater control and to govern their empire more effectively, they also wished to keep themselves independent of their powerful subordinates. As a consequence, the emperors were reluctant to create a united ministerial system, and Russia would not have an official prime minister before 1905. Until then, and even afterward, the autocrats played one minister off against another and were always ready to rely on favorites or create special agencies to elude the established bureaucracy.[24]

The perpetuation of the governors' viceregal status must be seen in this context, for the governors were one of the means the emperors used to circumvent the developing bureaucratic structure. Alexander I appointed a number of his influential personal friends to governorships and enhanced the power of the office both in the provinces and at the center.[25] Nicholas I gave governors he had chosen special assignments to carry out in his name.[26] More significant, in 1837 he pulled together all the existing legislation on the governors and issued

---

24. Orlovsky, *Limits*, pp. 1–12, presents an excellent discussion of ministerial power and the relation between the emperors and their ministers.

25. Marc Raeff, *Michael Speransky, Statesman of Imperial Russia, 1772–1839* (The Hague, 1957), p. 234.

26. "Zapiski V. M. Zhemchuzhnikova: Iz posmertnikh bumag," *Vestnik Evropy* 34 (February 1899): 657–58.

a new regulation for the office that preserved their dual position as imperial viceroys and ministerial agents.

The instruction (*nakaz*) to the governors was a substantial document of eighty pages and some 340 separate articles. It reaffirmed the governors' status as the chief representatives of the tsar and the central government in the provinces, guardians of legality, and the general supervisors of all local administration. The regulation listed specific areas of gubernatorial concern including the maintenance of law and order, famine relief, and public health. It also detailed the rights of the governors vis-à-vis local fiscal institutions, the courts and the military, outlined the procedures to be carried out when governors took over or surrendered a province, enumerated the kinds of reports they were to submit to different agencies, and stipulated the proper form of communication with various government institutions and officials. The instruction stated that the governor was a subordinate of the Ministry of Internal Affairs but affirmed his right to correspond with other ministries and they with him. Most important of all, the instruction stressed the governor's tie with the emperor, particularly the right of direct, personal communication.[27]

Nicholas's instruction was not an innovation and neither altered the position of the governors nor increased their powers.[28] But it made clear where they stood. At the same time, the *nakaz* demonstrated that the governorship was beginning to sink under the weight of its accumulated obligations. The enormous list of specific duties a governor was expected to carry out, the variety of papers he had to read and approve, the number of institutions he was supposed to inspect, and the quantity of reports he was required to make, all pointed to the fact that the burdens attached to the office had grown to such an extent that they now exceeded the capacity of a single person. Subsequent investigations by the MVD confirmed what the law implied. By the 1840s, the governors chaired eighteen committees and boards. Even a cursory handling of the many papers they received required over four hours daily.[29]

What had caused this lamentable situation? In large part it was the result of the ministerial system itself, which had fragmented provincial administration, vastly increased the amount of paper work the gover-

27. PSZ, 2d ser., 3 June 1837, no. 10303.

28. I. M. Strakhovskii, "Gubernskoe ustroistvo," *Zhurnal ministerstva iustitsii* 19 (September 1913): 68; S. Frederick Starr, *Decentralization and Self-Government in Russia, 1830–1870* (Princeton, N.J., 1972), p. 34.

29. I. Blinov, *Gubernatory: Istoriko-iuridicheskii ocherk* (St. Petersburg, 1905), p. 161.

nors had to contend with, and made necessary a variety of committees whose functions included coordinating the activities of the many independent gubernia agencies. Another problem was the general weakness of provincial bureaucracy. Local officials were too few and too poorly trained to handle the steadily increasing volume of provincial business. Their failure put even greater pressures on the *nachal'niki gubernii*.

Finally, there were the difficulties provoked by the provincial institutions of class self-administration. Existing legislation and governmental practice had rendered the corporate organizations of the nobility and the towns virtually impotent and hence unable to serve local interests effectively. The few quasi-governmental duties they exercised were carried out under heavy state tutelage. They could not lighten the governor's load, but may have increased it. Yet weak as they were, local class institutions, especially those of the nobility, could cause the governor trouble. They retained the ability to appeal to the center and even to the emperor. Thus they could bring down on the head of the *nachal'nik gubernii* the ire of St. Petersburg authorities.

In the context of a fragmented and underinstitutionalized provincial government, the governor found it increasingly difficult to exercise the power the laws afforded him. Instead, the *nachal'nik gubernii* was forced to engage in a kind of balancing act. Writing in 1827, Sergei Uvarov, who would later serve as Nicholas I's minister of education, aptly summed up the governor's dilemma:

> In order to maintain his authority, the governor is compelled either to form a party among the various [local] powers or engage in war with all of them. In the first case, there results a struggle of subtlety and intrigue, in the second, complete anarchy. . . . A conjunction of happy accidents, upon which a governor cannot always count, is necessary if he is to keep his equilibrium in such a dangerous situation. Truly, there is something peculiar in the position of a man who enjoys the title of chief without the corresponding authority and who can wield power only through guile or scandal.[30]

The government of Nicholas I was well aware of the deficiencies of provincial administration and the difficulties confronting the governors, but it restricted itself to a few palliatives. Only with the fall of Sevastopol and the start of a new reign did serious efforts at change begin. The reform era of the 1860s and 1870s once again took up the fundamental questions of provincial administration: decentralization,

30. Cited in Strakhovskii, "Gubernskoe ustroistvo" (September 1913), p. 62.

local institutional structures, public participation in governance, and the nature of gubernatorial power.

The *nachal'niki gubernii* were naturally concerned with these issues, and during the debate on the reforms they became an important lobbying group. Chief among their goals was the resuscitation of the vice-regal governorship and the reintegration of gubernia administration under their command. Governors wanted to reduce the ability of the central ministries to interfere at the gubernia level, and so they proposed to give to the provincial boards the power to coordinate the work of all local governmental agencies. The governors were particularly concerned to wrest control of gubernia treasuries from the Ministry of Finance and thereby reduce their own financial dependence on the center. But the governors were equally bold in demanding increased power vis-à-vis the provincial offices of the Ministries of State Properties and War.

The governors also addressed the problem of provincial under-institutionalization. A major concern of theirs was the police, which they saw as overburdened, poorly paid, corrupt, and inefficient. The governors urged a number of changes: make the rural police chiefs (*ispravniki*) appointed state officials; consolidate city and uezd police forces; and raise salaries. But this would not be enough; public and class institutions would have had to play a significant part in the reformed gubernias. Consequently, the governors backed a plan that would transfer a large portion of the economic duties of the police into the hands of new, elective institutions of self-government.[31]

The results of the reforms disappointed the governors' hopes. No significant devolution of power to the provinces took place. Instead, the local authority of the central ministries increased and, as a result, the *nachal'niki gubernii* became more dependent on the MVD.[32] The court and self-government reforms in particular heightened the fragmentation of gubernia administration. The restructuring of the judiciary in 1864 firmly separated the courts and the administration and ended the governors' power to intervene in legal proceedings or to confirm court decisions.[33] The zemstvo law (1864) and the statute on

31. Starr, *Decentralization*, pp. 129–33; Robert J. Abbot, "Police Reform in Russia, 1858–1878" (Ph.D. diss., Princeton, 1971), pp. 81–87.

32. George L. Yaney, *The Systematization of Russian Government: Social Evolution in the Domestic Administration of Imperial Russia, 1711–1905* (Urbana, Ill., 1973), pp. 242–43; 330–37.

33. On the new court system see N. N. Efremova, *Ministerstvo iustitsii rossiiskoi imperii, 1802–1917* (Moscow, 1983), pp. 70–72; Eroshkin, *Istoriia*, pp. 241–46; Samuel Kucherov, *Courts, Lawyers and Trials under the Last Three Tsars* (New York, 1953), pp. 32–36.

municipal government (1870) created elective institutions and gave them most of the economic and social functions once carried out by the gubernia administration.[34] Moreover, the prevailing ideology of the reforms—the "social" theory of self-government—deemed these institutions to be outside the state structure and thus largely independent of the governors.

The end result of the Great Reforms was to reduce significantly the power the governors could wield. To be sure, they remained viceroys, representatives of an autocratic sovereign whose power was unlimited. In law they continued to be independent of all ministerial hierarchies (*vnevedomstvennyi*). They still had general responsibilities for all that transpired within the provinces entrusted to their care. But the changes wrought in the early 1860s stripped the governors of most of their capacity for positive command, except within the narrow confines of police duties. In other areas, governors could stop, temporarily at least, agencies and individuals from taking actions that they believed were illegal. But the *nachal'niki gubernii* seldom had the last word in such disputes. Those who objected to the governors' actions could take their cause to the courts or to the Senate.

The reforms also failed to deal fully with the problem of under-institutionalization. Most notably, they did not create a firm administrative bedrock in the uezds. The introduction of self-government and the limited reform of the police were steps forward, but they did not provide the governors with a regular structure of subordinate agencies and personnel. As a consequence, the *nachal'niki gubernii* had few means to manage local affairs or to influence the world of the peasants directly.

Thus the governorship came out of the initial phase of the reform era transformed into an organ of supervision with a sharply limited sphere of operation. But this situation would not endure for long. Even before the 1860s waned, the government became convinced that the weakening of gubernatorial authority had been an error and moved to correct it. Unfortunately, the measures adopted never fully restored the power of the governors and, in fact, made their position within provincial government even more unclear.

In 1866 the central authorities commenced the process of augmenting gubernatorial authority. In the wake of Karakozov's attempt on

34. Of course, elective institutions were not introduced in all provinces. The zemstvos were confined to thirty-four, mostly Great Russian, gubernias. The law on municipal self-government was originally applied to some 423 cities, primarily in European Russia, and a modified urban statute was extended to the Baltic provinces in 1877.

the life of Alexander II, the government issued a law that expanded the governors' powers of supervision, giving them the right to make unannounced inspections of all state institutions in the provinces. The measure also increased their control over local personnel and made it possible for the governors to block the appointment or transfer of any gubernia official on the grounds of political unreliability. From now on, all proposals for rewarding or decorating provincial bureaucrats were to be made through the governors' offices.

Under the new statute, the governors' power to protect the social and political status quo also grew. They could close any organization or society engaged in antigovernmental activities and, through the police, were to watch for any actions threatening state security. Finally, the law reasserted the governors' power of active administration. Article five recalled the authority that the *nachal'niki gubernii* were entitled to exercise in dealing with criminal bands, public resistance to authority, famines, and plagues. Article eight required all state officials in the provinces, regardless of ministerial affiliation, to submit to the governors and to obey their lawful commands.[35]

During the decades that followed, the governors' sphere of activity steadily expanded. In 1876, they were empowered to issue binding regulations on matters dealing with local peace and security. After 1879, they could block the appointments of the zemstvos' hired personnel on the grounds of political reliability. The law of 14 August 1881 on increased security gave them broad authority in situations deemed to be serious threats to the state. The "counterreform" legislation of the late 1880s and early 1890s provided governors with increased leverage vis-à-vis local self-government and, through the land captains (*zemskie nachal'niki*), with a means of influencing peasant institutions. At the start of the twentieth century, the governors obtained virtually complete control of famine relief and acquired the right to place a tight ceiling on zemstvo budgets.[36]

But all these changes failed to render the governor "master of the province." Significantly, that title, embodied in article 358 of the gubernia statute of 1857, was not retained in subsequent redactions.[37] Gubernia administration remained fragmented as the local representatives of the several St. Petersburg ministries worked to define and to expand their spheres of influence. Self-government, though somewhat

35. PSZ, 2d ser., 22 July 1866, no. 43502.

36. PSZ, 2d ser., nos. 56203 and 59947; 3d ser., nos. 350, 6927, 8708, 6196, 18855, 18862.

37. "Obshchee gubernskoe uchrezhdenie," *Svod zakonov rossiiskoi imperii*, 2 (St. Petersburg, 1857). Compare articles 498 and 274 of the 1876 and 1892 editions of the second volume of the *Svod*.

diminished by the "counterreforms," continued to enjoy considerable authority. More important, the MVD failed to expand significantly the network of officials under the governor's command. The police and the provincial bureaucracy generally were, as before, understaffed, poorly trained, and ineffectual.

Nor did the governors acquire the means to coordinate the work of self-government and ministerial field agents. St. Petersburg legislators conjured up an ever-growing number of provincial standing committees (*prisutstviia*) in the hope that they might produce harmony in place of the cacophony of departmental demands. Composed of representatives of the concerned parties, the committees were designed to resolve differences and prevent inter-agency disputes. To a degree they were successful. But they neither increased gubernatorial power nor rationalized its exercise. Instead the committees simply enlarged the flow of government business, involved the governors in areas where they had little competence, and laid new and time-consuming tasks on their shoulders.

By the beginning of the twentieth century, the task set before the Russian governor had assumed herculean proportions. The volume of business confronting the *nachal'nik gubernii* in 1900 now exceeded that which had virtually overwhelmed his predecessors half a century earlier. Local staff and institutions continued to be inadequate. Yet, paradoxically, these weaknesses and difficulties often enhanced the personal role of the governor in provincial affairs. Because he could rely on neither command nor regular bureaucratic processes to achieve his ends, the *nachal'nik gubernii* became directly involved in many of the petty details of local affairs. This fact and his status as the tsar's representative made the governor appear as a special and superior source of help and justice in the eyes of many unsophisticated provincial denizens. Unable to understand or to cope with the chaos and inefficiency of the gubernia administration, frequently distrustful of zemstvos and city councils, ordinary citizens turned to His Excellency for aid and for the redress of grievances.

Like the autocracy, the governorship remained a "charismatic" office. The weaknesses of society and its institutions combined with bureaucratic underdevelopment to maintain the importance of the governor even as they undercut his actual power. As a result, the administering of a Russian province depended very much on a governor's personality, style, and administrative competence. The growing complexity of Russian life and the increase of political and social tensions made finding the right kind of man for this difficult job a matter of the greatest importance.

— 2 —

Fifty Good Governors

Writing in the early nineteenth century, the historian and literary figure N. M. Karamzin advised Alexander I that all would go well with his empire if the tsar could find in Russia "fifty wise and conscientious . . . [governors] to devote themselves zealously to the well being of the half million . . . [souls] entrusted to them, to curb the rapacious greed of minor officials and cruel landlords, to reestablish justice, pacify the land tillers, encourage merchants and industry and to protect the interest of the exchequer and the nation."[1] Much of what Karamzin said in his famous *Memoir on Ancient and Modern Russia* went unheeded. But his vision of a nation in the hands of good governors remained a goal of Russian administrators until the collapse of the old regime.

Given the importance of the office and the enormous significance of the responsibilities that devolved on it, a governor ought to have been a person of a very special stamp. Yet at no time did the Russian government ever formally define the requirements for holding a governorship. The law stated only that "governors [were] appointed and dismissed by the personal decree of the sovereign."[2] To be sure, in the course of the nineteenth century the Ministry of Internal Affairs gained virtual control of gubernatorial selection, for it drew up the lists of

---

1. N. M. Karamzin, *Memoir on Ancient and Modern Russia,* trans. by R. Pipes (Cambridge, Mass., 1959), p. 193.

2. "Obshchee uchrezhdenie gubernskoe," article 263, *Svod zakonov rossiiskoi imperii,* 2 (St. Petersburg, 1892).

potential governors for the tsar's approval. But the ministry's decisions on these appointments were not guided by any legal stipulations.

The absence of clear, specific criteria for holding one of the most important posts in the imperial service contributed to the notion that governors were chosen with little regard to their abilities. Instead, the Russian public, many administrators, and even some governors themselves assumed that an informal system of favoritism and patronage determined gubernatorial appointments. Men were picked to be governors because they had connections at court, were well known to important people, or had served in a particular province.[3]

There can be little doubt that a wide variety of forces influenced the choice of governors and that favoritism and connections had a significant impact. The fact that throughout the period under consideration somewhere between 25 and 30 percent of the *nachal'niki gubernii* held court rank (*pridvornye zvanie*) certainly gives weight to this assertion.[4] But a large body of evidence also suggests that selection was neither always arbitrary nor based primarily on personal ties. A study of the men who held governorships from 1880 to 1914 and an examination of the way in which they were picked indicates that over the course of three and a half decades the MVD developed and refined criteria for holding the office. Something like a gubernatorial corps, a pool of trained officials from which governors could be drawn, began to emerge.

To speak of the "professionalization" of the Russian governorship may be something of an exaggeration. Yet even before the 1880s there

---

3. I. Blinov, *Gubernatory: Istoriko-iuridicheskii ocherk*, pp. 263–67; V. I. Gurko, *Features and Figures of the Past: Government and Opinion in the Reign of Nicholas II* (Stanford, Calif., 1939), pp. 111, 355; I. F. Koshko, *Vospominaniia gubernatora (1905–1914): Novgorod, Samara, Penza*, pp. 13–14; idem, "Vospominaniia gubernatora, chast' II: Perm'," pp. 713–14, BAR, Koshko papers; E. M. Feoktistov, *Za kulisami politiki i literatury, 1848–1898*, ed. by Iu. G. Oksman (Leningrad, 1929), pp. 230–31; M. M. Osorgin, "Vospominaniia," Gosudarstvennaia biblioteka imeni Lenina, otdel rukopisei [hereafter GBL], f. Osorgina (215), papka I, delo 1, p. 2. In his study of the bureaucracy of late Imperial Russia, the distinguished Soviet scholar P. A. Zaionchkovskii also stresses the role of informal, nonservice related criteria in gubernatorial selection (*Pravitel'stvennyi apparat samoderzhavnoi Rossii v XIX v.* [Moscow, 1978]. pp. 210–211). The British historian W. E. Mosse joins in emphasizing the role of favoritism in the choice of governors ("Russian Provincial Governors at the End of the Nineteenth Century," *Historical Journal* 27 [1984]: 225–39).

4. I. V. Orzhekhovskii, *Iz istorii vnutrennei politiki samoderzhaviia v 60–70-kh godakh XIX veka* (Gor'kii, 1974), p. 81; Zaionchkovskii, *Pravitel'stvennyi apparat*, p. 214; *Spisok vysshikh chinov mestnykh ustanovlenii Ministerstva vnutrennikh del za 1913 g.* (St. Petersburg, 1913).

seems to have been a determination on the part of the government to improve the quality of the *nachal'niki gubernii* and, to a degree at least, specialize their in-service training. The studies of P. A. Zaionchkovskii and I. V. Orzhekhovskii both point to a sharp rise in the educational levels of governors between the last years of Nicholas I and the accession of Alexander III. The American scholar John Armstrong notes the emergence of a fairly clear distinction between high officials whose careers were centered in the capital and those, like the governors, who served primarily in the provinces.[5] By the beginning of the twentieth century a concern for the training and expertise of gubernatorial candidates appears to have become an important element in appointment decisions. Although favoritism and patronage might always help or hinder a man's advancement, the MVD was increasingly determined to pick governors from among those persons whose educations and previous service had prepared them to handle the responsibilities of the job.

The Ministry of Internal Affairs also sought to rationalize the selection process itself to identify and bring forward the kind of men who could carry out gubernatorial duties. During the late nineteenth century, the MVD pinpointed certain key offices—the vice-governorship and a number of major provincial posts—which, it felt, men aspiring to the job of *nachal'nik gubernii* ought to have held in the course of their careers. This trend toward a more regular system of preparation and selection is well illustrated when we compare the way in which two ambitious young men of different periods moved toward a governorship.

In 1866 Aleksandr Dmitrievich Sverbeev, who had recently left government after holding a diplomatic post in Germany, decided to resume his bureaucratic career. He headed for the capital determined to win an appointment to a vice-governorship. A graduate of Moscow University, Sverbeev had earlier worked on the staff of Riga's governor-general. He was known to a number of highly placed officials among them P. A. Valuev, the minister of internal affairs. Sverbeev's connections served him well. Turning directly to Valuev, he obtained vigorous support. The minister advanced him rapidly so that by the beginning of 1867 Sverbeev had acquired the rank necessary for a vice-governor. Valuev then assigned his protégé to Tver province where Sverbeev began to study gubernia and especially uezd institutions under the guidance of the local governor. After approximately three and a half months of on-the-job training in Tver, Sverbeev was posted to Kostroma as vice-governor. Although his advance to this point had been swift, Sverbeev would still have to serve as second-in-command at Kostroma for ten years before assuming a governorship in Samara in 1878.[6]

Just over thirty years after Sverbeev was sent to Kostroma, Aleksandr Nikolaevich Troinitskii received an appointment as vice-governor in Tobolsk. Like Sverbeev, Troinitskii was a young man with an excellent education and good connections. His grandfather had been assistant minister of internal affairs and his father, a former governor, was head of the MVD's statistical apparatus. Yet Troinitskii's path to high office differed markedly from that of his counterpart of the 1860s.

After being graduated from the School of Jurisprudence in St. Petersburg in 1891, the young Troinitskii immediately entered provincial service as a troubleshooter (*chinovnik osobykh poruchenii*) on the staffs of the governors of Olonets and Chernigov. He then worked his way through a series of important offices at the gubernia level. In 1895, he became a councilor (*sovetnik*) on the provincial board in Orel. In 1898, he held the post of permanent member of the Stavropol provincial committee on peasant affairs (*gubernskoe prisutstvie*). Four years later, in 1902, Aleksandr Nikolaevich was appointed vice-governor. He became governor in Semipalatinsk in 1908.[7]

The career patterns of Sverbeev and Troinitskii suggest both the continuities and changes in gubernatorial appointments over the span of three decades. In the late 1860s as in the early twentieth century, a vice-governor's office was the crucial stepping stone to a governorship. But the path a man traversed as he moved upward toward that preparatory post had undergone considerable alteration.

Personal connections appear to have had a more significant impact on Sverbeev's advance than they did on Troinitskii's. Sverbeev's use of his friendship with Valuev was blatant, and it allowed him to avoid the years of service that would have been required to attain the necessary rank. In the case of Troinitskii, the high position occupied by his father undoubtedly did him no harm, but he does not seem to have been able

6. A. D. Sverbeev, "Vstrechi i znakomstva, vospominaniia, 1916," Tsentral'nyi gosudarstvennyi arkhiv literatury i iskusstva SSSR (hereafter TsGALI) f. Sverbeevykh (472), op. 1, d. 104, pp. 76–77.

7. The outline of Troinitskii's career is based on information found in his personnel file: Tsentral'nyi gosudarstvennyi istoricheskii arkhiv (hereafter TsGIA), f. Department obshchikh del MVD (hereafter DOD), op. 47, 1911, d. 321.

Aleksandr D. Sverbeev, governor of Samara. Courtesy of TsGIA.

to use it to gain rapid promotions or choice assignments. Troinitskii moved upward at a steady, regular pace. His early postings were never in particularly desirable locations. His vice-governorship was in Siberia, and his first gubernatorial position was in Central Asia, on the Chinese border.

In terms of education and training Sverbeev and Troinitskii also differed. Both men had the equivalent of a university degree, but Sverbeev was a generalist, while Troinitskii was a specialist in the law. With regard to career experience, Troinitskii's on-the-job training was much more extensive and focused than Sverbeev's. It had been deemed sufficient for Sverbeev to study provincial and uezd institutions informally, for a few months, to prepare him for a vice-governorship, whereas Troinitskii had spent years in a series of posts which gave him direct contact with local government and its problems. More significant, from the offices he had held Troinitskii acquired a firsthand understanding of peasant needs and conditions, something virtually absent from Sverbeev's preparation.

In addition to specific considerations, a major difference between the careers of Sverbeev and Troinitskii was regularity. Sverbeev's advance was haphazard and informal. Troinitskii moved along a path that provided him with needed knowledge and skills. These two career patterns helped to produce governors of differing characters. Extensive reading in the surviving papers of both men reveals Sverbeev to have been a broadly cultured person with a wide range of literary and artistic interests. Troinitskii, by way of contrast, was definitely in the bureaucratic mold, focused on the day-to-day tasks of governance. Sverbeev was probably the more interesting person; Troinitskii may well have been the better administrator.[8]

Neither Sverbeev nor Troinitskii were typical governors of their respective generations. Yet their careers were not unique. The similarities and differences in their paths to high office point to broader developments in the MVD's recruitment practices. We can strengthen and deepen the impressions gained from the specific cases of Sverbeev and Troinitskii by examining in more detail available documents on

8. My impressions of Sverbeev are derived from various materials in his personal archive in TsGALI and from the article by A. N. Kurenkov, "Dnevnik samarskogo gubernatora A. D. Sverbeeva," *Istochnikovedenie i istoriografiia. Spetsial'nye istoricheskie distsipliny. Sbornik statei* (Moscow, 1980), pp. 19–21. My views of Troinitskii are based on a reading of his letters to his parents contained in TsGIA, f. N. A. Troinitskogo (1065), op. 1, d. 57, "Pis'ma Troinitskim N. A. i A. E. ot ikh detei, 1878–1913 gg."

the choosing of governors and vice-governors and by looking briefly at the evolution of the ministry's selection policy.

Between 1880 and the first years of the twentieth century, the MVD's choice of its top provincial officials does not seem to have been shaped by any clear-cut, overall design. The papers of the Department of General Affairs (*Departament obshchikh del*), that section of the ministry responsible for personnel selection, do not reveal any system for choosing governors and vice-governors. The surviving files, appear incomplete and fragmentary and lend credence to the idea that informal procedures were of considerable importance in appointment decisions.

What we find in department records for the years prior to the 1905 revolution are mostly letters recommending and supporting various individuals. This correspondence came from superiors, family, friends, and the office seekers themselves. Letters of support usually praised nominees for their serious attention to business and their general competence. Backers stressed the candidates' high moral standards and, on occasion, emphasized their ability to deal effectively with people of all social stations.[9] Occasionally a letter of recommendation might intimate that an individual was highly regarded by local people in the provinces to which he might be assigned.[10] Representations from the candidates themselves noted their own service and even tried to put the ministry under a sense of obligation. Some office seekers inferred that they had been promised rapid promotion when they had assumed their present jobs and called on the MVD to make good on its bargain.[11]

The criteria used by the ministry to sift the mass of suggestions it received are not entirely certain. Clearly, the MVD was interested in quality. Officials of the Department of General Affairs sought to investigate the past service of various candidates and to compare it to the achievements of those holding similar posts in the bureaucracy. When a prospective appointee was found wanting, consideration of his case was dropped.[12] This was true even when a candidate enjoyed august

9. Letter of recommendation from V. A. Dolgorukov on behalf of V. K. Shlippe, 15 December 1887, TsGIA, f. DOD, op. 45, 1877, d. 37, "O kandidatakh na dolzhnost' gubernatora," pp. 55–56. See comparable letters of support, ibid., op. 46, 1901, d. 35, "O kandidatakh na dolzhnost' gubernatora," pp. 4, 7–8.

10. Document titled "dlia pamiati," dated 13 June 1881, TsGIA, f. DOD, op. 45, 1881, d. 155, "O kandidatakh na dolzhnost' gubernatora," p. 14.

11. A. P. Engel'gardt to I. N. Durnovo [summer, 1892], TsGIA, f. DOD, op. 46, 1890, d. 63, "O naznachenii . . . Engel'gardta . . . ," p. 75; D. Volkov to I. N. Durnovo, 28 December 1892, ibid., op. 45, 1881, d. 152, "O kandidatakh na dolzhnost' vitse-gubernatora, ch. 2," p. 1.

12. See the materials relating to the candidacy of N. V. Saburov for the post of vice-governor, February–March, 1895 (TsGIA, f. DOD, op. 45, 1881, d. 152, pp. 67–68,

support.[13] The MVD did not respond kindly to suggestions that it had promised promotions to individual office seekers. The statement of one candidate that he had been told he would be given a governorship after a reasonable tour of duty as vice-governor elicited a large question mark in the margin of his letter. When an official seeking a vice-governorship tried to exert similar pressure, an MVD clerk investigated, then wrote laconically: "Information concerning a promise by the ministry to assign [the candidate] to a 'serious administrative post' cannot be found in the files."[14]

In the years before 1905, the MVD apparently did not look into the political convictions of the candidates. We can infer this from the fact that the files of the Department of General Affairs do not reveal any ministerial concern for these matters. Of course, such investigations could have been done independently by the police, but if they were not undertaken at all, it would not be particularly surprising. The military and civilian posts through which the candidates had already passed were sufficient to filter out "radicals" and most of those who were extreme "liberals". The MVD could assume the loyalty of the men under consideration, after which it was relatively unimportant whether a person held "advanced" or "conservative" views. This blindness to the political outlook of potential governors partly explains why even such conservative ministers as D. A. Tolstoi, I. N. Durnovo, and V. K. Pleve appointed and retained governors who were "liberal" in both opinion and practice.[15]

Once a prospective governor or vice-governor passed the initial screening, MVD officials inscribed his name on a list of candidates which contained information on education, service, source of recommendation, and a statement on where an individual might wish to be placed. These lists do not seem to have been inclusive of all persons being considered. (The largest list I saw for the pre-1905 period contained about forty names.) But as incomplete as these were, they served as a partial guide to the MVD and the emperor in appointing the two highest gubernia officers.[16]

The pre-1905 files on candidates for governor and vice-governor

75–76). Saburov was rejected because it turned out that he had handled his job as commissar for peasant affairs in a slipshod manner.

13. I. N. Durnovo to Grand Prince Sergei Aleksandrovich, 8 May 1895, ibid., p. 82.

14. Notation on Engel'gardt's letter to Durnovo, TsGIA, DOD, op. 46, 1890, d. 63, p. 75; memorandum attached to a letter from D. Volkov, [December, 1892], TsGIA, f. DOD, op. 45, 1881, d. 152, p. 4.

15. Pleve, for example, appointed at least three "liberal" governors in the first year of his ministry: S. D. Urusov, M. M. Osorgin and A. A. Lodyzhenskii.

16. TsGIA, f. DOD, op. 45, 1881, d. 155, pp. 1, 66–67; ibid., op. 46, 1901, d. 35, p. 1.

often appear jumbled and unsystematic, but they do not tell the whole story of the MVD's selection practices. Other documents from the late nineteenth century reveal a growing ministerial concern for the quality of the *nachal'niki gubernii* and their seconds-in-command. In 1895, for example, the MVD sought to boost the pay of its chief provincial officers. I. L. Goremykin proposed to the State Council that governors' salaries be raised from roughly 7,000 rubles to 10,000, and that those of vice-governors be increased from around 3,500 to 5,000 rubles. Gubernatorial and vice-gubernatorial salaries were already high when compared to those of other gubernia officials,[17] but Goremykin felt that they would not suffice to keep competent men at the top of the provincial administration. Unless the pay of governors was made commensurate with the duties of the job and the life-style it required, he argued, qualified men would shun the post. This would sharply narrow the field of potential prospects, and the MVD might be forced to choose "only wealthy (*sostoiatel'nye*) persons who had their own means of support."[18]

The MVD was ultimately successful in its fight for higher gubernatorial and vice-gubernatorial pay, but the ministry sought to improve the quality of these officials by other means as well. In particular, it tried to establish something like a ladder of service positions that ought to have been held before a person could aspire to the job of *nachal'nik gubernii* or his second-in-command. Toward the end of the 1890s, young men with gubernatorial ambitions were being told that before they could obtain even a vice-governorship, they would have to serve in certain key preparatory posts such as permanent member of the provincial committee on peasant affairs or marshal of the nobility.[19]

By 1903, the MVD was prepared to go even further. That year it proposed, in connection with a new law on the land captains, to restrict candidacy for vice-governorships and other lesser provincial offices *exclusively* to persons who had served in local administrative posts for at least three years. The office of land captain was singled out as a special rung on the ladder leading to a vice-gubernatorial position.[20]

17. The best discussion of the wages within the Russian bureaucracy is found in Zaionchkovskii's *Pravitel'stvennyi apparat,* especially pp. 86–91.

18. *Otchet po deloproizvodstvu Gosudarstvennogo soveta za sessiiu 1895–1896 gg.* (St. Petersburg, 1896), pp. 108–109.

19. Osorgin, "Vospominaniia," GBL, f. Osorgina, papka II, delo 2, p. 13. See also R. G. Robbins, Jr., "Choosing the Russian Governors: The Professionalization of the Gubernatorial Corps," *Slavonic and East European Review* 58 (October 1980): 542–44.

20. TsGIA, f. Zhurnalov departamentov Gosudarstvennogo soveta (1160), op. 1, d. 218, "Zhurnaly departamenta zakonov . . . , 1904, ch. 1," p. 209.

The State Council rejected the specifics of the MVD's proposal because it would have created too shallow a pool of selection. But the council accepted the ministry's basic premise.[21] As a result, the 1904 law on the land captains contained the stipulation that "the office of vice-governor . . . is to be filled *primarily* by persons [who have] served no less than three years in offices, no lower than VI class, of local peasant institutions or in one of the following posts: marshal of the nobility, chairman of the provincial [zemstvo] executive board, chairman of the provincial executive committee for the affairs of the zemstvo economy, and councilor of the provincial board."[22]

This new legislation formally linked vice-gubernatorial and, to a large degree, gubernatorial selection with both provincial and peasant related service. But it confirmed rather than altered established practice. The MVD had already come to the conclusion that its top provincial officers ought to have had considerable administrative experience at the gubernia level and be knowledgeable about peasant affairs. As a result, this aspect of the legislation of 1904 proved superfluous and ministry documents contain few references to those stipulations that concerned the choice of vice-governors.[23]

The revolution of 1905 did not cause a major shift in the ministry's selection policies. Rather, the MVD sought to refine the procedures it had already developed. Most striking was the acceleration of the trend toward choosing vice-governors and governors from among candidates experienced in local affairs and the problems of the peasantry.[24] Many who would have been acceptable earlier were no longer considered because they lacked this experience. As the Department of General Affairs explained to one candidate, the working conditions of a governor were now "extremely complex and demanded a thorough acquaintance with all sides of provincial life . . . as well as previous service in secondary offices at the local level."[25]

In the years after 1905 the ministry systematized the collection of information about both the moral and the service qualifications of

21. Ibid., pp. 209–10.
22. PSZ, 3d ser., no. 24388, 19 April 1904. (Italics mine.)
23. TsGIA, f. DOD, op. 46, 1905, d. 214, "Po khodataistvam o predstavlenii dolzhnosti vitse-gubernatora," p. 31.
24. Memorandum written in May, 1906, TsGIA, f. DOD, op. 47, 1906, d. 9, "O kandidatakh na dolzhnosti gubernatorov . . . ," p. 23.
25. Letter dated 8 January 1909, TsGIA, f. DOD, op. 47, 1909, d. 10, "O kandidatakh na dolzhnosti gubernatorov . . . ," p. 10. See also Stolypin's letter to Grand Prince Dmitri Konstantinovich rejecting a candidate because he "did not have . . . the opportunity to acquire the service preparation now required in such a responsible post as that of governor." Letter dated 30 October 1908, TsGIA, f. DOD, op. 47, 1906, d. 9, p. 268.

candidates. By 1906 the MVD was sending out a standardized letter to elicit such evaluations.[26] In 1911 the ministry began using a printed form on a regular basis to gather the opinions of governors on the qualities of vice-governors, councilors of the provincial board, and heads of chancellery. In doing so it sought to learn more about officials who might themselves eventually become aspirants for the post of *nachal'nik gubernii*.[27]

In 1911 the MVD also reaffirmed its determination to see that men who obtained a vice-governorship had the needed service experience. Prime Minister P. A. Stolypin stated that "from candidates for vice-governor the Ministry of Internal Affairs required the possession of solid administrative experience which the candidate could obtain only by passing through a number of less responsible offices before selection as vice-governor. This requirement, in addition to the personal qualities of the candidate, would guarantee his preparation for the job."[28]

What Stolypin had in mind when he spoke of preparatory steps on the road to a vice-governorship is illustrated when we look at his "long list" of vice-gubernatorial candidates. This document, dated 1910, is much more extensive and systematic than any similar lists compiled before 1905 and contains the names of just under 160 persons. Of these, three-quarters were currently engaged in provincial service and just a slightly smaller percentage (74.2) had made the provinces the main locus of their careers. Of the men then serving in provincial posts (120), 34 percent were permanent members of the provincial committee on peasant affairs. Beyond this, two-thirds of all candidates listed had held at least one post that had directly involved them in the peasants' problems.[29] Stolypin's list gives us a sense of the shape the gubernatorial corps might have taken had war and revolution not intervened. And it shows the ministry's determination to make good on its stated policies.

The available documents on the selection of the gubernatorial corps

26. For examples see two letters dated 16 June 1906, TsGIA, f. DOD, op. 47, 1907, d. 98, "O naznachenii . . . grafa Apraksina . . . ," pp. 7–8. The letters asked for "confidential and completely candid information on the service and moral qualities of . . . [the candidate] and . . . his readiness to assume a responsible administrative post."

27. For examples see, TsGIA, f. DOD, op. 47, 1911, d. 349, "Attestatsiia vitse-gubernatorov i chinov gubernskikh pravlenii za 1911–1917 gg.," p. 26 and passim.

28. Stolypin is quoted in an internal memorandum dated 8 October 1912, TsGIA, f. DOD, op. 47, 1911, d. 53, "Po khodataistvam o predstavlenii dolzhnosti vitse-gubernatorov 1911, 1912 g.," p. 203.

29. TsGIA, f. DOD, op. 47, 1910, d. 325, "Kandidaty na dolzhnosti vitse-gubernatorov po noiabr' 1910 g."

do not, of course, present a complete picture of its development. But we can confirm the impressions that we have gained to this point by looking at materials of a broader character. An examination of the social origins, education, and career patterns of the governors of European Russia in the years 1879, 1892, 1903, and 1913 provides us with a clearer picture of the kind of men governors were and how this select group changed during the reigns of the last two autocrats.[30]

Governors came from among the wellborn. Throughout the period under consideration, almost all the *nachal'niki gubernii* were hereditary nobles;[31] the majority had strong ties to the land. Roughly two-thirds held estates, and of those who did, most had inherited some portion of their property. The size of governors' land holdings varied, but until 1905 nearly half of the governors who were landowners (*pomeshchiki*) had more than 1,000 desiatinas. After the revolution of 1905 a noticeable shift occurred. The number of landed governors declined slightly and the proportion holding over 1,000 desiatinas dropped by almost 50 percent.[32]

The social composition of the gubernatorial corps requires some explanation, for only on the eve of World War I did this group begin to show the decline in the proportion of landed gentry that had been registered in almost all other segments of the upper bureaucracy.[33] Iu. B. Solov'ev's suggestion that this anomaly reflected the conscious policy of the tsarist regime to shore up the *dvorianstvo* appears to be at least partially justified.[34] A degree of concern for this traditionally

30. The benchmark years were chosen for several reasons. Eighteen hundred seventy-nine and 1903 were used by I. V. Orzhekhovskii and P. A. Zaionchkovskii in their studies of the Russian bureaucracy. Eighteen hundred ninety-two and 1913 were selected because they would allow me to examine the gubernatorial corps at the end of the counterreform era and on the eve of World War I. It should be noted that my sample of governors for 1879 and 1903 is slightly different from the samples of Orzhekhovskii and Zaionchkovskii. The Soviet scholars had access to certain files I could not see. Also they included in their samples only those governors who held office on January 1 of the years in question, whereas I tried to include information on any governor who served during 1879 and 1903.

31. Of the governors for whom I have biographical information, only one was of nonnoble origin, and he was the ward of a senator.

32. The statistical information presented here and in succeeding pages is derived from a variety of sources: the works of Zaionchkovskii and Orzhekhovskii previously cited, the service records of the governors held in TsGIA, DOD, *opisi* 44, 45, 46, 47, and various issues of the guidebooks *Adres kalendar'*, *Spisok grazhdanskim chinam pervykh chetyrekh klassov*, *Spisok litsam sluzhashchim po vedomstvu Ministerstva vnutrennikh del*, and *Spisok vysshikh chinov mestnikh ustanovlenii Ministerstva vnutrennikh del*.

33. Zaionchkovskii, *Pravitel'stvennyi apparat*, pp. 215, 222.

34. Iu. B. Solov'ev, *Samoderzhavie i dvorianstvo* (Leningrad, 1973), p. 171.

Table 1. Educational levels of Russian governors, 1879–1913

Level	1879		1892		1903		1913	
	No.	Percent	No.	Percent	No.	Percent	No.	Percent
Higher	31	53.4	31	60.7	36	67.9	29	58
Secondary	25	43.1	17	33.3	17	32.1	21	42
Primary	2	3.4	3	5.9	—	—	—	—
Totals	58	100.0	51	100.0	53	100.0	50	100.0

loyal class undoubtedly played a part in ministerial considerations, yet more seems to have been at issue than this. The MVD's continued reliance on the landed gentry for staffing its gubernatorial corps appears to have been a result of the fact that men drawn from this social element were the most likely to possess the combination of education, experience, special knowledge, and political skill which the ministry felt its governors needed.

The MVD wanted the governors to be well educated (see table 1). This is demonstrated by the steady rise of the educational levels of the *nachal'niki gubernii* during the last half of the nineteenth century. Indeed, the number of governors with higher education grew at a rate considerably faster than that of other comparable segments of the ministry's staff.[35] The MVD drew heavily on the graduates of three elite schools: the Alexander Lyceum, the School of Jurisprudence, and the Corps of Pages. In 1879 and 1903 fully one-third of the governors had been thus educated, by 1913, one half. Products of these institutions were noted for being well connected, well trained, and loyal.[36]

After 1905, however, the educational level of the gubernatorial corps declined. The number of highly educated governors fell from 68 percent in 1903 to 58 percent in 1913. The reason for this shift is not fully clear, though accidental factors may have been responsible in part. But several other explanations can be advanced. As noted above, in the period following the revolution of 1905 the MVD showed a

35. Robbins, "Choosing the Russian Governors," pp. 555; Zaionchkovskii, *Pravitel'stvennyi apparat,* pp. 207–214; Orzhekhovskii, *Iz istorii,* pp. 55, 81.

36. On the Alexander Lyceum and the School of Jurisprudence, see Allen A. Sinel, "The Socialization of the Russian Bureaucratic Elite: Life at the Tsarskoe Selo Lyceum and the School of Jurisprudence," *Russian History* 3 (1976): 1–31; on the Corps of Pages, see P. A. Kropotkin *Memoirs of a Revolutionist,* ed. J. A. Rogers (New York: Anchor Books, 1962), pp. 55–121, Paul Grabbe, *Windows on the River Neva* (New York, 1977), pp. 89–101; V. F. Dzhunkovskii, "Vospominaniia za 1865–1884 gg.," Tsentral'nyi gosudarstvennyi arkhiv oktiabr'skoi revoliutsii (hereafter TsGAOR), f. V. F. Dzhunkovskogo (826), op. 1, d. 38, pp. 13–24.

growing concern to have its high provincial officials be men who had acquired extensive practical experience in local administration. This growing emphasis on service criteria and career patterns may have led the ministry to pay less attention to formal educational attainment. Moreover, the events of 1905 put a premium on military skills. Certainly the number of governors who had been educated in military schools grew from just under 38 percent in 1903 to 46 percent a decade later (see table 2). Because the majority of military academies provided only secondary schooling, the proportion of governors with higher education was bound to decrease.

Yet if the MVD put less emphasis on higher academic training per se after 1905, it did not ignore educational criteria entirely, for the percentage of governors with legal training expanded steadily. In 1879 just under 10 percent of the governors had studied law. By 1892 the number had risen to 19.6 percent, and by 1903 to 22.6 percent. The events of 1905 did not interrupt this development. In 1913, 34 percent of the governors had been to law school. Like the rise in the number of governors with a military education, the substantial jump in governors with legal training after 1905 reflected the needs of a new period of Russian history. The complexities of massive land reform and the emergence of a quasi-constitutional regime required governors to have a greater awareness of the law and of legality.

When we turn from the educational background of the governors to an examination of their careers, we see another demonstration of the MVD's increasing determination to select men who were well prepared for the job. Throughout the period under consideration, the vast majority of governors had served for over twenty years in a variety of responsible posts before taking command of a gubernia. Moreover, from 1880 to 1913 the ministry steadily refined and sharpened its preparatory criteria.

As I have already suggested, the ministry regarded military experi-

Table 2. Types of education of Russian governors, 1879–1913

Type	1879		1892		1903		1913	
	No.	Percent	No.	Percent	No.	Percent	No.	Percent
General	17	41.5	19	37.2	17	32.1	9	18
Military	16	39.0	18	35.3	20	37.7	23	46
Legal	4	9.7	10	19.6	12	22.6	17	34
Technical	4	9.7	4	7.8	4	7.5	1	2
Totals	41	100.0	51	100.0	53	100.0	50	100.0

Table 3. Initial service of Russian governors, 1879–1913

Place of service	1879		1892		1903		1913	
	No.	Percent	No.	Percent	No.	Percent	No.	Percent
Military	23	46.0	27	53.0	23	43.4	25	50
Civilian	27	54.0	24	47.0	30	56.6	25	50
Central admin.	(11)	(22.0)	(10)	(19.6)	(13)	(24.5)	(14)	(28)
Prov. admin.	(9)	(18.0)	(8)	(15.0)	(10)	10.9	(11)	(22)
Unclear	(7)	(14.0)	(6)	(11.7)	(7)	(13.2)	—	—
Totals	50	100.0	51	100.0	53	100.0	50	100.0

ence as an important asset; almost half of all governors had begun their state service as army or navy officers (see table 3). But with the passage of time the MVD seems to have become chary about appointing military men who lacked intervening civilian experience. At no time did the number of governors who came to their posts *directly* from the armed forces exceed 20 percent, and usually it was lower. In 1879 and 1903 only 12 to 13 percent of the *nachal'niki gubernii* had been so chosen. After 1905, the governor with only military experience began to disappear, and by 1913 just two governors, 4 percent, had served solely as officers (see table 4).

If relatively few governors had only military experience, an overwhelming number had served as vice-governors. This was true of 60 percent of all governors in 1879, 50 in 1892, 68 in 1903, and 78 in 1913. On average, moreover, they had close to five years' tenure in that post. A vice-governorship was clearly an important training ground for future *nachal'niki gubernii* because vice-governors worked in close association with their immediate superiors, were deeply involved in the work of key provincial institutions, and often carried out gubernatorial duties.

Another path to a governorship was the position of provincial or uezd marshal. Marshals were elected by the local nobility for three-year terms and were usually men of considerable standing in the areas where they lived. Like a vice-governorship, this position immersed its occupant in the problems of provincial life and was a good preparation for higher office. This was particularly true of the uezd marshal because he often assumed functions in his locality comparable to those of a governor.[37]

The importance of a marshalship as a step toward a gubernatorial

37. Koshko, *Vospominaniia,* 149–50; G. M. Hamburg, "Portrait of an Elite: Russian Marshals of the Nobility, 1861–1917," *Slavic Review* 40 (Winter 1981): 586–87.

Table 4. Posts held by governors immediately before first governorship, 1879–1913

Post	1879		1892		1903		1913	
	No.	Percent	No.	Percent	No.	Percent	No.	Percent
Vice governor	30	60.0	25	49.0	34	64.1	36	72
Marshal	4	8.0	5	9.8	7	13.2	3	6
Zemstvo or city	2	4.0	—	—	—	—	—	—
Central official	3	6.0	6	11.7	4	2.5	5	10
Provincial official	5	10.0	5	9.8	1	1.9	4	8
Military	6	12.0	10	19.6	7	13.2	2	4
Totals	50	100.0	51	100.0	53	100.0	50	100.0

post rose in the period before 1905. By 1903 almost 38 percent of the governors had been marshals and over 13 percent had come from that position to the governor's office. After the 1905 revolution, the role of the marshalship as a stepping stone to high office seems to have changed. In 1913 just under 34 percent of governors had been marshals, but only 6 percent became governors directly after holding this position. This shift indicates that while the office continued to be a respected one, the MVD was increasingly eager to see that potential *nachal'niki gubernii* had also held the post of vice-governor.

A smaller proportion of the governors assumed their office directly from other positions in the provincial administration. Often they had been procurators of a judicial district or top local representatives of a ministry other than the MVD. The proportion of governors who came directly from posts in provincial service exclusive of vice-governorships fluctuated. But for most of the period it remained between 7 and 10 percent. Other governors came from the central bureaucracy. Frequently they had been heads of MVD departments or officials on special assignment. In 1879, 6 percent of the governors were appointed from positions in the center; this proportion rose to 10 by 1913.

Looking further back into gubernatorial careers, the picture becomes less sharp, but the general outlines are still visible. For those governors who did not come directly from the military, some kind of provincial service seems to have been almost essential. In 1879, 88 percent of my sample of governors had had provincial experience. By 1892 this proportion had fallen to 78 percent, but rose to about 80 percent by 1903. After 1905 the number of governors who had seen provincial service reached a remarkable 96 percent of the sample. All governors, except the two who had been selected straight from military posts, had worked at least briefly at the gubernia level. Of even greater importance was the growth of the average length of provincial service which rose from 11.5 years in 1879 to nearly 15 years in 1913. More significant still, the number of governors who had worked for more than fifteen years in the provinces jumped from 20 percent in 1879 to 54 percent by 1913 (see table 5).

The increasing importance of provincial service in gubernatorial careers is a unifying theme that runs through all the available material on the recruitment of these officials. This is perhaps best demonstrated when we look at the backgrounds of those governors who had been vice-governors earlier and consider the paths they took to that important preparatory post. An examination of the careers of governors in 1879 reveals that of those who had been vice-governors, approximately 17 percent had performed the bulk of their state service in the military field and just over 34 percent were products of the central bureaucracy. Slightly less than 49 percent of the sample had become vice-governors through working primarily in the provincial administration or locally elected posts such as marshals or zemstvo delegates.

By 1892 these percentages had changed significantly. Almost 21 percent of the governors who had earlier held vice-gubernatorial office had come to that post with a largely military background. But only 16.6 percent of the sample had gained vice-governorships from the central bureaus. Sixty-two and a half percent had become vice-governors after having served mainly at the gubernia level.

The trend toward selecting vice-governors from the ranks of those with extensive provincial service continued in the first years of the twentieth century. Of the 1903 governors who had been vice-governors, just under 17 percent had primarily military experience, and only 11 percent came from the civil service in the capital. Seventy-two percent had attained their vice-governorships after working for most of their careers in either appointed or elected office in the gubernias.

Table 5. Length of provincial service of governors, 1879–1913

Length of service in years	1879		1892		1903		1913	
	No.	Percent	No.	Percent	No.	Percent	No.	Percent
0–5	6	13.6	8	20.0	2	4.7	6	12.5
6–10	17	38.6	12	30.0	10	23.8	6	12.5
11–15	12	27.3	9	22.5	15	35.7	10	20.8
Over 15	9	20.4	11	27.5	15	35.7	26	54
Totals	44	100.0	40	100.0	42	100.0	48	100.0

Table 6. Paths to vice governorships, 1879–1913

Primary locus of service	1879		1892		1903		1913	
	No.	Percent	No.	Percent	No.	Percent	No.	Percent
Military	5	17.2	5	20.8	6	16.7	3	7.6
Central institutions	10	34.5	4	16.7	4	11.1	5	12.8
Provincial institutions	14	48.3	14	62.5	26	72.2	31	79.5
Totals	29	100.0	24	100.0	36	100.0	39	100.0

A decade later, the process of provincializing the gubernatorial corps was virtually complete. In 1913 just under 8 percent of the governors who had held vice-governorships were drawn from among career soldiers and only thirteen percent came from the ranks of central officials. Almost 80 percent were men who had served primarily in the gubernias. On the eve of World War I, the provinces, not the armed forces or the chancelleries of St. Petersburg, had become almost the sole source of top provincial officals (see table 6).

The emerging pattern of selecting governors from among officials with long provincial experience indicates that the Ministry of Internal Affairs had evolved the goal of assigning to the post of *nachal'nik gubernii* men who were specialized and expert in matters of local administration. By the outbreak of the war in 1914 the MVD had realized this intention and had defined its selection criteria even more sharply. Early in the twentieth century the ministry had also begun to attach greater importance to the peasant question. Increasingly it chose as governors men whose earlier careers had given them direct experience in the daily problems of rural life.

At the gubernia level, a number of posts gave a man significant contact with the world of the peasants. Among these were: uezd marshal, peace arbitrator (*mirovoi posrednik*), commissar for peasant affairs in one of the Polish provinces, land captain, and member of a county or provincial committee on peasant affairs.[38] In 1879 eighteen

---

38. Not all of these posts functioned simultaneously or in the same places. The peace arbitrators were established in 1861 and abolished for most of the Empire in 1874, but they continued to exist in the western provinces. The office of land captain was created in 1889. The uezd board for peasant affairs came into existence in 1874. After 1889 its functions were taken over by the county conference (*s''ezd*) of land captains. The provincial committee for peasant affairs had been established in 1861 and renamed the provincial committee (*gubernskoe prisutstvie*) in 1889.

governors of European Russia (36 percent) had held one or more of these positions. By 1892 this was true of 21 governors, 41 percent of the sample. In 1903 twenty-four *nachal'niki gubernii,* over 45 percent, had held posts that provided them with an opportunity to deal with peasant issues in detail. On the eve of the war, the number had risen still higher. Twenty-eight governors, 56 percent, had had peasant-related experience.

The statistical data on gubernatorial career patterns and the available documents on MVD selection policy lead to an inescapable conclusion. During the late nineteenth and early twentieth centuries, the tsarist government regularized considerably its recruitment of governors. On the eve of war and revolution, it was possible to select these officials from a sizable pool of men whose training had been both consistent and relevant to the job. The MVD had developed a specific career trajectory designed to produce governors who were experts in the area of provincial administration. The vast majority of governors and governors-to-be were passing along this path.

The emphasis on specialization and expertise had its limits, however. The ministry did not try to focus individual governors on particular provinces or areas of the country. Despite the vastness of the empire and the existence of a considerable number of ethnic, economic, and climatic regions, governors were assigned to provinces and transferred with little regard to their previous place of service. For example, A. P. Engel'gardt, longtime mayor of Smolensk and later vice-governor in Kazan, assumed his first governorship in Arkhangelsk. S. D. Urusov, a marshal and vice-governor in the Great Russian provinces of Kaluga and Tambov, found himself confronting, as governor, the problems of stormy, ethnically diverse Bessarabia.[39] The MVD did not want a governor to be too closely identified with the particular province over which he ruled.[40] Armed with general administrative skills, a governor was expected to be able to deal effectively with the problems of any segment of the tsar's realm.[41]

39. TsGIA, f. DOD, op. 46, 1891, d. 108, "O naznachenii . . . Engel'gardta"; Urussov, p. vi.

40. The MVD was reluctant to appoint men governors or vice-governors in provinces where they had estates, but there was no absolute prohibition of such a practice. Similarly, the ministry did not like to appoint as governors or vice-governors officials holding appointed or elective offices in the same province. See A. E. Timashev's letter to V. A. Lysogorskii, 23 April 1878, TsGIA, f. DOD, op. 44, 1878, d. 134, "O naznachenii . . . Andreevskogo . . . i Enakieva . . . ," p. 1, and I. N. Durnovo's letter to N. M. Baranov, 3 June 1895, ibid., op. 45, 1881, d. 152, pp. 89–90. Of course, there were always exceptions to these rules.

41. After 1905, the MVD came to feel that governors serving in Great Russian

The growth of gubernatorial specialization and the regularization of the process of training and selection are undeniable. But what did this mean for the governance of the empire? Did these trends produce Karamzin's fifty wise and conscientious governors zealously striving to meet the needs of the people whom the tsar had entrusted to their care? Did the *nachal'niki gubernii* emerge as professional civil servants whose knowledge and administrative skills were coupled with devotion to duty, honesty, and consistent behavior?

These questions are, of course, extremely difficult to answer. Statistics and the techniques of group biography tell us little about actual performance. Men with comparable educations and career patterns could and did act very differently in gubernatorial posts. In the end, the historian is forced to use subjective judgments and unquantifiable impressions in order to arrive at conclusions about the impact of changing recruitment patterns on the way Russia was ruled. Certainly the system of selection and training *could* work to produce governors who were competent, honest, and devoted to their duties. And occasionally we encounter materials that permit us to see, in individual terms, the process of creating such officials. Soviet archives hold a collection of letters from Aleksandr Nikolaevich Troinitskii to his father, Nikolai Aleksandrovich, that is particularly revealing.

The young Troinitskii was governor in Semipalatinsk and Tula provinces between 1908 and 1917. His career pattern, which saw him through a series of provincial offices and a vice-governorship, is a model of the trajectory the MVD evolved in the late nineteenth century. What Troinitskii's letters to his father enable us to observe is the impact of this path on the psychological development of a young official. In short, we can see how the bureaucratic steel was, or at least could be, tempered.

Of special relevance are the letters written during Troinitskii's tenure in lower level provincial offices, for these bear witness to the growth of his consciousness and sense of duty. The early correspondence from his days of service in Chernigov showed mundane social concerns taking precedence over service. Petty local squabbles, problems with housing, worries about the state of his wardrobe and the prospects for promotion weighed heavily on the mind of the young bureaucrat. The chance to accompany the governor on a tour of inspection of the northern uezds elicited some excitement, but the actual

provinces ought to have experience in zemstvo affairs, but it was never rigid about this. See, P. P. Stremoukhov, "Moia bor'ba s episkopom Germogenom i Illiodorom," *Arkhiv russkoi revoliutsii* 16 (1925): 5.

work itself seems to have been of little interest.[42] Troinitskii noted the filth and rain that greeted the inspection party in Starodub. The only bright spot on the trip was a stay with Count Kleinmichel and his charming young wife.[43]

Time and experience slowly changed Aleksandr Nikolaevich. After taking up his post as a permanent member of the Stavropol committee on peasant affairs, Troinitskii's letters show an increasing absorption with his duties. Descriptions of local intrigues and personal problems give way to detailed reports on his work. The climax of the process seems to come in the summer of 1899. In a letter written while on a tour of inspection of uezd institutions, Aleksandr Nikolaevich shows that he has pushed all other concerns aside and has plunged fully into his administrative responsibilities:

> Dear Papa,
>   I haven't written for a long while, but everything is going well and I am very busy with work. Our project on various fire prevention measures has been approved by the ministry and they are releasing 61,000 rubles for funding and so it is necessary to put the project into effect. The project was my creation, and I . . . have to write all the orders for getting [things] into motion. I hope it will be of value to the province. . . .
>   I've been sitting three days in the village of Moskovskoe, Stavropol uezd. I have inspected the *volost'* board and the court. . . .[I] stayed here an extra day or two in order to acquaint myself with several pieces of business I brought from Stavropol. . . . After the departure of the entire staff of the provincial committee for vacation, there has been no chance to work on major business since I have to write even the minor papers myself. Last night a fire was put out here. In the past there has been arson. How are things with you and the census? What's new in Petersburg? . . .
>   The heat [here] is terrible, and for work I have to get up no later than 5 A.M. I go to bed late, only after midnight. . . . On Thursday morning, or maybe even tomorrow night, I'll return to Stavropol. . . .[44]

Troinitskii's letter of 13 July 1899 marks the emergence of a professional official. After this date all the surviving correspondence between son and father is in the same vein. It is service oriented, with only the slightest reference to family and personal matters. The dominant

---

42. Letters of 11 November 1892, 19 March, 27 August and 21–23 November 1893, TsGIA, f. Troinitskogo, op. 1, d. 57, "Pis'ma Troinitskim . . . ot ikh detei," pp. 88, 78–79, 82–85.

43. Letter of 11 October 1893, ibid., pp. 80–81.

44. Letter of 13 July 1899, ibid., pp. 70–71.

themes of subsequent letters repeat and amplify those found above: concern for the development of the provinces, devotion to duty, and pride in achievement.

Making generalizations about the mental and moral evolution of Russian governors on the basis of a single example is, of course, dangerous. Nevertheless, the Troinitskii correspondence is both highly believable and suggestive. Clearly, these letters were not written with an eye toward history. Straightforward, homely, graceless, they are exactly what we would expect from a young man of Troinitskii's class and era. And what makes the letters seem so particularly relevant is the fact that by the end of the nineteenth century a large number of men were moving toward governorships along paths similar to Troinitskii's. Unfortunately, their letters home have not survived. Would they have been so vastly different from those of Aleksandr Nikolaevich? After reading the memoirs and private papers of many governors, I am persuaded that, in the main, they would not.

Yet if Troinitskii's development illustrates some of the general processes shaping the gubernatorial corps, there remained plenty of leeway for deviation from this pattern. Despite the trend toward regularizing recruitment, the MVD often selected governors who lacked the requisite training. Nor did all governors whose careers conformed to the pattern we have seen evolving display the virtues that they might have been expected to acquire during their service. Throughout the period under discussion there were always governors whose administrations were characterized by personal vice, inattention to duty, and even wild abuse. The process of professionalizing the gubernatorial corps had very real limits despite the advances made at the start of the twentieth century.

Of course, no group of officials, even one as small and as carefully chosen as the Russian governors, can ever be free of malefactors and incompetents. Of greater significance, perhaps, was the MVD's persistent inability or even unwillingness to weed out the unworthy in the gubernatorial ranks. This problem will be treated in a later chapter. Suffice to say here that the ministry's failure to establish firm controls over the *nachal'niki gubernii* inhibited both the development of a genuine professional consciousness among the Russian governors as a group and the evolution of a clear-cut and consistently applied code of behavior. The values and concerns developed by men like Troinitskii were not effectively championed by their superiors in the MVD. As a result, the Russian gubernatorial corps never fully jelled, and the process of professionalization remained incomplete.

Truncated as they were, however, the trends in the evolution of the gubernatorial corps had a decided impact. With their increasingly specialized training, the governors of the early twentieth century were more competent in the handling of day-to-day administrative problems than had been their predecessors at the beginning of the 1880s. Yet whether the governors of 1913 were "better" than those of the previous generation depends upon point of view. A zemstvo activist or a member of the "third element," eager to expand the role of the institutions of self-government, might see a governor who was well trained and desirous of influencing the course of local affairs as being intrusive and hostile. Central officials could find it difficult to control governors who had their own ideas on how provincial needs ought to be met. In the end, all evaluations concerning the quality and effectiveness of the governors involve a high degree of subjectivity. We should, therefore, defer judgment until after examining in detail the work of the governors and their relations with the central and local institutions that surrounded them.

— 3 —

It Comes with the Territory

An early twentieth-century European tourist, armed with *Baedeker* and Kodak, would have found little to detain him in the town of Vologda. With a population of 38,000, this provincial capital had few points of interest save the Cathedral of St. Sophia, built in the 1580s, a passable collection of ecclesiastical antiquities, and a house once occupied by Peter the Great.[1] A Russian traveler, too, would have hurried through, eager to shake the dust of the backwoods from his boots and pass on to the brighter lights of Moscow or St. Petersburg. There were few amenities and little culture to attract a person to this place; "society" in the province consisted of a small number of landowners and a sizable complement of political exiles.

Even some governors regarded their appointment in Vologda as a kind of exile.[2] Few would stay long.[3] But for those who ruled in this vast and dreary gubernia, there were compensations. Ten thousand rubles a year would buy sufficient creature comforts, and the official residence of the governor provided the setting for a life-style befitting the personal representative of the Russian emperor.

Built in the 1890s, the elegant two-story governor's house was situ-

---

1. Karl Baedeker, *Russia: A Handbook for Travelers* (1914; New York, 1971), p. 258.
2. "Vospominaniia Aleksandra Nikolaevicha Mosolova, 1866–1902," TsGAOR, f. Kollektsii otdel'nykh dokumentov lichnogo proiskhozhdeniia (1463), op. 1, d. 1115, pp. 94–95.
3. The average tenure of a governor in Vologda during the last quarter of the nineteenth century was just over three years.

ated on the embankment of the river that had given its name to both town and province. The mansion did not face the water, but rather looked out onto a large courtyard and garden, both of which were walled off from the street and the parade square. Visitors approached the residence via the courtyard and entered the building after passing under a portico covering the main doorway. Once inside, they found themselves standing in a large foyer, gazing up a formal, circular staircase.

The ground floor of the mansion was largely given over to the public aspects of the governor's work. To the right, off the foyer, was a chamber where petitioners wishing to speak with His Excellency could wait. When their turn came, they might be ushered into either the receiving room (*priemnaia*) at the back of the house or the business office that adjoined the waiting area. Also on the first floor were other rooms of a public character, among them a large dining hall and buffet for entertaining guests.

The remainder of the ground level and most of the upstairs constituted the private quarters of the governor and his family. This part of the house contained bedrooms, sitting rooms, the governor's private study, a nursery, and a classroom for the children. But even on the second story, there were places for the public as well. Next to the governor's office were a large hall and parlor for formal occasions.

The governor's house was well provided with comforts and conveniences. Several stoves heated the rooms and kept out the raw climate. The building also had indoor plumbing that included five water closets. A large service wing and servants' quarters had been constructed adjacent to the mansion so that the material needs of the governor and his family would be attended to properly.[4]

Compared with other gubernatorial mansions, the one in Vologda was somewhere in the middle range. The governors' homes in Nizhni-Novgorod and Vitebsk were much more imposing, those in Kostroma and Viatka rather modest.[5] But even an elegant exterior was not a sign that all was well within. In the early years of the twentieth century, the

4. Description based on plans found in TsGIA, f. Tekhnichesko-stroitel'nogo komiteta MVD (1293), op. 166-Vologodskaia gub., d. 102, "Chertezh kazennogo kamennogo doma zanimanemogo kvartiroiu gubernatora gor. Vologdy;" d. 104, "Chertezh general'nogo plana doma gubernatora v gor. Vologde;" d. 109, "Plan mesta . . . gubernatorskogo doma v gor. Vologde, 1890."

5. TsGIA, f. Tekh-stro. kom., op. 169, d. 947, "Gubernatorskii dom v N-Novgorode;" d. 131, "Gubernatorskii dom v Vitebske;" d. 674, "Kostroma;" d. 291, "Viatka."

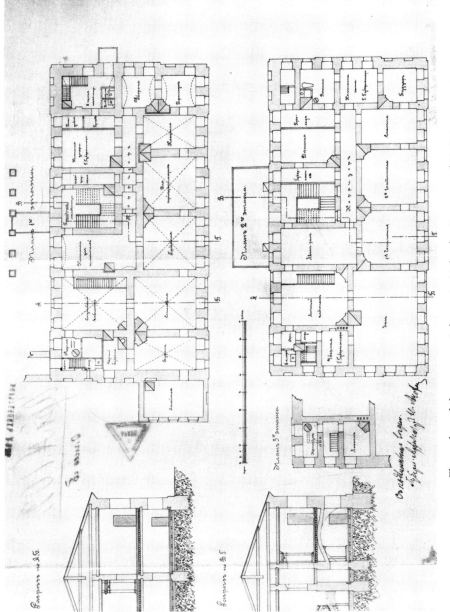

Floor plan of the governor's house in Vologda. Courtesy of TsGIA.

Governor's house in Vitebsk. Courtesy of TsGIA.

Governor's house in Kostroma. Courtesy of TsGIA.

governors' residences in Vilna and Perm were in such poor repair that they caused their occupants considerable annoyance and anxiety.[6]

For the most part, however, even the least of the governors' houses was impressive in the context of a provincial city where the majority of construction was still of logs in the traditional Russian manner. The residence of the governor, built of stone or brick and graced with a European facade, stood in sharp contrast to its surroundings. It was intended to be that way. Usually standing near the center of the town, the governor's mansion was a visible symbol of imperial power projected into the hinterlands. The face of authority was a matter of gravest concern. When a governor's house was being designed, bureaucrats in distant St. Petersburg worried lest the form and proportions of the structure produce an undesirable impression. Solid construction was not enough. The mansion had to have "a smart appearance" (*paradnyi vid*).[7]

The official residence of a governor underlined his dignity and power. It was also a place of business and a tool that helped the *nachal'nik gubernii* carry out his threefold duty as viceroy, administrator, and politician. Beyond this, the mansion, with all its attractive accoutrements, was a perquisite of office. It was a justified reward; the governors worked hard.

A Russian governor's day was long and full.[8] It usually began early. Soon after rising, between 7 and 8 A.M., the governor acquainted himself with the state of the provincial capital either by hearing a report from his police chief or by making a personal inspection of parts of the town.[9] Getting a police briefing undoubtedly saved time and energy, but a governor who relied exclusively on this method could miss the pungent realities of the urban life that surrounded him.

Visiting the market district of Chernigov shortly after he had assumed command of that province, Governor Evgenii Konstantinovich Andreevskii was nearly bowled over. At the meat stalls he encountered

6. V. V. fon Val', "Vil'na," TsGIA, f. fon Valia i Miasoedovykh (916), op. 1, d. 13, p. 5; I. F. Koshko, "Vospominaniia," p. 47, BAR, Koshko family papers.

7. Vypiska iz zhurnala tekhnichesko-stroitel'nogo komiteta, 28 April 1911, TsGIA, f. Tekh-stro. kom., op. 107, 1911, d. 37, "O postroike gubernatorskogo doma v g. Samare," p. 5.

8. The following account of a governor's work day is drawn primarily from the writings of governors themselves. Of particular value are the works of S. D. Urusov, V. V. fon Val', I. M. Strakhovskii, V. F. Dzhunkovskii, M. M. Osorgin, and N. P. Sinel'nikov.

9. M. M. Osorgin, "Vospominaniia," GBL, f. Osorgina, papka II, d. 2, pp. 158–59; N. P. Sinel'nikov, "Zapiski senatora N. P. Sinel'nikova," *Istoricheskii vestnik* 59 (1895): 383–84.

appalling filth: carcasses oozing blood and covered with dirty fat lay on unclean tables. The refuse of the butcher shops was indifferently thrown into alleys, where it rapidly putrefied. In the courtyards he passed, the governor noted "a mass of sewage, . . . consisting of cabbage leaves, potatoe and carrot peels, egg shells, livers and other internal organs." The situation seemed likely to produce serious contagion.

Andreevskii's morning tour prompted strong action. First, the *nachal'nik gubernii* demanded increased sanitary inspection, and later he imposed stricter rules for protecting the city from pollution.[10] In addition, the new governor learned a valuable lesson. Official reports were usually poor substitutes for on-the-spot, personal inspections.

An initial tour of the gubernia capital might leave a governor with his senses reeling, but that was only the beginning of his day. The real business of the morning commenced around ten or eleven with the reception of petitioners (*priem*). This activity consumed anywhere from three to five hours and was one of the most important parts of the governor's job. For His Excellency, the reception was a ritual that allowed him to assert his viceregal status and to establish direct contact with the people he ruled. For provincial citizens, it was an opportunity to escape the grip of local officials and to bring their problems to the attention of someone whom, they believed, had the power to deal with matters quickly and effectively. The *priem* reinforced in the public's mind the idea of a patriarchal and personal style of rule and so enhanced the governor's position and importance. But the attitude toward authority that the reception helped support could also result in false hopes and might engender exaggerated notions as to what the *nachal'nik gubernii* would actually be able accomplish.

Receptions were physically demanding and emotionally trying. The governor was on his feet most of the time as he stood waiting for petitioners to step forward with their requests or went around the reception hall talking to them. The petitions a governor received could be heart-rending and frustrating, especially when they presented him with problems that were beyond his power to solve.[11] Citizens of the province asked the governor's assistance in regard to their most basic needs. "The children did not have tea today and I cannot buy provisions for supper," wrote Evgeniia Lapitskaia to N. A. Troinitskii.

10. See Andreevskii's letter to the Chernigov police chief, 19 January 1894 and his instructions to the Chernigov police, December 1897, TsGIA, f. Kantseliarii Ministra vnutrennikh del (1282) op. 1, d. 1180, "Perepiska s chernigovskim gubernatorom," pp. 5–6, 10–14. Quoted passage on p. 5.

11. Urussov, pp. 24–25; Sinel'nikov, "Zapiski," *Istoricheskii vestnik* 59 (1895): 729–30.

"Your Excellency, I turn to you as a man and a governor. We are in a terrible situation. . . ."[12]
Financial necessity was central to many of the requests governors received. Frequently they came from women. Destitute, in a "hopeless position" (*bezvykhodnoe polozhenie*), they asked the *nachal'nik gubernii* to help them secure suitable employment.[13] But they were not alone. Recent graduates of higher educational institutions, retired bureaucrats trying to return to state service, persons seeking appointment in a particular area, all might approach the governor for help in landing a job.[14] Governors could also be asked to straighten out problems with an official's pension.[15] Sometimes the needs of petitioners were even more specific and limited. Gerasim Golovkov, a hired worker at the Academy of Arts in St. Petersburg, needed to travel to Belostok but lacked money to purchase a ticket. To whom did he turn? To the governor, of course![16]
Petitioners might involve governors in more intimate problems. A distraught mother begged Governor Sinel'nikov to help break up her son's romance with a soldier's wife. Anna Karlovna fon Verneke, a twelve-year-old orphan and heiress, petitioned V. V. fon Val' for his "protection and defense," asking that she not be placed under the guardianship of her two closest relatives. A teacher of German, accused of molesting the young boys in his classes, asked Governor D. D. Sverbeev what to do about this "slander."[17]

12. Letter dated 2 August 1879, TsGIA, f. Troinitskogo, op. 1, d. 52, "Pis'ma Troinitskomu ot raznykh lits," p. 1. In reconstructing the kind of things asked of governors during their receptions, I use a variety of letters and petitions found in governors' files and private papers. I am by no means certain that every document cited was actually handed to a governor at the time of the *priem.*

13. Petition of A. I. Vidutskaia, 21 July 1895, Leningradskii gosudarstvennyi istoricheskii arkhiv [hereafter LGIA], f. Kantseliarii petrogradskogo gubernatora (253), op. 3, d. 2063, "Po lichnoi perepiske nachal'nika gubernii, 2 II–15 XII 1885," p. 35; letter of M. Krasil'nikova to N. A. Bezak, 13 May 1880, TsGIA, f. Bezaka (895), op. 1, d. 54, p. 1.

14. Letter of Governor I. V. Lutkovskii to I. A. Zinov'ev, 10 July 1884, letter of A. Krizhanovskii to Lutkovskii, 5 February 1884, LGIA, f. Kants. pet. gub., op. 3, d. 1950, "Po lichnoi perepiske, 8 II–17 XI 1884, pp. 59, 2–3; Letters of Governor A. D. Sverbeev to M. A. Malinovskii and N. A. Gidman, September 1881, TsGALI, f. Sverbeevykh, op. 1, 468, "Predpisaniia samarskogo gubernatora, 1873–1893," pp. 12–15.

15. A. Berezhkovskii to N. A. Bezak, 18 May 1880, TsGIA, f. Bezaka, op. 2, d. 31, p. 1.

16. I. V. Lutkovskii to P. A. Gresser, 30 May 1884, LGIA, f. Kants. pet. gub., op. 3, d. 1950, p. 29. In this letter Lutkovskii passes on Golovkov's request to the St. Petersburg *gradonachal'nik.*

17. Sinel'nikov, "Zapiski," 59: 729–30; letter of fon Verneke, 30 December 1878, TsGAOR, f. fon Valia, op. 1, d. 94, "Perepiska . . . fon Valia . . . ," p. 8; Karl Boi to

When governors had to deal with requests from peasants or from minorities unfamiliar with Russian practices, receptions could become particularly troublesome and frustrating. Many times governors found that supplicants had traveled for days to deliver appeals that could just as easily have been sent by mail. Peasant and minority petitioners who sought to supplement their written requests with an oral presentation of their needs frequently became confused and confusing as cultural gaps and language barriers impeded both exposition and understanding. For minorities translators were often required. In the case of peasants, it was sometimes hard to comprehend their rambling discourse. Here a governor might draw heavily on his previous experience in rural areas. He and his aides needed a good understanding of customary law and local folkways in order to make sense out of what was being said.[18]

Throughout the reception, a conscientious governor tried to be patient, attentive, and above all, tactful. He had to decide rapidly whether a particular matter should be handled personally, turned over to local government agencies, or passed on to officials in St. Petersburg. Governors took considerable pride in their role as local problem solvers. Even when dispatching a case into other hands, it was not uncommon for them to append personal notes to guide and direct subordinates and to guarantee that the matter received proper attention.[19]

Gubernatorial pride seems to have been justified. The evidence suggests that a direct appeal to the *nachal'nik gubernii* produced action, if not always success, on behalf of the petitioner. Lapitskaia got the food she needed when Governor Troinitskii promptly brought her case to the attention of the Viatka charitable society. Sinel'nikov broke up the romance between the young man and the soldier's wife. St. Petersburg governor Lutkovskii made a more than good faith effort to secure a teaching position for Aleksandra Vidutskaia, who had petitioned for help in her "hopeless situation."[20]

Occasionally, requests made to governors could not be dealt with at once but required investigation at greater length. The case of the young

D. Sverbeev, 16 February 1900, TsGIA, f. Kants. MVD, op. 1, d. 1175, "Kurliandskaia guberniia," pp. 22–23.

18. See circular of Saratov governor to local police, 9 March 1888, in A. I. Kosich, *Tsirkuliary, ukazaniia i rechi g. nachal'nika saratovskoi gubernii General-Leitenanta A. I. Kosicha* (Saratov, 1891), p. 36; Urussov, pp. 24–25; Koshko *Vospominaniia*, p. 145.

19. Koshko, *Vospominaniia*, p. 145; V. F. Dzhunkovskii, "Vospominaniia za 1909–1910, TsGAOR, f. Dzhunkovskogo, op. 1, d. 49, p. 158.

20. Note on Lapitskaia's letter, TsGIA, f. Troinitskogo, op. 1, d. 52, p. 1; Sinel'nikov, "Zapiski," 59: 729–30; Lutkovskii's letters on Vidutskaia's behalf 24 August and 6 September 1885, LGIA, f. Kants. pet. gub., op. 3, d. 2063, pp. 36, 38.

heiress Anna fon Verneke, for example, proved more complicated than first thought. Governor fon Val' found out that the precocious preteen had attracted the attentions of a man more than twice her age who was planning to make off with both nymphet and fortune once his own ailing wife had passed from the scene. In the matter of Karl Boi, the German instructor accused of pederasty, a shocked Governor Sverbeev learned that the charges were true. Twelve students gave testimony that they had indeed been molested by their teacher. He had lured them to his apartment "where he kissed them, stuck his tongue in their mouths, sucked their lips and fondled their penises. . . ."[21]

Not only were receptions long and tiring, but they could also involve an element of danger as Governor N. M. Baranov of Nizhni-Novgorod discovered. On the morning of 21 August 1890, Baranov had received petitioners for three hours and was exhausted. He therefore broke off the interviews, asking those who had not been helped to return at 4:00 P.M. At this point the governor was approached by a young man with "a very unusual, but rather pleasant appearance." This petitioner stated that he could not come at four and was unable to wait until the next day to have his problem attended to. Baranov then agreed to meet the young man at two-thirty.

The governor was true to his word. But before he could keep his scheduled appointment, he encountered, on the stairs leading to his office, a weeping woman carrying an infant. Baranov ushered the woman into his study, briefly dealt with her problem, and dismissed her. He then called in the impatient youth from the morning's *priem*. The governor's annual report to the emperor tells the rest of the story:

> Being extremely tired . . . I did not want to talk standing up, and [so] I invited the petitioner to sit down and seated myself in a chair opposite him. Noticing the nervous twitching on the petitioner's face and the placement of his hand in his trousers' pocket, I moved over to another chair alongside the petitioner. [He] . . . became visibly confused by this and, after a brief hesitation, leaped from his seat and pulled out a large revolver with the intention of shooting me point blank. I easily succeeded in grabbing the hand with the revolver and, squeezing the wrist, twisted it behind the back of the criminal and threw him down on a divan. . . . But then, stepping in [some] filth left by the child of the [previous] petitioner, I slipped, and for several instants released the right hand of my opponent. Taking advantage of this, he grappled with me, striking a

---

21. Korbinskii to fon Val', 20 February 1879, TsGAOR, f. fon Valia, op. 1, d. 94, pp. 16–17; D. D. Sverbeev to MVD 30 March 1900, TsGIA, f. Kants. MVD, op. 1, d. 1175, p. 18.

blow to my side. But the finger of his hand, firmly pressed to the revolver, had probably become numb, and he was not able to get off a shot.[22]

Baranov's would-be assassin was quickly subdued, and the governor escaped with little more than an aching side and dirty shoes. But the dangers associated with receptions were a disquieting aspect of a governor's life. Somewhat sheepishly, I. F. Koshko recalled that in the wake of the upheaval of 1905 he held his receptions in the presence of a body of gendarmes. Only after order had been restored did the governor discontinue this practice.[23]

After the reception, the governor usually broke for his midday meal. Then came the meetings of one or more of the administrative bodies over which he had to preside. These sessions were never as dangerous as the *priem*, but they were equally tiring. Together with his advisers, the governor found himself confronting a wide range of legal questions, economic matters, and problems of social welfare. Even when no emergencies were involved, such meetings could last until late afternoon. At this point, if time permitted, the governor would receive reports from various provincial officials. These papers were frequently very detailed, contained extensive references to law codes and ministerial circulars, and demanded careful consideration.[24]

The hearing of reports usually went on until the dinner hour by which time most provincial bureaucrats were eagerly on their way home. But the governor's work continued. If the press of his regular duties allowed, the governor might make a number of business related calls on important people in the gubernia capital. Then at around eight, after his evening meal, the governor turned to the examination of still more reports, documents and miscellaneous correspondence. Much of the governor's work at this point was routine and simply involved signing his name, but a portion of these papers required closer attention. A governor could have his head of chancellery present the gist of this material in an official summary (*doklad*). Many *nachal'niki gubernii,* however, preferred to sift through the raw documents themselves, seeing this as the best way to keep their finger on the pulse of provincial life.[25]

22. TsGIA, f. DOD, op. 223, 1890, d. 249, "Vsepoddanneishii otchet o sostoianii . . . gubernii," p. 7.

23. Koshko, *Vospominaniia,* p. 144.

24. Osorgin, "Vospominaniia," GBL, f. Osorgina, papka II, d. 2, pp. 39, 158–59; Urussov, p. 25; Strakhovskii, "Gubernskoe ustroistvo," (October 1913): 103–104; Sinel'nikov, "Zapiski," 59: 383–84.

25. Urussov, pp. 25–26; Osorgin, "Vospominaniia," GBL, f. Osorgina, papka II, d. 2, pp. 158–59; Koshko, *Vospominaniia,* p. 145.

The reading and signing of official papers and the preparation for the next day's work often continued until well past midnight. By then the governor headed wearily to bed, but even now his rest might be interrupted. The late hours of the night could bring a frantic knocking at the gates, and the governor would confront a desperate citizen or an indignant political exile demanding action on a matter that could not wait for morning.[26]

The regular round of official duties did not encompass all of the governor's work day. Like a busy modern politician, he was constantly being called upon to be present at a variety of public functions. Could the governor attend the opening of an exhibit at the Institute of Civil Engineers? Would he be so kind as to come to a prayer service that was part of the graduation exercises at the zemstvo normal school? There was an almost endless number of ceremonial occasions that would just not be right without his presence: the dedication of a new hospital, the unveiling of a statue, the inauguration of a charitable lottery, school examinations. . . .[27] On top of this there was a wide range of social activities—parties, dinners, formal banquets, and balls—that the governor was expected either to give or to attend.

Social and ceremonial events could be of the greatest significance, for they enabled governors to escape the confines of bureaucratic routine. Meetings and informal situations gave a governor the chance to establish connections with local elites and to promote those programs he felt would be beneficial to the province. The ties a governor developed with prominent citizens could be crucial in determining the success of his administration, for a governor who lost the support of key elements in the province might find his usefulness at an end, be forced to retire, or transferred to another assignment.

The sphere of a governor's activities was not confined to the provincial capital. Worker or peasant disturbances in any part of the gubernia might bring His Excellency to the scene alone or at the head of a detachment of troops. Here the governor would be forced to deal decisively with the widest variety of situations. Often confronting barriers of distrust and incomprehension, the governor could find himself

---

26. P. B., "Neobychainyi gubernator (Stranichka iz vospominaniia)," *Na chuzhoi storone* 8 (1924): 163–64; Sinel'nikov, "Zapiski," 59: 384.

27. Director of the Institute of Civil Engineers to Governor S. A. Tol', 11 May 1892; Chairman of the St. Petersburg provincial zemstvo uprava to Tol', 18 May 1892, LGIA, f. Kants. pet. gub., op. 3, d. 2680, "Lichnaia perepiska nachal'nika gubernii, 27 I–26 IX 1892," pp. 20 and 23; see also the materials in TsGAOR, f. fon Valia, op. 1, d. 60, "Povesti i uvedomleniia fon Valiu o iavke na zasedaniia gubernskogo pravleniia, okruzhnogo sudia, razlichnykh obshchestv i uchrezhdenii."

in one of a number of roles from mediator or conciliator to stern judge dispensing corporal punishment.[28]

Strikes and riots were not the only occurrences that brought the governors into the uezds. More immediately connected with the day-to-day administering of the province were the regular tours of inspection the governors undertook. As the chief representative of governmental authority in the gubernia, the governor was empowered to make unannounced inspections of all local state institutions.[29] In fact, the law specifically required the governor to conduct a general tour of the province shortly after assuming office and to make other inspections at least once every two years.[30] During the course of these tours (*revizii*) the governor got away from his desk and traveled to the small towns and villages where the great majority of provincial inhabitants lived.

The frequency and the amount of time involved in these tours of inspection obviously varied according to local conditions and the personal qualities of particular governors. Some governors shirked this responsibility whenever possible.[31] But most took their duties seriously and conducted *revizii* on a regular basis. The initial months of a governor's tenure might be particularly hectic in this regard as the new *nachal'nik gubernii* sought to get a clear picture of the local situation through numerous inspections.[32] Even established governors, however, often toured their provinces and spent as much as two months a year on this kind of work. Many of these inspections took only a day or two, but some could last as long as three weeks, especially in the larger gubernias.[33]

---

28. An almost limitless variety of gubernatorial responses to lower class disturbances can be found in the volumes edited by A. M. Pankratova, *Rabochee dvizhenie v Rossii v XIX veke: Sbornik dokumentov i materialov* and in the *Krest'ianskoe dvizhenie* series. This subject will be discussed in greater detail in Chapter 9 below.

29. "Obshchee uchrezhdenie gubernskoe," art. 271, *Svod zakonov*, 2 (1892).

30. Ibid., art. 388.

31. TsGIA, f. Zemskogo otdela (1291), op. 32, 1903, d. 7, "Otchet . . . Savicha po proizvedennoi v 1903 revizii krest'ianskikh uchrezhdenii permskoi gubernii," p. 55; letter of Arkhangelsk governor Bibikov to MVD, 24 April 1913, TsGIA, f. DOD, op. 47, 1908, d. 75, "O naznachenii . . . Bibikova," pp. 117–18.

32. TsGAOR, f. fon Valia, op. 1, d. 57, pp. 15–33. These pages contain a series of communications from the new governor Shmit to fon Val' about his various travels. Between 2 May and 30 November 1877, Shmit made five tours of inspection.

33. The personnel files of governors often contain information on their tours of inspection. See TsGIA, f. DOD, op. 45, 1882, d. 78, "O naznachenii . . . Batiushkova," pp. 152–72; ibid., 1889, d. 136, ch. 2, "O naznachenii . . . Shlippe," pp. 35–98. Also A. N. to N. A. Troinitskii, 21 May 1910, ibid., f. Troinitskogo, op. 1, d. 57, "Pis'ma Troinitskim . . . ot ikh detei," pp. 11–12.

A gubernatorial inspection was hard work for everyone involved. In the provincial chancelleries, papers flew. A series of curt directives told local officials of the governor's intentions and ordered them to prepare the appropriate record books for examination.[34] Staff workers drew up an itinerary and a list of the institutions to be visited. The governor, too, readied himself for an ordeal. Plans often called for a long march in a short space of time with whirlwind visits to as many as twenty different agencies.[35] And travel was not easy. Although a train or river boat might take a governor to the starting point of his tour, most of the inspection would be made by more humble means. Riding over hard roads on horseback or in a carriage, His Excellency was frequently tormented by heat, cold and dust.[36]

Plans for governors' inspections were often tinged with an air of unreality, and the historian suspects that few were accomplished on time. Certainly this was true for V. F. Dzhunkovskii's sixty-mile journey from Bronnitsy to Ozery. Although the governor began at six in the morning and expected to reach his final destination by ten in the evening, unforeseen delays soon forced him to abandon the schedule. Unmindful of the hour, he conducted his last inspection—the *volost'* board and zemstvo school in Gori—at three in the morning and arrived at Ozery an hour later.

Along the way Dzhunkovskii must have left a trail of exhausted local officials, roused from half-sleep to greet him. His Excellency, however, was a man of iron constitution. Despite the rigors of the preceding day and night, Dzhunkovskii needed only a few hours' rest. By eight he was up and meeting a delegation of striking workers from a nearby factory.[37]

In conducting an inspection governors developed their own methods and their own particular goals. But, with variations, most *revizii* in-

---

34. See materials on gubernatorial inspections contained in Gosudarstvennyi arkhiv kalininskoi oblasti [hereafter GAKO] f. Kantseliarii tverskogo gubernatora (561). op. 1, d. 3641, "O poezdkakh g. nachal'nika gubernii v otpusk i po delam sluzhby, 1895," pp. 18–21.

35. TsGAOR, f. Dzhunkovskogo, op. 1, d. 118, "Zametki Dzhunkovskogo i dr. materialy o poezdke po moskovskoi gub., 1906 g.," p. 6; GAKO, f. Kants. tver. gub., op. 1, d. 17792, "O poezdke nachal'nika gubernii v gor. Ostashkov dlia revizii mestnykh uchrezhdenii, 1914," p. 11.

36. Koshko, "Vospominaniia," pp. 68, 133–34 BAR; A. N. to N. A. Troinitskii, 6 September 1909 and 31 May 1912, TsGIA, f. Troinitskogo, op. 1, d. 57, pp. 68, 234–35.

37. Dzhunkovskii, "Vospominaniia za 1905–1908 gg.," TsGAOR, f. Dzhunkovskogo, op. 1, d. 47, pp. 220–21; see also the account of the inspection carried in *Moskovskie vedomosti,* 17 June 1906.

volved one or more of the following: interviews with local officials, a tour of the main public institutions of the area, and meetings with peasant officials and land captains.[38] There were some governors, like the seemingly indefatigable Dzhunkovskii, who tried to do everything in a single sweep. An excerpt from a report on his inspection in Klin admirably shows Dzhunkovskii's style:

... The governor visited in the following order: the local church school, the municipal executive board, the girls' progymnasium, the city parish school, and the city bank; he looked over the vehicles of the city fire department [and] during that time the firemen conducted a drill. [The governor] noted that the girls' progymnasium was well housed and had exemplary instruction. The governor attended several classes in Russian language, arithmetic, geography, and French.

Then he visited the zemstvo executive board [and] the uezd conference (s"ezd) where the governor talked with ... five headmen from neighboring volosts and nineteen elders from nearby villages. [He also visited] the zemstvo jail, which he found to be in proper order, the zemstvo agricultural storage house (where he noted that there was only a small amount of seed oats on hand), the chancellery of the draft board, the uezd police department, and the treasury; the latter had an excellent safe.[39]

Almost always, governors sought to display concern and the personal touch. They tried to leave the impression that nothing—the food at a local hospital, the operations of a wine and fruit growing school, or the needs of hard pressed uezd officials—was too insignificant for consideration.[40] Sometimes a governor literally sniffed out problems. On the occasion of his inspection of the prison in Rzhev, A. N. Somov noted the following situation: "The outhouses were found to be in generally good condition, but on the day of the inspection a slight odor became noticeable. Clearly this occurred because the apertures of the toilet seats were not closed and the lids ... did not fit tightly."[41]

Governors gathered information from their tours in a variety of

38. Urussov, pp. 113–20; Koshko, "Vospominaniia," pp. 368–70, BAR; journal of the Kharkov provincial committee on peasant affairs, 3 October 1876, TsGAOR, f. fon Valia, op. 1, d. 117, "Zhurnaly khar'kovskogo gubernskogo po krest'ianskim delam prisutstviia i perepiska fon Valia," pp. 6–9; GAKO, f. Kants. tver. gub., op. 1, d. 19275, "O revizii nachal'nika gubernii v gor. Bezhetske, 1892," pp. 1–69.

39. TsGAOR, f. Dzhunkovskogo, op. 1, d. 114, "Zapiski ... ob osmotre ... goroda Klina," p. 2.

40. Ibid.; Urussov, pp. 116–17; Koshko, "Vospominaniia," pp. 338–69, BAR.

41. GAKO, f. Kants. tver. gub., op. 1, d. 19154, "O revizii nachal'nikom gubernii gorodov Rzheva i Ostashkova," p. 124.

ways. Some, like N. A. Bezak, put together systematic notebooks that listed findings under appropriate headings and provided a detailed description of the bureaucrats serving in rural areas.[42] Others, like V. V. fon Val', simply jotted down impressions on small scraps of paper.[43] Accompanying staff assembled statistical materials and pored through the records of inspected institutions. Later they combined the governor's impressions with various other findings into a final report. From this document the governor's subordinates drew smaller and more specifically focused directives that informed local and central officials about particular problems and suggested the means to correct them.[44]

By the beginning of the twentieth century, students of provincial administration and even some governors considered inspections an imperfect means of keeping tabs on the real situation in the gubernias.[45] There was too much to see and too little time, and officials eager to make a good impression frequently stage-managed encounters between the *nachal'nik gubernii* and local people. V. F. Dzhunkovskii recalled that during a tour of Moscow province a particularly officious district police officer herded a group of peasants down for a meeting. His effort to project an image of jollity failed, however, when the departing governor heard the policeman urge his charges: "Shout 'hurrah,' you bastards!" His Excellency was amused, but not impressed.[46]

Yet few governors would have abandoned the inspections altogether. These tours enabled them to observe local needs directly, deal quickly with the abuses they found, and meet and get to know local officials.[47] In the end, governors gathered a wealth of impressions that would guide their decisions in the months ahead. I. F. Koshko probably expressed the views of many of his colleagues when he wrote: "All

42. Bezak's notebooks are found in TsGIA, f. Bezaka, op. 2, d. 3, "Svedeniia po ekonomicheskomu polozheniiu uezdov nizhegorodskogo gubernii."
43. TsGAOR, f. fon Valia, op. 1, d. 63, "Materialy o revizionnoi poezdke . . . po iaroslavskoi gubernii," pp 52–72.
44. TsGAOR, f. Dzhunkovskogo, op. 1, d. 120, "Tsirkuliar moskovskogo gubernatora . . . o rezul'tatakh osmotra bogorodskogo uezda," pp. 1–3; GAKO, f. Kants. tver. gub., op. 1, d. 18900, "O revizii goroda Korchevy i sela Kimri, 1884," pp. 64–83; ibid., f. Tverskogo gubernskogo pravleniia (466) op. 1, d. 33706, "O revizii tverskim gubernatorom uchrezhdeniia goroda Kaliazina, 1897," pp. 1–38.
45. Blinov, *Gubernatory*, pp. 310–21; Koshko, "Vospominaniia," p. 334, BAR; A. Planson, "Detsentralizatsiia," TsGAOR, f. V. K. Pleve (586), op. 1, d. 316, pp. 10–12.
46. Dzhunkovskii, "Vospominaniia za 1905–1908 gg.," TsGAOR, f. Dzhunkovskogo, op. 1, d. 47, p. 333.
47. Urussov, p. 113; Koshko, "Vospominaniia," pp. 219–21, BAR; Osorgin, "Vospominaniia," GBL, f. Osorgina, papka II, d. 2, p. 196.

of these [impressions from inspections] remain, for the time being in a corner of your brain, and you are unaware even of their existence. And only during your practical work do they come forth, giving . . . firm examples of what to do, and how."[48]

Inspections were important for other reasons as well. Given the absence of a coherent uezd administration with a clear-cut chain of command, these *revizii* enabled governors to correct and energize the work of local officials. At the same time, inspections underlined the direct, personal, and even patriarchal character of gubernatorial rule. In the eyes of much of the public, the governor was an emperor-surrogate, and his presence in their town or village was a sign of the tsar's concern for his people.

Indeed, the governor's status as viceroy helped give inspections a festive air. His arrival was an excuse for all kinds of dinners, receptions, and entertainments. "Society" in the lesser provincial towns rapidly enveloped the distinguished visitor, and often he had to spend hours listening to the chatter of local officials and their wives. Nobles and merchants, too, were eager to wine and dine the *nachal'nik gubernii*, and their hospitality might put his talents as a trencherman to the test. The governor of Riazan, A. N. Obolenskii, making a one-day inspection of parts of Riazhsk uezd, was entertained at breakfast, served three separate main meals and, on his return to Riazhsk, was asked to have supper as well.[49]

The culinary adventures of I. F. Koshko in Ekaterinburg provide extreme examples of a governor's dietary duties and dilemmas. The "second city" of Perm province, too big and rich to be simply a county seat, used the governor's visit to demonstrate both its wealth and sophistication. Society here possessed more than a few rought edges, however, and had a tendency to go to extremes. On several occasions Koshko suffered at the hands of Madame Bibikova, one of the town's leading hostesses, who, in her zeal for feeding guests, "displayed the tyranny of a Nero and the cruelty of an Ivan the Terrible." Setting before the governor a mountain of delicacies, Bibikova bid—nay, commanded—him to eat. Thoroughly cowed, the "master of the province" cleaned his plate.[50]

Inspections, then, remained a vital part of the governor's work. But

48. Koshko, "Vospominaniia," p. 335, BAR.

49. Urussov, pp. 114–15; Koshko, "Vospominaniia," p. 331, BAR; Vladimir Korostovets, *Seed and Harvest*, trans. by Dorothy Lumby (London, n.d.), pp. 136–37; TsGIA, f. DOD, op. 47, 1911, d. 342, ch. 2, "Otchet . . . [N. Ch.] Zaionchkovskogo po obozreniiu deloproizvodstva riazanskikh gubernskogo pravleniia i kantseliarii gubernatora i revizii politseiskikh uchrezhdenii," p. 90.

50. Koshko, "Vospominaniia," p. 159, BAR.

they caused difficulties that went beyond the long days of travel and the spotlight of notoriety in dreary uezd towns. The *nachal'niki gubernii* frequently had to put aside important tasks when they went out into the country. A. N. Troinitskii complained that he had to delay writing his annual report to the emperor in order to conduct local inspections and that when he returned found himself confronting a backlog of unfinished business.[51] The weight of evidence suggests that Troinitskii was not alone. Nursing their livers and their saddle sores, facing desks full of unanswered correspondence and unread reports, many governors coming back from inspections must have asked: Was that trip necessary?

Of course, governors were not always public men. They also had private lives filled with pleasures and frustrations, joys and woes. The student of institutional history may see these matters as irrelevant. Yet given the personal character of gubernatorial rule, a few generalizations should be ventured, for these help us to understand better the circumstances in which the governors worked.

Governors' private lives mirrored an official existence cluttered with various competing demands on their time and energy. Moreover, financial worries were never far despite their high salaries. And because many *nachal'niki gubernii* held considerable estates or other forms of capital, they had to devote some portion of their day to seeing that their holdings were properly managed.[52] Nor were governors free from other mundane cares, as N. A. Troinitskii's correspondence demonstrates particularly well. Various letters show him encumbered with the petty details of household management: Would there be wine for the winter? How could one obtain a good rug? Where was the best place to stay during a stopover in Nizhni-Novgorod? And when Troinitskii moved on to a new post, he even had to write letters to the newspapers to which he subscribed informing them about the change of address.[53]

Families were both a burden and a joy. When separated from parents, wives, and children, as they often were, governors experienced loneliness and even despondency,[54] though when their loved ones

51. Letters to N. A. Troinitskii, 18 June and 11 July 1912 and 26 February 1913, TsGIA, f. Troinitskogo, op. 1, d. 57, pp. 157–58, 192, 238.

52. See for example materials in the papers of S. A. and S. D. Tol' and N. A. Bezak, TsGIA, f. Tolia (1064), op. 1, dd. 1, 2, 3, "Khoziastvennaia perepiska po imeniiam;" ibid., f. Bezaka, op. 2, d. 117, "Kniga prikhodov i raskhodov za 1869–1890."

53. TsGIA, f. Troinitskogo, op. 1, d. 2, "Kopii sluzhebnoi perepiski," pp. 16, 44, 234; ibid., d. 71, "Pis'ma . . . Romanusu," p. 31a.

54. See, for example, the letters of A. N. Troinitskii to his father, 6 September 1909 and 16 August 1910, TsGIA, f. Troinitskogo, op. 1, d. 57, pp. 55–56, 69; also the

were present, it was difficult for governors to find sufficient time for them. Having the children sit in on a business lunch or a few stolen moments of play was often all the busy *nachal'niki gubernii* could spare for their sons and daughters.[55] Inevitably, family life generated stresses that must have impinged on the governors' work. Childhood illness and adolescent rebellion were but a few of the many domestic concerns that could turn a governor from the task of running a province.[56]

The love lives of governors also deserve a moment's consideration for reasons beyond the purely prurient. The romantic involvements of the *nachal'niki gubernii* could have considerable political as well as personal import and may help to explain why such matters find a place in the works of some of Russia's greatest writers. A single governor, amiable and gallant, might gain great favor with the provincial ladies and become a much-sought-after addition to the social scene.[57] But a governor's amorous successes might also produce local jealousy and other pitfalls as well. Perhaps it is not accidental that Lev Tolstoi, with his unerring sense of Russian realities, had Aleksei Aleksandrovich Karenin's fate decided by matronly intrigue while he was a provincial governor.[58] And was there something of Karenin in Evgenii Osipovich Iankovskii who, at the age of forty-three, married nineteen-year-old Natalia Ivanovna Ziloti?[59] A young governor, though perhaps not a young man, was still a very fine catch indeed!

Relations between married governors and their wives were also of the greatest importance, because the *gubernatorsha* was often a figure of considerable significance in her own right who helped set the tone for provincial social life and directed the work of local charitable institutions. The impression she made on the leading figures of the gubernia was a matter of considerable gubernatorial concern.[60] Available evidence indicates that most governors loved their wives and were

letters of S. A. Tol' to his wife, ibid., f. Tolia, op. 2, d. 27, "Pis'ma i telegrammy . . . 1878–1899."

55. Osorgin, "Vospominaniia," GBL, f. Osorgina, papka II, d. 2, pp. 158–59.

56. N. A. Troinitskii to V. I. Romanus 24 April 1878, TsGIA, f. Troinitskogo, op. 1, d. 71, p. 31a; see also Ol'ga Koshko's account of her decision to run away from home and study at the higher courses for women in St. Petersburg. O. I. Koshko, "Vospominaniia," p. 33, BAR.

57. Urussov, pp. 16–17.

58. Leo Tolstoi, *Anna Karenina,* A. Maud trans., G. Gibian, ed. (New York: Norton, 1970), p. 461.

59. TsGIA, f. DOD, op. 44, 1879, d. 152, "O naznachenii . . . Iankovskogo . . . ," p. 29.

60. Osorgin, "Vospominaniia," GBL, f. Osorgina, papka II, d. 2, p. 231; D. N. Liubimov, "Vospominaniia," p. 62, BAR, Liubimov papers.

faithful to them. But conjugal devotion could be a drawback if it meant giving a willful *gubernatorsha* free reign to intrude on governmental matters. Dostoevskii's hysterical and hilarious Madame fon Lembke was obviously a grotesque caricature, but meddlesome gubernatorial spouses were not unknown. Their actions could provoke anger, conflict, and, over time, might cause serious problems for the *nachal'nik gubernii*.[61]

Of course, there were governors who strayed from their wives, and gubernatorial mistresses—if not always the equals of Saltykov-Shchedrin's "pompadouresses"—were frequent figures on provincial stages. Skillfully managed, a governor's affair of the heart might produce little more than the shaking of heads and the wagging of tongues. But when things got out of hand, as they often did, an extramarital adventure could rock a province, call authority into disrepute, and destroy a career.

The story of Konstantin Mikhailovich Shidlovskii is a useful case in point. While serving in Ekaterinoslav (1909–1910), the governor, forty years old, married, and the father of two, entered into a liaison with the wife of a certain M. de Laroche, a resident of the province. When the cuckold ultimately learned of the affair, he railed at Shidlovskii and challenged him to a duel. Matters never came to a pass of arms, but to satisfy the offended husband, Shidlovskii agreed to quit the province. In fact, the scandal had left him little choice.

Shidlovskii requested a transfer to another post, but the news of his escapades had not been well received in St. Petersburg. Displaying a droll humor not usually attributed to him, Prime Minister P. A. Stolypin proffered Shidlovskii the governorship of the former penal colony of Sakhalin Island.[62] The prodigal ex-governor declined to accept this cold comfort, however, finding something warmer close at hand. In September, 1911, he divorced his wife and, shortly thereafter, the twenty-five-year-old Madame de Laroche took Konstantin Mikhailovich as her third husband. Archival documents do not tell us if the two were happy, only that Shidlovskii's personal finances and his career were in ruins.[63]

61. Memorandum of 15 October 1911, TsGIA, f. DOD, op. 47, 1910, d. 278, "So spravkami o gubernatorakh kotorye prestavlialis' g. Ministru v 1910, 1911 gg.," pp. 118–19; ibid., 1913, d. 332, "Otchet . . . Zaionchkovskogo po komandirovke v gor. Vologdu," p. 2.

62. Memorandum of 15 October 1911, TsGIA, f. DOD, op. 47, 1910, d. 278, p. 118.

63. Memorandum on Shidlovskii, no date, TsGIA, f. DOD, op. 47, 1912, d. 19, "So spravkami o gubernatorakh kotorye predstavlialis' g. Ministru v 1912 godu i 1913 godu," p. 68.

The pressures on the governors, both public and private, appear to have caused a high incidence of illness among the *nachal'niki gubernii*. A large body of evidence shows the governors suffering from a multitude of complaints: intestinal catarrah, severe cough, shortness of breath, chest pains, extreme stiffness, swelling of the liver, dispepsia, migraine headaches, dietary difficulties, dizziness, insomnia, depression, and general exhaustion.[64] Not all of these problems were necessarily attributable to the burdens of office, but the observations of Governor I. M. Strakhovskii have the ring of truth: "Just as in the past there were known certain 'episcopal' diseases associated with a sedentary way of life, so at the present time various forms of overwork and nervous heart disorders, such as angina pectoris, are typical 'gubernatorial' maladies."[65]

How governors' illnesses influenced their official conduct is not entirely clear. Certainly they led the *nachal'niki gubernii* to request fairly frequent leaves of absence and, as a result, some governors were away from their provinces for considerable periods. Poor health may also have helped cause the fairly rapid turnover of governors in some of the more inclement gubernias and so added a measure of instability to provincial administration. Finally, the image of a governor who frequently suffered serious discomfort must be joined with that of an official whose days were extraordinarily busy and whose private life was often harried and cramped. At the very least, such knowledge should inform our judgments as we look more closely at the governors and the way they functioned in the various roles that their office imposed.

64. A variety of doctors' reports are found in governors' personnel files. See for example TsGIA, f. DOD, op. 44, 1874, d. 26, "O naznachenii . . . Erdeli," p. 32; ibid., op. 45, 1880, d. 147, "O naznachenii . . . Tomara," p. 307; ibid., 1887, d. 9, "O naznachenii . . . Terenina," p. 153; ibid., op. 73, 1906, "O naznachenii . . . Lodyzhenskogo," p. 2. Also of use are some of the letters governors wrote to their family and friends. See particularly the letters of A. N. Troinitskii to his father, and those of S. A. Tol' to his wife (TsGIA, f. Troinitskogo, op. 1, d. 57, p. 258 and passim; ibid., f. Tolia, op. 2, d. 27, pp. 83–86, 104).

65. Strakhovskii, "Gubernskoe ustroistvo" (October 1913): 105.

– 4 –

Viceroy and Flunky

Writing in exile after the revolution, former governor P. P. Stremou-khov made the following observation about the office he had once held: "In the complex administrative machine of the old order, the governors were the hundred or so bolts that held it together. One needed only to wrench them out of the machine and it would fall apart."[1] Stremoukhov may have been guilty of exaggeration, but his assertion contained an essential truth. The governors' work was determined by a series of connections with the center, local administration, and provincial society. Even if we do not see them as the essential element holding the tsarist system together, we must agree that the *nachal'niki gubernii* were truly men in the middle, subject to all kinds of pulls and pressures from both above and below. Each of the cords binding the governors to one or another segment of society or the administrative structure tugged in a different direction and each required them to assume an appropriate stance or function.

The links connecting the governor to the center were particularly important, but they forced him to assume three often contradictory roles. As the personal representative of the emperor, he was a viceroy, the local embodiment of the sovereign's power. Simultaneously, however, the governor was a state official who had to act as a general supervisor and administrative ombudsman, because he was outside the regular ministerial hierarchies. Finally, His Excellency was the chief

1. P. P. Stremoukhov, "Administrativnoe ustroistvo imperatorskoi Rossii po vospominaniiam gubernatora," section 1, p. 1, BAR, S. E. Kryzhanovskii papers.

provincial agent of the MVD, a subordinate capacity in which he functioned as an all-purpose manager and, on occasion, glorified errand boy.

In an ideological and emotional sense, the most important tie connecting the governors to the center was their link with the sovereign which gave them a sense of prestige and independence and strongly influenced their conception of office. In the tsar, the governors always felt that they had a unique source of support, an ultimate trump card in dealing with any central official, even the minister of internal affairs.

Direct contact between the emperor and his viceroys was, however, relatively infrequent and its incidence seems to have declined over the course of the nineteenth century.[2] By the early 1900s, the way in which the *nachal'niki gubernii* obtained access to the emperor had become encumbered by bureaucratic routine. A governor who wished to have an audience with the tsar usually made application through the MVD's Department of General Affairs (*Departament obshchikh del*), a process that allowed the minister to monitor and control these contracts. Beyond this, any interview with the tsar was likely to be extremely brief, no more than five or six minutes. In such circumstances, a governor could not hope to inform the sovereign about his assigned province or deal with any significant matter.[3]

However limited its value, governors often sought to make use of their right to address the tsar, particularly when embarking upon a new assignment and, judging from their memoirs, this experience was something memorable.[4] I. F. Koshko, who had three interviews with the emperor during his almost ten years as governor, admitted being excited to the point that he failed to notice any of the details of his surroundings. All Koshko's attention had been directed toward His Majesty.[5]

On occasion, a governor might enjoy a more intimate relationship with the emperor. While governor in Moscow, V. F. Dzhunkovskii also served Nicholas II as aide-de-camp, a largely honorific post that gave him a unique opportunity to approach the sovereign. During his brief stays in St. Petersburg, the governor often took tea or dined with the imperial family and was able to discuss many issues that concerned

---

2. Theodore Taranovski, "The Politics of Counter-Reform: Autocracy and Bureaucracy in the Reign of Alexander III, 1881–1894" (Ph.D. diss., Harvard, 1976), p. 110.

3. Koshko, "Vospominaniia," pp. 199–202, BAR, Koshko family papers.

4. Urussov, *Memoirs*, pp. 4–5; Sinel'nikov, "Zapiski," 60: 695–96; Sverbeev, "Vstrechi i znakomstva," TsGALI, f. Sverbeevykh, op. 1, d. 104, pp. 5–6.

5. Koshko, "Vospominaniia," p. 207, BAR.

the welfare of his province in these informal circumstances. Thus when the village of Tretiakovo burned down, Dzhunkovskii brought the problem to the tsar's attention and almost at once obtained a gift of 5,000 rubles to aid the needy.[6]

To appeal to the tsar in behalf of fire victims was one thing, to solve more complicated questions was something else again. Once a matter entered the embrace of the bureaucracy, even the emperor's charms had limited effect. Dzhunkovskii found this out when he tried to help some peasants whose land had been taken by the state for a railroad right-of-way. The Ministry of Finance had fixed the price of the condemned property well below its real market value, and when Dzhunkovskii tried to get the peasants what was properly due them, he encountered a wall of official indifference: the Ministry of Finance's evaluation had already been approved by the State Council and sanctioned by the emperor.

Undaunted, Dzhunkovskii turned to the tsar, who accepted the governor's contention that the peasants had been underpaid and approved an order giving them an additional 50,000 rubles as compensation. Yet, even the autocrat's command did not solve the problem. The emperor's memorandum simply passed from one ministry to another because no one could decide where the monies were to come from. The issue remained unresolved until P. A. Stolypin assumed responsibility and took the necessary sums from a special fund reserved for unforeseen expenditures.[7]

Because personal audiences with the tsar were infrequent and usually of limited worth, governors attached great value to their right to present His Majesty with an annual report. The *vsepoddanneishii otchet* (most loyal report) kept alive the mystique of the governors' imperial connection despite the efforts of the central bureaucracy to minimize its importance. Through their reports governors called attention to the needs of their provinces and, on occasion, raised broader questions as well. And when suggestions put forward by the governors met with the tsar's approval, they could have considerable impact. The sovereign's comments (*otmetki*) on the reports were discussed by the Committee of Ministers and in this way, governors' proposals could become catalysts for legislation or for economic programs.[8]

Over the course of the nineteenth century, the central ministries, and

6. Dzhunkovskii, "Vospominaniia za 1905–1908 gg.," TsGAOR, f. Dzhunkovskogo, op. 1, d. 47, pp. 32–37, 292–96.

7. Ibid., pp. 442–45.

8. Yaney, *Systematization*, pp. 299–301.

particularly the MVD, had done much to structure the annual reports and to define their contents.[9] By the early twentieth century, a governor's report consisted of two parts: the first, the *otchet* proper, was the personal representation of the *nachal'nik gubernii* to the emperor; the second, the printed survey (*obzor*), contained a large amount of statistical information. In terms of size, the second section far outweighed the first—the data it contained were important to the government bureaus in St. Petersburg—but the governor's direct communication with his sovereign was of greater significance. This was true because the emperors Alexander III and Nicholas II saw the reports as vital instruments for maintaining the autocratic system and their personal style of rule.

As George Yaney has pointed out, late nineteenth-century autocrats used the *otchety* both as a device for stimulating and coordinating ministerial activity and as a means for circumventing bureaucratic channels.[10] The governors, too, were well aware of the importance the emperors attached to the reports, for they received copies of the tsars' comments on a regular basis.[11] The governors even took the liberty of publicizing some of these *otmetki*, violating government policy and provoking vigorous, but probably futile, objections from the MVD.[12] The governors' actions demonstrate that in their eyes the *otchet* was more than just a way of informing the sovereign and influencing state policy. It was also a device for institutional and even personal aggrandizement. The report underlined the governors' direct connection with the emperor and asserted the viceregal status of their office.

Given the large number of potential usages, it is not surprising that governors' reports differed markedly in terms of style, focus, and content. Despite the fact that the form of the *otchet* had supposedly been standardized in 1870, meaningful generalizations about such documents are almost impossible. Still, a fairly extensive reading of gubernatorial reports suggests that, structure aside, three basic elements

9. Ibid., pp. 295–301; N. P. Diatlova, "Otchety gubernatorov kak istoricheskii istochnik," in *Problemy arkhivovedeniia i istochnikovedeniia* (Leningrad, 1964), pp. 247–48.

10. Yaney, *Systematization*, pp. 299–301.

11. Communications from the MVD to A. D. Sverbeev, 25 December 1885 and 26 November 1886, TsGALI, f. Sverbeevykh, op. 1, d. 459, "Tsirkuliary, otvety i vyzovy departamenta obshchikh del, 1877–1891 gg.," pp. 4–5; Letter of N. L. Obolenskii to N. P. Muratov, 15 October 1915, TsGIA, f. Muratova, op. 1, d. 4, "Pis'mo kurskogo gubernatora . . . Muratovu," pp. 1–3.

12. Circular of the MVD to the governors 31 January 1901, TsGIA, f. Kants. MVD, op. 3, d. 103, "Tsirkuliar ministra . . . o poriadke sostavleniia i predstavleniia otchetov . . . ," p. 3.

stood out: the strictly informational, the programmatic, and the personal. The balance of these elements, however, varied from report to report and from governor to governor.

Most governors contented themselves with the relatively simple task of presenting the emperor with general information about the state of the province. Such reports skimmed over the local situation and gave the impression that, in the main, all was well and in good order. On occasion, bland reports might be garnished by a discussion of a specific problem that could benefit from imperial attention.

The master of this style of *otchet* was P. A. Poltaratskii, who governed three provinces (Arkhangelsk, Ufa, and Kazan) for over twenty years before he was appointed to the State Council in 1904. Poltaratskii was always cautious, and his reports emphasized the positive even in the hardest of times. Although he was aware of the major trends in provincial life and willing to present these to the tsar, Poltaratskii avoided bold or striking suggestions. Nor did he assert his own importance as *nachal'nik gubernii*. In fact, the governor sometimes seemed to hide behind a mass of trivia. One of his reports, for example, devoted several pages to a description of a display of products produced by the inmates of Kazan's provincial prisons.[13]

Yet, even Poltaratskii had certain areas of concern that he stressed repeatedly. During his long tenure in Kazan (1889–1904), Poltaratskii pushed for the expansion of education as a means of stimulating local economic growth and overcoming the differences between the Russian and Tatar populations of the province.[14] The governor also lobbied for the expansion of railroad links between Kazan and the rest of the country.[15] But nowhere did he advance a general program for meeting the province's problems and needs.[16]

Although most gubernatorial reports were similar in style and tone to those written by Poltaratskii, the late nineteenth and early twentieth centuries saw a significant number of governors who sought to use their reports to develop plans for the economic, cultural, and even political growth of the provinces over which they presided. Often these governors went further and proposed solutions to problems with empire-wide significance. The names N. M. Baranov, A. P. Engel'gardt,

13. Report for 1890, TsGIA, f. DOD, op. 223, 1891, d. 190, pp. 5–6.

14. Reports for 1893, 1894 and 1903, TsGIA, f. DOD, op. 223, 1894, d. 212, pp. 9–11; ibid., 1895, d. 163, pp. 4–5, 9–10; ibid., op. 194, 1904, d. 124, pp. 7–16.

15. Reports for 1889, 1895 and 1896, TsGIA, f. DOD, op. 223, 1890, d. 240, pp. 1–12; ibid., 1896, d. 53, pp. 10–11; ibid., 1897, d. 55b, pp. 2–11.

16. A possible exception was Poltaratskii's final report (1903), TsGIA, f. DOD, op. 194, 1904, d. 124.

Aleksandr P. Engel'gardt,
governor of Arkhangelsk and Saratov

A. I. Kosich, S. V. Shakhovskoi, and P. A. Stolypin come quickly to mind but do not exhaust the list.

Of all the governors noted above, none made more consistent use of the annual report to present a developmental program for his province than A. P. Engel'gardt. For almost a decade as governor of Arkhangelsk, Engel'gardt not only outlined the specific needs of the gubernia to the emperor, but he also wrapped the individual requests in a broader plan for institutional and economic modernization. Beyond this, Engel'gardt tied the developmental concerns of Arkhangelsk with the greater destinies of the empire. He was, of course, not unique in discussing both the problems and the potential of Russia's northernmost province. His predecessors, notably N. M. Baranov and N. D. Golitsyn, had also pushed hard for the interests of the gubernia.[17] But

17. See, for example, Baranov's report for 1881, TsGIA, f. DOD, op. 70, 1882, d. 314, pp. 2–15, and Golitsyn's report for 1887, ibid., op. 223, 1888, d. 166, pp. 2–24.

Engel'gardt saw the requirements of Arkhangelsk most clearly and was able to present them in a convincing, systematic manner.

With regard to the problem of economic growth, Engel'gardt concentrated his efforts in three areas. First, his reports stressed the importance of expanding communications links between Arkhangelsk and the rest of the empire through the construction of railroads and telegraph lines. Second, he urged the tsar to increase colonization in the area and to strengthen the region's economy by supporting local shipping and fisheries.[18] Third, Engel'gardt worked to establish a major port facility on the Murman coast, emphasizing its importance both for the province and for the broader geopolitical concerns of the nation. The Murman area, warmed by the Gulf Stream, offered the prospect of a naval port that would be ice-free year round. Such a port, the governor argued, could not easily be blockaded, and from it the ships of the Russian fleet could steam forth to give "the mighty word of the Russian tsar . . . enormous significance in serious international disputes. . . ."[19]

Engel'gardt connected economic proposals with plans for the institutional modernization of Arkhangelsk. In his report for 1898, the governor pointed to the fact that the growth of the province was being stunted by the "stagnation and routine" that characterized the work of many of the local administrative bodies. Healthy initiative, he wrote, would be impossible "without vital institutions [capable of] answering the needs of the time."[20]

Engel'gardt proposed bringing to Arkhangelsk some of the positive achievements of the reform eras of the 1860s and early 1890s. To deal with the weakness of peasant institutions and the absence of proper supervision, the governor suggested the introduction of the "peasant chiefs" (*krest'ianskie nachal'niki*), a variation on the land captain that the government had recently developed to meet the special needs of Siberia. More significant, Engel'gardt recommended creation of a zemstvo-like body for the province. This institution would do for the north what the zemstvos had been doing for other gubernias: mobilize local talent and, working with the state, take steps to promote education, expand medical care, and deal with a variety of local economic and cultural needs. Such a quasi-zemstvo would have a special com-

18. See Engel'gardt's report for 1893, TsGIA, f. DOD, op. 223, 1894, d. 162 and pp. 66–70 of the attached survey. Also his reports for 1896, 1898, and 1900, ibid., 1897, d. 16, esp. p. 8; ibid, f. Kants. MVD, op. 3, d. 228, pp. 6–8; ibid., f. Komiteta Ministrov, op. 2, 1901, d. 5506, pp. 289–91.

19. Report for 1894, TsGIA, f. Komiteta Ministrov, op. 2, 1895, d. 5127, p. 605.
20. TsGIA, f. Kants. MVD, op. 3, d. 228, p. 2.

position and would function only at the gubernia level. Still, the governor asserted, it could be of great help both in energizing the population and presenting the needs of the province to state authorities at the center. Engel'gardt, who had been a zemstvo member in Smolensk, maintained that these bodies had extensive power to foster schools, hospitals, and other necessary institutions. In fact, he argued, "zemstvos were supplied by law with far greater authority (*polnomochiami*) than governors in non-zemstvo provinces despite all [the help] of provincial and even central institutions concerned with the managing of local economic problems. . . ."21

Although Engel'gardt's reports boldly put forth the needs of his province, relatively little of the governor himself intruded into these documents. This is in marked contrast to the flamboyant, self-serving style of N. M. Baranov, one of Engel'gardt's predecessors in Arkhangelsk and longtime governor of Nizhni-Novgorod (1882–1897). Baranov not only presented the needs of his gubernia clearly and in a programmatic manner but also included much about his own personal actions and achievements. These reports never made dull reading. In one, the governor described his life-and-death struggle with a would-be assassin, in another, how he scotched dangerous rumors during a cholera epidemic, in a third, his special technique for reviving drunks who passed out during the Nizhni-Novgorod fair.22

Baranov would often link accounts of his own deeds to larger questions. For example, the governor connected the story of how he personally intervened to save some 700 boats and barges threatened by the shallowing of the Volga with a broader proposal for improving the Nizhni-Novgorod harbor and the river as a whole. Baranov went on to develop these ideas in subsequent reports, and eventually, he put forth a grandiose scheme to expand Russian commerce into the Middle East by pushing a railroad down to the Persian Gulf.23 Yet in all his writings and plans one thing seems of paramount importance: Baranov's determination to prove that he was a vigorous, resolute man of action.

Although the governors' formal reports helped them to cut through red tape and stimulate ministerial activity, the number of concrete changes they could effect by this means seems to have been rather small. Obviously, ambitious projects, like Engel'gardt's scheme for a zemstvo in Arkhangelsk, that failed to elicit the emperor's enthusiasm

21. Ibid., pp. 3–6. Quotation on p. 6.

22. Reports for 1889, 1893, and 1887, TsGIA, f. DOD, op. 223, 1890, d. 249, p. 7; ibid., 1894, d. 226, pp. 12–13; ibid., 1890, d. 175, p. 33.

23. Reports for 1882 and 1886, TsGIA, f. DOD, op. 223, 1883, d. 120, pp. 2–4; ibid., Biblioteka, I otdel, op. 1, d. 56, pp. 1–4, 11–12.

did not have easy sailing through the bureaucracy.[24] But even when imperial support seemed firm and there was strong backing from one of the ministries, a governor's proposal could be sidetracked.

Engel'gardt's struggle to secure a major naval facility for the Murman coast is a case in point. Shortly before his death, Alexander III had decided to build a large port at Ekaterina harbor in the Murman area. The tsar did so on the basis of Engel'gardt's reports and a proposal by S. Iu. Vitte who warmly supported the project after he had toured the area with the governor. But Alexander's successor, Nicholas II, though initially inclined to accept his father's plans, yielded instead to pressure from military men who favored locating the facility at Libau on the Baltic. As a result, only the small port of Aleksandrov was constructed in the Murman region during Engel'gardt's tenure as governor. The harbor did not prove an economic success, and not until World War I would the governor's vision of a major ice-free port on the Kola peninsula be realized.[25]

In sum, the special link between the governors and the tsar had decidedly limited value. Its greatest importance, in both a positive and negative sense, lay in its psychological and ideological dimensions. As long as the viceregal status of the governors continued to exist, the position of the *nachal'nik gubernii* in the eyes of both the people and the state administration could never be that of a simple functionary. But while the prestige the governors enjoyed was undoubtedly pleasing to them personally and even of some use in practical political terms, it had disadvantages as well. Because they were viewed as the emperor's chosen representatives, the governors occasionally found themselves confronting popular expectations they could not hope to meet. More significant, the governors' ill-defined position in the state apparatus complicated their relationship with the Ministry of Internal Affairs and helped to make this crucial tie to the center a frequent cause of tension and conflict.

Viceregal status formed the basis for the special relationship between the governors and the sovereign. But important as that bond was, it could not compare in practical significance with the governors' tie to the MVD. Here was a connection rooted in unalterable mutual

24. *Svod vysochaishikh otmetok po vsepoddanneishim otchetam za 1898 g.* (St. Petersburg, 1901), p. 6.

25. S. Iu. Vitte, *Vospominaniia* (3 vols.; Moscow, 1960), 1, pp. 391–403, 2, pp. 7–13; "Libava ili Murman? Iz arkhiva S. Iu. Vitte," *Proshloe i nastoiashchee*, vyp. 1 (1924), pp. 25–39; I. F. Ushakov, *Kol'skaia zemlia: Ocherki istorii murmanskoi oblasti v dooktiabr'skii period* (Murmansk, 1972), pp. 395–407.

dependence. For the ministry, the governors were the primary link to the provinces. The *nachal'niki gubernii* were one of its major sources of information and its chief executive agents. The governors in turn understood that they had to work through the MVD, which selected, paid, rewarded, and promoted them. They also knew that they had to have its good will and backing to do their jobs effectively.

Yet a significant element of ambiguity and tension clouded the relationship between the ministry and the *nachal'niki gubernii*. The MVD seemed to have contradictory expectations of its governors because in addition to their being informants and obedient subordinates, the ministry also wanted them to act autonomously. Indeed, it counted on the governors to handle a variety of local problems without reference to St. Petersburg and to be, in short, the real "masters of the provinces."

For their part, the *nachal'niki gubernii* relished this independence. But they were realistic enough to understand their need for strong central support and sufficiently cynical to believe that they would not often get it. Consequently, many governors found the ministry's expectations of them to be both burdensome and frustrating. Its constant demands for information and endless barrage of circulars and regulations made them feel like harassed lackeys. Even more annoying, while subjected to the continuous scrutiny of central officials, governors were often denied access to their superiors in the capital. Finally, when they tried to act as "masters" of their provinces, governors frequently found ministerial backing to be inadequate or inconsistent. What were they, viceroys or flunkies?

The strain in governor-ministerial relations is illustrated when we turn to the question of information. Here the governors' obligations were enormous, and the MVD's demands apparently insatiable. From the moment he took control of his province, a governor was expected to present a detailed report on local conditions and to append a series of tables on various specific matters such as the status of paper work in provincial institutions, the amount of money on hand in various capital funds, and even the condition of local fire departments.[26] Beyond this, the law required the governor to have available information on such questions as population, crops, irrigation, transport and navigation, commerce and industry, medical establishments, and churches.[27] Governors might be queried on these and other subjects at any time and could be called upon to submit lengthy memoranda.

26. Kosich, *Tsirkuliary, ukazaniia i rechi*, pp. 1–5; TsGIA, f. DOD, op. 46, 1892, d. 235, "Ob obozrenii gubernatorami vverennykh im gubernii," pp. 1–25; ibid, 1894, d. 110, "O naznachenii . . . Chepelevskogo," pp. 118–44, 162–79.

27. "Obshchee uchrezhdenie gubernskoe," art. 294, *Svod zakonov*, 2 (1892).

Even the most cursory examination of MVD records and the personal papers of governors reveals that they were indeed asked to provide information on just about any subject. In the wake of the assassination of Alexander II, central authorities ordered governors to gather intelligence concerning the public's mood. As a result, they toured their provinces investigating matters firsthand and supplemented their own findings with those supplied by local marshals and zemstvo personnel. At other times the ministry queried the governors about problems connected with peasant migration or zemstvo proposals to introduce public tillage as a means to combat famine. The ministry's requests for information on the upkeep of provincial roads or for the most precise data on the property holdings of the nobility were also funneled through the governors' offices.[28] Nor did the MVD's demands for reports and analyses of provincial conditions end here. When major reforms were being considered, governors were often dispatched questionnaires soliciting their opinions on proposed changes. Finally, the ministry regularly summoned the *nachal'niki gubernii* to the capital so that they might participate in a variety of special commissions.[29]

Governors supplied vast quantities of information to St. Petersburg every year, but the MVD never seemed happy with its quality. Sometimes the ministry's discontent was fully justified. For example, governors who attended Pleve's conference to discuss legislation on the Jewish question floundered like ill-prepared schoolboys.[30] But governors were less responsible for another source of ministerial unhappiness; the lack of consistency that characterized many of the reports which came from the provinces. The great differences between the various regions of the empire meant that whenever the MVD surveyed its chief provincial agents on any given subject, it seldom obtained a

28. Circular of the Department of General Affairs, 23 May 1881, TsGALI, f. Sverbeevykh, op. 1, d. 459, pp. 1–3; circulars of the Zemskii otdel, 13 August 1882 and 28 August 1884, ibid., d. 462, "Tsirkuliarnye otnosheniia zemskogo otdela MVD . . . ," pp. 5–11; reports on provincial roads from the governors of Kaluga, Moscow, Penza, Tambov, Tula, and Vladimir, TsGAOR, f. Pleve, op. 1, dd. 49, 51, 52, 53; letter from V. K. Pleve to governors, 24 September 1902, TsGIA, f. Kantseliariia MVD po delam dvorianstva (1283), op. 1, II deloproizvodstvo, 1902, d. 29, "Po tsirkuliary gubernatoram o dostavlenni svedenii o dvorianskom zemlevladenii," p. 13.

29. George Yaney, *The Urge to Mobilize: Agrarian Reform in Russia, 1861–1930* (Urbana, Ill., 1982), pp. 14–21; Thomas S. Pearson, "Ministerial Conflict and Local Self-Government Reform in Russia, 1877–1890" (Ph.D. diss., University of North Carolina, 1977), pp. 170–79; S. A. Korf, *Administrativnaia iustitsiia v Rossii* (2 vols.; St. Petersburg, 1910), 1, pp. 441–52; Urussov, pp. 171–76.

30. Urussov, pp. 173–74.

clear-cut picture of the situation or consistent proposals for dealing with problems.[31]

Finally, the ministry was also critical of the governors' annual reports. The *otchety* and, even more important, the printed surveys were among the most consistently utilized body of information supplied to St. Petersburg officials. They were supposed to contain in "a short and condensed form" intelligence on harvests and food supply, local economic activities, taxes and tax collection, institutions of self-government, and the working of administrative and judicial bodies. In addition they were expected to present general conclusions and proposals. The printed surveys, often over one hundred pages long, were to include "all . . . statistical information and data that serve to confirm and buttress the conclusions and proposals presented in the reports." The law specified that these documents should be based on hard facts and not contain anything "speculative."[32]

The majority of reports and surveys never fulfilled the statutory requirements, however, and in December of 1895, Minister of Internal Affairs I. L. Goremykin went before the Committee of Ministers to complain. The reports were untrustworthy and unhelpful on a number of counts, he stated. Many of these documents simply repeated, year after year, the same stale information and sometimes used whole phrases from previous *otchety*. Goremykin charged that governors frequently ignored the proper form established by the law of 1870, and, instead, indulged in a kind of creative writing. The result, he continued, might be a lively, albeit one-sided, picture of provincial life, but such eccentric efforts were virtually useless for the ministry's purposes. According to Goremykin, the main problem with the reports was "the incomparability of the data contained in them not only . . . [with that from] other provinces, but also frequently . . . [with that from] the same province in different years."[33] The minister claimed that the statistical surveys suffered from identical weaknesses, and he lamented that earlier efforts to set matters straight had not been successful.[34]

The ministry's concern about the utility of the information con-

31. Yaney, *Urge*, pp. 14–15; see also the conflicting statements of the governors of Vologda and Viatka on the functioning of gubernia institutions, TsGIA, f. Kakhanovskoi kommissii, op. 1, d. 110, "Otzyvy gubernatorov o preobrazovanii gubernskoi administratsii," pp. 41, 96.

32. PSZ, 2d ser., no. 48502, 19 June 1870.

33. Vypiska iz zhurnala Komiteta Ministrov, 12 and 26 December 1895, TsGIA, f. Kants. MVD, op. 3, d. 80, "Delo ob izmenenii formy i vvedenii edinoobraziia v otchetakh gubernatorov o sostoianii gubernii," p. 14.

34. The MVD had attempted this in its circular to the governors dated 19 April 1895, ibid., pp. 178–79.

tained in the reports and surveys was well founded and has been shared by most modern scholars.[35] Yet, for all their deficiencies, these documents continued to be of crucial value if not for the MVD then at least for the other central institutions. Thus, when Goremykin suggested eliminating the statistical surveys altogether, the representatives of the other major ministries strongly objected arguing that the data supplied by the governors were indispensable for proper decision making.[36]

In the face of such protests, the new law on the governors' reports issued on 11 April 1897 did not change them significantly. Only the form of presenting the material was made less rigid, while the practice of submitting the survey to the emperor was abandoned.[37] As a result, the MVD continued to be unhappy. In January, 1901, it sent out a circular that again criticized the reports and surveys for being too long and burdened with unnecessary information.[38] But the ministry's admonition had no significant effect. As late as 1915 the government considered altering the form of the annual reports, but it produced no fundamental changes before the empire collapsed.[39]

The MVD's constant requests for information and dissatisfaction with the governors' efforts created a degree of tension between the ministry and its chief provincial agents that was further increased by the ministry's demands for action. Governors worked in a steady downpour of orders and circulars. I. M. Strakhovskii stated that governors received, on average, ten detailed communications from the center each day. These documents usually focused on major issues such as the implementation of reforms, the meaning and application of Senate decisions and the like. But this was only a small part of the "paper rain" that fell upon the *nachal'niki gubernii*. Other ministerial orders might concern much less significant subjects: how to fill out credit forms; what procedures to follow when issuing passports; and how to undertake the preservation of historical monuments.[40] The MVD also instructed the governors to set up conferences on peasant legislation and rural fires, demanded improvement in the work of local statistical agencies, and urged them to remove certain books from libraries. Fi-

35. See, for example, the opinion of B. G. Litvak, *Ocherki.istochnikovedeniia massovoi dokumentatsii XIX–nachala XX v.* (Moscow, 1979), pp. 185–86.

36. Diatlova, "Otchety gubernatorov," p. 233.

37. PSZ, 3d ser., no. 13950; Diatlova, "Otchety gubernatorov," p. 234.

38. Circular dated 31 January 1901, TsGIA, f. Kants. MVD op. 3, d. 103, "Tsirkuliar . . . o poriadke sostavleniia i predstavleniia otchetov . . . ," pp. 1–3.

39. Diatlova, "Otchety gubernatorov," pp. 234–35.

40. Strakhovskii, "Gubernskoe ustroistvo" (October 1913): 109.

nally, some circulars touched on highly sensitive matters such as government-zemstvo relations or when troops should be called out in case of public disturbances.[41]

The ministry's instructions could combine the serious with the slightly silly. In August of 1891, when much of central Russia was in the grip of a terrible famine, the governors received all kinds of orders on how to conduct relief operations. Yet Minister of Internal Affairs I. N. Durnovo also saw fit to send them the following circular marked top secret (*soversheno sekretno*):

> From information in the hands of the Ministry of Internal Affairs, it is clear that recently, in gardens where public entertainments take place, orchestras frequently play the "Marseillaise." The playing [of this song] is accompanied by the noisy approval of the public and by demands that it be repeated several times.
>
> Consequently, I feel it my duty to inform Your Excellency that public playing of the "Marseillaise," as the French National Anthem, was permitted solely in honor of the French squadron during its visit to Kronstadt [and that,] with the departure [of the squadron] from Russian shores, there is now no longer the basis for permitting the playing of the "Marseillaise" since it might become the cause of undesirable demonstrations.[42]

From the governors' perspective, the MVD's demands for information and its flood of orders were excessive and failed to take into account human limitations. As a result, the *nachal'niki gubernii* had to pass many assignments on to lower officials they knew to be irresponsible or incompetent.[43] But even when governors turned eagerly to their many duties, they confronted another complication thrown up by the ministry. For the MVD surrounded its chief provincial agents with a web of petty regulations that sharply limited their freedom of action. Initially designed to prevent the governors from abusing their powers, these restrictions had grown to the point where even the ministry realized that it had created a nightmare.

41. TsGAOR, f. Pleve, op. 1, d. 105, "Tsirkuliar . . . o sozyv . . . soveshchanii dlia peresmotra zakonodatel'stva o krest'ianakh," pp. 1–5; Koshko, "Vospominaniia," pp. 117–22, BAR; TsGIA, f. Kants. MVD, op. 3, d. 106, "Tsirkuliary po MVD za 1904 g.," pp. 8, 28; Circular of the Economic Department of the MVD, 10 February 1895, TsGIA, f. Khoziaistvennogo departamenta (1287) op. 27, d. 3114, "Po sekretnomu tsirkuliaru . . . o dostavlenii gubernatorami svedenii o kazhdom sluchae narusheniia predsedatel'stvuiushchimi v zemskikh sobraniiakh obiazannosti svoikh," p. 1; circular of the Department of Police, 16 April 1893, ibid., f. Kants. MVD, op. 3, d. 95, "S tsirkuliarami po ministerstvu vnutrennikh del," pp. 76–77.

42. TsGIA, f. Kants. MVD, op. 3, d. 93, "S tsirkuliarami po ministerstvu vnutrennikh del," p. 84.

43. Strakhovskii, "Gubernskoe ustroistvo" (October 1913): 110–111.

The degree to which this net bound the governors was revealed in 1903 when Minister of Internal Affairs V. K. Pleve tried to improve provincial administration by granting gubernia institutions the power to handle a number of functions that up to this time had required the approval of the center. From the list compiled by the reform commission we learn that in the first years of the twentieth century a governor had to have at least routine ministerial permission to authorize charitable lotteries, meetings, lectures, and exhibits. Many appointments of personnel concerned with local health and safety also needed sanction from St. Petersburg. Even the exhumation and movement of a corpse could not be done on a governor's own orders.[44] These restrictions constituted more than an encumbrance to gubernatorial activity; they indicated a lack of strong ministerial support for the governors and their work. No wonder that governors often felt themselves isolated from the MVD by a barrier of distrust.

The governors knew that the MVD expended considerable effort monitoring their activity, and they particularly resented the provincial agents of the Department of Police who regularly sent reports about them back to St. Petersburg.[45] They were also aware that ministry officials culled both provincial and capital newspapers for stories about problems at the local level. When such an article appeared, a letter from the minister or department head was likely to follow demanding that the governor attend to the matter in question and report back.[46] Nor could the governors have been ignorant of the fact that their personnel files, held at the MVD's Department of General Affairs, contained a variety of letters denouncing their activities. And while these complaints did not necessarily produce immediate action by the ministry, they were retained for future reference.[47]

After 1905, ministerial scrutiny of the governors expanded and "attestations" (*attestatsii*) describing their behavior began to appear regu-

44. "Perechen' . . . del kotorye mogli by byt' predostavleny razresheniiu . . . mestnoi vlasti . . . ," TsGIA, f. DOD, op. 194, 1903, d. 150, ch. 1, "Po gubernskoi reforme," pp. 295–301.

45. Stremoukhov, "Administrativnoe ustroistvo," sec. 2, p. 9, BAR; The governors' desire for greater control over the local police agents was expressed in 1903. See "Izvlechenie iz otzyvov gubernatorov po voprosu o preobrazovanii gubernskogo upravleniia," TsGIA, f. DOD, op. 194, 1903, d. 150, ch. 1, pp. 18–20.

46. TsGIA, f. Kants. MVD, op. 1, d. 1171, "Perepiska s saratovskim gubernatorom po povodu napechatannykh v mestnykh gazet zametok"; ibid., d. 1181, "Perepiska ministra . . . s arkhangel'skim gubernatorom po povodu napechatannoi v gazete 'Novoe vremia' zametki . . ."; ibid., f. Khoz. dep., op. 27, d. 254, "O . . . vrache I. I. Molleson," pp. 1–4.

47. See, for example, TsGIA, f. DOD, op. 44, 1871, d. 253, "O naznachenii . . . Ivanova i . . . Shevicha . . . ," pp. 76–79; ibid., op. 46, 1894, d. 110, "O naznachenii . . . Chepelevskogo . . . ," p. 391–414.

larly in official personnel files. In early 1911, P. A. Stolypin sought to systematize the collection of this kind of information and ordered the Department of General Affairs to solicit complete intelligence on governors' activities from the other departments of the MVD. The goal was to concentrate all such material in one place so that the department "could, at any moment, present at the demand of the minister, a detailed memorandum on every governor."[48] Later that year, the MVD would go even further, asking department heads to submit reports on the governors with special reference to acts that merited either ministerial praise or criticism.[49]

The MVD's increasing efforts to oversee the governors was no doubt disconcerting to the *nachal'niki gubernii*. But this was a manageable situation, provided they could maintain regular and effective communications with the minister and his top associates. Achieving this goal was not easy, however. Official channels were available to the governors and they used them very skillfully at times.[50] Yet Russia was a country where written documents could be delayed, ignored, or lost altogether. Not surprisingly, then, the *nachal'niki gubernii* gave the highest priority to direct, personal contact with leading St. Petersburg dignitaries and regularly sought permission to travel to the capital for consultation with the MVD.

But here, too, governors were frequently frustrated because the MVD kept them at arms' length by sharply limiting opportunities to converse directly with the minister. Before taking up his post, a new governor would usually have an interview with his chief and the main department heads during which he might be informed of the main problems he would encounter and what the ministry wanted him to do. He was also likely to get a dose of ritual pieties concerning the nature of his office and the great responsibilities before him.[51] Once a governor took over his province, however, MVD officers looked suspiciously at his requests to come to the capital. Often they queried him sharply about his agenda and made him reconsider his proposal.[52] As

48. Memorandum dated 26 February 1911, TsGIA, f. DOD, op. 47, 1911, d. 333, "Po zaprosam gg. nachal'nikov tsentral'nykh uchrezhdenii svedenii, kharakterizuiu-shchikh deiatel'nosti gubernatorov," p. 1. See also the Department of General Affairs' letter to other department heads, 3 March 1911, ibid., p. 2.

49. Memorandum dated 11 October 1911, ibid., p. 5.

50. See, for example, the *dokladnye zapiski* sent to the MVD by Moscow governor Dzhunkovskii (TsGAOR, f. Dzhunkovskogo, op. 1, d. 117, pp. 1–6).

51. Urusov, pp. 3, 8–9; Koshko, "Vospominaniia," p. 21, BAR; Osorgin, "Vospominaniia," GBL, f. Osorgina, papka II, d. 2, p. 232.

52. Letters between Governor Akhlestyshev and the MVD dated 12, 15, 25 November 1895, GAKO, f. Kants. tver. gub., op. 1, d. 3641, "O poezdkakh g. nachal'nika gubernii v otpusk i po delam sluzhbe, 1895," pp. 44–46.

a result, a governor would usually see the minister only once a year for about twenty minutes at the most.[53]

Circumstances at these interviews were not conducive to the leisurely discussion of major local problems; the press of business on the minister was simply too great for that. In his memoirs, I. F. Koshko recalled that he once went to St. Petersburg expecting an extended, serious talk with Stolypin on a host of important matters. Instead, Koshko found himself at the end of a long line of people awaiting an audience with the prime minister, a line that included six or seven other governors![54] During interviews, moreover, the minister's aides zealously guarded his time. Any governor who sought to prolong such contact was likely to be cut off by the official in charge of the reception.[55] As a result, some governors came to the conclusion that MVD staff was actually seeking to isolate them from their superiors.[56]

The available evidence makes it clear, however, that while the MVD wished to reduce the number of interviews between governors and its main officers, it also gave careful consideration to the proposals that the *nachal'niki gubernii* made when they came to the capital. The archive of the MVD chancellery contains a number of files that reveal the procedures used in dealing with issues raised by the governors in conversations with the minister. After the meeting took place, the requests of the governors were written up in a short summary form with a note directing them to a particular department of the ministry. These same files also contain the memoranda of various department heads outlining the measures they took on gubernatorial requests and complaints. Or, if they had not acted, the department heads presented information necessary for a decision on the questions posed.[57]

From the MVD's perspective, the main problem with direct contact between the governors and its high officials was the sheer volume and diversity of the matters that might be considered. Governors often tried to raise the greatest number of issues in the shortest possible time, and it was not unusual for six or seven separate questions to be broached at a single interview. The range of topics was enormous, too. Among the things governors discussed were the proper medical surveillance of

53. Strakhovskii, "Gubernskoe ustroistvo" (October 1913): 108.

54. Koshko, "Vospominaniia," pp. 12–23, BAR. See also P. P. Stremoukhov, "Moia bor'ba," 10, 15–16.

55. Strakhovskii, "Gubernskoe ustroistvo" (October 1913): 108.

56. Fon Val' to Durnovo, 26 October [1883?], TsGAOR, f. fon Valia, op. 1, d. 139, pp. 68–69.

57. See the files dealing with the visits of the governors of Viatka, Tula, Kherson, and Iaroslavl to the capital from 1900 to 1901; TsGIA, f. Kants. MVD, op. 3, dd. 335, 341, 343, 345.

prostitutes, the expansion of local educational institutions, the correct response to troublesome Senate rulings, the extension of telegraph lines, and the improvement of zemstvo accounting procedures.[58]

The variety of requests made by the governors placed considerable burdens on MVD staff, for they had to investigate these matters and, where warranted, attend to them. Consequently, it is understandable why the ministry sought to rationalize and regularize the process of arranging gubernatorial interviews. The MVD required the governors to submit detailed lists of matters they intended to discuss whenever they sent their requests to come to the capital. This procedure made good sense from the point of view of the central administration. But to the governors it must have seemed yet another bureaucratic barrier that minimized their importance, undercut the personal dimension of their office, and assigned them the position of simple cogs in the wheel.

The numerous requests for consultations with ministry officials were a clear indication of the degree of the governors' subordination to the MVD. But while these documents implied dependence, they also betokened the expectation of support. Governors turned to the ministry for advice on a wide range of questions because, initially, they counted on the MVD to back them up in dealing with local disputes and problems. Yet official records and governors' memoirs strongly suggest that these hopes were often unrealized. Confronted with difficulties in administering his assigned province, it was not unusual for a governor to find that he was supposed to handle the crisis on his own. At the very least, he would learn, firsthand, just how slowly and reluctantly the central bureaucracy responded to his needs.

Consider the case of A. A. Musin-Pushkin. As governor of Vologda in the late 1890s, he sought to improve the quality of life in the provincial capital by vigorously enforcing sanitary regulations. He also called on the city's merchants to lighten the burdens on their employees by closing shop at least once a week. These measures were not popular locally although they were in accord with overall government policy. Yet, when Musin-Pushkin's pursuit of these goals generated opposition, the MVD's support evaporated.

Musin-Pushkin's troubles began at a holiday banquet where he gave

---

58. Most of the agendas for these discussions are found in governors' personnel files. See, Poltaratskii to MVD, 26 December 1894, TsGIA, f. DOD, op. 44, 1874, d. 46, p. 138; B. B. Meshcherskii to V. F. Trepov, 27 January 1898, ibid., op. 46, 1891, d. 125, p. 103; E. O. Iankovskii to D. A. Tolstoi, 25 January 1889, ibid., op. 44, 1879, d. 152, pp. 202–204; A. A. Musin-Pushkin, to I. L. Goremykin, 28 October 1898, ibid., op. 45, 1886, d. 84, p. 91. See also the memorandum of the Economic Department of the MVD concerning the requests of I. M. Obolenskii, f. Kants. MVD, op. 3, d. 343, p. 18.

a speech encouraging merchants to suspend commerce on Sundays. Unfortunately, in the course of his talk the governor made offhanded use of the terms *obmer* and *obves* (false weight and false measure), and the businessmen exploded with indignation. Musin-Pushkin's words seem to have ignited all the animosity that had developed as a result of his cleanup campaign. Claiming that the governor had insulted their honor, the merchants held an illegal, secret meeting and framed a strongly worded complaint to the MVD. Musin-Pushkin, thoroughly astounded by the furor his remarks had caused, presented his own case to his superiors and asked permission to take action against those who had arranged the unauthorized gathering and protest.

The MVD's response was tepid. In a letter to the governor, Minister Sipiagin agreed that the merchants' complaint was largely unfounded. But he failed to authorize disciplinary measures against the protesters and, instead, admonished Musin-Pushkin to be more careful. In future, the governor should avoid misspeaking himself lest he demean governmental authority.[59] Musin-Pushkin was left to endure considerable embarrassment. Not surprisingly, the MVD soon transferred him to its central offices, then to a new governorship in Minsk.

Even when a governor moved to maintain law and order, he might encounter a frustrating lack of support from the MVD. In 1904, while governor of Grodno, M. M. Osorgin had to deal with a volatile situation at a glass factory in the village of Cherniana Ruda. The state had taken over the business because its owners had failed to pay fines levied against them. The managers had absconded, however, still owing the factory's 500 workers (many of whom were Belgians) 50,000 rubles in back pay. Moreover, they had left their former employees without food or medical care. The condition of the workers deteriorated dangerously, and when Osorgin toured the factory, he was reminded of scenes in Zola's *Germinal.* At one point, a riot broke out at the plant, and more violence threatened. The problem had to be resolved as quickly as possible.

Governor Osorgin turned to the MVD. He proposed selling some of the factory's land to nearby peasants and so raise the money to pay off the workers and send them home. The ministry rejected this idea, however, because it felt that the land was overpriced, and instead it sent Osorgin an emergency grant with which to mollify the workers. But the sum—a paltry 3,000 rubles—was so inadequate that the gov-

59. Musin-Pushkin to Sipiagin, 14 November 1899 and Sipiagin to Musin-Pushkin, 30 December 1899, TsGIA, f. Kants. MVD, op. 2, d. 2171, "Delo po zhalobe vologodskikh kuptsov na oskorblenie ikh grazhdanskim gubernatorom," pp. 5–10, 3.

ernor could neither satisfy the workers nor improve their conditions. Osorgin then approached his nominal superior, Governor-General A. A. Freze at Vilna, hoping to use the latter's good offices to obtain the needed funds. But the governor-general, who was new in his post, chose not to get involved. Instead, he encouraged Osorgin to go to St. Petersburg and present the problem directly to Minister P. D. Sviato-polk-Mirskii.

In the capital, Osorgin put forward a new proposal for resolving the crisis: take the money from the provincial food supply capital and use it to reimburse the workers. The borrowed sums could be repaid at a later date out of the proceeds from the sale of the factory's land. Sviatopolk-Mirskii hesitated. Osorgin's scheme was technically illegal because it violated the provision that food supply funds could only be used for famine relief. But by this time Osorgin's frustration had reached the point where he was prepared to throw caution to the wind. The governor boldly announced his readiness to take the risk of violat-ing the law in order to meet the needs of the workers. Sviatopolk-Mirskii reluctantly agreed if Osorgin would get Minister of Finance V. N. Kokovtsov to look the other way. The governor quickly cleared this final hurdle and the workers were paid off and sent to their homes. Osorgin's reward was the satisfaction of having defused a serious crisis and, no doubt, a few gray hairs.[60]

The burdens and frustrations that governors encountered in the course of their work helped to drive a wedge between central and provincial government and to weaken the MVD's controls. To be sure, governors rarely defied commands from St. Petersburg however much they might resent their superiors' unrealistic demands and uncertain support. But once they had held office for a time, *nachal'niki gubernii* understood that they could accomplish only a portion of the many tasks assigned to them, and this had a curiously liberating effect. Gov-ernors realized they were relatively free to choose which of the many ministerial directives they would attempt to carry out and which they would ignore. Some, of course, exercised their freedom in an eccentric manner. (V. K. Pleve told S. D. Urusov about a governor who simply refused to open any ministerial circular marked "secret.")[61] And while few governors behaved in such an arbitrary way, all knew that there would be occasions when they would have to act on the basis of their personal predilections and the circumstances of the moment.

The crises produced by periods of crop failure and famine often caused governors to operate with little regard to the orders from the

60. Osorgin, "Vospominaniia," GBL, f. Osorgina, papka II, d. 2, pp. 168–75.
61. Urussov, p. 3.

center. During these emergencies, ministerial orders frequently seemed irrelevant to the situation, and governors were forced to thread their own ways between what P. P. Stremoukhov termed the Scylla of inaction and the Charybdis of exceeding their authority.[62] During the famine of 1891, for example, a number of governors simply did as they pleased. A. F. Anis'in of Viatka illegally banned the export of grain from his province and for months refused repeated orders from I. N. Durnovo to cease. During the same time, Governor Baranov of Nizhni-Novgorod checked ministry attempts to question his policies with an angry threat to resign. Even the normally pliant P. A. Poltaratskii dug in his heels and ignored the MVD's demands to take a more vigorous personal role in the work of aiding the needy.[63]

For the most part, gubernatorial resistance to ministerial directives was brief, isolated, and sporadic. But examples of long-term, collective opposition can also be found. The fate of the MVD's attempt to force the governors to submit weekly reports on provincial events is a useful illustration. In October, 1864, the MVD first requested the *nachal'niki gubernii* to send in weekly reports. The stated purpose of these documents was to give the ministry a regular and accurate picture of provincial happenings and to free it from reliance on the information it received from the gendarmes and informal sources. The circular promised the governors that the reports would provide them with a new, direct, and strictly confidential link to the minister of internal affairs.[64]

Initially, the governors obeyed the MVD's request, but their compliance was apparently short-lived. By 1883 the ministry was complaining bitterly that the reports were incomplete and virtually devoid of significance. The MVD also charged that the governors dispatched the weekly reports irregularly and usually contented themselves with stating that nothing worthy of the ministry's attention had occurred in the province.[65] Six years later, the MVD again criticized the governors for their failure to obey the circular of 1864 but apparently to no avail.[66]

62. Stremoukhov, "Administrativnoe ustroistvo," sec. 1, p. 3, sec. 2, pp. 2–3, BAR.

63. Richard G. Robbins, Jr., *Famine in Russia, 1891–1892: The Imperial Government Responds to a Crisis* (New York, 1975), pp. 55–57, 126–30, 136.

64. TsGIA, f. Kants. MVD, op. 3, d. 69, "Delo po tsirkuliary . . . ob ustanovlenii poriadka dostavleniia grazhdanskimi gubernatorami ezhenedel'nykh sekretnykh svedenii," p. 8.

65. Circular of 4 November 1883, TsGIA, f. Kants. MVD, op. 3, d. 25, "Delo o priniatii mer k tochnomu ispolneniiu tsirkuliara ministera o dostavlenii gubernatorami ezhenedel'nykh zapisok o sobytiiakh v gubernii," p. 25.

66. P. A. Zaionchkovskii, *Rossiiskoe samoderzhavie v kontse XIX stoletiia* (Moscow, 1970), p. 183.

The distinguished Soviet historian P. A. Zaionchkovskii argued that the governors' refusal to send weekly reports was a sign of separatist tendencies or, at the very least, indicated their desire to keep the ministry in the dark about what was going on at the provincial level.[67] But an examination of some of the weekly reports that the governors actually submitted suggests that their failure to carry out the MVD's orders had another cause: physical exhaustion. If the governors had sought conscientiously to fulfill the obligation to prepare weekly reports, they would have consumed a considerable portion of their already limited time and would have been inhibited from carrying out their regular duties and functions.

The weekly reports sent in by Saratov's governor A. A. Zubov from 1882 to 1883 are revealing. After taking over the province in August of 1881, Zubov, full of zeal, tried to carry out his job according to ministerial instructions. His initial weekly reports were excellent, packed with detail and insights into the most varied problems. From Zubov's pen the MVD received information on fires, peasant disorders, counterfeiting operations, and murders. If vandals broke windows at the home of the inspector of the local gymnasium, the governor promptly informed the ministry. When a former member of the Saratov city duma was tried for corruption, Zubov attended the proceedings and wrote lengthy observations about the problems of urban self-government. Yet reports of this quality must have heavily taxed the governor and his staff. Thus, the denouement is not surprising. Zubov's diligence quickly faded, and by the end of the year, he, too, was submitting declarations that nothing of great significance had occurred in his province.[68]

By the beginning of the twentieth century, the MVD seems to have given up the idea of weekly reports, but it was still determined to force the governors to supply it with regular information about provincial happenings. In July 1903, the ministry reminded the governors of their duty to report any illegal activities by local officials and to relay the news of extraordinary happenings "without delay." Aware of traditional gubernatorial resistance to submitting this kind of intelligence, the MVD tried to obtain compliance by appealing to the governors' pride. The reports in question were not to be sent directly to the ministry but to the emperor as "most loyal memoranda" (*vsepoddanneishie donoseniia*). Reminding the *nachal'niki gubernii* that this had

67. Ibid.
68. TsGIA, f. Kants. MVD, op. 3, d. 187, "Ezhenedel'nye donoseniia grazhdanskogo gubernatora o proisshestviiakh v saratovskoi gubernii."

been a privilege reserved only for governors-general, the MVD urged them to cooperate and asked only that it be informed of the contents of these documents.[69]

The Ministry's ploy may have had some success, but it did not elicit more regular reports. Nor did it end the MVD's impotence in dealing with the problem. Consider the following memorandum concerning the activities of Governor M. N. Shramchenko: "On October 8, 1910, in the town of Griazovets, at the time of a visit by the governor, a clash took place between the chairman of the zemstvo executive board, General Levashov, and the land captain Shapanov that resulted in the murder of the latter by the former. Governor [Shramchenko] told . . . Minister P. A. Stolypin about this by letter, ten days after [the event], and not directly, but only as a result of an [official] inquiry." And what was the reaction of the powerful minister of internal affairs to Shramchenko's failure to keep his superior informed? "Concerning this matter," the memorandum concluded, "State-Secretary Stolypin expressed extreme surprise (*vyrazil krainee udivlenie*)."[70]

The governors' view of their office was another reason why they were not always perfectly subordinated to the MVD. The exalted position of the *nachal'nik gubernii* within provincial society and administration fostered a sense of autonomy. So did their uniform whose red-trimmed collars and cuffs signified their role as representatives of the tsar and set them apart from the "bureaucrats" of the MVD.[71] Political and judicial myth reinforced the feelings of independence fostered by status and symbol. Soon after being appointed governor of Bessarabia, S. D. Urusov read the sections of the *Svod zakonov* that concerned the rights and duties of his new job and concluded that he was not "merely" an official of the ministry of internal affairs but stood outside all governmental hierarchies. Urusov decided that while he would render all due respect to the minister of internal affairs, he would never permit that official to criticize his actions or treat him as a direct subordinate.[72]

The nature of the gubernatorial corps itself was an additional reason why the MVD often found it hard to make the governors obey. As a group, governors enjoyed a degree of economic independence increasingly rare among state officials. As noted in Chapter 2, the MVD

69. Circular of 15 July 1903, TsGIA, f. Kants. MVD, op. 3, d. 105, "S tsirkuliarami tsentral'nykh uchrezhdenii ministerstva vnutrennikh del," p. 109.

70. Memorandum dated 1 March 1912, TsGIA, f. DOD, op. 47, 1912, d. 19, "So spravkami o gubernatorakh kotorye predstavlialis' g. ministru v 1912 godu i v 1913 g.," p. 15.

71. Stremoukhov, "Administrativnoe ustroistvo," sec. 1, p. 2, BAR.

72. Urussov, p. 2.

consistently chose governors from the ranks of nobles with considerable estates, so the effect of any financial sanctions the ministry might apply was rather limited. More important, the MVD's selection criteria in the late nineteenth and early twentieth centuries had produced governors who were highly knowledgeable about local conditions and needs. This trend unquestionably improved the quality of provincial leadership, but it probably weakened ministerial control. With the governors' emergence as a group of professionalized provincial administrators, they were less willing than before to follow blindly the dictates of the center.

In his memoirs, I. F. Koshko recalls an incident which reveals the attitudes of these "new model" governors. While ruling in Perm (1911–1914), Koshko clashed with Minister of Internal Affairs N. A. Maklakov over a complex question of land redistribution. The issue was so serious and the dispute so bitter that the governor considered resigning. Ultimately, however, Koshko rejected the idea. "I did not retire as I had initially wanted . . . ," he wrote. "It was not worth it to disrupt my life and give up interesting work just because in [the post] of minister of internal affairs there accidentally happened to be a person who had absolutely no understanding of the matter." The governor resolved to go his own way, guided by conscience and the law.[73]

In the last analysis, however, the MVD itself was chiefly responsible for the weakness of central control over the governors because it failed to use the disciplinary tools at its disposal consistently. The ministry had many ways to make the governors hew to the line. It could reprimand them, deny them decorations and awards, transfer or dismiss them. Yet a survey of the governors' personnel files and other pertinent documents reveals that the MVD seldom punished these officials. Presumably this indicates that most governors obeyed the law and followed orders at least to the satisfaction of the ministry. Nonetheless, a large body of evidence from memoirs, government documents, and even governors' own reports points to a variety of gubernatorial misdeeds. The MVD was familiar with most of these activities but often it did nothing. This caution suggests that in its relations with the governors the ministry was torn between the desire to subordinate these officials and the need to have them able to act as real provincial "bosses."

The ministry never saw those two goals as mutually exclusive. Had it, the administrative history of late nineteenth- and early twentieth-century Russia would not have witnessed so many attempts to expand

73. Koshko, "Vospominaniia," pp. 553–54, BAR.

the governors' powers while integrating them more firmly into the MVD's hierarchy.[74] But combining the ideals of regular bureaucracy with active, independent local authority requires compromise: the men at the top must be prepared to loosen discipline over the officials below them.[75] This is what the MVD did in the case of the governors.

The ministers of internal affairs realized that much of a governor's ability to act at the provincial level depended on personal prestige and his status as the emperor's viceroy. Anything which tarnished that image would undercut a governor's usefulness, and for this reason the MVD saw the public reprimand of a governor as a dubious practice.[76] Nor was it possible for the MVD to discipline a governor secretly. As the leading figure in the province, the governor was at the center of attention, the object of discussion and gossip by bureaucrats and ordinary citizens alike.[77] Any action taken against him by the MVD was sure to leak and eventually would have had almost the same negative effect on a governor's ability to rule as sanctions publicly imposed.

A more stringent disciplinary measure was the transfer of an offending governor to a province with an unpleasant climate and few amenities. (Vologda seems to have been a favorite location). But such a step, though it might cause a governor grief, would not guarantee his becoming more pliant or check undesired activities. Moreover, governors sometimes brought along their confederates and, having set up shop in a new gubernia, continued business as usual.[78]

Dismissal was, of course, the MVD's ultimate form of disciplinary control, but this was also used sparingly. It was not unusual for a governor to have powerful supporters at court or in the government, and they could cause serious political trouble for the minister who removed him.[79] The difference that such protection could make is illustrated by the contrasting fates of two Vologda governors: A. A.

74. On efforts to reform the governors' office see the classic work by Korf, *Administrativnaia iustitsiia*, 1, pp. 291–320, 423–98, and the more recent book by Neil B. Weissman, *Reform in Tsarist Russia: State Bureaucracy and Local Government, 1900–1914* (New Brunswick, N.J., 1981), esp. pp. 38–52, 186–87.

75. Yaney, *Urge*, pp. 54–57.

76. Sinel'nikov, "Zapiski," *Istoricheskii vestnik* 61, no. 7: 42. For an illustration of the effect such a reprimand might have see TsGIA, f. DOD, op. 46, 1892, d. 211, "O naznachenii . . . Sukhodol'skogo . . . ," pp. 191a–191v.

77. Koshko, *Vospominaniia*, pp. 116, 173–74; fon Val', "Vil'na," TsGIA, f. fon Valia i Miasoedovykh, op. 1, d. 13, pp. 27–28.

78. See N. Ch. Zaionchkovskii's 1913 report on Vologda, TsGIA, f. DOD, op. 47, 1913, d. 332, pp. 2–9.

79. Stephen Sternheimer, "Administering Development and Developing Administration: Organizational Conflict in Tsarist Bureaucracy, 1906–1914," *Canadian-American Slavic Studies* 9 (Fall 1975): 290.

Lodyzhenskii and M. P. Daragan. Both men displayed what the MVD regarded as an excessive solicitude toward political exiles. But Lodyzhenskii, who had friends in high places, held on to his post, whereas Daragan, who apparently did not, lost his position.[80] Beyond this, there was another reason for the MVD's caution. The dismissal of a governor was an open admission that other, more limited means of control had failed, and this called into question both the power of the minister and his wisdom in selecting or retaining the errant official.[81]

Consequently, the MVD fired governors only when their actions undermined state security or threatened to bring serious disrepute on government service. In such circumstances, the ministry could act swiftly and decisively. With relatively little hesitation it cashiered P. V. Nekliudov for ordering the beating and imprisonment of a group of peasants,[82] N. P. Rokasovskii for having a disreputable citizen flogged,[83] and R. S. fon Raaben for failing to stop the disastrous Kishinev pogrom.[84]

Still the MVD was prepared to tolerate a wide range of questionable activities. Consider the case of V. A. Levashov, who served as governor in four provinces for sixteen years. Archival files reveal that at various times he was accused of abetting corruption in Vitebsk, violating a citizen's civil rights in Olonets, and encouraging a pogrom in Kherson. And while there seems to have been considerable substance to all of these charges, the MVD simply transferred the troublesome governor from one province to another. Only in 1910, when he had reduced the provincial administration of Riazan to near chaos, did the ministry remove Levashov and secure his appointment to the Senate.[85]

Other members of the gubernatorial corps engaged in activities of an even more shocking character. Levashov's successor in Riazan, A. N. Obolenskii and his vice-governor V. A. Kolobov became involved in an

80. P. B. "Neobychainyi gubernator," p. 160; TsGIA, f. DOD op. 44, 1878, d. 195, "O naznachenii . . . Daragana . . . . Zdes' zhe ob uvol'nenii," pp. 1–40.

81. I. Blinov, "Nadzor za deiatel'nosti gubernatorov (istoriko-iuridicheskii ocherk)," Vestnik prava 32 (September 1902): 74.

82. TsGIA, f. DOD, op. 44, 1879, d. 266, "O naznachenii . . . Nekliudova . . . ," pp. 206–208, 115–35. See also the published documents in Krest'ianskoe dvizhenie v Rossii v 1890–1900 gg.: Sbornik dokumentov (Moscow, 1959), pp. 183–87.

83. TsGIA, f. DOD, op. 45, 1881, d. 158, "O naznachenii . . . Rokasovskogo . . . ," pp. 189–95.

84. Urussov, p. 9; Materialy dlia istorii antievreiskikh pogromov v Rossii (2 vols.; Petrograd, 1919–1923), 1, pp. 335–39.

85. The following files contain materials on the activities of Levashov, TsGIA, f. Kants. MVD, op. 3, d. 937, pp. 13–15; ibid., op. 2, d. 2170, pp. 1–6; ibid., f. DOD, op. 46, 1902, d. 176, pp. 72, 148; ibid., op. 47, 1910, d. 278, p. 15.

attempt to blackmail the district procurator. The MVD's own investigator presented the details of the plot in a lengthy report supported by copious interviews and other documentary materials.[86] But the ministry's response was hardly firm. It promoted Obolenskii to the post of St. Petersburg *gradonachal'nik* (city governor) and made Kolobov governor of Kherson!

The careers of Levashov, Obolenskii, Kolobov, and others that could be cited here demonstrate the narrow range within which the MVD chose to use its disciplinary powers. The ministry punished only the most blatant misdeeds while it tolerated actions that simply strayed across the limits of legality and propriety. The inconsistency, indeed, timidity of ministerial discipline had serious consequences. It left a large gray area in which governors could operate with little fear of being called to account. This sense of impunity did more than give the governors the scope to act during emergencies. It undercut their willingness to obey the ministry's own commands.

In other countries the regular courts or the processes of administrative justice were used to insure the compliance of higher officials, and such reforms might have been introduced in Russia to keep the governors from abusing their office. But the MVD steadfastly opposed this kind of development because it believed that the rule of law would be a check on gubernatorial activity. Moreover, it would involve other institutions, particularly the Ministry of Justice and the Senate, in the work of disciplining the *nachal'niki gubernii* and further weaken the MVD's authority in the provinces.

The MVD made its position clear in the 1890s, when top government officials discussed the question of how to deal with governors who broke the law. It objected to proposals that would have strengthened the Senate's right to reprimand governors and order them to stand trial in the regular courts. Such an approach, I. N. Durnovo warned in April of 1893, would give undue weight to "purely legal considerations" and might inhibit the governors in meeting the many "special circumstances" that required them to take technically illegal actions.[87] Three years later the ministry made a similar argument and urged that the task of disciplining the governors ought to be given to the Committee of Ministers and, ultimately, the emperor.[88]

86. The report, by N. Ch. Zaionchkovskii, and various supporting materials are found in TsGIA, f. DOD op. 47, 1911, d. 342, ch.ch. 1 and 2.
87. Memorandum to the Ministry of Justice, 25 April 1893, TsGIA, f. DOD, op. 46, 1892, d. 113, "Po otnosheniiu ministra iustitsii ob izmenenii deistvuiushchikh pravil ob otvetstvennosti gubernatorov za prestupleniia dolzhnosti," p. 23.
88. MVD to Ministry of Justice, 19 March 1896, ibid., pp. 74–76.

On this point, the MVD held firm and won. When new regulations on the responsibility of governors for crimes committed in office were issued on 26 May 1897, they embodied most of the ideas put forth by Durnovo and his successor, I. L. Goremykin.[89] Yet the ministry's triumph had some ironic implications because at the same time as it prevented other agencies from meddling in its special relationship with the *nachal'niki gubernii*, the MVD weakened its own authority. The stress that the law of 26 May placed on the sovereign's disciplinary role reinforced gubernatorial autonomy by once more asserting the governors' viceregal status and their special link to him.

The Ministry of Internal Affairs never made an unambiguous, final choice between the goals of a rationalized, bureaucratic hierarchy and a vital, independent local authority. Its efforts at institutional reform aimed at the former; but its practice fostered the latter. Faced with the task of administering a vast and diverse empire, the ministers of internal affairs felt the need for an agent at the gubernia level who would be able to function decisively and go, when necessary, beyond the legal boundaries that were supposed to restrict ordinary officials. To achieve this end, the MVD sacrificed a significant measure of its power over the governors. Ultimately, it appears to have accepted Karamzin's dictum that the proper governance of Russia could best be achieved by finding fifty good governors and giving them the scope in which to act.

If, indeed, this was the ministry's perspective, it was not entirely false, for a successful governor needed to have those qualities of personality that are sometimes called charisma. And these gifts could not be displayed by an official who was too tightly controlled from the center. Yet there is another irony here. As subsequent chapters will show, the governor's ability to dominate the provincial scene was less than perfect. Because of the twisted knot of local bureaucracy and politics, the chief administrator of a province was far from being its master.

89. PSZ, 3d ser., no. 14151.

— 5 —

Prisoner of the Clerks

When members of Senator A. A. Polovtsov's inspection team began to examine the records of the Kiev provincial committee on peasant affairs in the fall of 1880, they encountered more than the expected bureaucratic tangles and backlog of unfinished work. They uncovered a mystery as well. A large portion of the files relating to the committee's current business had disappeared. Undertaking an immediate search, the inspectors soon located the missing documents in the quarters of the committee's registrar, Nikolai Vasil'evich Grishkov. But their discovery provoked another question: What had caused the clerk to take the files in the first place?

Grishkov's interrogation supplied the answer. Unable to support his family on a small government salary, the registrar had grown despondent. Then the death of one of his sisters and the debt incurred as the result of her funeral increased his misery and helplessness. "Often," he told the investigators, "I would go home not to eat, but to weep about my situation." Financial worries drained Grishkov of all energy. He had always been an exemplary worker, but now he could not carry out his duties. And the tasks before him were made more difficult because the committee did not have a secretary to guide its operations and its other members refused to provide the necessary leadership. As the number of papers awaiting his attention grew, Grishkov became desperate. He began to smuggle files out of the office, falsifying records to cover his traces. The clerk took these materials home, hoping to complete work on them after hours. But Grishkov could never seem to finish, though he sometimes labored through the night. Documents piled up steadily in his apartment, and the flow of business in the committee slowed. Delays of up to nine months were common.[1]

Because of his sincere repentance and the extenuating circumstances, Grishkov was not punished for his misdeeds. But his story illustrates administrative problems that could not be solved so easily. All across the tsar's empire, workers in government bureaus were troubled by many of the same things that broke Grishkov: low pay, inadequate staffing, and an ever-growing burden of work. Daily, thousands of demoralized petty functionaries and scribes toiled away, copying documents, sending papers from one office to another, filing, misfiling, covering up their mistakes whenever possible. In the process, they determined the pace and limits of imperial governance.

And while His Excellency the governor might seem far above the minor bureaucrats in the gubernia offices, he was, in fact, caught in the same web as they. The fulfillment of his orders depended on the dispatch of the office workers; their diligence and competence would frequently decide the governor's success in discharging his roles as imperial viceroy and ministerial leg-man. Assuming office for the first time, a governor might be proud of the tsar's commission and determined to meet the MVD's demands. But he soon realized that however high-sounding his titles, however vast his legal duties and responsibilities as *nachal'nik gubernii,* he was, to a large extent, limited in his ability to act. The governmental agencies through which he had to work functioned badly. The number of competent officials on hand was seldom large enough for effective management. To make things run right, the governor would have to rely on noninstitutional means: the personal loyalties and ties he could forge between himself and key members of the local bureaucracy. Yet these bonds might make His Excellency the prisoner of the clerks who served him.

Any survey of gubernatorial memoirs and unpublished papers leaves the reader with a strong impression of the degree to which governors were dependent on their staffs. Governors frequently noted how their work was eased or simply made possible by a competent official in the right place. But the same sources show that governors were highly vulnerable to the mistakes of local bureaucrats. Failure on the part of subordinates to handle papers properly, their dispatch to the wrong

---

1. Report of I. G. Danilov to A. A. Polovtsov, 23 December 1880, and statement of Grishkov to Danilov, 6 November 1880, Gosudarstvennaia publichnaia biblioteka im. Saltykova-Shchedrina. Otdel rukopisei [hereafter GPB], f. Revizii Polovtsova (600), d. 731, "Predpisanie . . . Polovtsova . . . Danilovu . . . i raport Danilova . . . ," pp. 7–11, 14–15.

institution or in the wrong form, could bring down on a governor the wrath of his superiors and even a reprimand from the Senate itself.[2]

The governors understood their situation. While praising the skill of some of their staffs, they were quick to assert that the personnel at their disposal was largely inadequate in numbers and ability. Throughout the entire period under discussion and from every quarter of the empire, the governors' complaints were similar. "I cannot now point to a single . . . [local official] distinguished. . . by something especially remarkable such as a strong talent, a broad understanding, [or] a notable influence on local society . . . ," wrote Arkhangelsk governor K. I. Pashchenko in 1884. Few good people would serve in the provinces for such paltry salaries, lamented Samara governor A. D. Sverbeev in his annual report for 1889. Five years later, his successor, A. S. Brianchaninov seconded and added to these words. Nor did governors restrict their grumblings to official channels. Writing to his mother from Semipalatinsk in 1910, A. N. Troinitskii told her that the majority of his staff could not be counted on because they believed "that they have to get paid but do not need to work."[3] The MVD agreed completely with the *nachal'niki gubernii* on the inadequate size and quality of provincial officialdom. In a memorandum dated 10 August 1910, Prime Minister P. A. Stolypin praised the "humble toilers" in the gubernia offices who "zealously and honorably" carried out their duties. But, he concluded, "the selection of the employees in the governors' chancelleries and in the provincial boards . . . [could] not be viewed as adequate."[4]

The problem of provincial staffing was a major concern for the *nachal'niki gubernii*. The first action a governor attempted after arriving in a new province was to familiarize himself with the officials in the state institutions and with the leading people of the various elected bodies. The governor's goal was simple and obvious: to discover who

2. Dzhunkovskii, "Vospominaniia za 1905–1908 gg.," TsGAOR, f. Dzhunkovskogo, op. 1, d. 47, p. 192; Ukaz of the Senate to the MVD, 23 April 1890, TsGIA, f. DOD, op. 45, 1886, d. 84, "O naznachenii . . . grafa Musina-Pushkina . . . ," pp. 31–38.

3. Pashchenko report dated 11 May 1884, TsGIA, f. Kants. MVD, op. 3, d. 228, "Po ezhenedel'nym zapiskam . . . ," p. 3; Sverbeev's report is in ibid., f. DOD, op. 223, 1890, d. 247, pp. 15–18; for Brianchaninov's views, see ibid., 1895, d. 181, pp. 8–10; Troinitskii's letter, dated 4 April 1910, is in ibid., f. Troinitskogo, op. 1, d. 57, "Pis'ma Troinitskim . . . ot ikh detei," p. 9.

4. Circular no. 37, found TsGIA, f. DOD, op. 47, 1910, d. 168, "Ob uluchshenii material'nogo polozheniia lichnogo sostava gubernskikh pravlenii i gubernatorskikh kantseliarii." This section of the *delo* is unpaged.

was competent and who was hopeless, who would prove cooperative, who obstructive.[5] Such an assessment was a necessary beginning, because the law gave the governors formidable, though not absolute, powers in the area of staffing. A governor's views had the greatest weight in the areas that were part of the MVD hierarchy, but he could also help to shape the personnel subject to other agencies. Article 286 of the gubernia statute stated that within a two-week period a governor could inform any ministry that its selection of a particular local representative was unsatisfactory and so block a troublesome appointment. In addition, other sections of the code made the governor responsible for the trustworthiness of all officials in the province and gave him enormous discretionary powers over the officers of elective institutions and those employed by them.[6]

Because his powers in the area of appointment appeared to be so significant, the arrival of a new governor caused considerable anxiety for gubernia officials. This was particularly true for the head of the gubernatorial chancellery (*pravitel'*) and the police chief of the provincial capital who had to work very closely with the *nachal'nik gubernii* and were dependent on his good will. But the concerns of local bureaucrats were sometimes engendered by political considerations. For example, a governor who came to a province with a reputation for "liberalism" might find that conservatives in the gubernia administration were fearful that their services would no longer be wanted.[7] In any case, local apprehension concerning the new governor was probably excessive, for his powers in the area of staffing were tempered by various factors. The governor's hirings and firings had to be cleared by the MVD. And though the ministry generally backed the *nachal'nik gubernii*, its approach to the question of dealing with officials was decidedly paternalistic. A bureaucrat who was not acceptable to a governor would not find himself kicked out on the street but was usually transferred to another post or province, often with a promo-

5. A. N. Mosolov, "Vospominaniia," TsGAOR, f. Otdel'nykh dokumentov . . . d. 1115, pp. 92–94; Koshko, *Vospominaniia*, pp. 113–14, 141; Osorgin, "Vospominaniia," GBL, f. Osorgina, papka II, d. 2, pp. 148–49; Urussov, pp. 13–14; Sinel'nikov, "Zapiski," *Istoricheskii vestnik* 59 (1895): 383.

6. "Obshchee uchrezhdenie gubernskoe," art. 282, *Svod zakonov*, 2 (1892); N. Driagin, "K voprosu o diskretsionnoi vlasti gubernatorov," *Pravo* (20 May 1910):1065–68; N. I. Lazarevskii, *Lektsii po russkomu gosudarstvennomu pravu* (2d ed., St. Petersburg, 1910), 2, pp. 230–31.

7. Koshko, *Vospominaniia*, p. 114; Osorgin, "Vospominaniia," GBL, f. Osorgina, papka II, d. 2, pp. 234–35, 238–39.

tion. Indeed, the governor himself had to help arrange for these changes, and this could take time.[8]

For example, I. F. Koshko recounts his difficulty in firing a certain Pesochinskii, the permanent member of the land settlement commission in Perm, whose ignorance of the law and of government guidelines made him virtually useless. At first, the governor requested Pesochinskii's resignation, but the latter refused. Koshko then asked the MVD to remove the undesired official and got some surprising results. The ministry took Pesochinskii off the land settlement commission but then made him a permanent member on the provincial committee on peasant affairs, a job for which he was equally unfitted! Only when irregularities in Pesochinskii's handling of the finances of the land settlement commission came to light was he removed from the provincial administration altogether.[9]

Despite the governor's powers, then, his attempts to change the provincial bureaucracy were often frustrated. This was true even of those offices such as head of chancellery and police chief about which the *nachal'niki gubernii* felt a special concern. An examination of the composition of gubernia offices in twenty-seven provinces following the installation of a new governor shows that about two-thirds of the heads of chancellery and police chiefs held on to their posts for at least the first year of a new administration.[10] And if these officials survived the initial sweep of the new gubernatorial broom, they might even outlast the *nachal'nik gubernii* himself.[11] The average governor's tenure of office in a particular province was six and a half years, but many served less than five.

The governor also encountered difficulty putting together his own local staff because he could seldom find competent men, particularly those with higher education, to fill the vacant posts. Pay scales were notoriously low and had not risen in over three decades.[12] Moreover,

8. Koshko, *Vospominaniia*, p. 114. The MVD apparently had few qualms about transferring incompetent officials from one province to another. See the memorandum of the Department of General Affairs dated 21 April 1915, TsGIA, f. DOD, op. 47, 1915, d. 23, "Po khodataistvam o predstavlenii dolzhnostei sovetnkov gub. pravlenii i o kandidatakh na eti dolzhnosti," pp. 24–25.

9. Koshko, "Vospominaniia," pp. 124–25, 126–32, BAR, Koshko family papers.

10. Information derived from *Adres-kalendary* for the years 1884, 1886, 1892, 1895, 1896, 1897.

11. E. N. Berendts, *O proshlom i nastoiashchem russkoi administratsii* (St. Petersburg, 1913), pp. 274–75.

12. Pay scales for provincial employees of the MVD were set by the law of 8 June

the problem of staffing remained even after the MVD had gotten around to increasing the salaries of its main provincial bureaucrats because the law of 21 January 1910 alloted but 1,160,000 extra rubles to augment the pay of workers in the governors' chancelleries and provincial boards.[13] Stolypin's subsequent admonition to the governors to upgrade the personnel of these institutions by hiring university and legally trained officers must have moved more than a few of the *nachal'niki gubernii* to wring their hands in despair.[14]

Some governors, of course, could solve their staffing problems by virtue of special charisma. S. V. Shakhovskoi, who ruled in Chernigov and Estland during the late 1880s and early 1890s, was able to recruit a large number of well-educated people for posts in his chancellery and the provincial board. They willingly took up these relatively lowly positions because of the governor's attractive personality and his special "Russifying" mission in Estland. According to M. M. Osorgin, Governor G. A. Tobizen had a similar ability to draw talented staff without, however, linking them to any particular cause.[15]

But few governors were as fortunate in their search for capable subordinates. Many relied on recommendations from friends, family, superiors, and even their colleagues wives, but often this advice proved useless.[16] We must assume that in the majority of cases governors depended on their own judgment and experience. They brought along a few trusted associates they had come to know during their earlier

---

1865 (PSZ, 2d ser., no. 42180). Under this statute, the head of a governor's chancellery had an annual salary of 1,500 rubles which remained fixed for the rest of the nineteenth century (Zaionchkovskii, *Pravitel'stvennyi apparat*, p. 88; TsGIA, f. DOD, op 194, 1903, d. 150, ch. 1, "Po gubernskoi reforme," pp 64–65). By 1910, the pay of a head of chancellery had risen to 2,000 rubles a year (Report of the Department of General Affairs, 29 June 1910, TsGIA, f. DOD, op. 47, 1910, d. 168, p. 5).

13 PSZ, 3d ser. no. 32939.

14. Stolypin's circular (no. 37) is dated 10 August 1910, TsGIA, f. DOD, op. 47, 1910, d. 168, unpaged; for a governor's comment see Dzhunkovskii's annual report for 1910, TsGAOR, f. Dzhunkovskogo, op. 1, d. 107, "Otchety . . . 1905–1914 gg.," p. 79.

15. On Shakhovskoi, see Umanets, *Vospominaniia*, pp. 19–20. Osorgin's comments on Tobizen are found in his "Vospominaniia," GBL, f. Osorgina, papka II, d. 2, p. 35.

16. For a variety of materials on governors' staffing problems see TsGIA, f. Troinitskogo, op. 1, d. 71, "Pis'ma N. A. Troinitskogo k V. I. Romanusu, 1874–1888 gg.," p. 21; letter dated 22 April 1880, ibid., f. Bezaka, op. 2, d. 70, "Pis'ma N. Martynova k N. A. Bezak," pp. 1–2; N. S. Brianchaninov to S. D. Tol', 22 November 1901, ibid., f. Tolia, op. 1, d. 2, "Khoziaistvennaia perepiska po imeniiam za 1900–1901 gg.," p. 347; Osorgin, "Vospominaniia," GBL, f. Osorgina, papka II, d. 2, pp. 189–90; Koshko, *Vospominaniia*, p. 144; letter of M. Zinov'ev to S. V. Shakhovskoi, 23 April 1889, GPB, f. Denmana, d. 75, "Shakhovskoi . . . perepiska ego . . . ," p. 26.

work and then, gritting their teeth, set out to make the best possible use of the human resources available in the province.

The difficulty that governors had in finding suitable personnel helps to explain why the *nachal'niki gubernii* frequently had very close ties to their main subordinates. If memoirs and personal papers are any guide, many governors saw at least a portion of their staff as family and their mutual relations were marked by real personal warmth.[17] Some governors displayed genuine fatherly concern. M. M. Osorgin, for example, learned what his officials liked to eat, and if by chance a particular bureaucrat's favorite dish were being served for lunch, the governor would send a servant to seek out the man and bring him to the table.[18] Much more often, governors helped subordinates secure special pensions or better jobs in other provinces. Even when dismissing an official, a governor might make him a small loan to help support his family during the search for new employment.[19]

The governors' involvement with their staff was more than a curiosity. It reflected the broader character and problems of provincial administration in the tsarist empire. The patriarchal and personal style with strong elements of patron-client relations was an important part of the Russian concept and practice of government. Beyond this, governors knew that given the low quality of most provincial bureaucrats, the only way they could get local institutions to function well was to find a few good men and to install them in the right places. A governor needed to form a strong link with his key officials and use it to elicit their best efforts. Unfortunately, this personal style could have negative consequences as well. Some governors ended up protecting subordinates from the consequences of their mistakes, accepting work that was clearly inadequate, and even shielding those guilty of offences that might have been prosecuted by the courts.[20] Such an approach might

17. Osorgin, "Vospominaniia," pp. 28–30; A. N. to N. A. Troinitskii, letters dated 11 November 1892 and 27 August 1893, TsGIA, f. Troinitskogo, op. 1, d. 57, pp. 88, 82–83; Umanets, *Vospominaniia*, p. 19; A. V. Ovchinnikov to N. A. Bezak, letter dated 26 October, 1882, TsGIA, f. Bezaka, op. 1, d. 18, "Pis'ma . . . Ovchinnikova . . . Bezaku," p. 8.

18. Osorgin, "Vospominaniia," GBL, f. Osorgina, papka II, d. 2, pp. 148–49.

19. N. A. Troinitskii to L. S. Makov, 13 May 1880, TsGIA, f. Troinitskogo, op. 1, d. 86 [miscellaneous correspondence], pp. 1–4; N. A. Troinitskii to G. M. Lapitskii, letters dated 22 May, 2 and 8 July, 1879, ibid., d. 2, "Kopii sluzhebnoi perepiski . . . ," pp. 138–39, 144–46; letters of V. V. fon Val' to G. Khokhuli, 11 March and 4 April 1880, TsGAOR, f. fon Valia, op. 1, d. 103, "Prosheniia . . . i dr. materialy ob ustroistve, uvolnenii, peremeshchenii po sluzhbe chinovnikov . . . ," pp. 7–15.

20. Osorgin, "Vospominaniia," GBL, f. Osorgina, papka II, d. 2, pp. 53–55; Sinel'nikov, "Zapiski," *Istoricheskii vestnik* 59 (1885): 763.

gain the governor the loyalty of his staff, but it could also slow and corrupt the processes of government.

Nowhere were personal qualities more important than in the relationship between the governors and their vice-governors. The association between these two men was a sensitive one. It contained the potential for serious conflict with disruptive consequences. Yet, it could also engender fruitful cooperation and mutual advantage.

Problems often developed because the relationship between the two officials was fluid and involved a combination of autonomy and dependence. Before the twentieth century, governors had almost no say in the selection of their vice-governors. This was a right the MVD retained and zealously guarded for at least two reasons. First, by making sure that the vice-governor was not the governor's creature, the ministry maintained a more or less independent check on gubernatorial activity and prevented a governor from becoming too powerful. Second, a vice-governorship was the chief training ground for future *nachal'niki gubernii* and control of the selection of vice-governors gave the MVD a means of determining the future shape of the gubernatorial corps.

Of course, these considerations did not stop governors from trying to influence the appointment of vice-governors. *Nachal'niki gubernii* wrote to friends in the capital asking them to put in a good word for a particular candidate and sometimes appealed directly to the minister. Usually they got nowhere.[21] Throughout the later nineteenth century, the MVD almost never queried the governors for their opinions about the selection of their seconds-in-command. So rigid was this policy that when long-time Nizhni-Novgorod governor N. M. Baranov was actually asked to suggest candidates for a vacant vice-gubernatorial post in his province, he expressed surprise and delight at this "benevolent question."[22] After 1903, an imperial order required the MVD to find out if a governor had objections to a proposed candidate.[23] But it appears that governors' vetoes were not always honored and that

21. Letter of Kostroma governor V. V. Kalachev to N. A. Bezak, 3 April 1887, TsGIA, f. Bezaka, op. 2, d. 45, "Pis'mo Kalacheva . . . ," pp. 1–2; Osorgin, "Vospominaniia," GBL, f. Osorgina, papka II, d. 1, p. 3.

22. Baranov to I. N. Durnovo, 3 May 1895, TsGIA, f. DOD, op. 45, 1881, d. 152, "O kandidatakh na dolzhnost' vitse-gubernatora," pp. 86–87.

23. This order is mentioned in a letter from A. D. Abrutsov to A. N. Kharuzin, 9 June 1905, TsGIA, f. DOD, op. 46, 1904, d. 132, "S perepiskoiu po snosheniiam s gubernatorami pri nazhnacheniiakh vo vverennye im gubernii vitse-gubernatorov," p. 23.

attempts by governors to have a positive influence on the selection were frequently rebuffed or ignored.[24]

The independence of the vice-governors was strengthened by the fact that, unlike their counterparts in the United States, Russian vice-governors played a significant part in the administration of the province. Their chief task was to direct the day-to-day work of the gubernia board and to manage its chancellery. Moreover, vice-governors frequently took on a number of other governmental duties and assumed the power of governor whenever he was on leave or touring the province. Thus, it was not unusual for a vice-governor to act as the *nachal'nik gubernii* for significant portions of the year.[25]

Because of their considerable autonomy and their proximity to power, many provincial seconds-in-command suffered from what I. F. Koshko called the "vice-gubernatorial disease," whose primary symptoms seem to have been a feverish ambition and a distended pride. Despite the fact that they carried considerable burdens on their shoulders, vice-governors often believed that their superiors ignored and slighted them.[26] Those who were ambitious might feel cramped and superfluous. "Personal initiative is closed to the vice-governor as is any self-sufficient, vital work that corresponds to the needs of the time and local conditions," complained A. P. Engel'gardt as he chafed in his position as Kazan's third citizen.[27]

In these circumstances, it is understandable that conflict between governors and vice-governors often developed and took a variety of forms. Discontented vice-governors frequently appear to have shirked their duties and engaged in petty intrigues.[28] At other times the frus-

---

24. See two communications from P. A. Stolypin asking that I. G. Knoll be made vice-governor (letter to A. G. Bulygin, 5 April 1905, ibid., p. 25 and an earlier memorandum written in February 1905, ibid., 1905, d. 213, "O kandidatakh na dolzhnosti vitse-gubernatorov," pp. 48–49). In the end Stolypin was successful, but his letters betray considerable frustration. See also the letter from E. A. Vatatsi to Governor Shlippe, 26 October 1904, ibid., 1904, d. 132, p. 15.

25. According to A. D. Sverbeev, while vice-governor in Kostroma (1868–1878), he carried out the duties of governor for a total of four years and four months (TsGALI, f. Sverbeevykh, op. 1, d. 455, "Proekt biograficheskogo ocherka . . . ," p. 5).

26. Koshko, *Vospomianiia*, p. 140.

27. Letter to I. N. Durnovo, n. d. [late spring, 1892], TsGIA, f. DOD, op. 46, 1890, d. 63, "O naznachenii . . . Engel'gardta . . . ," p. 75.

28. Letters of A. N. to N. A. Troinitskii, 7 March and 25 July 1910, TsGIA, f. Troinitskogo, op. 1, d. 57, pp. 304–305, 53–54; V. V. Kalachev to N. A. Bezak, 3 April 1887, ibid., f. Bezaka, op. 2, d. 45, pp. 1–2; V. D. Surovtsev to I. L. Goremykin, 26 November 1897, ibid., f. DOD, op. 46, 1897, d. 96, "Po sekretnoi perepiske," pp. 20–24; N. Ch. Zaionchkovskii's report on Tula, ibid., op. 47, 1911, d. 343, p. 18.

trations felt by vice-governors caused them to lash out at their superiors. In Arkhangelsk, the victim of one such outburst was not the governor but his wife. Administering the province in the absence of Governor Sosnovskii, A. F. Shidlovskii became convinced that he had been ignored by the *gubernatorsha* at a public function. Seized by an uncontrollable rage, Shidlovskii turned on the poor woman and, in the words of an official memorandum, "permitted himself . . . such unrestrained and insulting behavior . . . that [Mme Sosnovskii] suffered a nervous collapse (*zabolela nervnym rastroistvom*) and had to leave town to recover her health." For once a governor had something to say about the disposition of his second-in-command. At Sosnovskii's request, the MVD transferred Shidlovskii to Olonets.[29]

But there was more to conflict between vice-governors and governors than simple sloth and outbursts of pique. Some vice-governors spoke out against their chiefs during the meetings of various administrative boards and committees when they thought that the *nachal'nik gubernii* was in error or had overstepped his authority. M. M. Osorgin argued vigorously but unsuccessfully with Governor Tobizen concerning the acceptance of an inadequate report from a subordinate. As vice-governor in Samara, I. F. Koshko got into a serious and embarrassing dispute with Governor V. V. Iakunin on the question of disciplining a land captain. Iakunin refused to accept Koshko's proposal to turn matters over to the regular courts, and the result was a split between the two men at one of the sessions of the provincial committee on peasant affairs. Iakunin won, but Koshko felt that considerable bitterness had resulted from the clash.[30]

Sometimes, tensions reached a flash point and the vice-governor got a dose of gubernatorial abuse. Governor Nol'kin of Mogilev exploded after Vice-Governor Shidlovskii had challenged him on a number of procedural matters concerning the operation of the provincial board. The *nachal'nik gubernii* "banged his fist on the table and, raising his voice to the point of being heard in the neighboring rooms, shouted that *he* was governor, could make everyone obey his orders, . . . [and] would fulfill the task assigned to him by the sovereign emperor."[31]

Incidents of conflict between the two top officials of the gubernia

29. Memorandum dated 15 October 1911, TsGIA, f. DOD, op. 47, 1910, d. 278, "So spravkami o gubernatorakh kotorye predstavlialis' g. Ministru v 1910, 1911 gg.," pp. 118–19.

30. Osorgin, "Vospominaniia," GBL, f. Osorgina, papka II, d. 2, pp. 53–55; Koshko, *Vospominaniia*, pp. 117–118.

31. S. Shidlovskii to P. A. Stolypin, 30 January 1909, TsGIA, f. DOD, op. 47, 1909, d. 143, "Prilozheniia k otchetu . . . Zaionchkovskogo po komandirovke v mogilev-skogo gub. . . . ," p. 4 (italics mine).

could be dramatic, but they did not occur in most cases. Harmony, not altercation, seems to have been the rule. And how could it be otherwise since both the *nachal'nik gubernii* and his second-in-command had much more to gain from cooperation than from contention? Vice-governors, though not actual clients of the governors, could greatly benefit from their good will, and governors knew that their reputations depended on making things run smoothly. A clash with their *vitse* would be embarrassing and could do irrevocable damage to their careers.

Consequently, it is not surprising that when a new governor assumed command, he was likely to find the vice-governor eager to help. As Governor N. A. Bezak prepared to take up his post in Nizhni, Vice-Governor Vsevolzhskii wrote to welcome his new chief and to outline some of the problems he might face. Vsevolzhskii's solicitude verged on the obsequious as he informed Bezak that the governor's mansion was now in fine shape, with clean living-quarters, a large supply of wood, and a packed ice-house. Everything was ready, including the vice-governor. "Give me . . . the opportunity to be of real use to the service under your command [and] in accordance with the general direction ordered or approved by you," Vsevolzhskii concluded plaintively.[32]

Bezak's experience with Vsevolzhskii was not unique. When I. F. Koshko took over in Perm, Vice-Governor V. I. Evropeus made every effort to ease the new governor into his post. Even before Koshko had settled into his residence, his second-in-command had invited him to dinner together with the leading provincial officials and a few zemstvo figures. In this relaxed and informal setting, the new governor made the acquaintance of the men with whom he would have to work.[33]

Of course, solicitude could cut the other way too. M. M. Osorgin recalled that on his arriving as vice-governor in Kharkov, Governor G. A. Tobizen had greeted him at the train station, had helped his second-in-command get started by preparing a list of the people Osorgin was to visit, and advising him how to dress for each meeting. When Governor Shmit was on his way to assume control in Iaroslavl, he wrote to his vice-governor, V. V. fon Val'. In his letter the new governor expressed the hope that their association would be a good one and that he would be able to draw on fon Val's experience and knowledge of the province "which all . . . hold in the highest regard."[34]

32. Letter dated 3 March 1880, TsGIA, f. Bezaka, op. 2, d. 5, "Pis'ma Vsevolzhskogo . . . ," pp. 3–6.
33. Koshko, "Vospominaniia," p. 50, BAR.
34. Osorgin, "Vospominaniia," GBL, f. Osorgina, papka II, d. 2, pp. 28–30; Shmit

Once established, most governors continue to find their seconds-in-command valuable. A good *vitse* was someone on whom a governor could count to help shoulder the responsibilities of office, especially when he had to be away on business or vacation.[35] In time, a governor might unload a host of troublesome, unwanted duties on a talented and trusted subordinate, a practice particularly common among governors who had seen long service and had been worn down by the cares of office.[36] Of course, there were occasions when the governor proved incompetent, and the vice-governor was forced to assume the dominant position in the provincial administration.[37] But in most cases, there was no question of who was in charge, and governors developed an effective division of labor with their seconds-in-command. V. F. Dzhunkovskii, for example, found in Vice-Governor A. M. Ustinov a man to whom he could entrust the work of overhauling and managing the provincial board. Ustinov's competence and energy freed the governor from burdensome routine and enabled him to conduct much needed inspections of the gubernia.[38] Indeed, cordial relations often extended beyond the confines of business. S. D. Urusov recalled Vice-Governor Blok as "a never to be forgotten companion, a trusted assistant and an ally." Vice-Governor Evropeus and his wife were the Koshkos' closest friends in Perm and continued to be held in the highest regard long after service connections had been severed.[39]

A good working relationship and an effective division of labor between the governor and his second-in-command could do much to smooth the operations of the gubernia administration. Of almost equal importance was the governor's chancellery through which passed most of the paper work dealing with problems requiring his direct, personal attention. A governor's ability to manage affairs depended in large

---

to von Val', 23 April 1877, TsGAOR, f. fon Valia, op. 1, d. 57, "Uvedomleniia iaroslavskogo gubernatora fon Valiu . . . ," p. 14.

35. Vsevolzhskii to Bezak, 3–6 October, 1880, TsGIA, f. Bezaka, op. 2., d. 5, pp. 22, 32.

36. During the famine of 1891, Governor Poltaratskii assigned Vice-Governor Engel'gardt the chief role in relief operations (Robbins, *Famine in Russia*, pp. 127–30, 222); Tobizen turned over many of the day-to-day tasks of management to M. M. Osorgin (Osorgin, "Vospominaniia," GBL, f. Osorgina, papka II, d. 2, pp. 31, 42, 67–69).

37. TsGIA, f. DOD, op 47, 1911, d. 342, ch. 2, "Otchet . . . Zaionchkovskogo po obozreniiu deloproizvodstva riazanskikh gubernskogo pravleniia . . . ," pp. 87–89.

38. Dzhunkovskii, "Vospominaniia za 1905–1908 gg.," TsGAOR, f. Dzhunkovskogo, op. 1, d. 47, pp. 161–62.

39. Urussov, *Memoirs*, p. 26; Koshko, "Vospominaniia," p. 48, BAR.

measure on the efficiency, skill, and dedication of the chancellery staff because it gathered and systematized the information needed for the annual report and oversaw a far-ranging correspondence. The chancellery also handled those matters that were secret, or required special dispatch such as the calling out and dispositioning of troops.[40]

It is difficult to generalize about the operations of the chancelleries because so much depended on the personal predilections of the governors and the circumstances of the moment. Certainly most chancelleries had a scope of activity larger than that assigned to them by law because governors frequently assumed functions that rightfully belonged to other institutions.[41] As a result, the amount of business transacted by these bodies was very large. From 1904 to 1906, when the flow of official correspondence was undoubtedly extensive, information gathered from six provinces in various parts of the country suggests that on average a gubernatorial chancellery might process over 20,000 papers annually. Yet the amount of paper work was determined by the size, population, and importance of the gubernia. In 1904, for example, the Pskov chancellery dispatched some 8,147 papers, whereas the chancellery in Volynia processed 31,963 pieces of business.[42] In 1913 the Vilna chancellery handled 39,576 papers, and the one in Kiev 163,709.[43] In all cases, however, the number of people who handled this work was extremely small. The core of the chancellery staff consisted of nine individuals: a head (*pravitel'*), five assistants, a registrar, and two troubleshooters (*chinovniki osobykh poruchenii*). This basic list (*shtat*) of chancellery personnel, established in 1865, remained fundamentally unchanged until the end of the empire.[44]

Of course, core personnel could be augmented by hired assistants

40. PSZ, 2d ser., no. 42180, 8 June 1865.

41. "Zapiska chlena Gosudarstvennogo soveta senatora Kovalevskogo zakliuchaiushchaia materialy, kasaiushchiesia polozheniia i deiatel'nosti gubernskikh administrativnykh uchrezhdenii po dannym okazivshimsia pri revizii gubernii kazanskoi i ufimskoi" [hereafter Zapiska Kovalevskogo, no. 3], p. 38, in *Materialy po vysochaishe utverzhdennoi osoboi komissii dlia sostavleniia proektov mestnogo upravleniia* [hereafter *MVUOK*] (10 vols.; St. Petersburg, n.d.), 3: *Po senatorskim reviziiam*, pt. 1: *Zapiski senatora Kovalevskogo.*

42. TsGIA, f. DOD, op. 185, 1906, d. 73a, "O preobrazovanii uchrezhdenii gubernskogo upravleniia," pp. 424, 428, 430, 438, 440. The other provinces surveyed in this report were Kaluga, Saratov, Ekaterinoslav, and St. Petersburg.

43. TsGIA, f. DOD, op. 47, 1914, d. 43a, "Otchet . . . Zaionchkovskogo po komandirovke v g. Vil'nu . . . ," p. 93; ibid., 1915, d. 43a, "Prilozheniia k otchetu . . . Zaionchkovskogo po obozreniiu deloproizvodstvu kantseliarii kievskogo gubernatora i kievskogo gubernskogo pravleniia." (This section of the file unpaged.)

44. PSZ, 2d ser., no. 42180, 8 June 1865; Report of the Department of General Affairs, 29 June 1910, TsGIA, f. DOD, op. 47, 1910, d. 168, pp. 2–3.

who performed a variety of scribal and secretarial tasks, and though the number was not fixed, it generally ranged from seven to twelve.[45] In some provinces, however, governors built up considerably larger chancelleries. In 1883 Governor Somov of Tver had thirty clerical employees in addition to his main staff. The chancellery of the Kiev governor in 1915 had forty-one persons, which included twenty-six regular workers and a supplemental staff of fifteen—a small number considering the volume of business.[46]

By general admission, chancellery workers were grossly underpaid. At the beginning of the twentieth century, their salaries were fixed in accordance with the law of 9 March 1876, which together with an earlier statute (8 June 1865) set the annual wage of the head of chancellery at roughly 2,000 rubles. His senior assistant received 1,400, the junior 960. The troubleshooters got between 1,600 and 1,200, the registrar 800. These wage scales, already low in the 1870s, had become a scandal by the early 1900s. Indeed, the MVD itself stated that the living standards of government employees in the provinces had been seriously undercut by inflation and no longer met the rising cost of basic necessities.[47]

Given these circumstances, it is not surprising that the educational level of chancellery workers was also low. The head of the chancellery, in all likelihood, had finished secondary school or seminary, but most other employees had not risen even that high. Educational standards probably did not increase significantly during the course of the late nineteenth century, though an admittedly unscientific comparison between the schooling of the staff of the Tver chancellery in 1883 and the staffs of the Vilna and Kiev governors at the start of World War I suggests that there was some slight improvement under way.[48] A head of chancellery with a university education was something to be desired, but in 1911 was sufficiently unusual to elicit a government inspector's surprise when he encountered such a person in Tula.[49] Perhaps the most significant move in the direction of upgrading the quality of chancellery workers was the decision to employ women in various

45. "Deloproizvodstva v kantseliarii gubernatora i v gubernskom pravlenii," p. 1, in MVUOK, 3, pt. 2: Zapiski senatora Mordvinova; TsGIA, f. DOD, op. 47, 1914, d. 43b, "Prilozheniia k otchetu . . . Zaionchkovskogo po komandirovke v g. Vil'nu," p. 1

46. GAKO, f. Kants. tver. gub., op. 2, d. 481, "Formuliarnye spiski . . . za 1883 g."; TsGIA, f. DOD, op. 47, 1915, d. 43a, pp. 1–3.

47. Report of the Department of General Affairs, 29 June 1910, TsGIA, f. DOD, op. 47, 1910, d. 168, p. 1.

48. GAKO, f. Kants. tver. gub., op. 2, d. 481; TsGIA, f. DOD, op. 47, 1914, d. 43b, p. 1; ibid., 1915, d. 43a, pp. 1–3.

49. TsGIA, f. DOD, op. 47, 1911, d. 343, "Otchet Zaionchkovskogo po komandirovke ego v tul'skuiu guberniiu," p. 23.

clerical capacities because, as statistics from the Vilna chancellery suggest, their educations were consistently better than those of their male counterparts.[50]

For all their very real staffing problems and enormous work load, the governors' chancelleries appear to have functioned rather well. This was the general conclusion of government inspectors both in the 1880s and in the early years of the twentieth century. The tasks of the chancelleries were rationally divided among several departments, usually five. The most important work was concentrated in the first department, which handled the preparation of the governor's annual report, secret business, and a variety of police matters. In provinces with local institutions of self-government, there were departments of the chancellery devoted to the affairs of urban and zemstvo bodies. Aside from this, however, there seems to have been no uniform organizational scheme, and chancellery structure depended on tradition and the peculiar needs of each province.[51]

Moreover, from all indications the governors' chancelleries were reasonably efficient. Few government inspectors commented on any serious backlog of unfinished business, and in 1906 a general report on the status of provincial administration confirmed this.[52] In comparison with other provincial institutions, the governors' chancelleries seem to have been by far the most smoothly run. This relative success is not easy to explain, but the proximity of the chancellery to the governors must provide part of the answer. The governors knew that the correct processing of their personal papers contributed to the proper working of the administration, and consequently they were intimately involved in the chancellery's day-to-day operation. Also, because the governors recognized the paramount importance of their chancelleries, they must have staffed them with particularly competent heads. A first-time governor might, of course, be inclined to keep the incumbent who already knew the territory and could get a new administration off to a good start. But more experienced governors appear to have frequently brought along their own heads of chancellery from their previous assignment or some other official from former service.[53]

50. TsGIA, f. DOD, op 47, 1914, d. 43b, p. 1.

51. "Deloproizvodstvo v kantseliarii gubernatora i v gubernskom pravlenii," pp. 1–4, 11–13 in *MVUOK*, 3, pt. 2; TsGIA, f. DOD, op. 47, 1913, d. 254, "Otchet Zaionchkovskogo po komandirovke v khersonskuiu guberniiu," pp. 33–34; ibid., 1915, d. 43a, unpaginated section.

52. TsGIA, f. DOD, op. 47, 1911, d. 343, p. 23; ibid., 1913, d. 254, pp. 37–38; ibid., 1914, d. 43a, p. 57; ibid., op. 185, 1906, d. 73a, pp. 424, 426, 428, 430, 438, 440.

53. Dzhunkovskii, "Vospominaniia za 1905–1908, gg.," TsGAOR, f. Dzhun-

Available memoir literature and some correspondence suggest that relations between the governor and his head of chancellery tended to be businesslike and often cordial. Loyalties were based on close association and in common labor. But attachments were rooted in self-interest as well. A governor who had a trustworthy head of chancellery could count on him to provide a good summary of routine business and to point out matters of priority. Beyond this, the *nachal'nik gubernii* blessed with an efficient *pravitel'* could leave the province secure in the knowledge that he would be kept abreast of major developments at home. Governor A. D. Sverbeev of Samara seems to have found such a man in Gorshev, whose letters from 1883 to 1891 indicate how he kept his superior informed of events, sent him key documents, and even apprized him on the health of some of his associates' children.[54] Of course, firm ties with the governor could be of long-term advantage for the *pravitel'*. An outgoing governor might help him obtain a better posting, closer to the bright lights of the capital. N. A. Bezak's head of chancellery, A. V. Ovchinnikov, for example, looked forward to just such an opportunity when the governor took a new job in the Ministry of Transportation. Apparently, he was not disappointed.[55]

Ovchinnikov's letters to Bezak as well as other documents suggest, however, that the loyalties between a governor and his head of chancellery could pose a problem during a change of tenure. Upon taking over his province, a new governor might find the *pravitel'* entrenched, used to wielding considerable power, and set in his ways.[56] In Ovchinnikov's case, the situation appears even a bit more sinister. Bezak asked his head of chancellery to stay on and help the new *nachal'nik gubernii*, N. M. Baranov, get established, but the outgoing governor harbored some misgivings about his successor and expressed them to Ovchinnikov. Hence the latter's behavior toward his new chief was coldly formal despite Baranov's efforts to break the ice. Indeed, Ovchinnikov wrote to Bezak somewhat proudly, "I have not permitted myself to be frank and have tried to limit [our association] only to official reports, though His Excellency has been extremely kind. . . ."[57] In addition, Ovchinnikov

kovskogo, op. 1, d. 47, p. 192; Koshko, *Vospominaniia*, pp. 113–14, 142; Osorgin, "Vospominaniia," GBL, f. Osorgina, papka II, d. 2, p. 321; Umanets, *Vospominaniia*, p. 29.

54. TsGALI, f. Sverbeevykh, op. 1, d. 469, "Doneseniia pravitelia kantseliarii Gorsheva . . . o polozhenii v gubernii . . . , 1883–1890 gg.," *passim*.

55. Ovchinnikov to Bezak, letters dated 8 October and 29 November 1882, TsGIA, f. Bezaka, op. 1, d. 18, pp. 3, 10.

56. Fon Val', "Vil'na," TsGIA, f. fon Valia, op. 1, d. 13, pp. 14–15; Koshko, "Vospominaniia," pp. 521–22.

57. Letter of 26 October 1882, TsGIA, f. Bezaka, op. 1, d. 18, pp. 8–9.

was eager to pass on information and gossip about Baranov, a trait that would have been disconcerting to the new governor had he been aware of it.

The relationship between Bezak and Ovchinnikov was hardly typical, but their correspondence does underline once more the importance of personal rather than institutional connections in the functioning of provincial administration: a new governor might not be able to win over talented staff with the best will in the world because former loyalties were too strong. With the passage of time, successful *nachal'niki gubernii* would find it necessary to develop their own proteges and clients.

The governor's chancellery handled most of the paper work connected with his personal leadership. But in the administration of the province the governor was by no means a satrap managing everything himself. He was supposedly surrounded and, to a degree, restrained by other members of gubernia administration. Many decisions, especially those affecting the general welfare and the supervision of the police and other subordinate officials, were to be made collectively by the provincial board (*gubernskoe pravlenie*).

According to the *Svod zakonov,* the board was "the highest institution of the gubernia" empowered to act as both a legal and purely administrative body. Should an official suspected of offences be handed over to the regular courts for trial? What was to be done when the laws were unclear or in apparent conflict? Ought a bureaucrat be fined for dereliction of duty? These were the kinds of decisions the board made in its judicial capacity. As an administrative institution, the board's actions were even wider. The property rights of citizens, such as the establishment of trusteeships, matters involving the interests of the treasury, the firing and assignment of officials, emergency rulings for the control of threats to public health, the condition of prisons, the opening of eating and drinking establishments, and a host of other things were all subject to the board's rulings.[58]

The law code stipulated that the provincial board must have a two-fold structure. First, there was a general assembly (*obshchee prisutstvie*), the institution's decision-making body, which met under the chairmanship of the governor and consisted of the vice-governor, two councilors (*sovetniki*), the provincial medical inspector, the gubernia engineer (assisted by the provincial architect), the land surveyor, and

58. "Obshchee uchrezhdenie gubernskoe," arts. 436, 438, 493–97, *Svod zakonov,* 2 (1892); PSZ, 2d ser., no. 42180, 8 June 1865.

Main government office building in Nizhni-Novgorod, housing the provincial board, the provincial committee on peasant affairs, the fiscal chamber, and the provincial treasury. Courtesy of TsGIA.

the assessor. Paper work connected with the general assembly was handled by a small chancellery consisting of a secretary and a staff of about eight. The second section of the board was the main chancellery (*kantseliariia pravleniia*), which had a regular staff of about sixteen persons supplemented by several employees performing a variety of secretarial tasks. Most of its work was carried out under the direction of the two councilors, and overall supervision was vested in the vice-governor.[59]

The law was quite precise about the structure of the board's main chancellery. It was divided into five departments (*otdeleniia*): two were of a general executive (*rasporiaditel'nye*) character; the other three dealt with specialized matters such as construction, public health, and land surveying.[60] The two executive departments, each headed by a councilor, were further divided into four to six sections (*stoly*) altogether. The statutes, however, were not as clear on the functioning of the main chancellery. We can say that it received and processed all correspondence addressed to the board, gathered materials needed for its decisions, and issued the institution's orders and circulars. No general regulations assigned business to the various sections; custom and the specific needs of individual provinces determined such matters. Most board chancelleries had a section that dealt almost exclusively with problems of taxation and other financial questions, but beyond this, the apportionment of tasks between the sections appears to defy rational analysis.[61]

The *Svod zakonov* tells us that most of the board's decisions were arrived at collectively in the general assembly. All judicial questions and most important administrative issues were to be examined collegially and determination made by majority vote. Only matters that entailed the straightforward execution of the legal demands of various persons and institutions and some personnel problems could be decided individually by the governor, the vice governor, or the councilors.[62]

If the historian relied solely on the evidence of law codes, he would envision the provincial board as the nerve center of the gubernia, the

59. "Obshchee uchrezhdenie gubernskoe," arts. 441–42, 444, 446, *Svod zakonov*, 2 (1892); PSZ, 2d ser., no. 42180, and no. 55681, 9 March 1876.

60. "Obshchee uchrezhdenie gubernskoe," art. 454, *Svod zakonov*, 2 (1892).

61. "Deloproizvodstvo v kantseliarii gubernatora i v gubernskom pravlenii," pp. 4–5, 7–8, in *MVUOK*, 3, pt. 2: *Zapiski . . . Mordvinova*; TsGAOR, f. fon Valia, op. 1, d. 51, "Vremennoe polozhenie s iaroslavskom gubernskom pravleniem . . ."; TsGIA, f. DOD, op. 47, 1914, d. 43b, pp. 21–33.

62. PSZ, 2d ser., no. 42180, 8 June 1865; "Obshchee uchrezhdenie gubernskoe," arts. 493–501, *Svod zakonov* 2 (1892).

place where the main threads of local administration came together and where crucial decisions were made. But Russians were gifted creators of legal fictions, and the 168 articles of the *Svod zakonov* devoted to the provincial board stretched their capacities to the limit. Students of the state administration in the late nineteenth and early twentieth centuries agreed that the actual position and functioning of the provincial board bore almost no resemblance to the institution described in law. The highest administrative body in the province was anything but that: its collegial decision-making process was largely a sham, and it was unable to perform a meaningful advisory role because it was completely dominated by the governor. In fact, over the years it had been reduced to the status of his second chancellery.[63] Writing on the eve of the 1905 revolution, E. N. Berendts, an adviser to the minister of internal affairs, lamented this gap between law and life: "Does there exist somewhere in Russia a session of the provincial board under the chairmanship of the governor? We do not know. But we doubt that you can find a province in which . . . the board plays the role of a council to the governor or of a judicial collegium . . . participating in decisions with the full power accorded it by statute."[64]

Concerned as they were with the problem of legality, Russians at the end of the imperial period were often content to note the weaknesses of the provincial board and to let it go at that. On the threshold of the twenty-first century, an American historian may well ask some supplementary questions. How much and what kind of work did the board perform? How did the institution really function? If it was moribund, how do we explain it? What was the effect of the failure of the board on the processes of provincial governance and on the governor himself?

Certainly the board was the busiest of all provincial institutions. Official statistics show that at the beginning of the twentieth century these bodies processed an average of 45,000 pieces of business annually.[65] Nor were the matters decided entirely without interest, for they tell us much about the issues that affected the lives of ordinary men and women: petty corruption, police brutality, suspicious disappearances, widows' pensions, and land taxes.[66] Indeed, the range of

---

63. Lazarevskii, *Lektsii*, 2: 240.

64. Berendts, p. 271.

65. "Svedeniia o razmerakh deloproizvodstva v 1909 g. gubernskikh pravlenii 5–ti gubernii . . . ," TsGIA, f. DOD, op. 47, 1910, d. 168, unpaged section. The amount of work carried out by the boards varied widely from province to province. During 1909 the board in Arkhangelsk received 16,405 documents, in Kiev 109,340.

66. Journals of the Chernigov provincial board, 30 November 1879, 29 July 1880, GPB, f. Revizii Polovtsova, d. 1401, "Zhurnaly . . . pravleniia o zloupotrebleniiakh

things considered by the boards was so wide that it is impossible to generalize about the questions that dominated the work of these institutions. For example, data gathered by the senatorial inspectors in Chernigov suggest that during the late 1870s and early 1880s, three issues generated most of the work: the exile of persons convicted by the courts, the dismissal or assignment of state officials, and actions taken by the medical department under terms of the public health statute. In contrast, material from St. Petersburg province for a later period is dominated by complaints against the police and appeals by Jews for the right of continued residence in the region of the capital.[67]

Although provincial boards were unquestionably active, their operations were the subject of voluminous criticism. Illegality, injustice, and inefficiency were frequently charged, and it appears that these accusations were largely if not entirely true. Certainly the boards did not follow the procedures established by statute. Only a small number of their rulings emanated from collegial examination and discussion, and many of the most important matters were resolved by gubernatorial fiat.[68] It is difficult to be certain about the fairness of board rulings. Complaints were frequent,[69] yet materials in the archives of the St. Petersburg and Tver suggest that, on the whole, board members made a serious effort to see justice done.

On the question of inefficiency, however, it is easy to side with the boards' critics. These institutions always generated more than their share of red tape, and the situation does not appear to have improved over time. On the eve of the Great Reforms, an anonymous author, rumored to have been M. N. Katkov, wrote a brief comic masterpiece on the functioning of the bureaucracy. At one point he described in

---

meshchanskikh starost," pp. 1–6, 11–13; journals of the assembly of the St. Petersburg provincial board, 7 and 18 February 1903, LGIA, f. Petrogradskogo gubernskogo pravleniia (254), op. 2, d. 2911, "Zhurnaly 3–go stola . . . za 1903 g.," pp. 82–87, 93–95; journals of the Tver provincial board, 20 and 21 April 1892, GAKO, f. Tverskogo gubernskogo pravleniia (466), op. 2, d. 3814, "Zhurnaly . . . za aprel', mai, iiun' mesiatsy 1892 g.," pp. 71–74, 94–99.

67. GPB, f. Rev. Polovtsova, d. 1367, "Vedomost' o delakh v gubernskoe pravlenie . . . ," 1–4; LGIA, f. Pet. gub. prav., op. 2, d. 2911, pp. i–ii.

68. "Obozrenie deloproizvodstva chernigovskogo gubernskogo pravleniia," p. 12, in *MVUOK*, 3, pt. 3: *Zapiski senatora Polovtsova*, sec. 1; "Svedeniia o razmerakh . . . ," TsGIA, f. DOD, op. 47, 1910, d. 168, unpaged section.

69. See, for example, the Senate ruling in the case of Chernigov governor A. L. Shostak. The document cites at least seven major incidents wherein the provincial board under the governor's direction allowed the police to violate the rights of citizens without disciplining the offending officials. The abuses committed included crude insults and unjustified beatings (TsGIA, f. DOD, op. 44, 1878, d. 222, "O naznachenii . . . Shostaka . . . i ob uvol'nenii," pp. 39–45).

detail the labored passage of a piece of business through the entrails of the board. In fifty-four separate stages, the document went from registrars to secretaries to section heads to scribes. It reached the vice-governor only on the twenty-sixth step and the governor on the twenty-eighth.[70]

Katkov's description was certainly parody, but it contained large elements of truth. And official reports on the work of the provincial boards made in the early twentieth century show that their procedures continued to be cumbersome and slow. Papers were frequently lost and the backlog of business had attained crisis proportions in some provinces. A survey of forty-nine gubernia boards in 1909 showed that in only eleven had the amount of completed business exceeded the quantity of new paper received. In most provinces there was a reasonable balance between incoming and outgoing *dela,* but in twelve gubernias the excess of business received over what had been finished was greater than 10,000 items.[71]

How do we explain the weaknesses of the provincial board? Certainly, the absence of genuine collegiality in decision making stemmed from the governors' power over the councilors (*sovetniki*). Although legally MVD appointees, councilors were actually creatures of the governors who could oppose them only at the gravest professional risk.[72] The pliancy of the councilors and the almost certain support of the vice-governor made the decisions of the board's general assembly a mere formality. The general assembly atrophied, and most of the board's business centered in its main chancellery. Indeed, governors frequently bypassed the boards altogether and managed key issues by themselves.[73]

Inadequate staff was another major weakness of the board. Its regular work force, which probably did not exceed thirty persons in most cases, was small considering the enormous volume of business. In addition, the employees of the board were underpaid and poorly

70. *Rukovodstvo k nagliadnomu izucheniiu administrativnogo techeniia bumag v Rossii* (Moscow, 1858), pp. 5–7. For an ascription of this work to Katkov, see K. G. Mitiaev, *Istoriia organizatsii deloproizvodstva v SSSR* (Moscow, 1959), p. 73.

71. TsGIA, f. DOD, op. 47, 1914, d. 43a, pp. 3–4, 11; ibid., 1913, d. 254, p. 33; "Svedeniia o razmerakh . . . ," ibid., 1910, d. 168, unpaged section.

72. Yaney, *Systematization*, pp. 331–32; Zapiska Kovalevskogo, no. 3, p. 16, in *MVUOK*, 3, pt. 1; "Obozrenie deloproizvodstva kievskogo gubernskogo pravleniia," pp. 3–4, ibid., pt. 3, sec. 1. On the problems that might befall a councilor who opposed a governor see N. Ch. Zaionchkovskii's report on Riazan, TsGIA, f. DOD, op. 47, 1911, d. 342, ch. 2, p. 4.

73. Blinov, *Gubernatory*, pp. 278–82; see also Zaionchkovskii's report on Vilna, TsGIA, f. DOD, op. 47, 1914, d. 43a, pp. 4–5.

trained except for a limited number of specialists.[74] Discussing the makeup of the Vilna board, N. Ch. Zaionchkovskii noted that in a staff of twenty-three, only one (a councilor) had a university degree; four had completed gymnasium or seminary (one had failed that course); four had finished primary School (*uchilishche*); two had received equivalency diplomas; ten had been educated at home; and one (an assistant registrar) had graduated from the St. Petersburg School for the Deaf.[75] Nor was the quality of staff simply a problem for the backwoods. The high cost of living in major metropolitan areas made it almost impossible to find competent people willing to work for the wages the government could pay.[76]

The regular (*shtatnye*) workers on the board were frequently augmented by clerical employees hired to meet local needs and conditions. By the start of the twentieth century, the boards had begun to engage the services of women who, if the experience of the governors' chancelleries was any indication, were better educated than at least some of the regular male staff. These female clerks must have improved the work of the boards considerably, though in some places they were put to other than bureaucratic uses. When the MVD inspector N. Ch. Zaionchkovskii surveyed the *gubernskoe pravlenie* in Riazan, he noted the following situation:

> The seven young women employed to work in the provincial board call attention to themselves. Of these, six work in an extremely unsatisfactory manner, but to make up for it, they are distinguished by remarkable behavior. One . . . [of the women] was brought from Kursk by Vice-Governor Kolobov, and to this day he provides her with more than fatherly protection. Another was photographed at the apartment of the *kapel'meister* of one of the local regiments with two naked friends, and then they were also photographed separately, in the most debauched poses. (I have seen the pictures.) They say that this same girl, coming out of the office of the vice-governor, shouted loudly: "He kissed me, he kissed me, he kissed me! . . ." (Of course, this might be unsubstantiated boasting on her part.) A third, who only shuffles papers, also enjoys great favor with Kolobov; a fourth . . . has a close relationship with one of the clerks; a fifth lives openly with one of the secretaries . . . ; concerning the sixth, there circulate the most unambiguous rumors. I present this information because the Riazan provincial board is known in the city as the

74. Berendts, pp. 271–72.

75. TsGIA, f. DOD. op. 47, 1914, d. 43b, pp. 4–5; see also Zaionchkovskii's report on Voronezh, ibid., 1911, d. 305a, p. 29.

76. Annual report for 1909, TsGAOR, f. Dzhunkovskogo, op. 1, d. 107, "Otchety . . . 1905–1914 gg.," pp. 52–53.

harem of the vice-governor, [a title] that ill befits the highest institution in the province. In Tula and Voronezh women and girls also work for the provincial boards, but nothing like this is heard of there.[77]

Structural problems also inhibited the boards' operations. Because of the atrophy of the general assembly, most of the boards' work was handled in the main chancellery under the direction of the vice-governor. This was probably an efficient arrangement given the large volume of the boards' business, but not all the consequences of this practice were desirable. Some vice-governors were lazy, others, inexperienced. But even assuming that most vice-governors knew what they were doing, they lacked the authority needed to coordinate the work of the boards' staff and drive it forward because the councilors and other key personnel of the *pravlenie* felt dependent on the governor, not his second-in-command. As a result, they did not always follow the vice-governor's orders with the necessary diligence or dispatch.[78]

Of course, if a governor personally interested himself in the day-to-day work of the board, the problem might be mitigated. Still, it appears that the overwhelming majority of the governors left the main business of the institution in the hands of the *vitse*. This practice relieved the governor of a considerable burden and made his day easier. But it contributed to the further decline of the board's status and made it less effective as a governmental body and as a means of guiding provincial administration.

Because the governors had usurped so many of the board's functions and simultaneously had disengaged themselves from its regular activities, officials whose operations the board supposedly supervised showed little respect for the institution. They were reluctant to carry out orders issued in its name and occasionally would try to pass the responsibilities the board had assigned them to other governmental agencies.[79] This was particularly true of the police who were legally subordinated jointly to the governor and the provincial board.

The police were vital to the proper functioning of the board, for they were both its primary source of information and the chief executors of

---

77. TsGIA, f. DOD, op. 47, 1911, d. 342, ch. 2, p. 5. A careful search of the documents preserved in the archives failed to uncover the pictures Zaionchkovskii mentioned.

78. "Obozrenie deloproizvodstva kievskogo gubernskogo pravleniia," p. 10; and "Obozrenie deloproizvodstva chernigovskogo gubernskogo pravleniia," pp. 47–49, in *MVUOK*, 3, pt. 3, sec. 1.

79. "Obozrenie deloproizvodstva kievskogo gubernskogo pravleniia," p. 24, ibid.

its commands. Yet in neither instance did the police act satisfactorily. They were often unable or unwilling to supply the intelligence the board required and thus contributed to its inefficiency. Lack of information slowed the board's decision making and, not surprisingly, delays of over a year were common. Worse still, the police often ignored even the direct orders of the board, especially those that disciplined officers who had themselves broken the law. This was particularly true at the local level where police either refused to impose meaningful punishments on their fellows or delayed implementing board rulings for so long that they had no effect. As a result, the judicial functions of the board were undermined, and the police came to feel that they could act with impunity.[80]

The weakness of the provincial board had two contradictory consequences for the governors. On the one hand, it increased their personal authority, but, on the other, it rendered the exercise of that authority unsure and frequently ineffective. The failure of collective decision making made the governor appear as the only real power in the province and caused officials at all levels to bypass the board whenever possible. But this development in turn overburdened the governor with small matters which could have been handled effectively by subordinates had the board enjoyed greater respect. The board's inadequacies had a tarbaby effect, and the governors were sucked willy-nilly into a mass of needless detail.

Because the board was so often denied the information it needed for decisions and, consequently, got bogged down in its own paper work, governors sometimes could not make use of it even when they wanted to. In January 1875, for example, the governor of Kiev called on the provincial board to speed up the handling of business. Six months later, nothing had happened, so he tried again:

> On 25 January [His Excellency reminded the board] I forwarded to you a list of urgent papers from higher government bodies which had not been acted upon by the provincial board. [I also sent] an order to see to these

---

80. On the question of the police's failure to supply needed information see "Imennye vedomosti o delakh ne okonchennykh v 1880 g. s ukazaniem naimenovaniia del, vremeni ikh vystupleniia i prichiny ne razresheniia," GPB, f. Rev. Polovtsova, d. 674, esp. pp. 21–28; "Obozrenie deloproizvodstva chernigovskogo gubernskogo pravlenie," p. 30, in *MVUOK*, 3, pt. 3, sec. 1; TsGIA, f. DOD, op. 47, 1911, d. 342, ch. 1, pp. 220–21. On the problems of boards disciplining the police see "Materialy, kasaiushchiesia polozheniia i deiatel'nosti politseiskikh uchrezhdenii kievskoi gubernii," p. 48, in *MVUOK*, 3, pt. 3, sec. 2; *Istoriia pravitel'stvuiushchego senata za dvesti let, 1711–1911* (5 vols.; St. Petersburg, 1911), 4: 202.

matters and to reprimand those guilty for the delay. Seeing from memo-randa submitted by the board that from the entire list of undecided matters only one . . . has been properly dealt with, I consider it necessary to insist that the provincial board carry out the order of 25 January and present to me for confirmation the resolutions concerning the responsi-bility of those guilty of delay.

Writing five years later, Senator Polovtsov implied that the governor was still waiting.[81]

The weakness of the board also contributed to that aspect of provin-cial administration for which the governors were most consistently criticized; namely, arbitrariness (*proizvol*). Because the governors were frequently poorly advised and unable to rely on regular institutional procedures, they tended to take matters into their own hands. The result was inconsistancy. In the punishment of subordinate officials, for example, a governor might discipline one man with great severity and let another go free.[82] Frustrated by the inadequacies of the local institutional structure, governors often resorted to personal interven-tion in a wide range of matters. But given the growing complexities of provincial life, the frantic efforts of the *nachal'niki gubernii* to escape their confinement were usually ineffective and made them appear slightly ridiculous.

In addition to the provincial board, the governors were surrounded by a ring of institutions that we will call standing committees, each dealing with a specific aspect of provincial affairs. The number of these committees varied from province to province, and it was theoretically possible for a governor to chair nineteen committees and to participate in the work of at least four others.[83] The committees had emerged in the period after the emancipation and proliferated dramatically to-ward the end of the nineteenth century. They were a token of the expanding range of provincial government, the development of social and economic pluralism, and the growth of the activities of the several central ministries at the gubernia level.

When the Russian government began creating the standing commit-tees in the 1860s and 1870s, it saw them as a means of reducing the

---

81. "Obozrenie deloproizvodstva kievskogo gubernskogo pravleniia," pp. 13–14, in *MVUOK*, 3, pt. 3, sec. 1.

82. Ibid., pp. 7–8, 31–33.

83. S. K. Gogel, "Gubernskie prisutstviia smeshannogo sostava, kak organy admin-istrativnoi iustitsii na mestakh," *Vestnik prava* 36 (1906): 455–56.

administrative burdens on the governors.[84] By the start of the twentieth century, however, few governors or observers of provincial government believed that the committees had achieved their goal. Rather, these institutions had complicated the tasks of the *nachal'niki gubernii*, involved them in the work of officials not directly under their command, and forced them to make decisions on matters about which they had little expertise and few clear ideas.

Russians usually referred to these bodies as "provincial committees of mixed composition" (*gubernskie prisutstviia smeshannogo sostava*), an appellation which atoned for its clumsiness with general accuracy. Unlike the provincial board, the membership of the committees was varied. Depending on their duties, the committees included representatives of the MVD (in the persons of the governor, vice-governor, and sometimes permanent members), the local agents of other interested ministries, and the nobility (represented by the provincial marshal). Where warranted, spokesmen for the institutions of self-government in the gubernia might also participate.

The committees' functions were as varied as their composition. Generally speaking, the aim of the committees was to direct and coordinate the activities of the various provincial officials and elected representatives and solve any conflicts that might develop. The discharge of these obligations required the committee to assume both administrative and judicial duties. In the former capacity, they made decisions relating to their areas of competence and issued orders to the institutions and officers subordinate to them. In the latter role, the committees acted as courts in a growing system of administrative justice.

Because the regular courts of the empire lacked the power to deal with conflict between citizens and the organs of the state, Russia, like most other countries on the European continent, had created institutions of arbitration that functioned within the administration itself. The standing committees were the lowest instances in a structure that had its apex in the First and Second Departments of the Senate. Making decisions on the basis of equity and the public interest and not necessarily on the letter of the law, the committees adjudicated disputes among the government's agencies, their officials, and other public bodies.[85]

In view of the large number of standing committees and the great

---

84. Ibid., 407.

85. The major work on administrative justice in Russia is S. A. Korf, *Administrativnaia iustitsiia*. For a useful discussion in English see Taranovski's dissertation "The Politics of Counter-Reform," pp. 72–91.

differences in the areas of their competence, it is difficult to make generalizations about their functioning. Certainly the volume of business the committees handled was considerable, though far below that of the provincial board and the governor's chancellery. Moreover, the work of some committees vastly exceeded that of others. Data from 1904–1906 indicate that the busiest of the committees was the one for peasant affairs (*gubernskoe* or *gubernskoe po krest'ianskim delam prisutstvie*), which received an average of 14,000 pieces of business annually in the six provinces surveyed. The draft board (*gubernskoe po voinskoi povinosti prisutstvie*) was second, though its case load undoubtedly was inflated by the Russo-Japanese war. The committee on zemstvo and urban affairs (*gubernskoe po zemskim i gorodskim delam prisutstvie*) was the third busiest. Among the least burdened of the committees were those dealing with factory affairs (*gubernskoe po fabrichnym delam prisutstvie*) and commercial taxation (*gubernskoe po promyslovomu nalogu prisutstvie*). In 1904, for example, the average number of questions the factory committees received was 140; for the committee on commercial taxation the average was slightly higher, 269.[86]

The efficiency of these institutions differed considerably from province to province: one gubernia had committees that moved their business along smartly, whereas another saw the buildup of enormous backlogs. The reasons for these differences are difficult to pinpoint. The competence of individual staffs was certainly an important factor but so were internal organization, the respective procedures developed for handling documents, and the leadership that a governor or other key officials could provide.[87]

The governor's role in the several standing committees varied depending on the degree of his interest and competence. However, the committees that usually attracted the most attention from the *nachal'niki gubernii* were those dealing with peasant affairs and the activities of zemstvo and urban institutions of self-government. The questions touched on by these committees had the greatest relevance for the

86. TsGIA, f. DOD, op. 185, 1906, d. 73a, pp. 424, 426, 428, 430, 438, 440.

87. "Reviziia Litvinova," *Izvestiia zemskogo otdela* [hereafter *IZO*] (1908), no. 4, p. 241; ibid., no. 5, pp. 276–79; ibid., nos. 7–8, pp. 352–54; TsGIA, f. Zemskogo otdela (1291), op. 32, 1903, d. 7, "Otchet . . . [G. G.] Savicha po proizvedennoi v 1903 godu revizii krest'ianskikh uchrezhdenii permskoi gubernii." p. 156; ibid., op. 30, 1904, d. 253, "Otchet d.s.s. Gurko dlia revizii krest'ianskikh uchrezhdenii, kurskuiu, ekaterinoslavskuiu i nizhegorodskuiu gub.," pp. 2, 33–35, 53, 62–63; *Kurskoe zemstvo. Otchet po revizii proizvedennoi v 1904 godu senatorom N. A. Zinov'evym* [hereafter: Zinov'ev, *Kurskoe zemstvo*] (2 vols., St. Petersburg, 1906), 1, 234.

governor in his capacity as provincial leader because they frequently took a governor from his duties as administrator and brought him in to the arena of provincial politics.

In the first years of the twentieth century, the standing committee on peasant affairs had a regular membership of six persons. The governor chaired its sessions, and he was joined by the provincial marshal of the nobility, the vice-governor, the district procurator or his assistant, and at least two permanent members. The latter were chosen by the governor in conjunction with the provincial marshal and approved by the MVD.

Because the committee considered matters in a number of clearly defined areas, its membership was augmented as circumstances required. When judicial questions were being discussed, the chairman of the district court or one of its members sat in; when the committee turned to administrative problems, it included the fiscal administrator, the manager of state properties, and the chairman of the provincial zemstvo executive. Finally, during times of famine, the committee would examine relief measures in conjunction with the entire membership of the provincial zemstvo executive board.[88]

In its judicial capacity, the committee acted as an appeal instance in conflicts arising from the decisions of the uezd congresses and volost courts. In such matters its rulings were considered final and without appeal, though both the MVD and the Ministry of Justice could overturn a committee's rulings if either ministry perceived that the local body had acted illegally.

In the administrative area, the committee's purview was much more far-ranging and took up questions, complaints, and decisions concerning land settlement (*pozemel'noe ustroistvo*), migration, direct taxes, and the exile of peasants from local communes. The committee also supervised the work of the land captains, checked their decisions, and conducted inspections of their operations. It had the right to discipline the captains and could temporarily remove them from office or petition the MVD for permanent dismissal. As in the case of its judicial rulings, the committee's decisions in administrative matters were supposed to be final and without appeal, though the governor could block the implementation of a particular judgment or call the matter to the attention of the minister of internal affairs. The MVD, too, had the right to overturn the committee's administrative decisions if it felt a law had been broken.[89]

88. Korf, *Administrativnaia iustitsiia*, 2: 36.
89. Gogel, "Gubernskie prisutstviia," pp. 417–21.

The standing committee on zemstvo and urban affairs was usually composed of nine members. The governor served as chairman, and his colleagues included the provincial marshal, the vice-governor, the fiscal administrator, the procurator of the district court, the chairman of the provincial zemstvo executive board (*uprava*), the mayor of the provincial capital, and delegates elected either by the provincial zemstvo assembly or the city council (*duma*) of the gubernia capital. After 1900, the committee was expanded to include an appointed permanent member, and in some provinces a second was added. The permanent members had the right to vote and were in charge of managing the committee's paper work.

Like the committee on peasant affairs, the committee supervising zemstvo and urban self-government had both judicial and administrative functions. Its judicial operations were quite limited and concerned primarily the actions of zemstvos or city councils which had been protested by either the governor or a private citizen. If the institution of self-government did not alter a protested decision, the matter was examined by the committee, though its rulings would not be the final word, and if need be the dispute would then go to the Senate for a binding resolution.

In its administrative capacity, the committee could set aside the results of an illegally conducted election and could discipline a zemstvo's or duma's executive officials even to the point of removing them from office or remanding them for trial in the courts. In its disciplinary role, the committee was not subject to the Senate's review.[90]

As was the case of all provincial institutions, the standing committees were criticized a great deal by both scholars and governmental officials: there were too many of them; they did not function smoothly; there were times when committee members sat as judges in their own cases.[91] There was less of a consensus, however, on the governor's role in the committees or the ways in which the weaknesses of these institutions affected his ability to carry out his duties.

90. Ibid., pp. 412–13; Kermit E. McKenzie, "Zemstvo Organization and Role within the Administrative Structure," in *The Zemstvo in Russia*, ed. by T. Emmons and W. Vucinich (Cambridge, 1982), pp. 58–59; Thomas Fallows, "The Zemstvo and the Bureaucracy, 1890–1904," ibid., p. 183; "Polozhenie o gubernskikh i uezdnykh zemskikh uchrezhdeniiakh," arts. 134–136, *Svod zakonov*, 2 (1892).

91. V. Ivanovskii, "Obshchie nachala v ustroistve gubernskikh vlastei," *Zhurnal iuridicheskogo obshchestva pri imperatorskoi s-peterburgskoi universitete*, 26 (January 1896): 66; Gogel, "Gubernskie prisutstviia," pp. 458–59; Korf, *Administrativnaia iustitsiia*, 2: 9–10. The views of these scholars were supported by the reports from the senatorial inspections of the late 1870s and the inspection conducted under the auspices of the Zemskii otdel in the early twentieth century.

The legal scholars Korf and Gogel were inclined to argue that the governor had too much power vis-à-vis the committees and supported their judgments by pointing to his authority over the permanent members and his ability to block many of the committees' decisions. The views of these analysts were partly based on the evidence of senatorial inspectors gathered during the last years of Alexander II's reign, but later investigators also noted the excessiveness of gubernatorial power and its enhancement by the committees' inadequacies.[92] Other students, however, argued that a governor's ability to control the committees was extremely limited and that instead of enlarging his power, the committees actually fragmented provincial government and rendered it ineffective. Not surprisingly, many governors held this view; but they were not alone.[93]

Certainly, it is hard to accept the argument that the governors dominated the standing committees in the same way that they controlled the provincial board. The membership of the committees, which included many individuals not directly dependent on the *nachal'niki gubernii*, seems to have precluded this. Moreover, a survey of materials relating to the work of the committees, such as the records of the St. Petersburg committee on urban affairs, suggest that the governors' role, though considerable, was not overwhelming.

To be sure, in the committees that dealt with the institutions of self-government, the position of the *nachal'nik gubernii* was particularly formidable. He was the major source of the committee's business. He could protest the acts of elective institutions and have them reviewed, and he was also a conduit for complaints from the citizens who often came to his receptions in order to explain their grievances personally. If he thought that an issue merited investigation or action, the governor would turn the complaint over to his chancellery or designate a subordinate official to investigate and prepare materials for the committee's consideration.[94]

92. Korf, 2: 17–18; Gogel, pp. 458–59; "Zapiska senatora Polovtsova o sostoianii gorodskogo khoziaistva v gorodakh chernigovskoi gubernii," pp. 553–55, in *MVUOK*, 3, pt. 3, sec. 3; TsGIA, f. Zemskogo otdela, op. 30, 1904, d. 253, pp. 34–35.

93. Strakhovskii, "Gubernskoe ustroistvo" (October 1913): 110–11; Ivanovskii, 80–81; Gogel, too, argues that the pressure of committee business on the governors was excessive (pp. 456–57).

94. LGIA, f. Kants. pet. gub., op. 3, d. 2487, "Peredacha bumag i del v rasmotrenie peterburgskomu gubernskomu po gorodskim delam prisutstviiu," pp. 7–9, 15–16, 18; journal of the committee on urban affairs, 23 March 1888, ibid., f. Petrogradskogo gubernskogo po zemskim i gorodskim delam prisutstviia (259), op. 2, d. 4, "Zhurnaly zasedanii prisutstviia," pp. 95–96; "Zapiska o poriadke deloproizvodstva po gorodskim delam . . . ," GPB, f. Rev. Polovtsova, d. 1342, pp. 1–3.

When a piece of business came before any one of the committees, however, the governor did not necessarily dominate because many of the matters considered were straightforward and would be decided on the basis of established practice. Even in those cases where a governor held a strong opinion, his will did not automatically prevail, for as P. P. Stremoukhov pointed out, votes in the committees were not always initially in the governor's favor, and he had to use great "caution and tact" in working around those who opposed him.[95] Governors knew that they could lose a vote even when they pushed hard for a particular decision, and being overruled in committee was no doubt an embarrassment they sought to avoid.[96] How many times did *nachal'niki gubernii* backwater when confronting choppy seas? Or how often did they struggle to find a middle ground between opposing positions? The journals of the committees themselves tell us little about this aspect of provincial politics but we must assume that compromise was the norm.

A governor's ability to dominate a committee's work was further reduced when he confronted highly technical situations about which he knew virtually nothing. V. F. Dzhunkovskii was completely awash when he first tried to comprehend the business of the Moscow committee on commercial taxation. "At the initial session of the committee," the governor later wrote, "I only looked blank, agreed with the fiscal administrator or, to be more truthful, with the official reporter, and signed the journal. . . ."[97] Later, he mastered the complexities of the committee's work but only because Dzhunkovskii was a man of almost boundless energy and curiosity. One suspects that few of his colleagues would have gone to this trouble and instead would have continued to look blank and defer to the experts.

In sum, the diversity and weakness of the provincial standing committees meant that, like provincial board, the governor did not find them either a major source of power or a useful administrative tool. Because so many issues came before the committees, the governor had to limit his involvement and rely mostly on his staff and on those better informed about technical details. Frequently, a governor found that he

95. "Administrativnoe ustroistvo imperatorskoi Rossii po vospominaniiam gubernatora," sec. 2, p. 9, BAR, Kryzhanovskii papers.

96. For examples see: letter of Governor O. L. Medem to V. K. Pleve, 6 February 1903, TsGIA, f. Kants. MVD, op. 2, d. 1014, "Delo po doneseniiu novgorodskogo gubernatora," pp. 1–2; ibid, f. Zemskogo otdela, op. 32, d. 7, pp. 144–45; journal of the committee on urban affairs, 24 June 1888, LGIA, f. Pet. gub. po zem. i gor. del. prisut., op. 2, d. 4, pp. 122–24.

97. Dzhunkovskii, "Vospominaniia za 1909–1910 gg.," TsGAOR, f. Dzhunkovskogo, op. 1, d. 49, p. 171.

was evaluating not issues but personalities. "The governor chaired more than fifteen committees," P. P. Stremoukhov recalled: "It was absolutely impossible for him to know all the matters decided by . . . [these bodies] and the laws that guided their activities. But he had to know the capabilities of the committee's reporter or leading figure, to take these into account and to guide . . . [these officials] into the proper channel. I repeat, the management of people was . . . [the governor's] main task and, as is well known, this is the most difficult task of all."[98]

Thus, with the standing committees as in other aspects of provincial government, the *nachal'niki gubernii* found themselves prisoners of the clerks, dependent on them for information, often frustrated by their incompetence. The weakness, one is tempted to say virtual absence, of provincial bureaucracy put a premium on the personal qualities of the governor and on his ability to get the most out of the few people upon whom he could consistently rely. By no means did all governors possess significant skills in personnel management, and when they did not, provincial government could lapse into meaningless routine or explode into senseless conflicts. Moreover, even if a governor had the gift of leadership and sought to exercise it, he was often forced to go beyond the framework of the inadequate local institutions over which he presided, though this might raise the charge of *proizvol*. At the very least, the activist governor would find himself deeply involved in what can loosely be called provincial politics.

98. "Administrativnoe ustroistvo," sec. 2, p. 12.

– 6 –

The Issue of Their Charm

For weeks a growing mood of excitement had enveloped Perm "society." There would be a ball at the governor's mansion. Regular commerce in the city's shops came to a virtual halt as local merchants struggled to fill a large number of rush orders and to meet a sudden increase in the demand for dancing shoes. Wherever the leading citizens of the town gathered, speculation centered on the guest list: who had been invited; who had been left out? Those who were unsure of an invitation affected an air of indifference, though on receipt of the coveted card, they hastened to make up for lost time and to purchase the attire needed for the event.

Yet, for those who had received their invitations, there still remained a cause for consternation. What did the mysterious initials "P.P.O." mean? *"Prosiat prilichno odet'sia"* (You are asked to dress properly)? *"Pokorneishe prosiat otkazat'"* (Kindly refuse)? *"Permskii politsei-meister oboltus"* (The Perm police chief is a blockhead)? Eventually the ladies of the city began to phone the governor's wife and after the usual small talk, asked casually about the significance of the initials. In one day the *gubernatorsha* got ten such calls and became exhausted by having to explain that P.P.O. meant simply *pokorneishe prosiat otve-tit'*, the Russian equivalent of R.S.V.P.

When the long-awaited day arrived, guests found that His Excellency had spared no expense to make the ball a success. The center of the festivities was the main dining room of the mansion, a vast hall where 350 people could be seated. An adjacent glass-covered veranda had also been converted into a kind of winter garden for the occasion. The buffet was laden with all sorts of drinks, hors d'oevres, and sweets. The culinary high-point was the serving of a large wild goat that had been killed on the far northern reaches of the Kama River. Skillfully carved, and served on a great tray specially ordered from St. Petersburg, it produced a sensation.

Two orchestras drawn from local military units supplied the evening's entertainment, and the governor had also invited the best artists from a touring opera company to perform a small concert. But well lubricated with wine, the guests never ceased dancing. The opera singers joined with the crowd, and the revels continued until the dawn.[1]

Amidst the tumultuous events of the last years of the Russian Empire, the amusements that Governor I. F. Koshko arranged for the leading figures of Perm "society" may seem of little significance. But in the operation of provincial government, such occasions were of the greatest importance. Far from the source of power in the capital, forced to work through institutions that were generally poorly staffed and inefficient, the governors often had to rely on unofficial means to carry out their duties as viceroys and local administrators. Social functions were vital to a political process which could be both complicated and volatile.

Casting the governors in a political role may seem outlandish at first glance because their image as satraps has been so well established. Yet, the facts of the matter differ considerably from opinion. Whatever their reputations, governors never really ruled by command. Even when they issued orders in the name of the emperor, it was necessary for them to elicit support and cooperation from at least some quarters of provincial society. In doing this, the *nachal'niki gubernii* had to display considerable political skill because so much depended on their willingness to press the flesh and to strike bargains in informal situations.[2]

By the end of the nineteenth century, gubernia politics had at least three dimensions. The first of these was bureaucratic and involved the governor's relations with those officials and agencies outside the MVD chain of command but with whom he had to work on a regular basis. The second encompassed the institutions and officers of local self-government: the noble assemblies, the zemstvos, and the city councils

    1. Ol'ga I. Koshko, Untitled papers, section beginning with the words: "Bal u gubernatora!" pp. 1–2; I. F. Koshko, "Vospominaniia," pp. 658–68, BAR, Koshko family papers.

    2. Sinel'nikov, "Zapiski," no. 2: 384–86; "Zapiska ob ob'edinenii gubernskogo upravleniia," p. 1 in *MVUOK*, 3, pt. 2: *Zapiski senatora Mordvinova*; untitled general report, pp. 10–11, in *MVUOK*, 3, pt. 4: *Zapiski senatora Shamshina*; Berendts, pp. 270–71.

(dumas). These bodies reflected the views and desires of provincial "society" and handled a wide range of important quasi-governmental functions. The third dimension was less clearly defined and embraced a host of private groups and persons which occasionally the governor tried to mobilize for some specific goal.

To this field of play, governors came with certain advantages and liabilities. They were fairly familiar with the rules of the game, for most of them had served a good part of their careers in provincial institutions. At the same time, however, governors were usually strangers to the particular gubernias over which they presided. Being an outsider was not altogether a negative circumstance, for governors unencumbered by local connections might more easily set themselves up as honest brokers in provincial disputes. But as likely as not, the fact that they were not natives would also prompt one or more of the local leaders and groups to view them with suspicion if not hostility no matter how knowledgeable or well intentioned they might be. Wherever possible governors had to seek ways to eliminate the barriers of distrust that could impede their work.

In this endeavor, both the governors and their superiors in St. Petersburg placed great emphasis on something called "service tact" (*sluzhebnyi takt*). This term had no precise definition but in a broad sense meant the ability to maintain authority without giving offense, a willingness to cultivate and, if necessary, to appease powerful local forces, or the knack for reconciling conflicting parties and resolving differences. This kind of tact was an indispensable tool of provincial governance because much of the governor's power was only negative in character; that is, he could block the activities of various officials and agencies through his orders. Yet there was often very little a governor might do my means of command. Much of the governor's ability to lead depended on his charm, his powers of persuasion, and his ties with prominent figures in the local administrative agencies, the nobility, and the institutions of self-government.[3]

For this reason, the governor's mansion could become an institution that could rival the importance of many provincial boards and committees. "When you receive people at your home," Governor Koshko wrote,

> all distinctions based on service position fall away, and you all simply become acquaintances. Then if you can quickly overcome the usual stiffness between persons who know each other slightly and make them feel

3. Koshko, *Vospominaniia*, pp. 199–201.

relaxed, your house becomes [a place]. . . about which all will have pleasant memories. Thus [one's guests and fellow workers] develop straightforward relations rooted in mutual trust that will enable them to express themselves fully. At the very least, each of your acquaintances is sure to consider himself obliged. . . to avoid sharp conflicts with your views and wishes unless absolutely necessary.[4]

The importance of personality and tact in making or breaking a governor is illustrated in the case of Sergei Ivanovich Golikov, who became governor of Voronezh in 1909. Although he lacked vice-gubernatorial experience, everything else in Golikov's career pointed toward success. A graduate of Moscow University Law School, Golikov served for five years in the provincial offices of the Ministry of Justice and rose to the rank of assistant procurator before he retired to become marshal of the nobility in his home uezd in Tver province. Later, he assumed the post of permanent member of the provincial committee for zemstvo and urban affairs, a job he held for almost five years before again being voted uezd marshal. He served there until his appointment as governor.[5]

Two years after Golikov's posting to Voronezh, the MVD inspector, N. Ch. Zaionchkovskii, visited the gubernia, where he found the governor to be young, energetic, and well-prepared for his job. There was only one problem: no one seemed to have a good word to say about Golikov, and he was surrounded by people who wished him ill. Everyone from the provincial and uezd marshals to the chairman of the zemstvo executive, the procurator, even the head of the gendarmes disliked the *nachal'nik gubernii.*[6]

What had Golikov done to turn everyone against him? Zaionchkovskii could not point to anything terribly serious. Apparently, the governor was not very outgoing, and he compounded the problem by surrounding himself with a head of chancellery and a police chief who cut him off from provincial leaders. Moreover, he had made some tactless statements. When giving his opinion on the work of an uezd conference (*s"ezd*) of land captains, Golikov had used the phrases "the conference should have . . . " and "the conference has not attended to . . . the question . . . carefully enough. . . ." As a result, the Voronezh uezd marshal had taken umbrage.

4. Ibid., pp. 201–202.
5. TsGIA, f. DOD, op. 47, 1911, d. 305a, "Otchet . . . Zaionchkovskogo po obozreniiu deloproizvodstva voronezhskogo gubernskogo pravleniia i kantseliarii gubernatora," p. 80.
6. Ibid., p. 81.

But official words and phrases were not the only cause of Golikov's troubles; his lack of discretion extended to other areas. The strong emnity between the governor and the Voronezh uezd marshal, Baron Stal'-fon-Gol'stein, was based, as Zaionchkovskii learned from the police chief, on "their simultaneous pursuit of one and the same lady who had shown a decided preference for Golikov."[7] Lucky in love, the governor had offended local honor and soon became the victim of a series of petty slights. At the time of the meeting of the noble assembly, Golikov had invited the participants to dinner but the provincial marshal had arranged for a few of his colleagues to join him in a private party and thus had forced the governor to change the date of his own gathering. This kind of treatment led to an increase of tensions, so that Golikov eventually found himself in conflict with all the leaders of local self-government. Even the influential editor of the province's conservative newspaper viewed him with suspicion.[8]

Despite growing opposition, Golikov would rule in Voronezh for five years, though given his inauspicious beginnings, he could hardly have been very successful. Indeed, Voronezh was apparently his last gubernatorial post, for his service record does not indicate either a subsequent appointment, or an effort to seek one. More to the point, Golikov's example suggests the extreme sensitivity and volatility of provincial politics. Many governors came to their gubernias cautiously, even fearfully, well aware that their personal qualities and their ability to get along would do much to determine their success or failure. When he took over in Nizhni-Novgorod during World War I, Governor A. F. Girs recalled being awed by the local zemstvo and its long tradition of oppositionism. With some success, Girs made a strenuous effort to mollify the zemstvo members at the outset of his tenure.[9] Similarly, M. M. Osorgin sought to live down his reputation as a liberal as soon as he assumed the governorship in Tula and also worked to overcome the distrust his wife's connections in the province had generated in some quarters.[10]

Service tact was particularly important in the western provinces of the empire, where various national communities lived uneasily side by side. Most governors tried to establish good relations with the leaders of at least some of these ethnic groups and, where possible, to bring

---

7. Ibid.

8. Ibid., pp. 81–82.

9. A. F. Girs, "Pravitel'stvo i obshchestvennost'," pp. 25–26, BAR, Girs family papers.

10. Osorgin, "Vospominaniia," GBL, f. Osorgina, papka II, d. 2, pp. 234–35.

them together in the hopes of better accommodation.[11] In dealing with non-Russians a special sensitivity was often required. L. D. Liubimov recalled how his father, as governor of Vilna, had developed a rather precise linguistic etiquette for speaking with the local Polish aristocracy. Russian was used as the language of official business; but French was employed at social gatherings and in conversations with the fair sex.[12] During his rule in pogrom-racked Bessarabia, S. D. Urusov was determined to demonstrate his concern for the feelings of the Jewish community, and occasionally his good intentions were put to the test. Attending a Jewish religious service for the first time in his life, Urusov was thrown into a momentary quandary when the choir began to sing "God Save the Tsar." Official etiquette required that the governor remove his hat; the decorum of the synagogue demanded his head remain covered. What to do? Urusov solved his dilemma by holding his hand to the visor of his cap while the anthem was sung, thus satisfying at once his obligations to the emperor and to the God of Abraham, Isaac, and Jacob.[13]

Service tact was also at a premium when the governors dealt with the representatives of important agencies outside the MVD structure. The many provincial standing committees, of course, were important arenas where His Excellency could demonstrate political skills. But these formal meetings addressed only some of the potentially troublesome issues. In fact, the legal and bureaucratic problems that came before the committees were the most manageable of all: the rules of the game were known, the governor's position assured. Even if the decision of a given committee produced discontent and was appealed to a higher authority, the conflict usually proceeded along a well-worn track.

Outside the standing committees, however, governors were often likely to encounter situations where the limits of their power and the guidelines for action were unclear. Minor skirmishes were almost inevitable as various agencies sought to define their fields of activity and to protect their independence. Let a governor imply that the supervisor of an educational district was his subordinate or be less than punctilious in his communications with a local bishop, and complaints could be on their way to the center. And if such disputes arose, His Excellency

---

11. Fon Val', "Vil'na," TsGIA. f. fon Valia i Miasoedovykh, op. 1, d. 13, pp. 13, 23–24, 27–28.

12. L. D. Liubimov, *Na chuzhbine* (Moscow, 1963), p. 33.

13. Urussov, pp. 120–21.

frequently found that the minister of internal affairs would take the side of the offended party.[14] Yet, even when a governor went to extreme pains to base his relations on service tact, the whole construct could suddenly and unexpectedly come tumbling down like a house of blocks under the impact of a playful shove. Months of effort by Vilna governor D. N. Liubimov to bridge differences with the local archbishop collapsed in just this way because of a young boy's concern for his clothes.

The governor and Archbishop Nikandr had been at sword's point almost from the moment Liubimov had taken over the province. The bishop felt that Liubimov was too well disposed toward Jews and insufficiently supportive of Orthodoxy. He was also critical of the governor's wife, for she had gone so far as to converse publicly in Polish. But finally, a truce had been declared and, in the hope of establishing greater harmony between the church and the provincial administration, Nikandr had consented to pay the governor and his family a visit.

All went well until Liubimov's young son, Lyova, was introduced to the archbishop. The boy, outfitted according to the custom of the time in girl's clothing, was far less concerned about the decorum of a sensitive meeting than he was about the humiliation of being forced to wear a dress. So when Nikandr patted Lyova on the head and asked, "Tell me, how is it that you are so big and still wear a skirt?" the lad took offense. Fighting back tears, Lyova pointed at the archbishop's clerical garb and fairly shouted, "Well, you are wearing a skirt, too!" God had not granted His Eminence a sense of humor. Liubimov's peace effort collapsed, and soon Nikandr was complaining to the Holy Synod that, in addition to his other failings, the governor had raised his children as freethinkers with no respect for the highest dignitaries of the Orthodox faith.[15]

Personal disputes, scandals, and minor flaps lay at the heart of much of provincial politics. A governor had to be constantly on guard to avoid breaches of tact and to prevent small conflicts from getting out of hand. But issues of greater importance were also part of the provincial scene. As head of the gubernia administration, the governor had to

---

14. See, for example, the memorandum on Kharkov governor Katerinich, TsGIA, f. DOD, op. 47, 1912, d. 19, "So spravkami o gubernatorakh . . . ," p. 9; also see the material on the conflict between Saratov acting governor Boiarskii and Bishop Germogen, TsGIA, f. DOD, op. 47, 1906, d. 64, "Sekretnoe po saratovskoi gub.," pp. 31–32, 36.

15. Liubimov, *Na chuzhbine*, pp. 34–35.

contend with the local representatives of the powerful central ministries, most importantly those of Finance, War, and Justice. These officials were not fully subordinate to the governor's authority, and though they were supposed to obey his lawful orders, they looked to their superiors in the capital for instructions, guidance and support.

The fiscal administrator (*upravliaiushchii kazennoiu palatoiu*), the area military commander, and the district procurator were crucial to provincial governance. The fiscal administrator oversaw the operation of gubernia finances; the army commander helped to maintain peace and security; the procurator brought criminals to justice and kept watch on the work of the police and the local bureaucracy. Yet, these officials were also the agents of their particular ministry and sought to implement its larger policies; their efforts did not always conform either to what governors considered sound administrative practice or to the aims of the Ministry of Internal Affairs. Thus, the Ministry of Finance's desire to promote industrial development might engender local discontent by harming agrarian interests and increasing the tax burden on the peasantry. The War Ministry's determination to preserve the army's discipline and integrity could inhibit the use of soldiers in curbing local violence. Similarly, the Ministry of Justice's defense of the principle of legality would often be seen by both the governors and the MVD as a barrier to the adoption of firm disciplinary measures.

The way in which the clash of larger ministerial concerns could have a negative impact on the governors' ability to manage provincial affairs is illustrated by the fate of efforts to reform the system of famine relief during the 1890s. In the debate on this question, the Ministry of Internal Affairs sought to improve local administrative structures and so facilitate the supplying of aid to the victims of disaster. Conversely, the Ministry of Finance wished to keep costs to a minimum and to prevent too many resources from being tied up in the gubernias. In the end, the interests of the treasury prevailed, and the resulting law of 12 June 1900 was a truncated measure that not only failed to bring about needed administrative improvements but also complicated the governors' tasks. Moreover, because it excluded the zemstvos from relief work, the new statute contributed to the rise of political discontent in the provinces.[16]

Fortunately for the governors, few of the ministerial conflicts that took place in St. Petersburg had a direct impact on the local scene. The

16. Richard G. Robbins, Jr., "Russia's Famine Relief Law of June 12, 1900: A Reform Aborted," *Canadian-American Slavic Studies* 10 (Spring 1976): 25–37.

nachal'niki gubernii and the agents of the central ministries recognized that they had definite spheres of competence, and they were aware of the mutual dangers that could result should they transgress the boundaries between their areas of activity. Thus tact and caution usually dominated interagency relations. Still, differences between the tsars' chief advisers formed part of the "background noise" of provincial politics, and in times of stress it might be painfully amplified.

As a rule, governors appeared to have enjoyed the best relations with the fiscal chambers (*kazennye palaty*), fiscal administrators, and tax and factory inspectors. This harmony proceeded from the fact that the local representatives of the Ministries of Interior and Finance had much more to gain from cooperation than from dispute. The fiscal administrators needed the governors' police to help collect taxes, and governors relied on the fiscal chambers to approve their requests for monies from government coffers.[17] Beyond this, the structure of provincial government did not give the *nachal'nik gubernii* much of an opportunity to meddle in the affairs of the local agents of the Ministry of Finance. Although the governor oversaw the collection of taxes, he did not participate in the work of the fiscal chamber except when it considered some very specific types of contracts. The governor also had the power to review annually the amount of work undertaken by the fiscal chamber and to pass on information concerning improprieties to officials in St. Petersburg. Otherwise, the work of the fiscal chamber and its subordinate officers was almost completely sealed off from the gubernia administration.[18]

In the ordinary course of affairs, then, disputes between governors and the officers of the Ministry of Finance focused either on questions of personal behavior or on such routine matters as the inadequate support of the police in tax collection or the failure of one agency to supply information requested by another.[19] But during crises, such as the revolution of 1905, more serious conflict developed. As governors sought to maintain law and order and to prevent the spread of sedition, they found it necessary to invade the terrain of fiscal officials. For example, the governor of Tver asserted direct control over the work of the tax inspectors, and the governor of Kharkov suppressed a procla-

17. Yaney, *Systematization*, p. 305.
18. Blinov, *Gubernatory*, 329; Gogel, "Gubernskie prisutstviia," p. 455; "Obshchee uchrezhdenie gubernskoe," arts. 349–52, *Svod zakonov*, 2 (1892).
19. Koshko, "Vospominaniia," pp. 113–14, BAR; GAKO, f. Tver. gub. prav., op. 2, d. 3808, "Zhurnaly gubernskogo pravleniia za oktiabr', noiabr' i dekabr' mesiatsy 1890 g.," pp. 414–18; TsGIA, f. Kakhanovskoi kommissii, op. 1, d. 110, "Materialy . . . o gubernskikh i uezdnykh uchrezhdeniiakh . . . , tom 4," pp. 206–7.

mation sent out by the minister of finance himself.[20] The famine of 1891–92 provided a still more dramatic case of conflict between a governor and a local representative of the Ministry of Finance. During this crisis a violent clash erupted between Viatka governor A. F. Anis'in and I. V. Vinogradov, the fiscal administrator. Centered on the question of the proper response to the disaster, the dispute threatened to upset the operation of provincial government.

When the famine began, Governor Anis'in saw his first duty as protecting the well-being of the local population, and in conjunction with the provincial zemstvo, he initiated a series of dramatic but questionable measures to secure sufficient food supplies. He banned grain exports to other gubernias and gave the Viatka zemstvo the right to buy grain at low, fixed prices.[21] But Vinogradov, who looked at these policies from the perspective of the Ministry of Finance, insisted that Anis'in's actions were economically disruptive and a threat to the interests of the treasury, and he demanded that the governor follow established procedures. Vinogradov's refusal to support Anis'in shattered their close friendship and gave a dimension of personal bitterness and malice to official conflict. Moreover, the dispute sharpened when the Ministries of Finance and Internal Affairs became involved, both supporting the fiscal administrator against the governor. Anis'in brushed aside the objections of the center, but he grew increasingly disturbed because Vinogradov, who possessed his own informational source in the tax inspectors, continued to accumulate data that questioned the governor's program. Relations between the two men grew extremely tense. Anis'in publically affronted Vinogradov on a number of occasions and at one point threatened him with trial for allegedly exceeding his authority. The struggle culminated in Anis'in's undertaking an inspection of the work of the fiscal chamber, which was the governor's right under article 271 of the gubernia statute though it was rarely exercised. But in carrying out the inspection Anis'in calculatedly humiliated Vinogradov by not conducting the *reviziia* personally, as would have been proper, and instead turning the business over to subordinate officials.

From the outset, the governor's intentions were clear and threatening. The goal of the inspection was to uncover evidence that could incriminate Vinogradov and cause his removal. Anis'in also wanted to

---

20. TsGIA, f. DOD, op. 47, 1906, d. 16, "Sekretnoe po tverskoi gub.," pp. 23–24, 27–30, 31–32, 42; TsGIA, f. Ministerstva torgovli i promyshlennosti (23), op. 30, d. 46, "O stachkakh rabochikh na fabrikakh i zavodakh khar'kovskoi gub.," pp. 128–30, 134–35.

21. Robbins, *Famine in Russia*, pp. 55–57.

know what kind of information the fiscal administrator had been supplying the central government. Most important, the governor was determined to demonstrate to those who might have begun to question his authority that he was indeed *nachal'nik gubernii,* and in the words of the MVD's inspector, N. A. Troinitskii, to show "that [even] the approval of ministers was not enough to defend from the governor's wrath any person who dared evince even the slightest disagreement with his views."[22] Anis'in's *coup de main* failed, however, because the inspection of the fiscal chamber disclosed no significant irregularities and Vinogradov would be further justified by Troinitskii's subsequent investigation. The fiscal administrator held his ground, and Anis'in was once again reprimanded by the MVD.[23]

Clashes like the one between Anis'in and Vinogradov occurred very rarely in provincial life, and the careful attention the MVD paid the event is a clear indication of its singular character. Yet the episode tells us much about the nature and style of administrative politics at the gubernia level. First, it shows that the *potential* for conflict between the governors and the agents of ministries other than the MVD was constant. Particularly in an emergency, it was likely that their differing concerns would produce serious friction. Second, the course of the Anis'in-Vinogradov dispute illustrates the degree to which a governor was limited in his ability to control or to coerce ministerial field officers without strong support from the center. A fiscal administrator, or any other independent official for that matter, could defend his "patch" in the bureaucratic structure despite a governor's best efforts to break him. Third, the incident underlines the importance of "service tact" in gubernia politics and shows what could happen when a governor lacked this key quality. The issues involved might have been compromised or otherwise settled peacefully. But Anis'in, imperious by nature, would brook no challenge to his authority and would never seek to moderate differences with those he regarded as inferiors. The resultant discord was disruptive, time-consuming, and, ultimately, fruitless. Finally, N. A. Troinitskii's report on the events in Viatka also throws light on the question of the selection of governors. In trying to account for Anis'in's behavior, Troinitskii noted that Anis'in had made a dramatic rise from the post of uezd police chief to that of governor. Troinitskii stated that this unusual career pattern helped to explain

22. Report of N. A. Troinitskii to I. N. Durnovo, 20 May 1892, TsGIA, f. DOD, op. 46, 1892, d. 30, "O revizii viatskim gubernatorom mestnoi kazennoi palaty," pp. 91–101. Quotation on p. 101.

23. Project letter from Durnovo to Anis'in, ibid., p. 113.

why the *nachal'nik gubernii* was "arrogant and power-hungry to an almost pathological degree."[24] A more thorough examination of Anis'in's upward path shows that he never held any of the elective or administrative posts that so many of his colleagues had and suggests that he failed to acquire the strictly political skills that being a marshal, chairman of the zemstvo executive board, or even a permanent member might have provided.

There were, of course, governors who had all of the above mentioned preparatory experiences and who nevertheless displayed a grave want of tact. But the petty drama that played itself out in Viatka during the hungry years 1891–92 and the astute comments of former governor Troinitskii suggest strongly that the evolution of the MVD's criteria for selecting governors was based on a sound awareness of what made provincial government work.

In dealing with the military commanders stationed in their provinces the governors also had to develop a special brand of politics. Ties with the local army and navy units produced considerable tension and antagonism and placed great demands on a governor's skill at maneuver and compromise. To succeed, the *nachal'nik gubernii*, needed "the cunning of the serpent and the mildness of the dove."[25]

Generally, the institutional connections between governors and the military were not a major source of conflict. The governor chaired two standing committees in which the representatives of the military took part, the draft board (*gubernskoe po voinskoi povinosti prisutstvie*) and the quartering committee (*rasporiaditel'nyi komitet*). The first of these bodies supervised the raising of recruits and heard appeals concerning exemptions from service or requests for special status within the military. The quartering committee provided barracks for the troops and saw that they were afforded the proper grounds for drill and firing practice.[26]

The primary sources of dispute between governors and local military authorities involved differing conceptions of honor and institutional dignity. Such a conflict might seem strange at first glance because many of the governors of European Russia had been educated in military schools and had served in the armed forces. Yet, this shared experience did not result in mutual good will, and the recent work of John Bushnell and William Fuller help us to understand why.

24. Troinitskii report, ibid., p. 93.
25. Urussov, p. 58.
26. Gogel, pp. 433–35, 437–38.

According to Fuller, the Russian military's attitude toward civilians was shaped by the spirit of "negative corporatism." Officers were convinced that an antimilitary bias dominated the thinking of both educated society and state officials; this led in turn to a siege mentality and a touchy relationship with all outsiders. This problem was further compounded by the barrenness of life in provincial garrisons. Bushnell's study of these circumstances depicts a world of boredom, heavy drinking, and corruption. Isolated from local life, officers nursed a sense of superiority over the surrounding civilians, and in matters of their honor they demanded special respect. Officers often avenged real or imagined insults to the uniform by violent means.[27] But many governors who knew the military from the inside harbored few illusions about the officer corps. Indeed, they had consciously rejected army life and saw in civilian service a more fruitful and meaningful field of endeavor. Such men were unlikely to accept the military's claim to greater dignity and precedence.

At the same time, the commanders of the provincial garrisons frequently looked with disdain at the *nachal'niki gubernii*. Military men often dismissed those governors who had always been civilians as "civil service gentry" and acted as if cooperation with them was beneath their dignity.[28] Governors who had left the armed services posed a special problem. First of all, they had committed the sin of forsaking the brotherhood of officers. Second, the majority of such governors had never risen high in military rank. A general in charge of a division must have found it difficult to accept a former lieutenant or captain as his equal.

Because the prospect of civil-military conflict was ever-present, the *Svod zakonov* determined the relations between the governors and their counterparts in the armed forces by means of an elaborate set of rules. The appendix to article 406 of the gubernia statute extensively detailed how civilian and military officers were to pay each other the proper respect, what type of dress was to be worn and when, who was to visit whom in particular circumstances, and which official held precedence over the other on a given occasion. Under the terms of this law, a governor was equal in rank to a divisional commander, though in public events of a civilian character, the governor was to enjoy preeminence. In military parades and ceremonies, the division com-

---

27. William C. Fuller, Jr., *Civil-Military Conflict in Imperial Russia, 1881–1914* (Princeton, N.J., 1985), pp. 26–28; John Bushnell, "The Tsarist Officer Corps, 1881–1914: Customs, Duties, Inefficiency," *American Historical Review* 86 (October 1981): 755–62.

28. Urussov, p. 56.

mander assumed the position of honor.[29] Such an arrangement was simple and made good sense, but the fact that it required detailed exposition indicates just how touchy the associations between military and civilian authorities were and how easily they could erupt into hostility.

In 1897, for example, the governor of the Priamur region, S. M. Dukhovskii, invited a French admiral to the ceremonies marking the opening of the Chinese Eastern Railway and neglected, either through accident or design, to extend a similar honor to the commander of the Far Eastern Fleet and other dignitaries of the Russian navy. The result was an angry exchange of letters that ended in a ministerial rebuke to the governor.[30]

The military could of course be equally discourteous. Governor P. P. Stremoukhov recalled how on one national holiday, the chief of the garrison in the provincial capital decided on the time and place of the parade without consulting the governor, though the law required the two officials to work this matter out together. When Stremoukhov queried the division commander about the incident, the general did not respond directly but let it be known that he did not give a damn about governors. In the end, Stremoukhov appealed to the corps commander and secured the transfer of the offending officer.[31]

Occasionally such an incident, laughable in itself, could put a governor's *sang froid* to a serious test, as in 1913 when the governor of Estland, I. V. Korostovets, had to cope with a calculated affront from Vice-Admiral Gerasimov, commander of the naval fortress of Revel. The students of the city's Alexander Gymnasium were putting on a performance and reserved two tickets for the *nachal'nik gubernii*. But the admiral had seized Korostovets' tickets and proclaimed his primacy over the civilian authorities. An MVD memorandum noted that when students objected to his actions Gerasimov had asserted that though the governor would be angry, it meant nothing to him and that he, Gerasimov, "was the first person of the city and ought to sit higher than the governor." Although he had been clearly and deliberately insulted, Korostovets, who held the rank of general himself, decided not to escalate the incident. Opting, instead, for a dazzling display of service tact, the governor accepted tickets for two equivalent seats on

29. "Obshchee uchrezhdenie gubernskoe," art. 406 and appendix, *Svod zakonov*, 2 (1892).

30. Relevant letters are found in TsGIA, f. DOD, op. 46, 1897, d. 96, "Po sekretnoi perepiske," pp. 17–19.

31. P. P. Stremoukhov, "Administrativnoe ustroistvo . . . ," sec. 1, pp. 8–9, BAR, Kryzhanovskii papers.

the opposite side of the aisle from Gerasimov.[32] The atmosphere at the performance must have been electric.

Slights and confrontations of a personal character were but a small part of the difficulties that governors faced in their dealings with the military. Throughout the period under discussion, the *nachal'niki gubernii* found the army units garrisoned in their provinces to be a source of continuing trouble. In his annual report for 1884, Nizhni-Novgorod governor N. M. Baranov complained about the poor conditions of army life in the gubernia and cited the lack of cultural amenities, the isolation of the troops from cultivated society, and the easy availability of alcohol as major causes of the physical and moral decline of officers and enlisted men alike.[33] Bessarabia's governor S. D. Urusov noted that the troops' return to Kishinev after summer manuevers always resulted in an upsurge of thefts, fights, and debauchery.[34] I. F. Koshko encountered similar problems during his tenure in Perm.[35] The dissolute life that many army officers led caused other headaches. Governor Stremoukhov often had to hush up scandals involving officers and the local police. On such occasions, the governor sometimes had to take the side of the military against his own officials in order to keep peace with the army command, and similar motives explain his attempts to rescue officers from rapacious local moneylenders.[36]

In the western provinces with their sizable Jewish populations, military-civilian relations were especially troublesome because army officers and soldiers alike engaged in blatantly anti-Semitic behavior. A number of governors were well disposed toward Jews and found such activity appalling, but even they were occasionally forced to take unwanted steps to keep on the good side of the military. M. M. Osorgin recalled that while he was governor of Grodno, Vilna's governor-general Sviatopolk-Mirskii ordered him to arrest two Jews whose only crime had been to disarm a drunken Russian officer after the latter had threatened a crowd of their co-religionists. Despite Osorgin's pleas to let the matter drop, the governor-general insisted that he would not overlook such a serious "insult" to the Russian uniform. The arrested Jews were released only after Minister of Internal Affairs V. K. Pleve had intervened on their behalf. Similar problems faced Governor

32. Memorandum dated 15 November 1913, TsGIA, DOD, op. 47, 1912, d. 19, "So spravkami o gubernatorakh . . . ," p. 86.

33. TsGIA, f. DOD, op. 223, 1885, d. 217, pp. 15–16.

34. Urussov, p. 62.

35. Koshko, "Vospominaniia," pp. 501–3, BAR.

36. Stremoukhov, "Administrativnoe ustroistvo," sec. 1, p. 9.

Urusov in his efforts to both protect the Jews of Kishinev and preserve the "honor" of the army.[37]

Sometimes a governor's indignation at the military's abuses caused him to overstep his legal bounds and intervene directly in army matters. During his rule in Perm, I. F. Koshko became involved in a case wherein an enlisted man wounded an officer and subsequently had been executed for the crime. Koshko was convinced that the mistreatment the soldier had suffered at the hands of his commanders had driven him to desperate action. The garrisons of the province were poorly disciplined and badly led, the governor believed, and the unfortunate incident was the result of this mismanagement. The governor conveyed his impressions to the MVD and to the head of the Kazan military district, an act that exceeded his lawful authority. But Koshko justified his intervention on the grounds that "the representative of the sovereign power could never remain indifferent to any abuse, whatever its source might be."[38]

Few governors were as willing as Koshko to risk offending the military because most *nachal'niki gubernii* saw the presence of army units as an important means of maintaining the well being of the province. A garrison was a source of revenue for the area and could have a significant positive impact on local economic life.[39] Beyond this, governors often had to turn to the army in the event of natural disasters or civil disturbances. Calling out the troops to suppress riots was something that occurred with regularity, if not great frequency, during the last years of the empire. Indeed, by the early 1900s the number of incidents involving the use of soldiers had risen dramatically, and the violence of these disturbances had also increased.[40] The ominous threat from the lower classes had forced civilian and military officials into each other's arms.

Yet, local emergencies could produce serious civil-military conflict. No army likes to be used as an internal police force, and the assignment of military units to such duty was bound to rankle. Moreover, the rules that determined when and how a governor might call out the

37. Osorgin, "Vospominaniia," GBL, f. Osorgina, papka II, d. 2, p. 176; Urussov, pp. 59–62.

38. Koshko, "Vospominaniia," pp. 501–3, BAR.

39. See the annual report of Vologda governor V. Z. Kolenko for 1892 in which he complains about the decision to move a garrison from the provincial capital. TsGIA, f. DOD, op. 223, 1893, d. 216, pp. 7–8.

40. P. A. Zaionchkovskii, *Samoderzhavie i russkaia armiia na rubezhe XIX–XX stoletii* (Moscow, 1973), p. 35; Fuller, *Civil-Military Conflict*, pp. 89–91.

troops were elaborate and involved a large number of formalities.[41] Many governors came to view them as an encumbrance to the effective use of force and an ideal excuse for foot dragging on the part of a reluctant military.[42] Gubernatorial objections notwithstanding, the detailed and cumbersome regulations on the use of troops were probably justified. Their aim was to avoid unnecessary violence and to spare the army the shedding of Russian blood, and in fact, they were necessary because governors often overreacted to perceived dangers. During the cholera epidemic of 1892, for example, a number of *nachal'niki gubernii* called out the army when it was not needed but failed to supply it with proper information and even usurped the prerogatives of its commanders.

Disturbed by this development, the MVD sent the governors a special circular admonishing them to observe the greatest caution when using troops during civilian disturbances. They should employ the armed forces only after they had exhausted all other means for the restoration of order or when it had become clear that normal methods of control would not suffice.[43] This order had little effect, however, and the governors' continued misuse of their authority deepened civil-military tension.[44]

Yet the governors' reluctance to abide by formal regulations did have a rational basis. For those who ruled in particularly tense gubernias, the statute's slow-moving procedures could prove a source of trouble. A rapid deployment of soldiery could frequently avert serious outbreaks, but if a governor went strictly by the rules, matters might quickly reach the point where a much greater application of force would be needed to restore civil peace. In fact, S. D. Urusov confronted just such a situation when he took over Bessarabia in the wake of the terrible Kishinev pogrom. Significantly, he dealt with the problem by personal rather than institutional means. Working directly with the district commander and the head of the Kishinev garrison, he developed a system of special passwords that eliminated unnecessary paper work and formalities. This practice lessened the time required to get

41. Fuller, *Civil-Military Conflict*, pp. 79–80; "Obshchee uchrezhdenie gubernskoe," appendix to art. 316, *Svod zakonov*, 2 (1892). The application of these regulations will be discussed in more detail in Chapter 8.

42. Stremoukhov, "Administrativnoe ustroistvo," sec. 1, pp. 9–10; Urussov, pp. 57–58.

43. Circular of the Department of Police, 16 April 1893, TsGIA, f. Kants. MVD, op. 3, d. 95, "S tsirkuliarami po ministerstvu vnutrennikh del," pp. 76–77.

44. Fuller, *Civil-Military Conflict*, pp. 93–94.

troops to trouble spots and made the military a much more effective ally of the civilian police.[45]

Relations between the governors and the local representatives of the judicial system also placed a heavy burden on personality and tact. In institutional terms, the links between the gubernia administration and the courts were tenuous after the 1860s. The reform of 1864 had, to a large degree, sealed off the work of the judiciary from the intervention of the governors. The new statutes stripped the *nachal'niki gubernii* of most of their powers in legal affairs and dismantled much of the apparatus of procuratorial supervision of the administration. Yet, remnants of the old order survived and were a continued source of friction.

Governors could get involved in the work of the regular courts in at least two special circumstances. They participated in general meetings of the judicial chamber (*sudebnaia palata*) when it discussed questions involving conflict between the courts and other government agencies and when it made awards for damages resulting from the activities of administrative officials.[46] Beyond this, as chairmen of a variety of standing committees the governors took an active part in the system of administrative justice. After 1889 their judicial role was especially large in the provincial committee on peasant affairs, which acted as an appellate instance for decisions made by land captains and uezd congresses. In addition, governors chaired a special conference, composed of the head of the provincial gendarmes and the local procurator, that was concerned with crimes against the state.[47]

Similarly, the power of the judicial system impinged on the work of the governors in a number of ways. At the center, the Senate stood ready to review and overturn gubernatorial decisions on a wide range of matters. Closer to home, local courts and judicial officials might seem to hamper a governor's ability to deal with social and political problems. Finally, the police, in general subordinated to the *nachal'nik gubernii*, had a number of obligations to the local judicial institutions: informing them of possible crimes, conducting investigations, and carrying out various duties assigned by the courts. In these operations, the police worked under the supervision of the procuracy and were subject to its discipline. If police officials committed misdeeds in the course of their investigations or while working under court orders, the pro-

45. Urussov, pp. 58–59.
46. "Obshchee uchrezhdenie gubernskoe," art. 266, *Svod zakonov*, 2 (1892).
47. Blinov, *Gubernatory*, pp. 330–31.

curators could warn the offenders or even remand them for trial.[48] Thus, whatever the justice in a particular case might be, it was easy for governors to feel that the courts were undercutting their control over key subordinates and even interfering with the maintenance of local peace and security.

Indeed, differing conceptions of law and justice lay at the root of most clashes between the governors and the judiciary. As the officials charged with preserving order in the provinces, governors wanted the law and the courts to be supportive of that end and were often impatient with legal niceties. The procurators and other judicial officers, quite naturally, viewed their task more broadly, and though not indifferent to the need to suppress criminal activity and sedition, they were, nevertheless, concerned with maintaining the principle of legality itself. Given Russia's slowness in developing a "legal consciousness," the representatives of the judiciary felt constrained to uphold the letter of the law even if this sometimes complicated or frustrated the work of the gubernia administration.

Consequently, the majority of governors, even those who had a strong appreciation of the importance of legality, periodically confronted situations where the law either inhibited them from carrying out their duty to maintain local peace and security or simply ran counter to their sense of fair play. It was not unusual for governors to be forced to choose between inaction or illegal measures that enabled them to deal with a crisis swiftly or to right a perceived wrong. Indeed, governors frequently preferred the latter course, even if, as a result, they might face civil suits or administrative discipline.[49]

In most cases, governors who bent or even broke the law in the course of carrying out their duties did not find themselves entangled with the local representatives of the courts. But occasionally governors could blunder on to judicial territory with embarrassing and chastening consequences. P. P. Stremoukhov discovered this in the late 1890s when he was vice-governor of Kalysh province in Poland. Just after Stremoukhov had assumed his post, the governor went on vacation and left his second-in-command holding the reins. As acting governor, Stremoukhov took disciplinary measures against a group of peasants who had illegally cut timber and had offered resistance to the police who had

48. A. D. Gradovskii, *Nachala russkogo gosudarstvennogo prava: Organy mestnogo upravlenie*, in *Sobranie sochineniia* (9 vols.; St. Petersburg, 1899–1904), 9, pp. 340–46.

49. Recall Osorgin's handling of the strike at Cherniana Ruda discussed in Chapter 4; see also Dzhunkovskii, "Vospominaniia za 1909–1910 gg.," TsGAOR, f. Dzhunkovskogo, op. 1, d. 49, pp. 170–71.

tried to make them desist. During the preliminary hearing of the case, Stremoukhov suggested to the judicial investigator (*sudebnyi sledovatel'*) that the peasants be punished by incarceration as an example to the other villages in the region and so prevent an epidemic of illegal timbering. The judicial investigator concurred, and ordered that the peasants be detained. But shortly thereafter, Stremoukhov was visited by the distraught wives of the jailed peasants who begged him to release their husbands because of the onset of the harvest season. Without their menfolk, their families faced economic ruin. Moved by the women's pleas, Stremoukhov stated that he would free the men if they would return the stolen lumber and promise not to commit such crimes in the future. The women accepted in the names of their spouses, and the stolen wood was brought back. It was now the acting governor's turn to keep his end of the bargain. At this point, however, he encountered unexpected and unresolvable problems with the courts.

Stremoukhov applied to the judicial investigator for the release of the peasants only to be told that the investigator did not have the power to free them. He turned next to the procurator, but the latter informed him that the punishment had already been confirmed by the district criminal court in Warsaw and that this body alone could change the decision. Considering it to be very important that the representative of the emperor be able to keep his word, Stremoukhov journeyed to Warsaw where he explained to the chairman of the district court that the punishment had achieved its desired effect and continued incarceration threatened the peasants with extreme hardship. The chairman of the court, however, remained deaf to Stremoukhov's pleas. When Stremoukhov stated that being unable to keep the promise he made to the peasant women would cause the representative of the emperor to appear foolish, the chairman replied caustically that administrators should not involve themselves in matters that belonged to the judiciary.

There was nothing Stremoukhov could do. Forced to accept the action of the court, he later reflected on what appeared to him to be the lack of cohesion between justice and administration. "The disorders had been terminated, which seemed most important of all to the government; the accused[, however,] were unnecessarily ruined and the representative of authority placed in a ludicrous position. But none of this was of concern to the organs of the court. They decided these questions on an ideal basis, beyond time and space."[50]

50. Stremoukhov, "Administrativnoe ustroistvo," sec. 1, pp. 11–12. Quotation on p. 12.

But if one governor discovered the representatives of the judiciary to be excessively rigid and punctilious, another might see them as maddeningly lenient. The governor of Vologda, M. N. Kormilitsyn, found the procurator of the district court, A. A. Zelenetskii, a constant source of trouble because of the latter's unwillingness to defend law and order. In an official report, the governor described Zelenetskii as "a completely honest and kindhearted person" but then went on to complain that the procurator failed to display "definite and constant convictions" in his work. Zelenetskii was not firm in prosecuting peasants guilty of disorders, and because of this, the governor felt that he could not rely on him.[51] Lack of trust led Kormilitsyn to use unusual procedures in dealing with the procurator. Instead of employing simple oral communications with Zelenetskii, the governor resorted to the device of creating a special advisory committee (*osoboe soveshchatel'noe prisutstvie*) when measures to deal with serious incidents had to be developed. Kormilitsyn apparently reasoned that the procurator would respond only to decisions taken in a formal institutional setting.

But even this approach did not work. When peasants in several *volosti* of Totemskii uezd made armed attacks on the police collecting grain arrears, the governor organized a special committee to decide on a course of action. The body ordered the arrest of the leading rioters, and the procurator pledged that he would undertake a a vigorous investigation to identify the main perpetrators and bring them to justice. But when Zelenetskii arrived at the scene of the riots he did not live up to his word and instead released most of those being held by the police. The procurator was primarily interested in determining the economic condition of the peasants and based many of his legal decisions on this criterion. He even freed a man who had allegedly incited a mob to kill the police because the accused was poor. Zelenetskii stated that he would be "ashamed" to put such a person in jail.

Kormilitsyn found Zelenetskii's actions highly disturbing because they set a bad example of excessive leniency and encouraged further peasant resistance to authority. Yet, procuratorial independence left the *nachal'nik gubernii* unable to do anything at the local level. Kormilitsyn applied to the MVD for permission to go to Moscow to appeal to the procurator of the chief regional court, but in the end, he was saved the trip. News of Zelenetskii's erratic behavior had reached Moscow by other channels, and V. A. Sokolov, an assistant procurator of the

51. Kormilitsyn to I. N. Durnovo, 4 January 1892, *Krest'ianskoe dvizhenie v Rossii v 1890–1900 gg.*, p. 117.

regional court, journeyed to Vologda to investigate matters himself. Sokolov supported Kormilitsyn against Zelenetskii, and set aside the local procurator's lenient decisions. The leaders of the peasant riot were rearrested, and shortly thereafter the governor could write the minister with satisfaction that "the authority of the administration had not only been reestablished but remained unshakable."[52]

The incidents involving Stremoukhov and Kormilitsyn illustrate the degree to which governors found themselves constrained and even helpless in dealing with the representatives of the courts. But cases of this sort were relatively rare. A much more common source of friction between the governors and the local officers of the Ministry of Justice was the tension that often developed between the procurators and the police. Inefficient and usually corrupt, the provincial constabulary was a regular affront to the ideal of legality (*zakonnost'*). Frequently procurators were highly critical of the police and supported those who complained against their abuses.[53] But governors had to depend on the police and were often unable or unwilling to discipline them effectively. They strongly resented what seemed to them unwarranted procuratorial meddling.[54] Most governors simply endured. Others vented their anger in personal slights and the abuse of judicial personnel.[55] On at least one occasion, however, a governor went further and sought not only to break procuratorial supervision of the police but also to destroy the career of a member of the judiciary.

The incident occurred in Riazan in 1911. The city police chief, V. V. Gofshtetter, had been accused of various acts of criminal misconduct and sought to avoid prosecution by blackmailing the local procurator, N. G. Popov, and his wife. Threatening to charge the Popovs with extorting money from him, Gofshtetter demanded that the investigation into his activities be stopped. The police chief was backed by Governor Obolenskii and Vice-Governor Kolobov, who saw an opportunity to undermine the procurator's authority. The scheme might have worked, but M. V. Kirilov, a councilor of the provincial board whom the governor had told to produce a report incriminating the procurator, refused to join in the plot. Kirilov stood firm against his superiors and even brought the matter to the attention of the local gendarmes. Popov then took the offensive and forced Governor

52. Ibid., 118–21.

53. TsGIA, f. DOD, op. 47, d. 43a, "Otchet . . . Zaionchkovskogo po komandirovke v g. Vil'nu . . . ," p. 15.

54. A more detailed discussion of relations between the governors and the police can be found below, Chapter 8.

55. TsGIA, f. DOD, op. 47, 1911, d. 305a, pp. 81–82.

Obolenskii to remove Gofshtetter from office. The scandal shocked the province and provoked an angry report from the MVD's own investigator, N. Ch. Zaionchkovskii, though for reasons that remain obscure neither the governor nor his *vitse* suffered serious consequences.[56]

Few cases of serious conflict between governors and officers of the courts resulted from the kind of calculation involved in the escapades of the Riazan administration. Most appear to have been caused by blundering on the part of governors who simply had no idea what legality was all about. A preference for "prereform methods" was understandable, if not forgivable, of governors whose formative experiences had taken place during the reign of Nicholas I.[57] More disturbing is the fact that even at the start of the twentieth century a governor like Ufa's I. N. Sokolovskii could actually attempt to influence directly the outcome of a major court trial. In the course of his efforts, he exiled several defense attorneys from the province after confiscating important legal documents, publicly insulted the procurator because the latter had dared to defend due process, and ultimately, by his boorish and threatening behavior, forced a change of venue.[58]

Of course, documenting instances of crisis and conflict is always easier than discussing ongoing cooperation. Yet we must keep in mind that harmony between the governors and the local judiciary was undoubtedly the norm. Tact and common sense usually prevailed. Even governors who admitted to difficulties with the representatives of the courts were often quick to add that, on the whole, their relations with the procurators and court personnel were mutually supportive.[59] For every Baranov who saw the independent court system as a barrier to effective law enforcement, there was an Engel'gardt who regarded the

56. Materials relating to this episode are found in Zaionchkovskii's report on Riazan and appended documents. TsGIA, f. DOD, op. 47, 1911, d. 342, ch. 2, "Otchet Zaionchkovskogo . . . ," pp. 4, 87–88, and ch. 1, "Prilozheniia k otchetu . . . ," pp. 111–12, 128, 132.

57. See, for example, N. M. Baranov's defense of his use of corporal punishment at the time of the Nizhni-Novgorod fair (Report dated 30 January 1890, TsGIA. f. DOD, op. 223, 1890, d. 175, "Vsepoddanneishei otchet . . . za 1888 g.," pp. 10–11 [this *delo* contains two reports]).

58. Report of D. E. Rynkevich to S. S. Manukhin, Minister of Justice, 15 October 1903, TsGIA, f. Ministerstva Iustitsii (1405), op. 105, 1904, d. 11059, "O zabastovke rabochikh na zavodakh v g. Zlatouste," pp. 177–95.

59. Stremoukhov, "Administrativnoe ustroistvo," sec. 1, p. 12. See also the report of S. A. Lopukhin to V. V. Davydov, 19 January 1895 in *Krest'ianskoe dvizhenie . . . v 1890–1900 gg.*, pp. 277–80. This document shows how the governor and the local procurator in Orel worked together to prevent overzealous subordinates from exaggerating the significance of a peasant disturbance.

judicial institutions as a positive development in the moral life of the gubernias.[60]

Thus while it was traditional for governors to view the judiciary with a somewhat jaundiced eye, maintaining an attitude of cool reserve toward the courts, the more perceptive of the *nachal'niki gubernii* took a flexible stance. S. D. Urusov felt that governors had much to learn from local judges and procurators because they were close to the life of the gubernias and were generally free of the "slime" into which many provincial officials had sunk. Urusov developed a warm friendship for the procurator, V. N. Goremykin, and they frequently conferred on a wide range of problems. "I do not know whether we exchanged three documents during our common service," Urusov recalled, "but then it was seldom that three days passed without our discussing some service question that not infrequently had but little to do with the business of the attorney. Goremykin became well posted on Bessarabian matters before I did, and was constantly informed, both by his colleagues and by the the judges of instruction, of what happened in the district. By placing at my disposal this special knowledge, he enabled me to verify the police reports, and to watch, to some extent, the conduct of my subordinate district officials."[61] As in so many other areas of provincial governance, however, the governor's ability to form useful connections was based on personality, charm, and tact. Regular institutional links were far less valuable than informal ties.

60. Baranov report dated 30 December 1888, TsGIA, f. DOD, op. 223, 1890, d. 175, pp. 37–38; Engel'gardt's comments are found in his 1896 report on Arkhangelsk, ibid., 1897, d. 16, pp. 8–9.
    61. Urussov, p. 84.

– 7 –

Persuaders-in-Chief

Tension and conflict between the governors and the local field agents of the central ministries were a significant part of provincial politics, but they were not a major source of difficulty. Whatever their institutional affiliations, all the chief provincial officials were members of the same team. The disputes that emerged were, by and large, exceptional, occasional, and more the result of a clash of personalities and the less than perfect meshing of gubernia institutions than endemic interagency warfare. They could usually be averted or ameliorated by liberal doses of tact, patience, and compromise.

More complex and harder to contend with were the problems arising from the relationships between the governor and provincial institutions of self-government. In the assemblies of the nobility, the zemstvos, the urban dumas, and their elected leaders, the governors confronted persons and agencies that stood outside the MVD's chain of command and represented significant segments of provincial society. They were (or could claim to be) the spokesmen for native interests, and their cooperation was essential to the proper administration of the gubernia.

The gubernia and uezd marshals of the nobility were involved in a host of governmental functions. The provincial marshal sat on the major standing committees and participated with the governor in decisions affecting all sides of life in the gubernia. The uezd marshals were pivotal in local administration because they coordinated the work of the various institutions at the county level. The zemstvos and the urban dumas carried out important work in the areas of education, public welfare and philanthropy, famine relief, property insurance, the development of trade and industry, public health and veterinary services, the maintenance of roads and church buildings, and the like.

The governor had a limited capacity to give orders to these institutions and persons. Indeed, his ability to guide and direct them was even less than the power he might exercise in his dealings with field agencies outside the MVD structure. The assemblies of the nobility were not normally subject to gubernatorial interference. A governor's protest could block the implementation of certain decisions by the zemstvos and city councils, but it was possible to appeal his actions to the Senate. Conversely, the governor might propose that self-governing institutions undertake specific measures. But the noble assemblies, zemstvos, and urban dumas had the right to dispose of his suggestions as they saw fit. As in his relations with independent governmental offices, the formal institutional connections were often less significant than personal ties and associations: a governor's ability to persuade was more vital, and often more real, than his power to command.

The ties between the governors and the local nobility, for example, were complex, often frustrating but never unimportant. As a corporate entity, the gentry had little impact on the gubernia administration, yet its influence was all-pervasive. The *dvorianstvo* set the tone for the public life of the province, and its chief elected officers, the marshals (*predvoditeli*), were at the center of political influence, social prestige, and practical governance. Many of the most important local officials, especially those who dealt with the peasantry, came from the gentry, and its members also dominated the zemstvos. Without cooperation from the nobility, a governor could not rule effectively.[1]

Always sensitive, these relations became even more troubled at the turn of the century. By that time, Russia's noblemen had palpably suffered from an economic and political decline that had begun with the emancipation. A long agrarian crisis had hastened the impoverishment of their estates, and in increasingly specialized bureaucracy drew more of its recruits from other social groups and thus curtailed the nobility's access to state service. As a result, the gentry retreated to the provinces in a mood that was touchy, even surly. More and more, it came to view government officials as an alien, intrusive element unconcerned with local needs. Despite their own roots in the gentry, gover-

1. For a thorough discussion of the nobility's role in local administration, see A. P. Korelin, *Dvorianstvo v poreformennoi Rossii, 1864–1904 gg.* (Moscow, 1979), pp. 179–233. Also useful is P. N. Zyrianov, "Sotsial'naia struktura mestnogo upravleniia kapitalisticheskoi Rossii (1861–1914)," *Istoricheskie zapiski* 107 (1982): 273–83.

nors were also targets of this anger. To be sure, this black mood would not persist, and was considerably dissipated in the wake of the revolution of 1905. Yet just enough tension endured to color provincial politics and to maintain something of a barrier between the *nachal'niki gubernii* and the noble estate.[2]

Law and symbolism reinforced the gentry's sense of separation from the governor and his administration. The *nachal'nik gubernii* was forbidden by statute to attend the meetings of the triennial provincial noble assembly, even in those rare instances when he might be a local landowner and so entitled to participate.[3] Moreover, when the nobles gathered, the governor's role was largely confined to ceremonies that seemed designed to emphasize his powerlessness. On the opening day of the assembly, when the nobility congregated in its meeting hall, the governor was escorted to the scene by two gentry deputies. Only after the marshal's official welcome and the reading of the formal proposal for the opening of the assembly did His Excellency invite the noblemen to church, where, following services, they took the required oath to the emperor. At the initial gathering, the governor might also make a brief address. Speaking in the blandest tones, His Excellency would thank the nobles for their past cooperation and express his hope for continued good relations. The governor could then propose various matters for the assembly's consideration, after which he swiftly departed and left the nobles to their own affairs.[4]

The governor would not return to the noble assembly again until its formal closing, though this did not mean that he could not indirectly influence what transpired at its meetings. The convocation of the assembly was not simply a time for electing officers and discussing the needs of the class, it was an occasion for parties, dinners, and all kinds of get-togethers.[5] The governor was often a participant in these fes-

2. Roberta T. Manning, *The Crisis of the Old Order in Russia: Gentry and Government* (Princeton, 1982), pp. 3–64; Ruth D. MacNaughton and Roberta T. Manning, "The Crisis of the Third of June System and Political Trends in the Zemstvos, 1907–1914," in *The Politics of Rural Russia, 1905–1914*, ed. Leopold H. Haimson (Bloomington and London, 1979), pp. 184–209. Manning's position on the crisis of the nobility and its return to the land is not universally accepted. See the recent work by Seymour Becker, *Nobility and Privilege in Late Imperial Russia* (DeKalb, Ill., 1985), pp. 9–13, 32–34.

3. Gradovskii, *Nachala russkogo gosudarstvennogo prava: Organy mestnogo upravleniia* in *Sobranie sochineniia*, 9, p. 372.

4. Stremoukhov, "Administrativnoe ustroistvo . . . ," sec. 2, p. 5, BAR, Kryzhanovskii papers; TsGAOR, f. fon Valia, op. 1, d. 54, "Teksty rechei fon Valia pri otkrytii iaroslavskoe gubernskoe dvorianskogo sobraniia," p. 3; Gradovskii, *Sochineniia*, 9, pp. 395–96.

5. G. M. Hamburg, *The Politics of the Russian Nobility, 1881–1905* (New Brunswick, N.J., 1984), pp. 48–49.

tivities and with good reason—here was his chance to meet again the leading local power brokers, to learn firsthand their concerns and wants, and to lobby for his own views. This was how his Excellency became involved in gentry politics and attempted to shape the decisions of the assembly.

During its sessions, the nobles' assembly was obliged to consider proposals from the governor, and the marshal would report to him all the resolutions it had adopted. But the nobility was not restricted to discussing or voting on suggestions made by the governor, it was free to express its views on a wide range of subjects. The assembly had the right to address the governor, the minister of internal affairs, and the tsar on matters of concern. Members could complain about abuses committed by the local administration. In this way, the gentry protected its basic interests and checked the exercise of gubernatorial power.[6]

From the governor's perspective, the most important decision of the nobles' assembly was the election of the gentry marshal, for His Excellency would have almost continuous relations with this officer and with his colleagues, the uezd marshals. Indeed, the provincial marshal's status in the gubernia was second only to the governor's. Elected for a three-year term, confirmed in office by the emperor (on the recommendation of the minister of internal affairs), the provincial marshal was in no way a subordinate of the *nachal'nik gubernii*. In fact, in terms of service rank, the two men were often equals. The marshal had the right to communicate directly with the governor and the minister of internal affairs, and not even the provincial board, "the highest institution in the province," could issue an order to the gubernia marshal or demand information from him.[7] As a member of all the important standing committees and chairman of the provincial zemstvo assembly, the marshal was privy to most of the decisions affecting governance. His views could not be ignored with impunity, for the marshal not only enjoyed great local influence but was also likely to have powerful connections in St. Petersburg. If offended, he could make life very uncomfortable for the governor by undercutting his position both in the gubernia and in the capital. This kind of leverage sometimes enabled a marshal to "devour" or dominate a governor.[8]

Because of the great impact the provincial marshals could have on local administration and on the general political atmosphere in the

---

6. Gradovskii, *Sochineniia*, 9, pp. 389–90.

7. Ibid., pp. 402–3; Korelin, pp. 220–21.

8. P. D. Stremoukhov, "Nizhegorodskii gubernator A. N. Murav'ev (Iz moikh vospominanii)," *Russkaia starina* 106, no. 5: 355–61; P. P. Stremoukhov, "Administrativnoe ustroistvo . . . ," sec. 2, p. 5, BAR.

gubernia, the governors and their superiors in St. Petersburg watched the results of the nobility's elections intently and were occasionally tempted to influence their outcome. While ruling in Volynia in the period before the Great Reforms, V. P. Sinel'nikov actually used the threat of exile to prevent one member of the nobles' assembly from vigorously supporting an undesirable candidate for the marshal's post. But blatant intervention by local and even central authorities was dangerous and did not always have the desired effect. In 1866, for example, central authorities dismissed Riazan's provincial marshal A. N. Retkin for failing to check the political liberalism of the assembled gentry. But Retkin was triumphantly reelected by his colleagues, and the government backed down. The results of this episode were highly discomfiting to Governor P. D. Stremoukhov and to the MVD as well.[9]

Because the consequences of meddling in the selection of a provincial marshal were potentially explosive, most governors must have limited themselves to fretting on the sidelines. Contemplating the resignation of gubernia marshal Count Kapnist, Kharkov's governor, G. A. Tobizen, worried that finding a suitable replacement would not be easy. The best candidate was not actually a "native" (korennoi) Kharkovian, so his election might create problems, but the other potential gubernia marshals all had strikes against them. One was a confirmed playboy who would never take the job seriously, a second was inexperienced, and the remaining contenders were not really linked economically to Kharkov because most of their business dealings and properties were in other provinces. The governor had plenty of additional complaints about the character of the local nobility and its leaders, but to the crucial question "What to do?" Tobizen gave no answer.[10]

Despite the care and caution that characterized the relations between the governors and the second citizens of the provinces, breakdowns and ruptures occurred from which the governor might come out the loser. In the early twentieth century, for example, Tambov's governor N. P. Muratov and provincial marshal V. N. Chelokaev

---

9. Sinel'nikov, "Zapiski," no. 2: 392–93; P. D. Stremoukhov, "Iz vospominanii o grafe P. A. Valueve," *Russkaia starina* 117, no. 11: 283–85; G. M. Hamburg, "Portrait of an Elite: Russian Marshals of the Nobility, 1861–1917," *Slavic Review* 40 (Winter 1981): 589–90.

10. Letter of Tobizen to D. S. Sipiagin, 7 February 1900, TsGIA, f. Kants. MVD, op. 1, d. 1172, "[Perepiska] s khar'kovskim gubernatorom . . . ," pp. 7–12. In his report for 1895 Tver governor Akhlestyshev indicated his disapproval of the activities of the "liberal" party among the *dvorianstvo* but implied that he could only watch and worry (GAKO, f. Kants. tver. gub., op. 2, d. 588, pp. 14–15).

clashed on a number of issues that included the governor's refusal to confirm one of the uezd marshals in office. Venomous relations between the two men resulted. Muratov slighted Chelokaev on various occasions, failing to receive him in his study, refusing to sit with him during business discussions, and demonstratively absenting himself from the table when someone proposed to toast the marshal's health. The minister of internal affairs was not amused by this turn of events, but his wrath fell on the governor, not the marshal. Stolypin's warning to Muratov to cease his blatant insults was motivated less by a concern for good manners than by the fear that a breach between the governor and Chelokaev could disrupt the administration of the gubernia.[11]

The governor's position vis-à-vis the uezd marshal was theoretically stronger than in regard to the gubernia *predvoditel'*. Although elected by the local nobles, the uezd marshal was confirmed in office by the governor, so there was a slight implication of subordination. Indeed, the uezd marshal did carry out many administrative assignments under the direction of the *nachal'nik gubernii* such as supervising and coordinating the work of the land captains, and chairing various uezd standing committees.[12]

Yet the actual power a governor could exercise over an uezd marshal was virtually nonexistent. Confirmation, in most cases, amounted to little more than a certification that the marshal's election had been carried out in a legal manner. Even in minor matters, there was no way for a governor to compel a marshal to act, and he might offer resistance on such a relatively unimportant question as the proper form of communication with the *nachal'nik gubernii*. And while a governor could propose that a marshal be turned over to the courts if he had committed crimes in office, this did not constitute effective discipline. The marshal had wide latitude. His actions might cause a governor trouble or generate complaints from the citizens of the uezd and still be within the limits of the law.[13]

The duties carried out by the uezd marshals were so varied and so important that governors wanted strong competent individuals in this

11. Memorandum on Muratov, 27 March 1910, TsGIA f. DOD, op. 47, 1910, d. 278, "So spravkami o gubernatorakh . . . ," p. 39.

12. Korelin, pp. 221–25.

13. P. P. Stremoukhov, "Administrativnoe ustroistvo . . . ," sec. 2, p. 5, BAR. On the question of the form of address see the letter of the governor of Stavropol to the Department of General Affairs, 18 December 1899, TsGIA, f. Kants. MVD po delam dvorianstva (1283), op. 1, I deloproizvodstvo, 1899, d. 73, "O forme snosheniia uezdnykh predvoditelei dvorianstva s gubernatorami," p. 1. (The letter notes the attempt of an uezd marshal to use the same form of communication as the provincial marshal, i.e., implying equality with the governor).

post even if they might prove difficult from time to time. Unfortunately, good men were hard to find. In the early twentieth century, absenteeism and dereliction of duty were common, and even a well-intentioned, conscientious marshal, like A. D. Golitsyn, might spend an inordinate amount of time away from his district.[14] Despite this, few governors would have agreed with George Yaney's contention that the uezd marshals had become virtually irrelevant by the early 1900s. Instead, they complained bitterly about the large number of weak marshals and the fact that these officers were poorly integrated into the administrative structure of the gubernias.[15]

Yet let a governor try to correct this situation, and he might have a fight on his hands. Disgusted by P. S. Sheremetev's long absences from his district and by his failure to perform the essential functions of his marshal's office, Moscow governor Dzhunkovskii decided to send him a letter reminding him of his obligations. Sheremetev replied in what the governor considered "a completely improper tone," but there was little Dzhunkovskii could do to bring the marshal into line. Because his administrative means of discipline were extremely limited, the governor resorted to informal, personal channels and turned to the provincial marshal, A. D. Samarin. "Take upon yourself the task of thrashing out this unfortunate incident in the comradely circles of the marshals of the nobility," the governor wrote in an almost plaintive vein. "Help me to end [matters] in a dignified way, without putting the question on an official plane which would be undesirable for me . . . [given my] feelings of respect for the nobility."[16]

In the end, Samarin was able to bring a chastened Sheremetev to make his apologies to the *nachal'nik gubernii*. But the conflict and the way it was resolved, while doing credit to Dzhunkovskii's tact, point up the inability of the governors to control or direct the elected representatives of the nobility. Of course, members of the powerful Sheremetev clan were not to be trifled with, but Dzhunkovskii was, after all, both *nachal'nik gubernii* and an aide-de-camp to the emperor himself. If such a favored individual could not ask an uezd marshal simply to do his duty without suffering a serious affront, what could a governor with less impressive connections hope to accomplish? A

14. Koshko, *Vospominaniia*, pp. 149–50; Dzhunkovskii, "Vospominaniia za 1905–1908 gg.," TsGAOR, f. Dzhunkovskogo, op. 1, d. 47, pp. 199–200; Korelin, p. 230; Yaney, *Systematization*, 341–42.

15. Yaney, *Systematization*, p. 342; Dzhunkovskii, "Vospominaniia za 1905–1908 gg.," pp. 199–200, 333; Stremoukhov, "Administrativnoe ustroistvo . . . ," sec. 2, p. 5.

16. Quoted in Dzhunkovskii, "Vospominaniia za 1905–1908," p. 286.

marshal may have seen himself as a state servant just as the governor did. But the marshal rendered that service on his own terms, and the *nachal'nik gubernii* had little chance to exercise leadership. As in almost all other aspects of provincial governance, the governor had to use persuasion, not power, to achieve his ends.

An even more significant problem than that of the marshals of the nobility was posed by the zemstvos, the institutions of rural self-government established in 1864 at both the provincial and uezd levels. The complex and sometimes volatile relationship between the *nachal'niki gubernii* and the zemstvos illustrated the difficulty of reconciling the principle of absolutism with local initiative. On the one hand, both the original zemstvo law of 1864 and the later statute of 1890 gave these institutions considerable power to deal with economic concerns and a host of matters affecting life in the gubernias. On the other, tradition and existing legislation also made the governor ultimately responsible for the well being of the province and hence for the policies adopted by self-government.

As a consequence of overlapping duties and concerns, the association between the governor and the zemstvos was frequently an adversarial one. The governor's basic task was to exercise supervision (*nadzor*) over the zemstvos as he did over all state and private agencies in the gubernia. In addition, the legislation defining zemstvo rights and obligations gave the governor a number of specific means by which he could check the activities of these institutions.[17]

The original statute of 1864 enabled the governors to block, at least temporarily, any zemstvo resolution they deemed illegal or "contrary to general state interests." Gubernatorial sanction was also required for zemstvo budgets and expenditures as well as for measures concerning local trade, commerce, and transportation. Beyond this, the law of 19 August 1879 gave governors a degree of control over zemstvo personnel, for it allowed them to prevent the appointment or secure

---

17. For a good, convenient survey of the main legislation concerning the zemstvos and their powers vis-à-vis the administration, see Kermit E. McKenzie, "Zemstvo Organization and Role within the Administrative Structure," in *The Zemstvo in Russia*, pp. 31–78. In referring to the zemstvo statutes (and later to the urban statutes as well), I will use the 1876 and 1892 editions of volume 2 of the *Svod zakonov*. In the 1876 edition, all articles were numbered consecutively throughout the volume, so materials on self-government institutions begin with article 1817. In the 1892 edition of the *Svod*'s second volume there is a separate "Polozhenie o gubernskikh i uezdnykh zemskikh uchrezhdeniiakh" with its own pagination and article numbers. The city statute is also separate.

the dismissal of any individual in zemstvo service whom they regarded as "untrustworthy" (*neblagonadezhnyi*).[18]

The "counterreform" zemstvo statute of 1890 increased the governors' powers over the zemstvo. Governors could now block measures that "clearly violated" the interests of the local population.[19] Such grounds were ill defined at best, and this stipulation encouraged the *nachal'niki gubernii* to see themselves as the defenders of the provincial citizenry against the abuses of elective bodies. At the same time, the creation of the committee on zemstvo and urban affairs rendered gubernatorial supervision more comprehensive. This collegial institution, with a large non-zemstvo membership, now served as a forum in which disputes over zemstvo activity could be examined. As noted earlier, governors took a strong interest in the work of this committee and often dominated its proceedings.

The law of 1890 also altered the process by which matters in dispute between the governors, zemstvos, and local citizens could be appealed. The original zemstvo legislation had made the Senate the final arbiter of those conflicts between the zemstvos and the administration which could not be resolved at the local level. The new measure restricted the role of the Senate, which now ruled only when the legality of a zemstvo measure was challenged, and expanded the powers of the MVD and the Committee of Ministers by permitting them to make binding decisions on almost all other matters disputed between the zemstvos and the governors. Understandably, the MVD and the Committee accorded great weight to the opinions and wishes of the *nachal'niki gubernii*.[20]

Zemstvo statutes also gave the governors considerable control over the executive boards (*upravy*) of these institutions. The original law had empowered the governors to confirm the chairmen of the county boards in their posts, whereas the minister of internal affairs confirmed the chairmen of the provincial boards. The measure passed in 1890 expanded gubernatorial authority by allowing the *nachal'niki gubernii* to confirm all members of the provincial board, except the chairman, and the chairmen and the entire membership of the county boards.[21] "Counterreform" zemstvo legislation made the chairmen and the members of the zemstvo executive boards state servants subject to administrative discipline by the committee on zemstvo and urban af-

18. *Svod zakonov*, 2 (1876), arts. 1825, 1906; McKenzie, "Zemstvo Organization," p. 58.

19. "Polozhenie o . . . zemskikh uchrezhdeniiakh," art. 87, *Svod zakonov*, 2 (1892).

20. Compare *Svod zakonov*, 2 (1876), arts. 1910–1912 and "Polozhenie o . . . zemskikh uchrezhdeniiakh," arts. 88–89, *Svod zakonov*, 2 (1892).

21. *Svod zakonov*, 2 (1876), arts. 1864, 1872; "Polozhenie . . . ," art. 118, *Svod zakonov*, 2 (1892).

fairs or the council of the MVD, which could remand them to the courts for trial.

In keeping with the altered status of the *uprava,* the governor was now empowered to inspect both the board and its subordinate institutions. He could then bring any irregularities to the attention of the board and ask that they be corrected. Should the zemstvo executive refuse, the dispute was then turned over to the committee on zemstvo and urban affairs for a binding decision. If the executive board continued to object to the committee's ruling and the zemstvo assembly supported the executive, they could appeal the matter to the Senate for final resolution.[22]

The governors' powers to supervise and to interfere with zemstvo activity inevitably created a degree of tension between these institutions and the provincial administration, though the nature and scope of that tension has been considerably distorted. A significant body of literature—mostly of a liberal persuasion—portrays the governors as regularly engaging in the arbitrary abuse of their authority vis-à-vis the zemstvos. According to this interpretation, governors consistently blocked zemstvo efforts to expand their functions and to improve the quality of life in the gubernias. The leitmotif of all the governors' actions was the determination to subdue the zemstvos and make them pliant instruments of the state. This same school of thought depicts the zemstvos as resolutely fighting back, defending the interests of provincial society against the agents of autocracy.[23]

Conflict between governors and zemstvos was certainly real enough, and there were governors who clearly engaged in acts of arbitrariness (*proizvol*). Yet, recent scholarship in the Soviet Union and the west has revealed a more subtle and balanced picture of this side of provincial politics. We see that governor-zemstvo clashes have often been exaggerated and that points of agreement and cooperation have frequently been ignored.[24] An outstanding article by Thomas Fallows illuminates particularly well the true nature of relations between the *nachal'niki*

22. "Polozhenie . . . ," arts. 124, 132–37, 103.

23. Blinov, *Gubernatory,* pp. 282–310; V. M. Gessen, *Voprosy mestnogo upravleniia* (SPb., 1904), pp. 213–20; Khizhniakov, *Vospominaniia,* pp. 176–80; Jacob Walkin, *The Rise of Democracy in Pre-Revolutionary Russia* (New York, 1962), pp. 153–80.

24. P. A. Zaionchkovskii shows that cases of open government-zemstvo conflict were rare (*Rossiiskoe samoderzhavie,* pp. 208–16). N. M. Pirumova also notes that while the government sought to destroy the political self-sufficiency of the zemstvos, it cooperated with them in local economic affairs (*Zemskoe liberal'noe dvizhenie: Sotsial'nye korni i evoliutsiia do nachala XX veka* [Moscow, 1977], pp. 51–52). For western works that put zemstvo-government relations in a new perspective see Manning, *The Crisis of the Old Order;* Robbins, *Famine in Russia;* Emmons and Vucinich, eds., *The Zemstvo in Russia;* Yaney, *Systematization,* esp. pp. 346–60.

gubernii and the zemstvos. On the basis of an analysis of Senate decisions concerning the zemstvos, Fallows shows that strictly political questions were involved in only a relatively small portion of the disputes between governors and rural self-government. Most conflicts concerned economic questions, especially zemstvo levies and expenditures, and in many cases governors did not simply act on their own but responded to the pressure of citizens upset by rising taxes. As for the emotionally charged question of *proizvol,* it would appear that both the governors and the zemstvos demonstrated a tendency to exceed their legitimate powers. Provincial politics was a complicated, troubled process of give and take in which the *nachal'niki gubernii* and the institutions of self-government struggled to define their mutual relations. Important issues divided the two sides, and neither had a monopoly on right and virtue.[25]

Moreover, the conclusions about governor-zemstvo relations which Fallows reached are supported by other, more varied but less comprehensive materials such as gubernatorial reports and memoirs, which do not betray any general or consistent hostility toward the zemstvos. To be sure, some governors expressed concern that the zemstvos were wielding more power than they ought,[26] and others felt that zemstvos could do more to encourage local economic growth.[27] But overall, the impression derived from available sources is that governors viewed the zemstvos as valuable adjuncts to the gubernia administration. And *nachal'niki gubernii* who ruled in those parts of the empire where zemstvos had not been introduced often looked enviously on their colleagues whose provinces benefited from the work of these institutions.[28]

The usually friendly disposition of the governors toward the zemstvos is also illustrated by the fact that the number of gubernatorial protests of zemstvo resolutions was not excessive in absolute terms. Unfortunately, there are no nationwide statistics on this question, but

---

25. Thomas Fallows, "The Zemstvo and the Bureaucracy, 1890–1904," in *The Zemstvo in Russia,* pp. 184–93.

26. Pskov governor B. A. Vasil'chikov to V. K. Pleve, 16 December 1902, TsGAOR, f. Pleve, op. 1, d. 553, "Pis'mo Vasil'chikova . . . Pleve," pp. 1–2; TsGIA, f. DOD, op. 194, 1912, d. 48, "S kopieiu vsepoddanneishego otcheta o sostoianii viatskoi gubernii za 1911 g.," pp. 5–6. See also N. M. Baranov's criticism of the zemstvos during the famine of 1891–92 (Robbins, *Famine in Russia,* pp. 131–35).

27. Koshko, "Vospominaniia," pp. 517–18, BAR; TsGIA, f. DOD, op. 223, 1888, d. 168, "Vsepoddanneishii otchet o sostoianii saratovskoi gubernii za 1887 g.," p. 46.

28. Stremoukhov, "Administrativnoe ustroistvo . . . ," sec. 2, pp. 7–8; TsGIA, f. DOD, op. 194, 1905, d. 115, "S kopieiu vsepoddanneishego otcheta o sostoianii grodenskoi gubernii za 1904 g.," p. 8.

some partial data are suggestive. The papers of the Polovtsov inspection, for example, contain some useful information on the Chernigov zemstvo. During the period 1878–1880 (a time of considerable anti-government agitation in Chernigov), the zemstvos of the gubernia adopted a total of 2,077 resolutions, of which the governor, A. L. Shostak, blocked only twenty-four. Of the 292 resolutions passed by the *provincial* zemstvo, just two elicited a gubernatorial veto. The inspection of Senator S. A. Mordvinov in Voronezh uncovered a similar picture of zemstvo-administration relations: from 1878 to 1880, the governor protested only thirty-two zemstvo decisions. Of equal significance was the fact that in the majority of cases the zemstvos of Chernigov and Voronezh accepted the validity of the governors' vetoes and did not appeal to the Senate for redress.[29]

By the end of the century, the number of gubernatorial protests seems to have risen considerably. For example, in Viatka during the seven years from 1897 to 1903, 435 zemstvo decisions were examined by the committee on zemstvo and urban affairs, and in the overwhelming majority of cases the governor had protested the resolution. The same was true in Kursk, where more than half of the zemstvo-related cases that came before the committee had originated in gubernatorial vetoes. But as in the earlier period, the zemstvos demonstrated a proclivity to accept the decisions of the gubernia administration and appealed only a minuscule number of committee rulings to the Senate.[30]

Although governor-zemstvo conflict was a relatively small part of the provincial political sense, tensions undoubtedly increased in the initial decade of the reign of Nicholas II. There are a number of reasons for this development. First, the counterreform zemstvo statute gave governors more excuses for intervening in zemstvo affairs. Second, the rise of gentry discontent and activism turned the zemstvo assemblies, especially at the gubernia level, into political forums for the discussion of current issues. Third, the marked expansion of zemstvo budgets after 1890 caused local resistance and growing concern in St. Petersburg that the zemstvos were burdening the peasants and absorbing

29. GPB, f. Revizii Polovtsova, d. 1572, "Kratkaia vedomost' postanovleniiam zemskikh sobranii chernigovskoi gubernii, oprotestovannym gubernatorom za 1878–1880 gg."; ibid., d. 1353, "Protesty gubernskoi administratsii protiv postanovlenii gubernskikh i uezdnykh zemskikh uchrezhdenii chernigovskoi gubernii za 1878–1880 gg."; "Zemskie uchrezhdeniia v voronezhskoi gubernii," p. 40, in *MVUOK*, 3, pt. 2: *Zapiski Mordvinova*.

30. *Otchet po revizii t.s. Zinov'eva zemskikh uchrezhdenii viatskoi gubernii* [hereafter: Zinov'ev, *Otchet po viatskoi gubernii*] (3 vols.; SPb., 1905), 1, pp. 282, 285–88; idem, *Kurskoe zemstvo*, 1, pp. 196–97; idem, *Otchet po moskovskoi gubernii*, 1, p. 84.

too lage a share of potential tax revenues. Finally, the MVD became increasingly alarmed about the expanding influence of the often radical experts employed by the zemstvos and saw this "third element" as a force leading the zemstvos in a direction harmful to the autocracy.

Because of these developments, the governors were pressured to monitor the zemstvos carefully and to block some of their activities. From above and below, governors were urged to draw the line against zemstvo budget increases, to prevent zemstvo members from making unwarranted political statements, and to purge local self-government of untrustworthy staff.[31] In the meantime, the rise of gentry oppositional feeling made relations between the zemstvos and the governors increasingly difficult. Even a relatively minor breach of tact on the part of the *nachal'nik gubernii* could produce an explosion. Thus, Governor Obolenskii's reproof of the Kharkov zemstvo for what he regarded as sloppy financial management provoked charges that the governor was guilty of abusing his powers, and an appeal of his actions ultimately reached the Senate.[32]

The institutional weakness of the gubernia administration also helps to explain the rise of governor-zemstvo altercations because at the beginning of the twentieth century the *nachal'niki gubernii* no longer had the means to oversee zemstvo operations effectively. The amount of business transacted by the zemstvos was large and growing steadily; it was too much for a single person to examine in a serious way. Of course, the provincial committee on zemstvo and urban affairs helped the governors study the protests made against zemstvo decisions, but it did not assist in the work of initial supervision. Even the establishment of a permanent member for the committee in 1901 was of relatively little help to the governors when it came to shouldering the enormous burden of keeping tabs on the work of both uezd and provincial zemstvos.[33]

The size of the task they confronted made it almost impossible for governors to examine the activities of the zemstvos in detail. Instead they usually relied on "bureaucratic" means; that is, they studied texts of resolutions rather than concrete facts and problems. This practice in turn caused supervision to assume a political character. Gubernatorial actions and objections to zemstvo measures increasingly became based

31. Circular dated 10 February 1895, TsGIA, f. Khoz. dep., op. 27, d. 3114, "Po sekretnomu tsirkuliaru M-va Vn. Del . . . o dostavlenii gubernatorami svedenii o kazhdom sluchae narusheniia predsedatel'stvuiushchimi v zemskikh sobraniiakh obiazannosti svoikh," p. 1; Fallows, pp. 219–20.

32. Fallows, p. 213.

33. Strakhovskii, "Gubernskoe ustroistvo" (November 1913): 142–43.

more on broad abstract principles emanating from St. Petersburg (such as the limits of administrative and zemstvo authority)[34] than on specific local realities and needs. Experienced governors understood that it was always better to keep their supervision of zemstvo activity concentrated on hard facts rather than on vague points of law and administrative theory.[35] But as Governor I. M. Strakhovskii noted, detailed inspections of zemstvo operations were cumbersome and gubernatorial staff was usually too small to carry out this kind of work on a regular basis.[36] Moreover, even when governors did choose to examine the details of zemstvo work (the conditions of hospitals or the management of schools, for example), they often found that their efforts to set things right met with indifference or obstruction on the part of self-government.[37] Frustrated by such circumstances, a governor might resort to arbitrary actions and elicit the familiar charge of *proizvol*.

Institutional deficiencies also contributed to another sore spot in the relations between rural self-government and the *nachal'niki gubernii*. Zemstvo spokesmen frequently accused governors of abusing their discretionary powers in blocking measures passed by the zemstvos and challenging their appointments to staff positions. Under the law, the governor had two weeks to approve or reject a zemstvo enactment or appointment, but they often failed to meet the deadline. This practice kept the zemstvo and its would-be employee in a state of unpleasant suspense. As a result, zemstvos were forced to delay the start of needed projects or found it increasingly difficult to find good personnel because talented workers were unwilling to subject themselves to a lengthy period of uncertainty.[38] No doubt, zemstvo leaders felt that governors were deliberately slow in making decisions in order to harass them. This was true in some cases, though in most, these delays resulted from the

34. Zinov'ev, *Kurskoe zemstvo*, 1, p. 239; idem, *Otchet po viatskoi gubernii*, 1, pp. 301–4.

35. P. G. Kurlov, *Konets russkogo tsarizma: vospominaniia byvshego komandira korpusa zhandarmov* (Petrograd–Moscow, 1923), pp. 23–26; Zinov'ev, *Kurskoe zemstvo*, 1, p. 239; N. N. Kisel'-Zagorianskii, "Les Mémoires du Général Kissel-Zagorianskii," pp. 190–91, BAR, Kisel'-Zagorianskii papers.

36. Strakhovskii, "Gubernskoe ustroistvo" (November 1913): 142–43.

37. Dzhunkovskii, "Vospominaniia za 1905–1908 gg.," pp. 329–30; see also the exchange of letters between Governor Somov and the chairman of the Tver uezd zemstvo on conditions at the Zatverskaia hospital, 2–31 July 1886, GAKO, f. Kants. tver. gub., op. 1, d. 18996, "O revizii nachal'nikom gubernii . . . zatverskoi zemskoi bol'nitsy," pp. 1–4, 16, 22–25.

38. N. Driagin, "K voprosu o diskretsionnoi vlasti gubernatorov," *Pravo* (20 May 1901): 1065–68; Zinov'ev, *Kurskoe zemstvo*, 1, pp. 186–89.

inadequacy of gubernatorial staffs and the brevity of the time allowed to gather the necessary information. Moreover, the zemstvos themselves were frequently unable or unwilling to do the required background investigation and so contributed to the problem.[39]

In sum, it is probably true that governors tended to be over zealous in their scrutiny of zemstvo activity, but in fairness to them we must recall how they were constantly being asked by St. Petersburg to keep local self-government in line and to prevent "untrustworthy" elements from entering zemstvo service. This was particularly so during the decade prior to the 1905 revolution, although in the years that followed the MVD came to see that governors were too strict, especially in the matter of personnel decisions. In February 1911, Prime Minister P. A. Stolypin sent a circular to the governors, urging restraint in the use of their power to block zemstvo appointments. He noted that the gubernatorial practice of excessive vigilance was causing dangerous and unnecessary resentment among zemstvo leadership.[40]

Thus the increase in zemstvo-governor conflict at the turn of the century must be seen in perspective. Perhaps the best way to do this is to look briefly at the question of zemstvo budgets, an issue that caused considerable dispute between the governors, the central ministries, the institutions of self-government, and the general public. As we have noted, governors faced heavy pressure, both from St. Petersburg and from the local population, to check the expansion of zemstvo budgets and the concomitant rise in levies. But even governors who complained about zemstvo expenditures did not do so out of hostility to the institutions or their programs.

In his 1895 annual report, for example, Saratov's governor B. B. Meshcherskii expressed alarm about the impact that the increase in zemstvo taxation was having on the peasant economy. But the very next year he made it clear that for him the main problem was how to choose from among a number of desirable goals. "Of all the expenditures of the Saratov zemstvo," Meshcherskii wrote, "you cannot point to one that was not justified on the basis of expedience. All expenditures are useful. But the chief delusion consists in [thinking] that every expenditure on a useful goal is possible."[41]

That most governors shared Meshcherskii's supportive but cautious

---

39. D. N. Shipov, *Vospominaniia i dumy o perezhitom* (Moscow, 1918), pp. 104–106; Driagin, pp. 1065–68; Zinov'ev, *Kurskoe zemstvo*, 1, pp. 186–89.

40. Dzhunkovskii, "Vospominaniia za 1911–1912 gg.," TsGAOR, f. Dzhunkovskogo, op. 1, d. 51, pp. 29–30.

41. The 1895 report is in TsGIA, f. DOD, op. 223, 1896, d. 28b, pp. 15–16. The quoted passage is in the report for 1896, ibid., 1897, d. 30b, p. 4.

view of zemstvo levies and expenditures was demonstrated after 1900, when the *nachal'niki gubernii* acquired the means to restrict zemstvo budgets if they so desired. The law of 12 June sharply limited zemstvo powers in financial matters and thereafter zemstvos could expand their budgets by only 3 percent a year on their own authority.[42] Increases beyond this point required the approval of the governor. Because zemstvo budgets had been growing at a yearly rate of about 7 percent for the decade 1890–1900, the new law provided the governors with a device to check local self-government.

Yet few of the *nachal'niki gubernii* consistently exercised this new power. Even in the years immediately after the promulgation of the law of 12 June, zemstvo budgets grew by 4.2 percent, and the period 1903–1906 saw them expand by over 8 percent. For the entire decade 1903–1913, zemstvo budgets went up at a rate of 14 percent a year.[43] The cold figures of zemstvo budgetary increases were a sign that despite clear encouragement from the central government to restrain zemstvo activity and the means to do so, governors preferred to cooperate with these institutions in developing the provinces. In fact, these statistics suggest that beneath the surface of zemstvo-administration conflict there lay extensive cooperation between the *nachal'niki gubernii* and rural self-government. This should not be surprising, for the solid basis of this harmony was the common class background of governors and zemstvo leaders and a broad range of mutual interests.

As pointed out in Chapter 2, the governors of late nineteenth- and early twentieth-century Russia came overwhelmingly from the landed gentry, the same social class that dominated the zemstvos, particularly at the more politicized gubernia level. Moreover, an ever-increasing number of the *nachal'niki gubernii* had been involved in provincial politics and zemstvo activity, for years. Of course, one need not assume that as governor, a former zemstvo member or gentry marshal would fail to defend the interests of the state should push come to shove, but simply that governors did not bring a purely bureaucratic mentality to their jobs. In fact, they were attuned to the zemstvos' sensitivities and often sympathetic to their concerns. Beyond this, the governor and the *zemtsy* both had a vested interest in cooperation. The governor realized that an open break with the zemstvo was likely to raise questions about his ability to manage local affairs. Conversely,

42. PSZ, 3d ser., no. 18862.

43. Dorothy Atkinson, "The Zemstvo and the Peasantry," in *The Zemstvo in Russia*, p. 100; Zinov'ev, *Kurskoe zemstvo*, 1, pp. 209–10; N. A. Mel'nikov, "Russkoe zemstvo v proshlom i nekotorye mysli ob ego budushchem," pp. 28–30, BAR, Mel'nikov papers.

zemstvo members well understood that if the governor turned against them, he could obstruct zemstvo operations through his protests, deny state support for the collection of local imposts, or fail to back zemstvo requests from the center.

As a result of these circumstances, governors and zemstvo leaders often went to considerable lengths to avoid confrontation. As governor of Perm, I. F. Koshko faced a sensitive situation when A. F. Cherdyntsev was elected as a member of the provincial executive board. Cherdyntsev had been a Kadet agitator during 1905, and Koshko felt that he could refuse to confirm him on political grounds. Yet the governor did not want to create a breach with the zemstvo, so he sought a compromise. He arranged a meeting with Cherdyntsev and asked him to avoid overt political activity while serving on the board. Cherdyntsev accepted Koshko's terms and was duly confirmed in his post.[44] Of course, efforts to head off conflict came from the zemstvo side as well. When the Moscow activist D. N. Shipov found that Governor D. S. Sipiagin was prone to veto zemstvo measures on dubious grounds, he carefully combed through proposals before they were considered by the assembly. Wherever possible, Shipov tried to eliminate stipulations that might elicit a protest.[45]

The governors' desire for cooperation with the zemstvos resulted not simply from a concern about the damage a clash might do to their image or even to their ability to maintain control at the local level. As the officials ultimately responsible for the general well-being of the provinces governors had to work hand-in-hand with the zemstvos in a variety of local emergencies, most notably famines. In these situations, zemstvo successes were likely to be the governors' successes.

Managing crises or achieving any kind of positive goal required a degree of trust and mutual support. Despite his authority, a governor could not force a zemstvo to do anything,[46] and many of these institutions were slow in carrying out even those responsibilities that the law assigned them. As always, good personal relations between the governor and key figures in the zemstvo structure could help stimulate necessary action, but it was not uncommon for the *nachal'nik gubernii* to turn directly to the rank and file delegates and seek their support for various programs. The opening of the annual assembly of the gubernia

44. Koshko, "Vospominaniia," pp. 55–56, BAR.

45. Shipov, *Vospominaniia,* pp. 107–10.

46. The original zemstvo statute had given the governor the right to fulfill zemstvo obligations at zemstvo expense should it fail to carry out its lawful duties (*Svod zakonov,* 2 [1876], art. 1826). This right was apparently little used and was not included in the law of 1890.

zemstvo gave a governor a chance to put forward a list of measures he felt ought to be accomplished. Carefully mixing compliments with criticism, a governor could lend support to those who were working to move the zemstvo in the direction he desired.[47]

The activities of A. I. Kosich in Saratov during the late 1880s and early 1890s illustrate the positive role a governor could play in zemstvo affairs. When Kosich, an army general with a distinguished record arrived on the scene, the Saratov zemstvo was in a state of near somnolence.[48] Determined to stimulate the economic development of the province, Kosich tried to encourage the zemstvo to enact more ambitious programs, and in particular to increase its efforts in the areas of agriculture and food supply. The governor argued that the serious decline of local farming resulted in part from the poor state of the peasant economy and that matters could be significantly improved if the zemstvo placed greater emphasis on educating the rural dwellers and providing cheap credit so the peasants could more easily improve their lands and herds. Kosich also chided the zemstvo for neglecting the improvement of roads, which would be of immediate benefit to the province, while they agitated for the expansion of railways, whose economic impact was, in the short run at least, disruptive. Beyond this, Kosich stressed the inadequate size and condition of the grain reserves stored against crop failure and famine. The governor recognized that the peasants had been loath to put aside grain in good times, but he insisted that there was no excuse for this situation to continue. The zemstvo was responsible for gathering and protecting the grain, and it had to exercise the leadership necessary to achieve this goal.

Governor Kosich's public statements to the zemstvos contained many stinging criticisms, yet his approach did not provoke a negative response. On the contrary, the zemstvo adopted many of his ideas and the *nachal'nik gubernii* came to enjoy considerable popularity in zemstvo circles because he always combined his remarks about the zemstvo's shortcomings with expressions of respect for the institution and solicitude for its well-being. This approach must have been particularly encouraging as the "counterreform" of the zemstvos loomed on the horizon. In 1888 Kosich assured zemstro members that the intended legislation would not affect the functions of local self-government. And when the new law was finally issued, he told the assembly that opened in December 1890 that the zemstvo would continue to be "the

47. B. B. Veselovskii, *Istoriia zemstva za sorok let* (4 vols.; SPb., 1909–1911), 4, pp. 487, 624–25.
48. Ibid., p. 381.

most hopeful element for the proper development of the province and for the satisfaction of its most important needs."[49]

Kosich's success in managing relations with the zemstvo underlines once more the importance of tact and personality in governing the provinces. The zemstvos were not monolithic but contained in almost every case a wide variety of "parties," often rooted as much in family and group ties as in political ideology. Any governor, be he "liberal" or "conservative," could probably find some basis of support in the zemstvo assembly or even the executive board. A governor's relations with the zemstvos thus depended less on objective conditions and political currents than on subjective factors—a tolerance for a measure of dissonance in zemstvo operations, an ability to compromise, and a willingness to see zemstvo activity in terms of the half-full rather than the half-empty glass. Moreover, the primacy of personality meant that an incoming governor had a good chance of avoiding conflict with the zemstvo if he did not arrive with a host of preconceived notions and if he were patient enough to get his bearings before undertaking to guide the province.

Of course, not all governors possessed the requisite tact, and for this reason there were wide swings in governor-zemstvo relations as one *nachal'nik gubernii* succeeded another, especially in places like Tver, where the zemstvo's high degree of political consciousness had defined party lines clearly. But even in less politicized gubernias, rapid shifts in governor-zemstvo relations often occurred.[50] These changes, however, did not significantly interrupt the process of defining the balance of power between the administration and self-government or prevent their cooperation in the work of local development.

In concentrating on the relations between the governors and zemstvos, students of the Russian provinces have paid almost no attention to the relations between the *nachal'niki gubernii* and urban institutions. This is surprising because disputes between governors and city councils (dumas) appear to have been at least as frequent as clashes with the zemstvos. Moreover, it would seem that the relative tact and decorum that characterized governor-zemstvo disputes were often absent from governor-duma quarrels.

49. Kosich, *Tsirkuliary, ukazaniia i rechi*, pp. 53–64. Quoted passage is on p. 60.
50. See for example, the last report of Tver's Governor Somov (GAKO, f. Kants. tver. gub., op. 2, d. 531, "Otchet za 1889 g.") and one of the first submitted by his successor, Governor P. D. Akhlestyshev (ibid., d. 549, "Otchet za 1891 g."). Somov's report contains no anti-zemstvo rhetoric, Akhlestyshev's is full of it. See also Veselovskii, 4, pp. 376, 407, 486–87.

The legal position of urban self-government under the terms of both the original city statute of 1870 and the "counterreform" measure of 1892 was very close to that of the zemstvos; and the powers that the governors enjoyed *vis-à-vis* these institutions were virtually identical.[51] The municipal law of 1870 asserted the basic autonomy (*samostoiatel'nost'*) of city government. The governor's fundamental task was to supervise the legality of the decisions taken by the dumas and their executive boards. Objections to these measures, when made either by the governors or private citizens, were to be examined by the committee on urban affairs. In almost every case, its rulings could be appealed to the Senate.[52]

The 1892 regulations tightened controls considerably and greatly enhanced the power of the governor. The new law listed a large number of specific duma measures that required the approval of the *nachal'nik gubernii*. Beyond this, the governor was to examine city council decisions for both their "correctness" and their legality. He could protest measures that he felt broke the law, exceeded the limits of municipal government's authority, did not correspond to the general needs of the state, or "clearly" violated the interests of the local population. As with the 1870 law, matters protested by the governor were turned over to a standing committee (now renamed the committee on zemstvo and urban affairs). But appeal of committee decisions to the Senate was limited to those questions that concerned the legality of council actions.[53]

The 1892 statute also expanded gubernatorial control over the executive boards of the dumas. Under the 1870 law, governors had confirmed only the mayors of uezd towns in their posts; now they continued to confirm not only these mayors but also the members of all the executive boards in the province. Only the mayor of the gubernia capital required MVD approval.[54] In addition, article 101 of the new statute gave governors the right to conduct inspections of the work of town executives and to report what they regarded as misdeeds to the city council. Should the council fail to act on the governor's suggestions for change, the conflict would then be examined by the committee on zemstvo and urban affairs.

51. For a convenient survey of the legislation defining the powers of city governments, see Walter Hanchett, "Tsarist Statutory Regulation of Municipal Government in the Nineteenth Century," in Michael F. Hamm, ed., *The City in Russian History* (Lexington, Ky., 1976), pp. 91–114.

52. *Svod zakonov*, 2 (1876), arts. 1952, 1948, 2095–2100.

53. "Gorodovoe polozhenie," arts. 78, 11, 83–85, *Svod zakonov*, 2 (1892).

54. Compare *Svod zakonov*, 2 (1876), art. 2039 and "Gorodovoe polozhenie," art. 118, *Svod zakonov*, 2 (1892).

Although the legal position of urban self-government closely resembled that of the zemstvos, governors seemed more likely to intrude on the work of urban institutions than on the activities of rural self-government. Gubernia administrations regularly bombarded the dumas of even small uezd towns with a variety of proposals, from requests for information on taxes and arrears to procedures for the selection of church elders. Nothing suggests that governors engaged in a policy of "benign neglect."[55] For this reason conflicts between urban institutions and the gubernia administration appear to have been more plentiful than governor-zemstvo disputes. Statistics gathered by N. A. Zinov'ev at the beginning of the twentieth century show that the majority of cases coming before the committees on zemstvo and urban affairs stemmed from decisions taken by municipal institutions. This is, of course, not surprising in a place such as Moscow province where 177 out of 230 matters discussed by the committee between 1902 and 1903 concerned urban issues. But that it should have been true as well for rural provinces such as Viatka and Kursk indicates just how closely the *nachal'niki gubernii* supervised city governments.[56]

On the substance of the matters examined by the committees, we have, unfortunately, no comprehensive information. Using materials gathered during Senator Polovtsov's inspection in Chernigov, we can suggest that questions of taxation, land use, public health, and local commerce were the most frequently discussed, and these were followed by disputes concerning duma elections. Budget items, internal council organization, and materials concerning contracts and obligations made up a rather small proportion of committee business.[57]

How do we account for the fact that governors seem to have intruded more regularly into the affairs of urban government than they did into those of the zemstvos? Part of the answer lies in tradition. Since early times, the city in Russia had been a creation of the state, subject

---

55. Zapiska Kovalevskogo, no. 3, pp. 68–69, in *MVUOK*, 3, pt. 1: *Zapiski senatora Kovalevskogo;* "Zapiska senatora Polovtsova o sostoianii obshchestvennogo upravleniia i khoziaistva v gorodakh kievskoi gubernii," pp. 456–57, ibid., pt. 3: *Zapiski Polovtsova*, sec. 1; GPB, f. Revizii Polovtsova, d. 1724, "Svedeniia o predlozheniiakh sdelannykh nachal'nikom kraia i gubernatorom krolevatskoi-nezhinskoi gorodskim dumam za 1878–1880 gg."

56. Zinov'ev, *Otchet po moskovskoi gubernii*, 1, p. 84; idem, *Otchet po viatskoi gubernii*, 1, pp. 282–83; idem, *Kurskoe zemstvo*, 1, pp. 196–97. For a discussion of governor-duma conflicts in the 1870s and 1880s see V. A. Nardova, *Gorodskoe samoupravlenie v Rossii v 60-kh–nachale 90-kh godov XIX v. Pravitel'stvennaia politika* (Leningrad, 1984), pp. 152–80.

57. GPB, f. Revizii Polovtsova, d. 1723, "Vedomost' o deiatel'nosti chernigovskogo gubernatora i chernigovskogo gorodskogo prisutstviia, 1878–1880 gg."

to heavy government tutelage.[58] This pattern was hard to break, despite the "golden words" of the 1870 law guaranteeing the independence of urban institutions. Beyond tradition lay the matter of class prejudice and experience. When governors surveyed the work of the zemstvos, they were dealing with institutions that were dominated by members of their own social class. Municipal government, especially in the smaller towns, was in the hands of merchants whose attitudes and folkways were very different from those of the gentry. Many governors, moreover, had considerable experience in zemstvo affairs; relatively few had served in urban bodies. Social differences and general unfamiliarity with the workings of city government may have prompted the governors to watch these institutions more closely than the zemstvos.

More specific reasons for the governors' greater involvement in city affairs were the proximity and activity of municipal government. Governors spent most of their time in urban areas and saw their problems at first hand. Also, the governors' chief subordinate agents, the police, were concentrated in the towns and gave the *nachal'niki gubernii* a ready means of influencing the course of events there. Moreover, the urban dumas were much more active on a day-to-day basis than were the zemstvos. Under the terms of the 1870 statute, the city councils met at will, whereas the 1892 law limited the number of regular meetings to no more than twenty-four a year.[59] In contrast, zemstvos ordinarily convened in a single annual assembly. All told, the volume of business urban self-government could generate was considerably greater than that of the zemstvos and required more consistent gubernatorial supervision.

Tensions between governors and municipal self-government did not flow simply from the specific decisions that the urban dumas made. The institutional practices of both the city councils and the gubernia administration were also important. Governors frequently complained that the dumas' sloppy financial management made proper supervision virtually impossible. They also maintained that corruption was a fact of life in urban politics.[60] In Kiev, for example, Governor F. F. Trepov

---

58. J. Michael Hittle, "The Service City in the Eighteenth Century," in Hamm, ed., *The City in Russian History*, pp. 53–60.

59. *Svod zakonov*, 2 (1876), art. 2003; "Gorodovoe polozhenie," art. 64, *Svod zakonov*, 2 (1892).

60. Report of Governor Zubov, 25 January 1882, TsGIA, f. Kants. MVD, op. 3, d. 187, "Ezhenedel'nye donoseniia grazhdanskogo gubernatora o proisshestviiakh v saratovskoi gubernii," pp. 9–10; "Gorodovoe khoziaistvo v tambovskoi gubernii," p. 21, in *MVUOK*, 3, pt. 2: *Zapiski Mordvinova*.

had to intervene to prevent the city fathers of Radomysl from budgeting a considerable sum of money for the purpose of bribing St. Petersburg officials.[61] Urban institutions had their grievances, too. Most frequently they charged the governors with being lax in controlling the city police. As a result, the police were dishonest, failed in their duty to protect the people, and often refused to enforce the dumas' rulings.[62]

Available sources illustrate many points of conflict between the governors and the institutions of municipal self-government. But one issue was clearly the source of the greatest contention: the quality of urban life itself. By general admission, Russian towns were appallingly filthy. Surveying the situation in Tambov in the early 1880s, Senator Mordvinov stated that only two streets in the entire city were in satisfactory condition. "The rest," he continued, "are covered, during the rainy season, with a thick, deep layer of mud. Some of them, especially in the spring and fall, are almost impassable. . . . In the very center of the city, there runs a big ditch that is almost dried out toward the end of spring and serves as a place for the dumping of all kinds of filth, so that it is impossible to go near the ditch without noticing the stench. In the outlying districts of the town, which . . . are very near the center, manure lies not only in the courtyards . . . but also even under the windows."[63] Smaller towns suffered from situations that were similar and usually worse. In the late 1880s the Viatka administration, for example, undertook a survey of conditions in some of the provincial cities and recorded the results in the journal of the gubernia board. This document vividly described the dangers a pedestrian faced on the muddy streets of Glazov and concluded that sanitary conditions in the town of Nolinsk were "a threat to the health of its inhabitants."[64]

Governors were painfully aware of these problems. Indeed, if there were any consistent theme in their writings about local conditions, it was the need for making the cities and towns more livable. But almost as often, the *nachal'niki gubernii* expressed frustration with the inactivity of the city fathers. Writing in 1890, Governor Kosich criticized the Saratov city duma for failing to take measures to improve local

61. Trepov to Sipiagin, 1 February 1900, TsGIA, f. Kants. MVD, op. 1, d. 1182, "Perepiska ministra vnutrennikh del s kievskim gubernatorom o napravlenii predpologaemoi k postroike kievo-kovel'skoi zh. d. cherez gor. Radomysl'," pp. 1–6.

62. Khizhniakov, *Vospominaniia*, p. 85.

63. "Gorodovoe khoziaistvo v tambovskoi gubernii," p. 35, in *MVUOK*, 3, pt. 2: *Zapiski Mordvinova*.

64. Zhurnal obshchego prisutstviia viatskogo gubernskogo pravleniia, 20 July 1888, TsGIA, f. DOD, op. 223, 1888, d. 142, "Vsepoddanneishii otchet o sostoianii viatskoi gubernii za 1887," pp. 99, 105.

sanitation, and a decade later, Kosich's successor, B. B. Meshcherskii, wrote essentially the same report. At the beginning of the twentieth century, Riazan's governor N. S. Brianchaninov also complained about duma passivity and demanded increased powers to deal with the situation.[65]

When governors pressured city institutions to improve urban conditions and especially to upgrade sanitation, they often created tensions and anger that ultimately burst into the open. The charge of the Vologda merchants that Governor Musin-Pushkin had insulted them appears related, in part, to administration demands for greater urban cleanliness.[66] On the other hand, when city dumas failed to act with sufficient dispatch, governors sometimes took matters into their own hands. Using police powers and their right to issue decrees, they would resolve a question to their satisfaction without reference to the wishes of the city council. Frustrated by the duma's refusal to order the cabs operating in St. Petersburg to be covered, *gradonachal'nik* V. V. fon Val' ended this "hazard to public health" summarily by sidestepping the council altogether and forcing the committee on urban affairs to issue the necessary decree. Later, fon Val' was equally high-handed when it came to getting the proper designations on streets and houses in Vilna.[67] In much the same style, Chernigov's governor A. L. Shostak had the police forcibly settle a question of land use and urban pollution which the duma had proposed to handle in a somewhat more leisurely and legal way.[68] Of course not all governors supported urban improvements. Some sided with those forces that were opposed to upgrading local conditions. On occasion, such activity was linked to broader political struggles. Kharkov's governor M. K. Katerinich, for example, saw urban reformers as part of a larger movement with subversive intentions and used his powers to frustrate them.[69]

65. Meshcherskii's reports for 1889 and 1899, TsGIA, f. DOD, op. 223, 1890, d. 226, pp. 10–11; ibid., Biblioteka, 1 otdel, op. 1, d. 81, pp. 11–13. Brianchaninov's reports for 1900 and 1902, ibid., f. Kants. MVD, op. 3, d. 538, p. 17; ibid, f. DOD, op. 194, 1903, d. 110, pp. 5–7.

66. See above, pp. 80–81.

67. Zhurnal sanktpeterburgskogo obshchego stolichnogo po gorodskim delam prisutstviia, 10 October 1892, LGIA, f. Petrog. gub. po gor. i zem. del prisut., op. 2, d. 4, "Zhurnaly zasedanii prisutstviia 2 fev. 1887–10 okt. 1892," pp. 242–45; fon Val', "Vil'na," TsGIA, f. fon Valia, op. 1, d. 13, pp. 13–14.

68. Khizhniakov, *Vospominaniia*, pp. 86–87; "Zapiska o sostoianii gorodskogo khoziaistva v gorodakh chernigovskoi gubernii," pp. 556–59, in *MVUOK*, 3, pt. 3: *Zapiski Polovtsova*; GPB, f. Revizii Polovtsova, d. 1834, "Perepiska gubernatora s chernigovskim gorodskim golovoi . . . ," pp. 69–71.

69. Michael F. Hamm, "Khar'kov's Progressive Duma, 1910–1914: A Study in Russian Municipal Reform," *Slavic Review* 40 (Spring 1981): 23–30.

Gubernatorial conflicts with urban institutions were only a part of the picture of city politics, however. As in the case of the zemstvos, governors also had a positive leadership role to play. In times of emergency such as a major disaster, the appearance of the governor on the scene could have the effect of both calming the population and mobilizing local forces for action. This was certainly the case following the terrible fire that ravaged the town of Kashin in June 1883 and did up to a million rubles' worth of damage. Arriving shortly after the fires had been put out, Tver governor A. N. Somov inspected the situation and summoned Kashin's city council into emergency session. He addressed the duma and urged immediate steps to begin reconstruction and to aid the needy. At the governor's suggestion, the council set up a committee to assist the victims, appropriated local funds for that purpose, and petitioned the central government for additional moneys. The city then undertook to quarter the homeless in buildings that had been intended for use by the military, agreed to suspend local taxes for those who had been ruined in the blaze, and requested that St. Petersburg provide similar relief. Finally, the mayor committed the town to rebuild in accordance with the established city plan and to adopt safety measures that would help prevent a similar fire's occurring in the future.[70]

Not all gubernatorial leadership efforts were as dramatic or as successful as Somov's. Perm's governor I. F. Koshko worked vigorously to bring the Verkhoture city duma and several state agencies together on a complicated land exchange only to have his compromise unravel as the result of an ill-advised outburst by a local government official. But tact and the willingness of the governor to efface himself saved the day. Realizing his own limitations in this particular situation, Koshko decided to enlist the aid of one of the province's representatives to the State Duma who persuaded the Verkhoture council to change its stand. The deal, beneficial to all parties, was finally consummated.[71]

The nobles' assemblies, zemstvos, and city councils were the chief institutions of self-government in the provinces. But with the revolution of 1905 a new element was added, the State Duma. Strictly speaking, the Duma was not a provincial institution, but the elections held to select its deputies became a major event in local politics. The existence

70. GAKO, f. Kants. tver. gub., op. 1, d. 18884, "O revizii nachal'nikom gubernii gorodov Kashina i Kaliazina, 1883 g.," pp. 52–59.
71. Koshko, "Vospominaniia," pp. 177–81, BAR.

of the national parliament would create new problems for the *nachal'niki gubernii*.

The October Manifesto, which introduced a quasi-constitutional regime into Russia, caught the governors by surprise. A number of them were shocked by the tsar's decision to share power with the elected representatives of the people and resigned in disgust and disappointment. Once the dust raised by the 1905 revolution had settled, the governors adjusted to the situation though the changed circumstances made many of them uneasy. With the Duma came national politics, political parties, and unseemly agitation. Unfamiliar groupings emerged at the provincial level which were influenced by forces from outside the gubernia and beyond the governors' control. A new brand of politician appeared who could be a thorn in a governor's side.

A Duma deputy was a force to be reckoned with. He occupied a position from which he could publicly, in a national forum, question and criticize the actions of a governor and his administration.[72] Furthermore, the deputy might also be an officer of one of the provincial institutions of self-government whose actions the governor was supposed to supervise and with whom he might have quarreled over any number of local matters.[73] As a participant in a national institution, a Duma deputy enjoyed a status that, in the eyes of some governors, gave him excessive influence in the capital. And there were times when a deputy could put a governor in the shade. Writing in exile, Governor P. P. Stremoukhov complained that "a member of the State Duma, backed by his party, often had more influence with the Ministry of Internal Affairs than did a governor. [Thus] some local doctor who supported the opposition [could] come to the minister wearing a sport coat and be admitted at once, whereas a governor, dressed in uniform, might wait a week to be received and meet with less attention than the Duma deputy. In these circumstances, a governor's position was extremely difficult."[74]

For the most part, the governors' activities impinged on the State Duma only at election times, particularly during the early years of the constitutional experiment. The careful research of Terence Emmons into the conduct of the first parliamentary campaign reveals a wide range of administrative interference such as the prohibition and disruption of party meetings and the arrest of prominent oppositionists.

72. Ibid., pp. 88–96.
73. Stremoukhov, "Administrativnoe ustroistvo," sec. 1, p. 4.
74. Ibid.

The governors also put heavy pressure on government workers in an attempt to keep them from participating in party politics. According to Alfred Levin, similar abuses took place during elections to the Second Duma.[75]

Yet for all their efforts, the governors did not prove very successful in managing the elections. Despite government strictures, campaigning was vigorous, and the outcome disappointing. In the First Duma, the Kadets, the party deemed most dangerous by the authorities, emerged the clear winner; the second, was even more radical thanks to the participation of the socialist parties. Clearly, the governors had much to learn about electoral politics and about ways that administrative pressure could be used to achieve desired results.

Stolypin's coup d'état and the revision of the suffrage law in 1907 produced a more tractable situation. With a considerably narrowed voting base, local elections provided the forces of the left with less room for play. Moreover, after the "mad summer" of 1905, the political currents in the provinces flowed in an unmistakably conservative direction. Party activity declined, and politics reverted to a more traditional style rooted in personality, family, and faction.[76] Altered circumstances made it possible for governors to relax and adopt a more olympian stance.

In Penza, which had been a cauldron of revolution during 1905 and 1906, Governor Koshko was able to observe the campaign for the Third Duma almost passively. "Of course, I followed the elections with great interest," he wrote in his memoirs, "attempting to eliminate any . . . illegal influence. When the qualities of this or that candidate were discussed in private conversation, I gave my opinion; but in all honesty, this could hardly be called pressure. . . . Every elector, even one wishing to take into account the governor's views, cast his vote in secret."[77] Moreover, when the ballots were counted, Koshko invited the victors to dinner, and he himself sat next to Akimov, a newly elected peasant deputy, because he wanted to be able to come to Akimov's aid should the latter be ill at ease in the unaccustomed social circumstances.[78]

75. Terence Emmons, *The Formation of Political Parties and the First National Elections in Russia* (Cambridge, Mass., 1983), pp. 181–83; Alfred Levin, *The Second Duma: A Study of the Social-Democratic Party and the Russian Constitutional Experiment* (2d ed., Hamden, Conn., 1966), pp. 62–65.

76. MacNaughton and Manning, "The Crisis of the Third of June System," in *The Politics of Rural Russia*, pp. 194–97; Leopold H. Haimson, "Conclusion: Observations on the Politics of the Russian Countryside (1905–14)," ibid., pp. 270–71.

77. Koshko, *Vospominaniia*, p. 221.

78. Ibid., pp. 221–22.

Most governors tried to stay out of electoral politics during the calm provided by Stolypin's "bonapartist" regime, but some became willing participants and others were dragged in against their wishes.[79] In the western provinces, Governors A. F. Girs and A. A. Eiler gave active support to candidates of the Nationalist party in various local elections, as well as in those of the Fourth Duma, but when Volynia's governor A. P. Kutaisov failed to back the Nationalists, he had to endure the wrath of the local aristocracy. As a result of their pressure, the MVD removed him from office.[80]

On the whole, the ability of a governor to influence Duma elections was rather slight. And sometimes, inaction might produce more desirable results than intervention. In his memoir-essay, P. P. Stremoukhov relates an amusing and illustrative incident that occurred in 1912 while he was governor of Saratov. During the campaign for the Fourth Duma, Stremoukhov received a telegram from the Balashov uezd police chief informing him that F., a notorious radical earlier banished from the province, had returned. Worse still, F. had just been chosen as a delegate to the gubernia electoral assembly.

A day later, the governor got more bad news. F., who had gone into hiding after his election, had surfaced in Saratov. He made an appearance at one of the electoral meetings in the city where he delivered a fiery antigovernment speech to an enthusiastic audience. Fearing that F. might be selected as a Duma representative and so acquire immunity from incarceration or rebanishment, Stremoukhov ordered the police to arrest the agitator at once. After some delay, the city police chief reported to the governor that F. was ensconced in the apartment of one of the local opposition leaders, surrounded by his comrades; an arrest could be effected only by the use of armed force. Despite the dangers involved, Stremoukhov told the police to do their duty.

By this time, it was already late in the evening. But around midnight, the governor received an unexpected visit from K. N. Grimm, the highly respected chairman of the gubernia zemstvo's executive board. Grimm, an adherent of the Octobrist party, had learned of F.'s impending arrest and of the likelihood that force would be employed. This prospect frightened the chairman because he was convinced that if violence took place, F., wrapped in the aura of martyrdom, would be sure to win a seat in the Duma, whereas if the authorities did nothing, F. was certain to be defeated.

79. Ibid.; Koshko, "Vospominaniia," pp. 154–55; Kisel'-Zagorianskii, "Mémoires," unnumbered page, BAR; Stremoukhov, "Administrativnoe ustroistvo," sec. 2, pp. 4–5.

80. Robert Edelman, *Gentry Politics on the Eve of the Russian Revolution: The Nationalist Party, 1907–1917* (New Brunswick, N.J., 1980), pp. 130–36, 148–52.

Grimm's revelation confronted Stremoukhov with a difficult choice. Failure to arrest F. would clearly be a dereliction of duty, but the consequences of F.'s election to the Duma could be even worse. A dangerous radical would be free to roam the province, stirring up the population with his inflammatory rhetoric. Weighing these alternatives, the governor was inclined to defer the arrest. Yet he hesitated because he knew that the right-wing elements in the province, especially V. N. Oznobishin, the gubernia marshal, would be indignant if he let F. go untouched, and their complaints to the MVD could have the most unpleasant consequences for Stremoukhov personally.

Turning to Grimm, the governor proposed not arresting F. if the board chairman would go to the marshal and enlist his support for the plan. Now it was one o'clock in the morning, but Grimm roused Oznobishin, won him over, and shortly thereafter the marshal appeared at Stremoukhov's to ask that F. be left alone. At this point, the governor was beginning to enjoy himself, and he decided to play a little game at the marshal's expense. He reminded Oznobishin sternly that a governor was duty bound to arrest a wanted antigovernment agitator. The marshal retorted that F.'s election to the Duma would be a terrible stain on the honor of the province. Stremoukhov countered sarcastically by wondering aloud how Oznobishin, an ultrarightist, could express such solicitude for a dangerous revolutionary. In the end, the governor yielded to the marshal's pleas, but only after the latter presented him with a formal request in the name of the entire provincial nobility.

F. spent the night in peace, and Stremoukhov, too, got a few hours of well-deserved rest. At the elections the following day, the revolutionary was defeated as Grimm had predicted. Violence had been averted and the honor of the province saved by an exercise of patience and common sense.[81]

If tact and personal charm were important as determinants of relations between the governors and the elected institutions of the provinces, then they were even more vital when *nachal'niki gubernii* sought to mobilize elements of the general public for the attainment of civic goals. This type of gubernatorial activity was most common in the field of local charity where both the governor and his wife were frequently honorary members of leading provincial societies. Often the governor functioned *pro forma* and left most of the work to his spouse, though some governors insisted on being more directly involved. During his

---

81. Stremoukhov, "Administrativnoe ustroistvo," sec. 2, pp. 5–6.

rule in Tomsk and Kharkov, G. A. Tobizen was very supportive of local charitable efforts and helped energize a number of organizations engaged in assisting the needy.[82]

Aid to the poor, of course, was only one of the areas in which governors worked to stimulate the activity of provincial "society" with the aim of promoting moral, economic, or cultural growth. Orphanages, schools, public monuments, and local nature societies all might be the objects of gubernatorial solicitude. *Nachal'niki gubernii* were often very proud of their accomplishments in these spheres, and they figure prominently in their memoirs and reports.[83] In the governors' minds, this kind of work was one way in which they might leave an enduring mark on the provinces they ruled, though at times ambition exceeded capability (S. D. Urusov noted how he had dreamed "Manilov-like" of a grandiose and unrealizable scheme to improve the water supply in Kishinev).[84] But whatever the goals, governors advanced toward them by persuasion and not by command.

The papers of N. A. Troinitskii contain some correspondence that show how, as governor, he encouraged the building of a theater and concert hall in Viatka. Soon after he took command of the province, Troinitskii decided to champion the construction of this important cultural institution despite the fact that a previous effort had failed because sufficient funds could not be raised. In his effort, the governor turned to leading figures of the province, using the prestige of his office and appealing to the civic and individual pride of the intended patrons.

In a letter to Ia. A. Prozorov, for example, Troinitskii pledged his own "lively and active participation" in the work of building the new theater and urged the prospective subscriber to join him in this worthwhile effort. Not above employing flattery, the governor assured Prozorov that he had turned to him because of the patron's well known "willingness to come to the aid of any worthy cause in Viatka."[85]

With Alfons Fomich Paklevskii-Kozello, Troinitskii took a different tack. After praising Paklevskii's generosity, the governor strengthened

---

82. Adele Lindenmeyr, "Public Poor Relief and Private Charity in Late Imperial Russia" (Ph.D. diss., Princeton, 1980), pp. 177, 183–84, 191.

83. Kosich, *Tsirkuliary, ukazaniia i rechi,* pp. i–iii; Urussov, pp. 93–95; fon Val', "Vil'na," TsGIA, f. fon Valia, op. 1, d. 13, pp. 15–17; Gorshev to A. D. Sverbeev, 9 July 1883, TsGALI, f. Sverbeevykh, op. 1, d. 469, "Doneseniia pravitelia kantseliarii . . . ," pp. 2–3; Koshko, "Vospominaniia," pp. 258–59; Khoromanskii, "Vospominaniia," pp. 2–4, BAR, Khoromanskii papers; Sinel'nikov, "Zapiski," 59: 732–33; Baranov's report for 1890, TsGIA, f. DOD, op. 223, 1890, d. 249, pp. 9–10.

84. Urussov, pp. 97–98.

85. Letter dated 24 September 1876, TsGIA, f. Troinitskogo, op. 1, d. 2, "Kopii sluzhebnoi perepiski Troinitskogo s uchrezhdeniiami i litsami," pp. 35–36.

his case by pointing out the value that theatrical productions could have in raising public consciousness and morals. "Everyone knows," Troinitskii argued, "that in theatrical performances society sees, as in a mirror, the good and evil sides of life. . . . No moral book, no moralistic lecture can have the kind of powerful corrective influence on a person as [can] a play in which all the ugly and beautiful actions of the human soul are shown . . . by means of living example."[86]

Once the necessary pledges had been made and the construction of the threater was underway, the governor continued his interest in the project, prodding contributors and making sure that the materials needed for the building were delivered on time.[87] And when the work was completed successfully, Troinitskii gained not only personal satisfaction for a job well done but also the gratitude of Viatka's leading citizens. Long after he had left for a new post, Troinitskii continued to receive letters that thanked him for his efforts, informed him of plans to hang his portrait in the theater, and granted him honorary life membership in the Concert Hall Society.[88]

The survey of provincial politics found in the preceding two chapters reveals a governor who was more salesman than satrap, and a style of rule which depended less on power than on persuasion. This side of local governance reflected the pluralism that had developed in Russia since the time of the Great Reforms. By the beginning of the twentieth century, authority at the gubernia level had become highly fragmented. Autonomous officials, institutions, and social groups had multiplied; all demanded recognition and respect. As holder of the tsar's viceregal commission, the governor continued to occupy the center of the stage. But increasingly, he had to defer to the other actors.

In these complex and potentially volatile circumstances, a governor needed to both maintain his authority and give the various forces of the gubernia their due. In accomplishing this task, personal qualities, especially tact, were all-important, for the "persuader-in-chief" needed good will in many quarters. A sense of balance, a willingness to compromise, the ability to flatter and to cajole could greatly help a governor gain and keep the necessary support. A *nachal'nik gubernii* who lacked these skills or was unwilling to employ them faced the possibility of serious opposition.

86. Letter dated October, 1876, ibid., pp. 38–41a. Quotation on p. 39.

87. See letters to V. A. Paklevskii-Kozello dated March 1877, ibid., pp. 51–52, 57.

88. Letters of the council of the Viatka Concert Hall Society, 13 November 1882 and 9 June 1883, ibid., d. 5, "Bumagi ob uchastii Troinitskogo v raznogo roda obshchestvennikh organizatsii," pp. 2–4.

All this is not to say that governors never used their powers of command or that they lived in constant fear of ruffling local feathers. They often took stands they thought were necessary and right even though unpopular and sometimes personally distasteful. But instances of governors' blatantly abusing their authority were relatively rare. Moreover, when such arbitrariness did occur, it was likely the result of momentary frustration or misunderstanding and not of abiding ill will.

Of course, the kind of politics we have been discussing was confined to the world of the educated and the privileged. In dealing with the lower classes, governors were much more inclined to be arbitrary and to employ compulsion. Yet even here, governors encountered limitations. As the next two chapters will show, the governors' powers were theoretically great but the instruments of force available to them were often inefficient and unsteady. In addition, workers and peasants had definite expectations of the way that *nachal'niki gubernii* ought to behave. Governors who disappointed them ran very real risks. As in their relations to the upper strata of society, governors had to learn the rules of the game and keep to them.

— 8 —

Instruments of Force

Peace was the governor's profession. Among the many duties assigned to His Excellency, none was more central than the maintenance of law and public order. The *Svod zakonov* listed numerous obligations: protecting the state against its enemies, preserving the security of the tsar's subjects from attacks by thieves, swindlers, and bandit gangs, suppressing civil disturbances, and upholding public morality.[1]

Regular statutes provided the governors and their subordinate agents with wide powers to deal with almost all forms of criminality. But, in the latter half of the nineteenth century, a series of special measures augmented the authority of the *nachal'niki gubernii*. The law of 13 July 1876, for example, empowered governors to issue "binding regulations" (*obiazatel'nye postanovleniia*) affecting public order and security.[2] These regulations were not supposed to contradict existing statutes regarding crimes and punishments, but were designed to deal with specific cases not precisely covered by legislation already on the books. Governors were required to inform the MVD when issuing such regulations, and the ministry might overrule them if it saw fit or if it was convinced by the complaints of private citizens that the measures were improper. But once approved by the MVD, gubernatorial regulations would remain in force until the ministry or the governors, acting with the sanction of the MVD, decided to modify or to abolish them.

1. "Obshchee uchrezhdenie gubernskoe," arts. 314, 315, 316, 317, *Svod zakonov*, 2 (1892).
2. PSZ, 2d ser., no. 56203.

The law of 13 July gave the governors a significant, albeit strictly circumscribed, legislative authority. But the power accorded them by this statute paled when compared to the potential for control created by the infamous decree on "measures to preserve state order and public tranquility" (14 August 1881).[3] This law, designed to protect the state against sedition and terror, permitted the minister of internal affairs to place a section or sections of the country in an "exceptional situation" (*iskliuchitel'noe polozhenie*), which were of two kinds—"heightened security" (*usilennaia okhrana*) or "maximum security" (*chrezvychainaia okhrana*). In each of these the authority of the ministry or of the governors might be dramatically increased.

The state of "heightened security" was of special relevance to the governors because they were empowered to issue binding regulations to prevent activities that menaced the existing political and social order. Governors could arrest people who disobeyed these decrees, fine them up to five hundred rubles, or incarcerate them for as long as three months. In the areas where "heightened security" had been declared, governors could also close public or private assemblies and trading or commercial establishments, and expel any person. During this state of emergency, *nachal'niki gubernii* had the right to dismiss all employees of elected institutions they deemed to be "untrustworthy" (*neblagonadezhnyi*).

The law further gave governors the means to insure that local authorities used the power accorded them. Article 22 of the statute stated that officials who were found guilty of dereliction of duty (*bezdeistvie*) could be punished to the full rigors of the law and even to a degree that exceeded normal statutory limits. And because this stipulation might be applied to governors as well as to their subordinates, the *nachal'niki gubernii* themselves were under special pressure to employ all the means which the law now placed at their disposal.

Those articles of the law concerning the state of "maximum security" did not appear to give the governors any special powers. The enormous authority defined by the statute was to be exercised only by the MVD, governors-general, or by individuals especially commissioned by the tsar. Persons in command of an area during the state of "maximum security" enjoyed all the powers granted state officials during "heightened security" as well as a host of other rights. They could issue orders to all civilian officials in the region and could augment local police forces by establishing special military-police commands. When "maximum security" had been declared, basic civil rights

3. PSZ, 3d ser., no. 350.

were suspended. Officials in charge of the affected region were permitted to remove certain kinds of crimes from the purview of the regular courts, handle them by administrative means, or turn them over to military tribunals. They could seize property used for "criminal" purposes, and imprison any person violating their regulations for up to three months or fine them as much as 3,000 rubles. State authorities could remove the elected officers of the zemstvos and dumas, block any of their proposed measures, or forbid their meetings. Finally, governmental officials in areas under "maximum security" had the power to suppress newspapers and periodicals and close educational establishments for up to a month.

The existence of these extraordinary statutes undoubtedly increased the confidence of the governors and of their subordinates, but it is important to remember that until the revolution of 1905 relatively few provinces saw the law of heightened security applied.[4] During that crisis the government greatly extended the use of emergency measures, gave governors positions of command in situations where "maximum security" had been declared, and under certain circumstances permitted them to introduce such a state on their own authority.[5] Many of these extraordinary powers were terminated after order had been restored, though as late as 1912 all but five million Russians were governed by a type of "exceptional" measure.[6]

One further gubernatorial prerogative deserves mention here; namely, the right granted by a secret ministerial circular (31 May 1885) to employ corporal punishment in the suppression of peasant disorders. The governors themselves had urged this measure and saw it as appropriate to the problem of peasant violence and in accord with the peasants' intellectual level and world view. Designed for exceptional circumstances, this right was widely used by the *nachal'niki gubernii* and gave a brutal and arbitrary cast to their authority.[7]

4. In 1881 ten provinces (St. Petersburg, Moscow, Kharkov, Kiev, Volynia, Podolia, Chernigov, Poltava, Kherson, and Bessarabia) were placed in a state of "heightened security." By the early 1890s, the last four provinces had been removed from the list; but later in the decade one more gubernia (Ekaterinoslav) was added. See Donald Rawson, "The Death Penalty in Late Tsarist Russia: An Investigation of Judicial Procedures," *Russian History* 11 (Spring 1984): 44–45.

5. Wayne D. Santoni, "P. N. Durnovo as Minister of Internal Affairs in the Witte Cabinet: A Study in Suppression" (Ph.D. diss., University of Kansas, 1968), p. 198 and passim.

6. Hans Rogger, *Russia in the Age of Modernization and Revolution, 1881–1917* (London and New York, 1983), p. 52.

7. Zaionchkovskii, *Rossiiskoe samoderzhavie*, pp. 170–72; Nancy M. Frieden, *Russian Physicians in an Era of Reform and Revolution, 1856–1905* (Princeton, N.J., 1981), p. 186.

On paper, then, the governor appeared to be a genuine satrap, wielding awesome power, free from accountability to the people over whom he ruled. Yet, the preceding chapters have shown that there was a wide gap between law on the one hand and reality on the other. When the governor tried to exercise the authority provided by the statutes and ministerial circulars, he often found that the instruments necessary for maintaining public order and security were dangerously weak.

A major stumbling block to effective law enforcement was the absence of a coherent uezd administration. A genuine governmental hierarchy did not exist at the county level and the number of state officials there was very small. Much of the real power was in the hands of the local marshal, who was imperfectly subordinated to the governor. The several uezd standing committees were supervised by the *nachal'nik gubernii* through their gubernia instances, but his control was limited and indirect. Indeed, fragmentation, weakness, and irresponsibility were the chief characteristics of uezd government.

As a result, the governor was heavily reliant on the local police who were, without question, his direct subordinates. The governor appointed the police chiefs (*ispravniki*) and their seconds-in-command and exercised discipline over them and all lesser officers through the provincial board. But a variety of deficiencies made the police a frail reed in the governors hand, and his position of command did not beget real control.

The major weakness of the police force was its size. Even after the police reform of 1903, which created a new category of lower ranking constables (*strazhniki*), the ideal ratio of officers to citizens in rural areas was not supposed to *exceed* 1 to 2,500. In reality it was much worse. Things were better in urban areas, but the goal of one policeman for 500 civilians (400 after 1905) was achieved only in the capital. Official statistics suggest that a police-citizen ratio of one to 700 existed in most towns, but these figures may have been inflated.[8] Governors and almost all informed observers felt that the limited number of policemen precluded an effective struggle against crime and other forms of violence.

The small local police forces were overburdened with work. A list of their major obligations ran five closely printed pages in the *Svod zakonov* and contained over seventy items. In addition to the uphold-

8. PSZ, 3d ser. no. 22906, 5 May 1903; Rogger, *Russia*, pp. 56–57; "Politsiia," *Entsiklopedicheskii slovar'*, 24, p. 329; Neil B. Weissman, "Regular Police in Tsarist Russia, 1900–1914," *Russian Review* 44 (1985): 47–48.

ing of law, order, and public safety, the constabulary had a variety of bureaucratic, economic and welfare duties that were of the greatest significance to the public. The law code thus contained more than a distant echo of Peter the Great's decree on municipal administration which had proclaimed the police to be the "soul of civil society." Indeed, according to one legal scholar the tasks of the policeman in the late 1890s exceeded those of the tsar reformer's time.[9]

The police were expected to do almost everything, but their rewards were few. At the beginning of the twentieth century a police chief's salary was about 1,500 rubles a year; for lower ranks it could be as little as two hundred rubles. And these pay scales, established for the most part in the 1860s, were ideal norms. In practice, salaries were usually lower.[10] Conditions of work, too, were often deplorable. Describing the police station in Riazan in 1911, an MVD inspector noted a dilapidated and neglected building, dark, narrow, poorly ventilated cells, appallingly filthy outhouses, and a crowded and unsafe office area.[11]

Such conditions meant that few good men would willingly enter the service. Educational levels were abysmal. In the early 1900s, only 3 percent of all police chiefs had higher education and only 21 percent had had secondary education. Nor had the situation improved by 1914.[12] The district officers (*stanovye pristavy*) and sergeants (*uriadniki*) were even more hopeless; some were barely literate. Training for all ranks was almost nonexistent and the majority of policemen were simply former soldiers who had failed to achieve promotions and had been mustered out. At least one governor found it ironic that a man who in the army could not become head of even a small detachment might, as a police officer, be made responsible for the supervision and protection of thousands of people.[13]

Not surprisingly, turnover in police ranks was high. This seems to have been particularly true in the urban constabulary. In his report for 1887, Governor A. I. Kosich stated that in the city of Saratov there had been 230 staff changes in a force of 250 men during a single year. In

9. Ivanovskii, "Obshchie nachala," 76.

10. "Politsiia," p. 329; Yaney, *Systematization*, p. 335; Weissman, "Regular Police," p. 52.

11. Report of N. Ch. Zaionchkovskii, TsGIA, f. DOD, op. 47, 1911, d. 342, ch. 2, p. 66.

12. Weissman, "Regular Police," p. 55; A. Planson, "Detsentralizatsiia," TsGAOR, f. Pleve, op. 1, d. 316, pp. 7–8.

13. TsGIA, f. DOD, op. 223, 1888, d. 168, "Vsepoddanneishii otchet o sostoianii saratovskoi gubernii za 1887 g.," pp. 18–19.

Tsaritsyn the governor calculated that 300 different men had passed through the sixty positions on the local force during the same period.[14] The mayor of Chernigov complained that the turnover of the police took place so quickly that the city council's executive board had no idea what man was holding which post.[15]

Rapid changes in the police force had two effects: first, it caused instability and demoralization; second, it vitiated the possibility of meaningful discipline. How could the threat of administrative sanctions deter abuses among the police when an offender would have very likely left the force by the time any decision on the charges made against him had been reached?

Indeed, these circumstances combined to ensure that police forces remained corrupt, often incompetent, and difficult to control. Low pay made bribe taking a necessity, for few local officers could live on their salaries, especially those at the bottom of the chain of command. But even the higher echelons of the police were driven to take bribes, not always for personal gain but from administrative considerations. Clerical staff was vital to the proper management of paper work, but the sums provided were insufficient for hiring the necessary secretaries and scribes. It was apparently quite common for police chiefs to pay these supplementary personnel out of their own pockets and to make up the difference by accepting "gratuities." Governors had no choice but to wink at such practices.[16] Yet even when extra help was added to the force, police operations remained terribly sloppy. Business was transacted either extremely slowly with a maximum of red tape or very quickly in a careless and slipshod manner.[17] Such inefficiency, troubling for its own sake, served as a cover for a variety of police abuses.

The huge quantity of work that fell on the shoulders of the police exhausted their patience and led them to ignore their duties to the citizenry. Uneducated and untrained sergeants and constables frequently lorded it over the peasants they were supposed to protect, ignored their rights and abused them into the bargain.[18] But when seeking a redress of grievances against the police, the average denizen

---

14. Ibid., p. 19.

15. "Zapiska o sostoianii gorodskogo khoziaistva v gorodakh chernigovskoi gubernii," p. 552, in *MVUOK*, 3, pt. 3: *Zapiski Polovtsova*, sec. 3.

16. Urussov, pp. 30–31; Kurlov, *Konets russkogo tsarizma*, p. 70.

17. "Materialy, kasaiushchiesia polozheniia i deiatel'nosti politseiskikh uchrezhdenii kievskoi gubernii," p. 38, in *MVUOK*, 3, pt. 3: *Zapiski Polovtsova*, sec 2; "Zapiska po voprosam . . . otnosiashchimsia k politseiskim uchrezhdeniiam," p. 10, in *MVUOK*, 3, pt. 4: *Zapiski Shamshina*.

18. Weissman, "Regular Police," pp. 58–59.

of the village or provincial town was likely to find his complaint sidetracked, ignored, or lost. Lower police officials were reluctant to administer punishments to a subordinate lest the matter reflect on them, so they processed appeals with infinite slowness and used bureaucratic inefficiency to maximum advantage. The provincial board, itself virtually drowning in a sea of paper, could not hope to give proper attention to all the cases of abuse that reached it and was undoubtedly selective in its disciplinary role. Frustrated and feeling helpless, a citizen who wanted justice might turn to the governor.[19]

Confronting that citizen's petition, however, His Excellency might also experience a sense of frustration. To be sure, he would probably be able to solve the particular case before him, right the wrong, and punish its perpetrator, yet his action in this matter could have undesirable repercussions throughout the provincial police. Beyond this, even the most determined and well-intentioned governor undoubtedly realized that he could never hope to remedy the broader problem of police corruption and abuse.[20]

As we know, a governor's helplessness resulted primarily from the weakness of gubernia institutions. His small staff, the excessive burdens on the provincial board, and his own multitudinous duties all made effective supervision of the police practically impossible. Besides, the governor had relatively few means for keeping tabs on the police personally. Tours of inspection could uncover police misdeeds, but the number of such tours had to be limited.[21] Complaints from citizens were a useful source, yet they represented but a small part of police abuses. Many people feared police retaliation and so were timid about making charges against them.[22] Moreover, the *nachal'nik gubernii* knew that he had to move with tact and decorum lest he disrupt the constabulary to the point where he could not rule effectively.

In effect the governors were dependent on the police force, however much they might inveigh against its corruption and inefficiency. The police was one of the few institutions of the state that extended into the villages, and governors understood this. The police were their admin-

19. "Materialy, kasaiushchiesia polozheniia . . . politseiskikh uchrezhdenii," p. 46, in *MVUOK*, 3, pt. 3: *Zapiski Polovtsova*, sec. 2; Berendts, pp. 269–70.

20. Kurlov, *Konets russkogo tsarizma*, pp. 69–70; Skoropyshev, "Tobol'skaia guberniia v piatidesiatykh godov," in *Viktor Antonovich, Artsymovich—vospominaniia—kharakteristiki*, p. 35.

21. Urussov, p. 113; Kisel'-Zagorianskii, "Mémoires," pp. 188–89, BAR, Kisel'-Zagorianskii papers.

22. "Zapiska po voprosam . . . otnosiashchimsia k politseiskim uchrezhdeniiam," pp. 16–17 in *MVUOK*, 3, pt. 4: *Zapiski Shamshina*.

istrative eyes and ears and helped governors keep abreast of the main currents of local life.[23] They could query the police on a variety of specific matters from the truthfulness of rumors to information on a particular political prisoner.[24] Without their constables, governors could not hope to evaluate candidates for state and zemstvo service.[25] Moreover, when governors wanted something accomplished—improved fire protection, preparations for meeting an impending food supply crisis, or keeping bicyclists from riding in unauthorized places— they had to rely on these much maligned officials.[26]

The governors' dependence often made them reluctant to punish policemen or at least very cautious in disciplining them. Sometimes it was better to have a corrupt chief of police (*ispravnik*) who knew his job than an honest greenhorn who could not handle the position.[27] Competent men were rare, and governors had to make sure that in disciplining the police they did not either demoralize the force and increase the problem of turnover or undermine them in the eyes of the public and imperil thier effectiveness. The governors were encouraged in this by their superiors in St. Petersburg, as demonstrated by the example of Kursk governor N. N. Gordeev, who publically reprimanded an uezd police chief for allowing "complete chaos and lack of efficiency" in police ranks.[28] Minister of Internal Affairs V. K. Pleve in turn criticized the governor's action as "undesirable" because it indicated the existence of "abnormal relations between the governor and officials subordinate to him."[29]

In these circumstances governors were likely to defend the police from attack and sometimes even went to absurd lengths. In his report on the inspection of Kiev province, Senator Polovtsov noted a case where a district police officer forced a local noblewoman, Mlle Zaionchkovskaia, to submit to an examination for syphilis. The humiliated

---

23. TsGALI, f. Sverbeevykh, op. 1, d. 470, "[Materialy] o deiatel'nosti politsii, 1879–1890," pp. 19–39.

24. Troinitskii to Pasynkov, 23 September 1876; Troinitskii to A. P. Lysenko, 12 and 19 May 1879, TsGIA, f. Troinitskogo, op. 1, d. 2, "Kopii sluzhebnoi perepiski," pp. 37, 135–37.

25. GPB, f. Revizii Polovtsova, d. 1348, "Vypiska iz del . . . o nevypolnenii zemskimi uchrezhdeniami pravil ob utverzhdenii dolzhnostnykh lits gubernatorom . . . ," pp. 3–6.

26. Kosich, *Tsirkuliary, ukazaniia i rechi*, pp. 39–41, 52–53; circular to police 16 July 1893, LGIA, f. Kants. pet. gub., op. 3, d. 2691, "Tsirkuliary nachal'nika gubernii," p. 12.

27. Skoropyshev, in *Artsymovich*, p. 35.

28. *Kurskie gubernskie vedomosti, chast' neofitsial'naia*, 10 June 1903, no. 120, p. 2.

29. Memorandum dated 30 June 1903, TsGIA, f. DOD, op. 46, 1902, d. 135, "O naznachenii . . . Gordeeva," p. 36.

girl later attempted suicide. But despite both the subsequent scandal and a direct order from the governor-general to remove the offending *pristav*, Governor N. P. Gesse kept the man at his post.[30]

Nor was the Kiev incident an isolated occurrence. We have mentioned on several occasions the protection Riazan's governor Obolenskii afforded the clearly criminal police chief Gofshtetter. And in Nizhni-Novgorod, even more curious events took place. There the abuse of authority by the police was abetted by both the *nachal'nik gubernii* and his wife. Governor M. N. Shramchenko, it seems, enjoyed spectacular success with the local ladies, though he reserved most of his energy for a certain Berezina. Mme Shramchenko, unable herself to keep tabs on her husband's activities, enlisted the aid of Nizhni police chief Charnoluskii, who used his plainclothes detectives to follow the governor to his various rendezvous and inform His Excellency's wife. She in turn made Charnoluskii a special favorite, and her support emboldened the police chief to the point where his abuses became a public scandal. The governor, too, backed Charnoluskii and defended him as an "extremely attentive, businesslike, and honorable man, able to do much for the good order of the city." Did Shramchenko praise his police chief because the man knew too much, or was the governor too distracted by his pleasures to carry out the task of supervision?[31]

All this is not to say that governors were unable to exercise power over the police. A determined governor could shake up the local force, get rid of incompetents, and bring in new men, often with extremely good results.[32] Still the weight of evidence from both gubernatorial memoirs and surviving correspondence suggests a rather high degree of indulgence for police foibles. I. F. Koshko, for example, tolerated as Perm police chief a certain Chereshkevich, whose propensity for telling tall stories undercut the governor's confidence in the official reports the man submitted.[33]

A letter from the archive of Viatka's governor N. A. Troinitskii is also revealing. On 2 February 1882, the governor wrote to V. K. Pleve defending the work of the police chief of Kotel'nicheskii uezd, one

30. GPB, f. Revizii Polovtsova, d. 672, "Predstavlenie . . . o narusheniiakh poriadka deloproizvodstva v kievskom gubernskom pravlenii i kantseliarii kievskogo gubernatora."

31. Memorandum on Shramchenko dated 1 March 1912, TsGIA, f. DOD, op. 47, 1912, d. 19, "So spravkami o gubernatorakh . . . ," p. 15.

32. See two reports of N. Ch. Zaionchkovskii, TsGIA, f. DOD, op. 47, 1913, d. 254, "Otchet . . . po komandirovke v khersonskuiu guberniiu," pp. 118–21; ibid., 1914, d. 43a, "Otchet . . . po komandirovke v g. Vil'nu," p. 120.

33. Koshko, "Vospominaniia," p. 49, BAR, Koshko family papers.

Domashevskii. The *ispravnik* had been attacked by local people for reasons the governor did not fully spell out, though if we read between the lines he seems to say that Domashevskii was an effective but despotic police chief. A list of his achievements included a cleanup of the county seat, an improvement in tax collections, and the expansion of the local police force—tasks not likely to be accomplished without pressure. Moreover, Troinitskii himself was forced to admit that Domashevskii did have a commanding figure and a loud voice "that gave the majority of his requests the sense of being orders."[34] The rest of Troinitskii's letter was a further, more specific defense of Domashevskii, but the letter closed with the governor's stating that he was reluctantly transferring him to another uezd.

Governor Troinitskii was certainly capable of removing a police official when he had to.[35] But his defense of Domashevskii illustrates the nature of the constraints on governors in their dealings with the police. Good men, willing to serve in places like Viatka, were very difficult to come by. Even if they had some rough edges, caused a degree of local discontent, and led, as in Domashevskii's case, to "a mass of unpleasant and boring correspondence,"[36] governors were often willing to tolerate these shortcomings for the sake of a more effective constabulary.

Until the 1890s, the police were the only officials who gave the governors a direct link with the peasant world. Then, as a result of the "counterreforms," the administrative structure below the uezd level became more complicated. In 1889 the government created a new post, that of land captain (*zemskii nachal'nik*). The introduction of these officials marked a significant attempt by the government to regulate and direct peasant life. The land captains were to supervise the peasants and their institutions of self-government and, it was hoped, to end what St. Petersburg officials had come to see as a situation characterized by chaos and wild abuse.

Governors selected land captains from a list of candidates drawn up by the uezd marshal and the minister of internal affairs confirmed them in office. Ideally, the captains were nobles native to the bailiwick (*uchastok*) where they worked and were thus close to the people they supervised. In addition, the law required land captains to have either

---

34. TsGIA, f. Troinitskogo, op. 1, d. 2, "Kopii sluzhebnoi perepiski," p. 196.

35. See the letter dated 26 July 1876, in which the governor fired A. E. Porshnev, the Malmyzhevskii uezd *ispravnik* (ibid., pp. 28–29).

36. Letter to Pleve, 2 February 1882, ibid., p. 195.

higher education or sufficient experience in provincial administration to prepare them for their many duties. Combining local roots and expertise, the *zemskii nachal'nik* was to be a beneficent, "patriarchal" authority able to lead the peasants forward to both moral and economic development.

The power a land captain could wield over peasants and their institutions was extensive. He had to approve the agendas of the meetings of canton (*volost'*) assemblies and could suspend decisions taken by those bodies or by any peasant commune. He also had broad authority over elected or hired peasant officials. He heard complaints against them and could arrest, fine, or temporarily remove them from office. Further, the land captain was empowered to discipline any peasant who failed to obey his orders. The land captain also carried out a variety of judicial functions. These included rendering decisions in certain kinds of civil suits, particularly those involving peasants with local nobles, and in criminal cases in which the maximum punishment was not more than one year in jail or a fine of five hundred rubles. Nor were his powers limited by the letter of the law. The land captain could punish anything a peasant might do which, though technically legal, had caused personal injury or damages.

Finally, the land captain was charged with protecting peasants from themselves and from others. He could stop the sale of grain at exorbitant prices, punish usurers, and prevent employers from violating the pay clauses of contracts made with peasants. The land captain also had considerable power in the area of family law, particularly in cases of child abuse.[37]

Because the government introduced the land captain in order to improve law and order in the rural areas, the governors welcomed the new office.[38] Indeed, the establishment of the land captaincy was, to a significant degree, a response to gubernatorial complaints about mismanagement and abuses in peasant administration.[39] But from the perspective of the *nachal'niki gubernii* one significant problem plagued their relations with the land captains: the new officials enjoyed a large measure of independence and were not a part of the chain of command

37. This outline is based on James Mandel, "Paternalistic Authority in the Russian Countryside, 1856–1906" (Ph.D. diss., Columbia University, 1978), pp. 216–27.

38. Ibid., p. 230. Mandel suggests that the governors were not altogether honest in their praise of the new institution and said in their reports what they thought St. Petersburg wanted to hear. My own research leads me to believe that the initial enthusiasm was, indeed, genuine, but that later developments led to a cooling of the governors' ardor.

39. Thomas S. Pearson, "The Origins of Alexander III's Land Captains: A Reinterpretation," *Slavic Review* 40 (Fall 1981): 397–99.

directly controlled by the governors. Why land captains were given this special position is a matter of some conjecture and dispute.[40] The question remains open, but in terms of practical administration, the results were clear. The peculiar status of the land captains meant that although the governors played a significant role in their selection, these officials were subordinate to the MVD, which alone could remove them, and not to the head of the provincial administration.

The law that established the land captains also provided a means of control that was highly uncertain and operated at considerable distance from the *nachal'niki gubernii*. Immediate supervision of the captains was vested in the uezd conference (*s"ezd*), a body composed of *zemskie nachal'niki* and, depending on circumstances, a few other uezd officials. As a result, land captains often acted as judges in cases involving their own decisions and actions. Beyond the conferences, the only other local officials who had direct responsibility for checking on the captains were the uezd marshals. But they were frequently derelict in their duties and worked independently from the governors' chain of command.

At the gubernia level, the provincial committees on peasant affairs, chaired by the governors, supervised the land captains. But these bodies, too, were inadequate to the task because of their small staffs, high case loads, and voluminous paper work. Nor were the governors able to keep watch on *zemskie nachal'niki* through regular inspections, for with an average of fifty-seven captains in each province, the job was simply beyond their capacity. And matters got worse in the early years of the twentieth century. As central officials sought to take on the job of reshaping rural life, they imposed a growing number of duties on the land captains, which made the task of supervising their work more and more complex, and, in the end, governors could do little more than examine the proceedings of the uezd conferences. But these "paper inspections" were clearly insufficient. Governors were bound to remain in the dark about a great number of situations that called for guidance or for disciplinary action.[41]

The evolving peasant policy of the MVD which thrust ever greater governmental duties on the *zemskie nachal'niki* put the governors in a curious and frustrating position.[42] As the chief officer of the province,

40. For three conflicting views compare the arguments of P. A. Zaionchkovskii (*Rossiiskoe samoderzhavie*, pp. 92–95, 433–34), Mandel ("Paternalistic Authority," 205 and passim), and George Yaney and Thomas Pearson (*Urge*, pp. 79–96; "Origins," p. 402).

41. Mandel, "Paternalistic Authority," pp. 300–312.

42. On the "bureaucratization" of the land captains, see Mandel, "Paternalistic Authority," esp. chap. 6, and Yaney *Urge*, p. 95 and passim.

they were supposed to work closely with the land captains, but the peculiar status of these lesser officials made leadership difficult. Land captains could and did take their own courses of action no matter what governors might order, and such defiance of gubernatorial authority, though not an everyday occurrence, caused both administrative conflict and popular disaffection.[43] Yet governors could do little but wring their hands and complain to their superiors when they confronted unwanted behavior. Nizhni-Novgorod's governor P. F. Unterberger summed up the situation well when he noted that the land captain was "almost beyond the sphere of the direct influence of the governor who, witnessing improper action on [a land captain's] . . . part and his inattention to his duties, [was] unable to put pressure on the careless land captain to the degree that he could do so in regard to all other officials; [although] the governor's responsibility for the one [was] the same as for the others."[44]

Governors criticized the land captains for incompetence as well as insubordination, and such criticism was frequently well informed. By the early twentieth century many governors had previously served as land captains and knew well both what these officials were supposed to do and how to do it. Such governors were appalled by the low quality of the land captains and by the difficulty of finding suitable people to fill the post.[45] Moreover, they found the abuses of land captains, especially in some of the more distant provinces, shocking. Surveying the situation in Perm, Governor I. F. Koshko stated that the misdeeds of local land captains would have produced large scandals had they occurred in his home province of Novgorod.[46]

Yet all the governors' complaints failed to generate a significant change in either the quality or the status of the land captains. The MVD declined to undertake major reform even though the *zemskie nachal'niki* failed to act effectively in the crisis caused by the revolution

---

43. The famine of 1891–92 produced a serious case of resistance by land captains to gubernatorial policy. See Robbins, *Famine in Russia*, pp. 155–63. Nor was such opposition confined to periods of crisis. See Governor B. B. Meshcherskii's account of the problems he had with one of his land captains, TsGIA, f. DOD, op. 223, 1896, d. 28b, "Vsepoddanneishii otchet o sostoianii saratovskoi gubernii za 1895 g.," p. 11.

44. TsGIA, f. Kants. MVD, op. 3, d. 555, "Vedomost' o rassmotrenii del, voznikshikh v MVD po otmetkam Nikolaia II na ochetakh gubernatorov," pp. 120–21.

45. Osorgin, "Vospominaniia," GBL, f. Osorgina, papka II, d. 2, pp. 187–89. Governors' concerns were well founded. According to data supplied by the zemskii otdel, only 31 percent of the captains had higher education and only 40 percent had served in positions that had prepared them for the job. See A. A. Liberman, "Sostav instituta zemskikh nachal'nikov," *Voprosy istorii*, no. 8 (August 1976): 204.

46. Koshko, "Vospominaniia," pp. 230–36, BAR.

of 1905. The ministry refused to subordinate the land captains to the governors because that would have constituted an affront to the nobility and have led to the loss of the best captains still in service.[47] Thus when the tsarist regime sought to use the land captains as a means of effecting its great land reform, the governors still lacked the power to guide and direct these officials. Moreover, as George Yaney has shown, the MVD often intervened to check governors who pushed land captains too hard.[48] The tension between these two offices remained unresolved until both were abolished in the wake of the February Revolution in 1917.

In addition to the police and the land captains, the governors could be assisted in the task of maintaining law and order by the political police and the army. Both these agencies were independent of the *nachal'niki gubernii* and often took actions not fully in accord with those of the provincial administration. As a consequence, many governors looked on the local leaders of the gendarmes and the military with a certain suspicion, and this feeling was frequently shared by their opposite numbers.

Until the early twentieth century, the political police consisted of the local representatives of the corps of gendarmes who were directly subordinated to the Department of Police in St. Petersburg. The size of the gendarme detachments was quite small. In the mid-1890s there were about 370 officers and 2,500 subordinates for the entire empire. The period following the 1905 revolution saw the corps grow to 1,000 officers and 10,000 subordinates, though the number of agents actually in the field was never that large.[49] The gendarmes were supplemented and sometimes rivaled by the much more secretive security divisions (*okhrannye otdeleniia*). Originally limited to St. Petersburg, Moscow, and Warsaw, the security divisions spread through the tsar's domains after 1905.

The primary duty of the gendarmes and the security divisions was to combat threats to the established political and social order: major urban or agrarian disturbances and the activities of revolutionary organizations. The *nachal'niki gubernii* welcomed this aspect of their work, especially during the rising tide of opposition at the start of the

---

47. Mandel, p. 454.

48. Yaney, *Urge,* pp. 297–301.

49. Zaionchkovskii, *Rossiiskoe samoderzhavie,* pp. 163–64; A. P. Martynov, *Moia sluzhba v otdel'nom korpuse zhandarmov. Vospominaniia* (Stanford, Calif., 1972), p. 74.

century. Moreover, the years between 1900 and 1907 saw a general upsurge of political violence, and governors frequently became the targets of Socialist Revolutionary terrorists. In 1906 alone, at least five governors were victims of assassination attempts, three of which were successful.[50] And threats of attack continued to hang over the heads of the governors long after the revolutionary crisis had subsided.[51]

Still, common interests and a joint struggle against sedition and terror did not prevent tensions from developing between governors and the political police. The heads of the gendarmes and security divisions were careful to make clear their independence of the governors. They were punctilious in using a form of address, both in writing and verbally, that would remind the *nachal'nik gubernii* that in presenting him with information they were not giving a formal "report" (*doklad*), an act that would have implied subordination. Thus the head of the local gendarmes might employ the rather curt phrase "I am informing Your Excellency" ("*soobshchaiu Vashemu Prevoskhoditel'stvu*"), something that many governors found slightly offensive.[52]

The independence of the political police undoubtedly prompted a bit of gubernatorial jealousy, especially because the gendarmes and the *nachal'niki gubernii* were under the control of the same ministry. But most governors understood that the vital question of internal security should be handled by officers directly responsible to St. Petersburg.[53] What rankled was the fact that on some occasions the security forces kept the governors in the dark about what was going on in their provinces. In 1902, for example, the Department of Police sent out a confidential memorandum ordering its local agents to conduct their operations with their own personnel and not to inform the governors of the content of top-secret circulars.[54] The governors also knew that the gendarmes often sent reports to the capital which criticized the work of the provincial administration. These denunciations heightened

50. A. I. Spiridovich, *Partiia sotsialistov revoliutsionerov i ee predshestvenniki, 1886– 1916* (2d ed.; Petrograd, 1918), pp. 298–305.

51. Martynov, *Moia sluzhba*, pp. 120–26.

52. Ibid., pp. 129–30.

53. Dzhunkovskii, "Vospominaniia za 1913 g.," TsGAOR, f. Dzhunkovskogo, op. 1, d. 53, pp. 22–23.

54. Circular dated 30 October 1902, no. 6862, in Ministerstvo vnutrennikh del. Departament politsii, *Sbornik sekretnykh tsirkuliarov obrashchennykh k nachal'nikam gubernskikh zhandarmskikh upravlenii, gubernatoram i pr. v techenie 1902–1907*, p. 8 (unpublished materials held in the Slavonic Division of the New York Public Library).

the governors' sense of vulnerability and burdened them with the task of explaining their actions to their superiors in St. Petersburg.[55]

Often the governors had good reason to feel dubious about the gendarmes. As with all security organs, their work involved a degree of mystification that was far less impressive when examined closely than it appeared to be at first glance. For example, Saratov governor S. S. Tatishchev told A. P. Martynov, head of the security division in the province, how he had discovered the weakness in the gendarme's intelligence at the local level when seeking information concerning the political loyalty of T., a rural midwife. The governor had asked the head of the gendarmes and the uezd police chief to conduct separate investigations, but both their reports contained the identical phrase: "for the past thirty years [T.] has illegally cohabited with zemstvo doctor K." The reason was obvious: the gendarmes and the regular police had made use of the same source of information, a local police sergeant. So much for the myth of the security forces' wide-flung net of spies![56]

Of course, the gendarmes were frequently fully justified in sending in critical reports about the *nachal'niki gubernii*. Gubernatorial misdeeds were common enough to make the secret communications of the political police a useful means of central control.[57] Moreover, the gendarmes sometimes had reason to feel that governors did not fully support efforts to suppress dissent. Governor Baranov, for example, questioned the value of administrative exile and made use of politically suspect people during a time of national crisis.[58] From the gendarmes' point of view, Vologda governors Daragan and Lodyzhenskii both appeared to be overly solicitous of the welfare of political exiles.[59]

As for the secretiveness of the political police, it, too, was rationally

55. Stremoukhov, "Administrativnoe ustroistvo," sec. 2, p. 9, BAR, Kryzhanovskii papers.

56. Martynov, *Moia sluzhba*, pp. 73–74.

57. Report of V. Gofman, head of Mogilev gendarmes to F. F. fon Taube, 17 February 1909, TsGIA, f. DOD, op. 47, 1909, d. 143, "Prilozheniia k otchetu . . . Zaionchkovskogo po komandirovke v mogilevskuiu gub.," pp. 13–18; Memorandum on Governor Shramchenko, 1 March 1912, ibid., 1912, d. 19, p. 15. Collecting this kind of information and dispatching it to the center was one of the original reasons for establishing the corps of gendarmes (P. S. Squire, *The Third Department: The Establishment and Practices of the Political Police in the Russia of Nicholas I* [Cambridge, 1968], pp. 184–94 and passim).

58. George F. Kennan, *Siberia and the Exile System* (2 vols.; New York, 1891), 1, pp. 276–77; Robbins, *Famine in Russia*, p. 138.

59. See above, p. 88.

based. Security in gubernatorial offices was frequently lax, and confidential materials did leak to revolutionary groups. In Saratov, for example, a love affair between a leading local Menshevik and the wife of a highly placed official threatened to create a conduit through which information vital to the security of the province might pass into radical hands.[60] I. F. Koshko recalled that for a time he employed as the head of his chancellery in Penza a man who communicated with radical emigrés. (The governor noted that his *pravitel'* engaged in this kind of activity only while drunk.)[61] M. M. Osorgin was surprised to learn that revolutionaries knew of secret and highly sensitive political measures undertaken by the government almost as soon as they occurred. Writing in the 1920s, Osorgin ruefully conceded that had the government's intelligence system been as effective as that of its opponents, the outcome of the struggle against the revolution might have been different.[62]

The tension between governors and the political police was probably inevitable and even had some desirable consequences. But it must have reduced efficiency when a common struggle of all government forces against the enemies of order was called for. Such problems could be overcome, of course, but they were surmounted on an individual rather than on an institutional basis. When a governor saw that the leading figures of the security forces were competent and well intentioned, excellent relations might ensue. Likewise, when the head of the gendarmes became convinced that a governor had a serious concern for security problems, the two might work closely together in handling sensitive matters.[63] But such breaches in the distrust separating the *nachal'niki gubernii* from the political police were usually the product of "accidental" factors such as tact or personality.

As concerns cooperation with the military, the governors also found themselves on difficult ground. We have already looked at this problem in an earlier chapter, and here we should only examine in more detail the rules concerning the use of military force by the governors and gubernia authorities. Governors had the power to summon military units to assist civilian authorities when the regular police were unable to control events. They could use troops to maintain order at festivals, protect state property, aid the population in times of fire, flood, and pest infestation, transport prisoners, track down bandits,

60. Martynov, *Moia sluzhba*, pp. 143–44.
61. Koshko, *Vospominaniia*, p. 142.
62. Osorgin, "Vospominaniia," GBL, f. Osorgina, papka II, d. 2, p. 175.
63. Ibid., pp. 205–206; Martynov, *Moia sluzhba* pp. 129–30, 143–44.

and prevent or suppress all kinds of civil disturbances.[64] Governors made their requests for assistance from the military in written form, though in times of extreme emergency the law permitted oral communications either directly or through an authorized subordinate.

When calling for military assistance during civil disorders, governors were required to tell the troop commanders about the nature and size of the immediate problem and the possibility of further outbreaks. On the basis of this information, the military itself decided on the number of soldiers dispatched and whether artillery was required. When military units arrived on the scene of trouble, the governor or his authorized subordinates gave the commanders instructions on the goals in the specific situation, the places that were to be guarded, and the persons to be arrested. Guided by these orders, the military then took the required action, maintaining open lines of communication with the civilian authorities at all times.

The most difficult question in the event of civil disorder concerned the use of arms. Here the law divided responsibility between civilian and military leaders. Civilian authorities decided whether to employ weapons after they had determined that all other means had been exhausted. Once a resort to arms had been ordered, however, the military took charge and acted on its own, though the law again stipulated that troops were to shoot only as a last resort. Moreover, army commanders were required to warn the crowd of their intentions and to signal three times by drum or trumpet before issuing the order to fire. Once shooting began, civilian control of the situation would not resume until the soldiers had restored order or ceased their operations.

This law on the use of force seemed designed to permit both civilians and the military to pass the blame for shedding Russian blood to one another. Arms could not be used without civilian authorization, but orders to fire must come from the troop commander. (Thus the sequence of events made famous by Leonid Andreev in his short story *The Governor:* "The wave of a white handkerchief, shots, blood," was, legally at least, impossible.)[65] Oddly enough these cumbersome

64. Rules governing the use of troops were spelled out by the law of 3 October 1877 (PSZ, 2d ed., no. 57748). They were included in the *Svod zakonov* as an appendix to article 316 of the gubernia statute, 1892 edition. Reference here is to the *Svod*. For a thorough discussion of the military's role in repressing civil disturbances see Fuller, *Civil-Military Conflict,* pp. 75–110.

65. L. N. Andreev, "Gubernator," in *Krasnyi smekh: Izbrannye rasskazy i povesti* (Minsk, 1981), p. 265. Stremoukhov, "Administrativnoe ustroistvo," sec. 1, p. 10, BAR. The Andreev story appears to have been based loosely on the events of the Zlatoust massacre of 1903. But there the order to fire into the crowd was given by the military

rules, which were intended to prevent unnecessary loss of life, might have the opposite effect. By slowing official reaction to disturbances, they could make government functionaries appear weak and indecisive and so encourage the resistance and the violence the statute sought to avoid.

And beyond the question of the use of force lay another, broader problem. Military units were spread thinly across the vast empire, and even in times of peace they were not always available to meet local emergencies. What would happen if a war, which drew the army to a distant front, were to coincide with major disturbances at home? Would civilian-military relations, difficult in the best of circumstances, be able to weather the strain?

Consideration of the means governors had for maintenance of law and order again shows the pattern we have noted with regard to the rest of the provincial administration. The *nachal'niki gubernii* had to work through institutions that were inadequate, lacked cohesion, and were difficult to control. On many occasions, the instruments of force created trouble instead of preserving the peace and security of the gubernia. This was particularly true of the police and land captains who provoked resentment and sometimes resistance through their corruption and abuse. The army, too, was a frequent source of discontent, as were the gendarmes with their seemingly constant spying.

Though well aware of these problems, governors were often inhibited in their efforts to set things right. If they attempted to discipline the police force, turnover in the ranks would increase, and its already abysmal efficiency would decline still further. As for the land captains, the *nachal'niki gubernii* exercised no direct control over them but had to rely on the backing of the MVD and the support of the local nobility, both of which were uncertain at best. Relations with the army were always complicated, delicate, and even volatile. Finally, in the struggle against sedition, the governor might rely on the gendarmes but could not command them. Any attempt to restrain or direct the security forces was likely to generate a complaint against the governor himself.

As a result of this situation, much of the power that a governor supposedly wielded as imperial viceroy and provincial "chief" was illusory. But ironically, the many institutional difficulties that weakened the governor had the effect of dramatizing his *personal* role in provincial life. Exasperated by the insolence of office and the slowness

---

commanders after warnings had been given. This incident will be discussed in some detail in the next chapter.

of regular methods of redress, a citizen, whether noble or peasant, was likely to turn to the *nachal'nik gubernii*. And His Excellency, who could not hope to exercise general control over his police or land captains, might deal swiftly with a specific problem and thereby enhance the image of his authority. In this way the shortcomings of provincial administration kept alive the myth of the satrap and increased the number of occasions when the governors would have to handle matters themselves or when their personal appearance at some event was anticipated if not required. The expectation that His Excellency could solve matters on his own was particularly strong among the lower classes of society. Many times their naive faith involved the governors directly in those rituals of command and persuasion, defiance and submission, that took place when the instruments of state authority touched the lives of the common people.

– 9 –

Their Compulsory Game

The arrival of a governor at an unruly peasant village or at a factory besieged by striking workers was by no means an ordinary event and usually came after the efforts of lower officials—police, land captains, factory inspectors—had proved insufficient to resolve the developing conflict.[1] On occasion—and this was particularly true in industrial disputes—the workers or peasants might specifically request His Excellency's intervention. But invited or not, the governor's appearance automatically raised the stakes in the game, underlining the seriousness of the problem at hand and heightening the expectations of its speedy and just resolution.

For the governor personally, much was at risk. Although he might be backed by a detachment of troops and accompanied by key local officials, the uezd marshal, the district procurator, the head of the provincial gendarmes, His Excellency was essentially on his own. He would have to act knowing that excessive lenience could lead to the rapid spread of the disturbances and that the unjustified use of force could bring authority into disrepute. Failure to strike the proper balance might destroy his reputation and career. Physical danger, too, was

---

1. The following general discussion of the relations between governors, peasants, and workers is based on a variety of sources. Of great value are the volumes in the *Krest'ianskoe dvizhenie* and *Rabochee dvizhenie* series. Also important are the many gubernatorial memoirs already cited, especially those of Dzhunkovskii, Koshko, O-sorgin, and Urusov.

always close by, and in confrontations like these it was not uncommon for a governor to experience the bitter taste of fear.[2]

When governors met with workers or peasants the world of the state and educated society touched that of the common people. The vast gulf between these two worlds would influence the outcome of the confrontation, for the two sides held very different myths about and expectations of each other, and each had different goals. In the ensuing process of maneuver and negotiation, each party would try to make the other act in accordance with its own preconceptions and desires. To the extent that both were at least partially successful, there could be compromise and even harmony. Failure would produce violence and, possibly, death.

Looking at the peasants or workers, His Excellency saw them as essentially childlike. Ignorant, easily deceived and confused, the lower classes were at the same time basically decent. Their lives were hard; the poverty and misery they endured often led them to hopes and demands that were utterly fantastic. Yet for all their childishness and lack of realism, peasants and workers were rational human beings who might see things as they actually were if authorities could remove or force into submission the pernicious individuals leading them astray. But governors were aware that stubbornness also characterized the lower classes. Sometimes, no explanation, however tactfully made, would convince peasants or workers of their error; no concession, however reasonable, would restore order. When such a point was reached, governors might have to apply force: arrests, beatings, and on occasion, even bayonets and bullets. Still, the *nachal'niki gubernii* usually tried to avoid the more extreme means of compulsion, for they realized that spilled blood and lost lives disrupted the traditional patterns of command and obedience and put all parties to the dispute on unknown and uncertain ground.[3]

Governors tended to view both peasants and workers in much the same light, though they also saw certain crucial distinctions between the two classes and tailored their approaches accordingly. Governors looked at peasants through eyes familiar with the flow of rural life, experience gained as landowners, gentry marshals, and provincial functionaries. Peasants belonged to a traditional social system that

2. Koshko, *Vospominaniia,* p. 62; Dzhunkovskii, "Vospominaniia za 1905–1908 gg.," TsGAOR, f. Dzhunkovskogo, op. 1, d. 47, pp. 228–31.

3. See, for example, Dzhunkovskii's comments on dealing with a workers' strike during 1905: "Vospominaniia za 1905–1908 gg.," pp. 163–64.

governors believed was legitimate and basically just. Consequently, they usually regarded peasant disturbances with stern disapproval. On occasion, to be sure, a peasant claim might be justified and the governors would take measures to rectify a problem or at least mediate a dispute,[4] but in the main they sought to make the peasants obey and to accept the "proper" order of things. To achieve this end, they tried to use the peasants' natural conservatism and reverence for constituted authority.

Dealing with industrial workers was something different. Although close to the village in many ways, proletarians were part of a far from traditional system. Relations between the workers and their bosses were still ill defined and often harsh. In the eyes of many governors the wretched life-style of the factory hands was shocking and seemed much worse than the familiar poverty of the rural areas. Consequently, when governors encountered industrial disturbances, they often felt little sympathy for the system that existed in the factories. The grievances of the workers appeared justified, though their methods of protest were impermissible. In these circumstances, governors were inclined to see their duty as involving more than the restoration of order. They had an obligation to protect the oppressed and to remove the causes of future conflict. While trying to make the workers submit to the legal authorities, governors often struggled to find compromises on some of the basic economic issues in the dispute.

The attitudes of peasants and workers also influenced the course and results of their confrontations with governors. To a significant degree, what Soviet historians term "naive monarchism" colored the outlook of the lower classes. Seeing the *nachal'niki gubernii* as the direct representatives of the tsar, the workers and peasants gave them a measure of respect they denied lesser officials. The number of times peasants and workers summoned governors to hear their grievances, the almost unvarying politeness with which they initially received them, testifies to the high level of their expectations. The lower classes often felt that governors were able to dispense a direct and personal kind of justice and to remedy situations that lower-ranking bureaucrats could not or would not handle.

But just as governors saw peasants and workers differently, the expectations of these two groups regarding the *nachal'niki gubernii*

4. See, for example, the report of Vilna's governor N. A. Grivenets to Durnovo, 12 November 1891, in *Krest'ianskoe dvizhenie 1890–1900 gg.*, p. 114; report of acting governor of Pskov, A. V. Adlerberg, to Durnovo, 1 June 1895, ibid., pp. 295–98. Also of interest is the report of the chancellery of the Department of Court Lands (*udelov*) dated 11 December 1892, ibid., pp. 158–64.

were also markedly distinct. Peasants often held extravagant ideas about what a governor could actually do, such as overturn decisions made by the courts or even the Senate, and frequently they were overly confident that they could convince His Excellency about the rightness of their cause.[5] At the same time, peasant hopes were combined with wariness, rooted in a general distrust of all officials and, sometimes at least, tinged with guilt for having defied authority. Accustomed to a patriarchal style of rule, peasants hoped that the governor might dispense the fatherly mercy of the tsar, though stern judgment came as no surprise, and arrests, even beatings, were not unexpected. One even suspects that peasants accepted these punishments because such measures helped them to justify, in their own minds, their inevitable submission to the power of the state.

Conversely, workers had a clearer, more realistic idea of what they wanted governors to do and had a better understanding of what they could accomplish. Drawing on considerable experience, workers believed that if a governor came to the scene and saw their problems firsthand, there was a very good chance he could remedy them. Individuals might be arrested or fired, they reasoned, but as a group they were likely to benefit.[6]

A governor generally proceeded by a series of fairly well-defined steps in dealing with lower-class disturbances. First, if the peasants or workers were actively engaged in violence, he sought to end it. Often, he had already dispatched troops to the scene who might have restored order by the time he arrived. If not, the governor's presence usually sufficed to terminate disruptive activity, at least temporarily. Second, the *nachal'nik gubernii* sought to make the discontented elements submit once more to the constituted authorities. To accomplish this, he tried to persuade them that their path was wrong and futile. In the case of the peasants, the governor strove to make them recognize the "criminality" (*prestupnost'*) of what they were doing. In that of the workers, the governor would state categorically that their strike was illegal and that nothing could be done about their grievances until they stopped breaking the law.

Reaching the second goal was not always easy, especially when it came to peasants. The villagers were usually convinced that their actions—taking a piece of land, plowing a disputed field, cutting down

---

5. For an example of peasant fantasies, see the documents relating to the attempts of the peasants of Sukho-Karbulakskaia *volost'* in Saratov province to secure possession of the piece of land called the "Shakhmatovskaia pustosh'" (ibid., pp. 67–77).

6. Daniel R. Brower, "Labor Violence in Russia in the Late Nineteenth Century," *Slavic Review* 41 (Fall 1982): 417–31.

timber, refusing to pay a tax—were entirely just and that they were exercising rights to what was really theirs. Making them see that their convictions were wrong required considerable powers of persuasion, for it was here that peasant "darkness" and stubbornness would be most apparent. In such a situation the exchange of opinion between the peasants and the *nachal'nik gubernii* could be lively indeed.[7] The governor would have to draw on his knowledge of the peasant world and attitudes in order to explain matters comprehensibly and to negotiate without compromising his authority or dignity. When unsuccessful, however, he would have to resort to arrests or the birch in an effort to make the peasants "see reason."[8] Once resistance had been overcome either by persuasion or by force, the final act of the drama ensued. The governor extracted expressions of repentance and the promise, usually in the form of a collective resolution (*prigovor*), not to repeat their misdeeds. The matter was then usually considered closed, and His Excellency, along with the other representatives of state authority, withdrew.

Governors' dealing with factory workers usually took a different course. The *nachal'niki gubernii* had no need to convince strikers or those engaged in other kinds of industrial disturbances that what they were doing was a violation of the law. Indeed, governors knew that the workers often deliberately committed illegal actions to force a change in conditions the *nachal'niki gubernii* themselves were frequently inclined to see as unjust or inhumane.[9] The goal of the governors at this point was to assure the workers that their grievances would be examined once order had been restored and the strike ended. In many cases, such guarantees proved sufficient, and the factory hands terminated or suspended the walkout. If workers refused to return to the bench, a

7. See report of Chernigov governor Anastas'ev for 1885, in *Krest'ianskoe dvizhenie v 1881–1889 gg.*, pp. 444–45.

8. Cases of governors using corporal punishment to bring peasants to submission abound in the *Krest'ianskoe dvizhenie* volumes. Usually these incidents occurred as the result of a breakdown in communications, peasant stubbornness, or the inability of the governor to get his point across. Sometimes there was an element of genuine sadism on the part of the governors. See, for example, the report of the Kharkov procurator to the minister of justice concerning the beating of peasants in the village of Gaponovo by Governor fon Val' (report dated 4 June 1891, *Krest'ianskoe dvizhenie v 1890–1900 gg.*, pp. 132–33). Even more dramatic and unjustified were the actions of Orel's Governor Nekliudov at the village of Oboleshevo (ibid., pp. 180–97).

9. Osorgin, "Vospominaniia," GBL, f. Osorgina, papka II, d. 2, pp. 168–75; see also the comments of Tver's governor Akhlestyshev on factory working conditions, *Rabochee dvizhenie v Rossii v XIX veke: Sbornik dokumentov i materialov*, ed. A. M. Pankratova and L. M. Ivanov (4 vols; Moscow and Leningrad, 1950–63), 3, pt. 2, pp. 150–51.

governor might employ limited force and arrest some of the strike leaders, or he could ask management to pay off and dismiss those refusing to return to work.[10]

With calm restored at the factory, it was also common for governors to take up at least a portion of the workers demands and negotiate with the factory owners and administrators to secure concessions. Here governors often enjoyed considerable success. The improvement of conditions, the reduction of working hours, and the increased pay that often resulted from their efforts were enough to gain industrial peace for some time.[11]

In addition to peasant and working-class disturbances, a governor might also have to cope with another manifestation of lower-class violence: the urban riot. Triggered by fire, epidemic, or racial tensions, usually anti-Semitism, these explosions severely tested the personal qualities of a governor. Firmness, judgment, sense of timing, and physical courage were all at a premium. A governor could often check a riot in its infancy if he appeared in the midst of danger, removed or punished those trying to stir up trouble, or simply took small but visible measures to avert public panic. Conversely, if a governor became confused, indecisive, dilatory, or cowardly, an otherwise manageable situation was almost certain to get completely out of hand.

It is extremely difficult to generalize about governors' reactions to peasant disturbances (*volneniia*), workers' strikes, and urban riots. But it is worth looking at some examples of governors' behavior during such crises. The cases that follow are not "typical"; rather, they illustrate the kinds of actions governors took in the face of lower-class disaffection. Just as important, they indicate how governors used a variety of means—ritual, psychology, concession, force—to restore and maintain law and order.

In the summer of 1884, Chernigov's governor S. V. Shakhovskoi faced a major challenge. During the spring a group of peasants in the

---

10. Report of the head of the Tver gendarmes, 25 February 1892, ibid., 3, pt. 2, pp. 146–47; report of the head of the Vladimir gendarmes, 23 June 1893, ibid., pp. 367–68. See also report of V. N. Pavlov to the minister of transportation, 30 June 1903, *Rabochee dvizhenie v Rossii v 1901–1904 gg.:Sbornik dokumentov* (Leningrad, 1975), pp. 200–203.

11. Report of Vladimir's Governor Terenin to Durnovo 8 July 1893, *Rabochee dvizhenie*, 3, pt. 2, pp. 368–71. Also see the report of Irkutsk's governor-general to Minister of Transportation, M. I. Khilkov, 8 November 1902, TsGIA, f. Ministerstva putei soobshchenii, Upravlenie zheleznykh dorog (273), op. 12, d. 226, "Sekretnaia perepiska 1902, ch. 2," p. 130.

village of Chelkhov had illegally begun to plow the fields of a certain Plekhanov, a landowning merchant. Chelkhov was a large settlement composed of two communes, each governed by a separate "assembly" (*skhod*). In this case, members of only one of the communes were involved in the transgressions, but in spite of the relatively small number of people who took part, local peasant officials and the police had proved unable to stop them.

When the trouble started, Shakhovskoi was away on leave, and the vice-governor, using both police and troops, had restored order. But the peasants remained convinced that they were right. Soldiers were quartered in the village, and their presence was sufficient to prevent a resumption of the illegal plowing, though it was clear that the peasants would once again take over the disputed land should the military withdraw. Shakhovskoi returned to Chernigov determined to end the standoff, but the means at his disposal were few. The governor considered employing force, then decided it was too risky and in the end resolved to use his presence and powers of persuasion. This, too, entailed dangers, for as he noted, "success . . . could depend on a mass of accidental factors that were impossible to foresee or to avoid."[12]

Shakhovskoi proved to be a master of "dosage," moving deliberately in a series of carefully conceived steps. First, he ordered the uezd police chief to select six of the ringleaders of the rebellious commune and escort them to Chernigov for a private conversation. During the interview, Shakhovskoi condemned their actions in severe terms, and the peasants appeared to be contrite. But the governor felt that their repentance was feigned, sent them home, and told them he intended to visit their village soon. His Excellency journeyed to Chelkhov on 24 July, but before he arrived he sent word that the village's two assemblies should gather in front of the church. He ordered the soldiers drawn up in formation together with two piles of birch rods. Shakhovskoi himself appeared at the scene at 11:00 A.M., accepted the traditionally proffered bread and salt from the commune that had not participated in the illegal actions, and praised its members lavishly for their exemplary conduct. Rejecting the bread and salt from the mutinous assembly, Shakhovskoi verbally chastised them for their disobedience, refused to listen to any protestations of innocence, and ordered the arrest of one vociferous member of the crowd. The governor explained that their actions had been improper and had violated not only man's law but also God's injunction against coveting their neighbor's goods. He also reminded them that they had ignored the tsar's com-

---

12. Shakhovskoi to D. A. Tolstoi, 6 April 1884, in *Krest'ianskoe dvizhenie v Rossii v 1881–1889 gg.*, p. 394.

mand to obey gentry marshals, and finally, Shakhovskoi spoke of the terrors awaiting the guilty in the next world.

The governor's speech had the desired effect. The offending peasants spontaneously fell to their knees and remained there while His Excellency talked for almost twenty minutes. At the end, the peasants were fully subdued, bowed low to the ground, recognized their "guilt," and promised not to commit the offense again. But Shakhovskoi was not satisfied. He announced that he would not believe the peasants' declaration of submission unless they were willing to let the uezd marshal be the guarantor (*poruchnik*) of their behavior. The villagers agreed, and the marshal himself questioned them, receiving renewed assurance of repentance. At this point the governor was ready to take the commune's offering of bread and salt. But he stated that he would forgive them and accept their promises only on the condition that they join him in eating the gift. Shakhovskoi ordered the bread cut up and dipped in the salt. Each of the more than three hundred peasants approached their governor in turn, recieved from his hand a small piece of bread, made the sign of the cross, and uttered the words: "May God be witness to my repentance and to the truth of my promise." The "communion" service complete, Shakhovskoi again addressed the peasants, reminded them of the punishments God reserved for those who broke faith, and recalled to them the crime and fate of Judas. The speech produced a powerful impression on the now pacified villagers. Successful and satisfied, the governor and the troops withdrew.[13]

Shakhovskoi's handling of the Chelkhov disturbance was unique. But the account of his actions demonstrates most of the ingredients that produced success for governors confronting similar situations: style, tact, and timing were crucial; the governor must be stern, aloof, and cool. He needed to make his case without being unduly offensive and be sensitive enough to the peasants' mood to know when to relent and forgive. When speaking to peasants, the *nachal'nik gubernii* sought to touch the proper feelings, to utilize their basic respect for authority, reverence for God's law and the tsar's command, and fear of divine retribution. Shakhovskoi's dramatic communion service drew heavily on all these things as well as the sense of community which still existed between members of the noble estate and the lower classes. All the while, the governor never let the peasants forget that the sanctions of force, the sticks and the soldiers, were available to him should everything else fail.

Two decades later, S. D. Urusov defused a similarly difficult situation in the Bessarabian village of Korneshty, and his account suggested

13. Ibid., pp. 395–96.

that the elements that went into Shakhovskoi's success could be effectively recombined to meet differing circumstances. Approach the peasants as rational people, Urusov advised. Avoid shouts and threats, for a dispassionate manner and a "certain amount of bonhomie" could do much to secure mutual understanding. Then work on the peasants' basic respect for law and order and their desire to see matters settled in a "proper manner." But, the governor added, be prepared for trouble. "Have in reserve, as a sort of *ultima ratio,* a disciplined military force. . . ."[14]

If the examples of Shakhovskoi and Urusov help us to see how a governor might cope successfully with peasant *volneniia,* then Riazan's governor N. S. Brianchaninov's handling of the strike at the Khludov textile mill in Egorevsk demonstrates how a *nachal'nik gubernii* could treat worker disturbances. On 25 May 1893, some 3,000 workers laid down their tools. They complained of low and infrequent pay, an increase in the work load, the introduction of a night shift, and a variety of other abuses by the factory management. The work stoppage was accompanied by considerable violence. Strikers broke windows at the factory, stole account books, robbed the company store, wrecked several machines along with some of the finished goods, and forced open a cash box containing several thousand rubles. When it became clear that the local authorities could not terminate the disturbances, Brianchaninov dispatched his vice-governor and two batallions of troops. They restored order and temporarily closed the plant. In the early morning of the twenty-seventh, the governor, who had been on a tour of inspection in an outlying region of the province, appeared at the scene.[15]

At the outset, the governor met with the elected representatives of the workers, and after listening to their complaints, read them a stern lecture. Their actions were illegal, and their demands, presented in such a way, could not be met. At the same time, the governor held out the hope of change. He urged the workers to turn to management and ask that they reopen the plant as soon as was feasible. He advised them that they could not make *demands* on their employers though they might *request* improvements in conditions. Of course, he added, all decisions concerning the factory depended "entirely on the will of the owners."[16] The majority of the workers appeared willing to accept the governor's dictates, but a minority remained unreconciled.

14. Urussov, pp. 105–111.

15. Background derived from Brianchaninov's report for 1893, TsGIA, f. DOD, op. 223, 1894, d. 207, pp. 13–14.

16. Brianchaninov to I. N. Durnovo, 21 July 1893, *Rabochee dvizhenie,* 3, pt. 2, pp. 315–16.

Although he had calmed the workers and defused the immediate prospect of further violence, Brianchaninov recognized that the situation was still explosive. He therefore turned to the factory owners and assumed the role of mediator in the dispute. The governor proposed that the administration of the plant undertake a number of specific measures. While the shop was closed, workers who lived at the factory should be allowed to obtain food from the company store, the cost of which could be deducted from future wages. Workers should also be given the pay they were owed at the time the strike began. The governor further stressed that the factory ought to be reopened as soon as possible and urged that the complaints of the workers be thoroughly investigated. Beyond this, he called on management to make a number of specific concessions, such as paying the workers twice instead of once per month, reducing the length of the night shift, and ceasing night work before Sundays and holidays. The employers indicated that they were willing to follow some of the governor's suggestions. With peace restored and a process of negotiation and reform under way, Brianchaninov returned to Riazan on the first of June.[17]

Nevertheless, the governor continued to be involved with the situation in Egorevsk. Once in Riazan, Brianchaninov assembled a task force of leading gubernia officials and representatives of the courts to study the Khludov factory and its problems. Brianchaninov himself moved in two directions. Using his police powers, he removed many of the strike leaders from the factory and the town and simultaneously pressured management to reopen the factory and to effect needed reforms. By 10 June, he had achieved his goals. Work resumed at the plant; the owners abolished night work before major holidays and took steps to see that the day shift on Saturdays ended promptly at 5:00 P.M. The owners also indicated that they would be willing to meet other demands the workers had made.

Brianchaninov felt that circumstances at the factory were still dangerous, however. He was particularly concerned because the burdens of the Khludov workers were exceptional when compared to conditions at other factories in the area. The night work imposed by the factory administration was physically demanding and financially unrewarding. Workers were paid according to the quality of the goods they produced, and those who worked at night tended to make more mistakes than those who did not. In addition, the governor believed that as long as the Khludov factory continued to be managed by Mr. Rigg, an Englishman, things were not likely to be very stable. With almost no

17. Ibid., 316–18.

knowledge of Russian, Rigg was dangerously limited in his ability to negotiate directly with the workers.[18]

During the summer, the factory owners dealt with many of the problems the governor had pointed out. They fired Rigg and several lesser factory officials, began paying their employees twice monthly, cut the length of the night shift to six hours, and again reviewed other complaints of the workers. But Brianchaninov was convinced that more extensive reforms were needed. In particular, he urged that workers not be paid in accordance with the quality of their product because this practice gave management the means of abitrarily reducing wages. As a result, Khludov hands averaged ten to forty rubles less a month than did comparable workers in Moscow.[19]

Brianchaninov's assessment of the situation at the Egorevsk factory proved correct. The lingering discontents of the workers flared again in a strike that lasted from October second to the seventh, after which the hands gradually began returning to the mill. On the eleventh the governor issued a proclamation to the remaining strikers and once more stated that work stoppages and demands for pay increases were illegal and no action could be taken on their outstanding grievances while they remained in violation of the law. At the same time, Brianchaninov sought to assure the workers that he was proposing measures to improve conditions and alleviate abuses.[20] The governor's approach was apparently successful because by the thirteenth the factory was again operating with a full crew.[21]

Brianchaninov also tried to push for further reforms at the factory and in a report to the minister of internal affairs again outlined his belief that the workers' claims were generally reasonable and just. The governor informed his superior that he was putting heavy pressure on management to meet the workers at least half way, though in November he had only received assurances that changes would be made. Writing to the emperor sometime later, Brianchaninov once more stated that the factory owners had abolished night work before Sundays and holidays, removed some of the more abusive lower echelon supervisors, and established a special office to look into worker complaints on a regular basis. The governor expressed optimism that in the future disputes at the Khludov works could be resolved peacefully.[22]

18. Ibid., 319–20.
19. Brianchaninov to Durnovo, 10 September 1893, ibid., pp. 329–32.
20. Ibid., 341–42.
21. Report for 1893, TsGIA, f. DOD, op. 223, 1894, d. 207, p. 15.
22. Report to Durnovo dated 18 November 1893, *Rabochee dvizhenie*, 3, pt. 2, pp. 342–49; report to the Emperor, TsGIA, f. DOD, op. 223, 1894, d. 207, pp. 15–16.

Brianchaninov's actions during the Khludov strike illustrate many of the basic techniques that governors employed in settling industrial disputes. Firmness in the restoration of order was combined with an openly declared mediating role which often made the *nachal'nik gubernii* a spokesman for workers' interests not only with the factory management but also with the MVD and the emperor. By asserting that the majority of the workers' demands were just, the governor could pressure management and develop support for a compromise solution to the conflict. Indeed, the documents dealing with the Khludov strike and other instances of labor conflict indicate that Brianchaninov and many of his colleagues possessed an anti-industrial if not an anti-capitalist bias and regarded factory conditions as inherently exploitative. In addition, they saw the workers as a dangerous force that had to be mollified if possible. Available evidence also suggests that workers often sensed the governors' underlying assumptions, so that, in the case of the Khludov factory, mill hands were not afraid to resume their strike when the desired reforms were slow in coming. They did so, confident that the *nachal'nik gubernii* was more likely to renew pressure on management than to use force to crush resistance at the plant.

The rather intricate interplay between governors, workers, factory managers, and central authorities which characterized many industrial disputes differed markedly from the handling of most peasant disturbances. The latter situations were starker, and the prospects for mediation and compromise correspondingly fewer. Most cases of peasant resistance involved conflicts over the ownership or usage of land or some other kind of property. Here it was difficult to find a middle ground, and should moral pressure and fatherly persuasion fail, the governor would have had to employ force. In factory disputes, ownership of property was almost never at issue, and as a result a governor could find more room for maneuver. In these circumstances, patriarchal authority could take on a protective guise and may explain why workers were often more receptive than peasants to the intervention of governors in their affairs.

Although examples of governors dealing successfully with peasant and working-class disturbances are quite common, it is considerably more difficult to find material that show *nachal'niki gubernii* at work preventing urban riots. First, the number of such outbursts was considerably smaller than that of peasant *volneniia* or industrial strikes, and once riots started, handling them effectively was much more difficult. Indeed, the only real success a governor might enjoy was seeing that no kind of urban violence took place at all. But nonevents cannot be documented. Occasionally, however, a governor's reports can give us insight into how potential riots might have been forestalled. As governor of Nizhni-Novgorod, N. M. Baranov believed that he had done this several times.

Baranov apparently learned a good deal from his experiences in June 1884 when he had not been able to prevent an anti-Semitic pogrom. Although he had rushed to the scene as soon as it had broken out, the governor had underestimated the size and seriousness of the disturbance. He tried to stop the riot with only a small detachment of police, and though he had been able to disperse one fairly large crowd, he could not break up a much more formidable mob. Seeing the magnitude of the danger, Baranov called in the troops and with their assistance restored order, but not before rioters had killed nine Jews and damaged much property.[23]

As a result of the pogrom and the investigation that followed, Baranov drew a number of conclusions that appear to have guided him in dealing with similar riots later on. First, he learned that riots have small beginnings: in the case of the 1884 pogrom, rumors that Jews had kidnapped a young girl set things off.[24] Second, Baranov saw the value of publicizing his commitment to law and order, so he permitted the Jews to stage a funeral procession for the pogrom victims and kept troops at the ready in case of need. Beyond this, Baranov published his orders to the police affirming his determination to protect the Jews of the city: "All Jews living in Nizhni-Novgorod, baptized or unbaptized, are loyal subjects [of the Tsar] just as we and, therefore, the killing or robbing of Jews ought to be punished with the same severity as like crimes committed against Christians."[25] Two years later, when it seemed that another pogrom was about to occur, the governor acted with dispatch. He ordered the arrest of several individuals whom police had pinpointed as potential riot leaders, and because there was not enough evidence for a court trial, Baranov dealt with them by "administrative means." Two of the chief suspects were publicly, vigorously, and illegally flogged.[26]

Baranov again confronted a potentially explosive situation when cholera swept into the Volga region following the famine of 1891 and provoked considerable panic. In a number of places, riots broke out, stimulated by rumors and sometimes abetted by misguided and inept

23. Report dated 9 October 1884, TsGIA, f. DOD, op. 223, 1884, d. 196, pp. 6–8.
24. Ibid., pp. 8–9.
25. Ibid., p. 12. See also S. M. Dubnow, *History of the Jews in Russia and Poland* (3 vols; Philadelphia, 1918), 2, pp. 360–62.
26. Report for 1886, TsGIA, Biblioteka, I otdel, op. 1, d. 56, p. 8. The tsar's comment was: "Well done."

government policies.[27] Sensing the dangers to civil order, Baranov strongly supported the anticholera measures adopted by local physicians and took a number of steps that had both administrative and propagandistic significance. He kept the Nizhni-Novgorod fair open despite pleas to cancel it and also scotched tales regarding the causes of cholera which might have led people to distrust doctors and the treatment they were prescribing. Putting his deserved reputation for toughness to good use, Baranov also threatened rumormongers with swift punishment.

Later, when the number of cholera cases threatened to overwhelm the city's medical facilities, Baranov ordered that six or seven houses be rented as temporary places for treatment and, as an example, turned the governor's mansion into a hospital. The governor saw his gesture as having primarily moral significance in two ways: it would stand as a symbol of the tsar's concern for the people's welfare; and it showed that the gubernia administration not only supported the medical profession in its measures to check the disease but also that its highest representative had willingly taken on the burden of the struggle.[28] On the whole, Baranov's measures seem to have been successful. Although the epidemic that hit Nizhni was a severe one, no serious cholera-related disturbances occurred.

In all these examples of gubernatorial activity, it is clear that the successes enjoyed by the *nachal'niki gubernii* were based largely on their ability to tap the feelings of respect for authority, in particular gubernatorial authority, which were still strong in the lower classes during the 1880s and 1890s. Force might be the ultimate arbiter in disputes between representatives of the government and the lower classes, but persuasion and compromise played a significant part. By the beginning of the twentieth century, however, submission to the dictates of state officials, even those as highly placed as governors, had become less automatic than formerly.

The reasons for this are unclear. The economic downturn that took place after 1898, renewed crop failures and famines, and a decline in agricultural wages, undoubtedly played a part. So did a change in farming practices by landlords, the spread of education, the growth of class consciousness, and the expansion of revolutionary propaganda. In any case, the period from 1902 to 1903 forced a number of gover-

27. Frieden, *Russian Physicians*, pp. 138–53.
28. Report dated 7 November 1892, TsGIA, f. DOD, op. 223, 1892, d. 124, pp. 16–23.

nors to confront situations wherein the traditional methods of control
no longer worked. Meeting the challenge posed by these new circumstances would prove extremely difficult.

In late March and early April 1902, a series of peasant disturbances
swept Poltava and Kharkov provinces; during the summer of that year
similar but not as serious uprisings occurred in Saratov. The size of the
insurrection was extraordinary. In the two western provinces alone,
some 174 villages and as many as 38,000 people took part in attacks
on 105 different estates.[29] The scope of the peasant movement and the
swiftness with which it spread caught local administration largely un-
awares. Indeed, the success of the revolt exposed and highlighted the
weaknesses of the police and other institutions whose task it was to
supervise the peasantry.

According to the report of G. G. Kovalenskii, a Senate official who
took part in the judicial investigation that followed the revolt, the
land captains had been inattentive and had ignored clear warnings of
the troubles ahead. Then, when the storm broke, some simply hid out
until the governors and troops reached the scene. The local police also
proved ineffective, though not as cowardly as the land captains. The
low level of police performance was the result, Kovalenskii argued, of
long-standing problems of inadequate pay, understaffing, a lack of
clerical assistance, and a too extensive sphere of responsibility.[30]

The unexpected and unprecedented character of the revolt made it
impossible for the governors to use effectively the means of negotiation
and persuasion that had long served them so well. Particularly in
Poltava and Kharkov, the governors relied, to varying extents, on
extreme measures—punitive expeditions, mass arrests, beatings, and
even a form of indiscriminate terror—to bring things under control
once more.[31] It seemed that a governor's success depended on his
ruthlessness, his willingness to go beyond the normal methods used in
dealing with peasants.

The suppression of the peasant revolt in Poltava and Kharkov is a
tale of two governors. Poltava's *nachal'nik*, A. K. Bel'gard, was ad-

---

29. P. N. Pershin, *Agrarnaia revoliutsiia v Rossii: Istoriko-ekonomicheskoe issledovanie* (2 vols; Moscow, 1966), 1, pp. 227–28.

30. Kovalenskii's report is undated, *Krest'ianskoe dvizhenie 1902 g. (Materialy po
istorii krest'ianskikh dvizhenii v Rossii, vypusk 3)*, (Moscow, 1923), pp. 89–90, 94–
95.

31. In Saratov the situation did not apparently become as critical as in the west. But it
forced Governor A. P. Engel'gardt, by all accounts an extremely cultivated and humane
man, to make considerable use of corporal punishment (S. Dubrovskii and V. Grave,
"Krest'ianskoe dvizhenie nakanune revoliutsii 1905 goda [1900–1904 gg.]," in *1905.
Istoriia revoliutsionnogo dvizheniia v otdel'nykh ocherkakh*, vol. 1, ed. M. N.
Pokrovskii [Moscow, 1926], pp. 274–76, 388–89).

judged a failure and would be summarily dismissed; Kharkov's chief, I. M. Obolenskii, was seen as a success, rewarded with imperial favor, and made the object of an abortive Socialist Revolutionary assassination effort.[32] What accounted for the differences in the fate of the two men? Qualities of personality were probably decisive, but experience was important, too.

Bel'gard, who had ruled his gubernia since 1896, was immersed in the routines of his office and spread thin over his many duties.[33] In the past, as Kharkov's vice-governor, Bel'gard had had occasion to handle peasant disturbances by more or less peaceful methods,[34] and during most of his tenure in Poltava, the province had been quiet.[35] It is not surprising, then, that Bel'gard was slow to believe reports that suggested a major uprising was imminent. But when the crisis broke, the governor failed to make effective use of cavalry, did not post sufficient garrisons in pacified areas to prevent the resumption of violence, and held back from the systematic use of corporal punishment.[36]

In contrast, Governor Obolenskii had just arrived in Kharkov when the troubles began. He had had no time to familiarize himself with his staff or the procedures of gubernia administration, but he was determined to act swiftly and decisively. Because the vice-governor was on leave, Obolenskii handed the regular administration over to a committee of top local officials and immediately went out with the troops to put down the revolt. Obolenskii's military skills (he held the rank of general) apparently served him well, for the tactics he adopted were markedly different from those of the hapless Bel'gard. Whereas the latter simply followed in the trail of the rebels, Obolenskii positioned his detachment of Orenburg Cossacks in the main path of the developing revolt and checked its spread.[37] As a result of this strategy, the extensive use of corporal punishment, and the practice of allowing lesser officials to engage in indiscriminate beatings, Obolenskii suppressed the Kharkov disturbances in a matter of days, but the uprisings in Poltava just burned themselves out.[38]

32. Edward H. Judge, *Plehve: Repression and Reform in Imperial Russia, 1902–1904* (Syracuse, N.Y., 1983), p. 42; Spiridovich, *Partiia sotsialistov revoliutsionerov,* pp. 122–24.

33. Kovalenskii report, *Krest'ianskoe dvizhenie 1902 g.,* p. 97.

34. Bel'gard to I. N. Durnovo, 11 September 1894, *Krest'ianskoe dvizhenie . . . v 1890–1900 gg.,* pp. 262–66.

35. See "Khronika krest'ianskogo dvizheniia," ibid., pp. 629–48.

36. See the reports of A. A. Lopukhin, 11 April 1902, and Kovalenskii, *Krest'ianskoe dvizhenie 1902 g.* pp. 25, 111–12.

37. A. D. Golitsyn, "Vospominaniia: Obshchestvenno-politicheskii period," p. 61, BAR, Golitsyn papers.

38. Lopukhin and Kovalenskii reports, *Krest'ianskoe dvizhenie 1902 g.,* pp. 25, 108–10.

The lessons of Poltava and Kharkov, while not immediately clear, were ultimately disturbing. They suggested that force, vigorously applied, would be sufficient to keep the peasants in submission, and that leniency or even negotiation might be counterproductive. Kovalenskii noted that the mood of the peasants in Kharkov following Obolenskii's brutal repressions was better than in Poltava, where the much less severe administration had been ineffective.[39] Prince A. D. Golitsyn, an uezd marshal in Kharkov province made a similar observation.[40] Yet, other signs portended a sea-change in peasant attitudes: an unwillingness to accept the moral authority of government officials no matter how much force they employed. Kovalenskii's report contains the account of a Poltava peasant who, despite a furious beating in the presence of Governor Bel'gard, continued to snarl imprecations at his tormentors. When the flogging finally ended, the peasant stood, turned to the governor, made a low bow, and said: "I humbly thank you." Then he disappeared into the crowd.[41]

If the riots in Poltava and Kharkov during 1902 showed that traditional methods of handling peasant disorders were declining in value, then the tragedy that occurred in Zlatoust the following year indicated that the same was true of industrial strikes. Events began normally enough. Workers at a state armaments factory had become agitated when management introduced new account books (raschetnye knigi). In early March a sizable walkout took place, and the authorities dispatched troops. The governor of Ufa province, N. M. Bogdanovich, hurried to the scene, but before his arrival, the police had jailed two worker representatives engaged in negotiations with management. The arrests produced a massive demonstration. Factory hands demanded the release of their representatives; the police refused. Then authorities compounded problems by telling the crowd that the prisoners had been transferred to Ufa and could not be freed immediately. This falsehood was quickly exposed, however, and Zlatoust officials were discredited. When Governor Bogdanovich reached the strike-torn city on 12 March, he found the situation tense, the workers hostile, and the local administration in disarray.[42]

---

39. Ibid., p. 113.

40. Golitsyn, "Vospominaniia," p. 62, BAR.

41. Krest'ianskoe dvizhenie 1902 g., pp. 112–13.

42. Background is derived from M. L. Mandel'shtam, *1905 god v politicheskikh protsessakh: Zapiski zashchitnika* (Moscow, 1931), pp. 105–106, and documents held in the archive of the Ministry of Justice: report of V. Kazem-Bek, procurator of the Ufa district court, to the procurator of the Kazan district court, 22 March 1903; circular of Ufa governor Sokolovskii to police chiefs of the province, 30 January 1904, TsGIA, f. Ministerstva iustitsii (1405), op. 105, 1904, d. 11059, "O zabastovke rabochikh na zavodakh v g. Zlatouste," pp. 13–15, 116–17.

Available sources do not give us a completely consistent picture of Governor Bogdanovich or his actions in Zlatoust. M. L. Mandel'shtam, a defense lawyer for the workers later accused of inciting the disturbances, stated that Bogdanovich was "not the worst of the pompadours of that long-suffering province. He did not revel in administrative ecstasies, and by nature he was not a bad person, but he was a coward."[43] The head of the Kazan court who heard the case also charged a failure of nerve on the part of both provincial and local officials during the crisis.[44] But V. Kazem-Bek, the Ufa procurator who was an eyewitness to the events, as well as the protocol of the workers' trial, paint a more positive picture of the governor's actions.[45]

Bogdanovich was undoubtedly alarmed by the situation he confronted, and his concern may have been increased by local reports that exaggerated the hostility of the workers.[46] Still, he first attempted to use normal procedures to defuse the crisis: he received the petitions presented by a large group of workers on the day of his arrival and told them he would consider their requests. The gathering broke up, and matters appeared headed for a peaceful resolution.

The following day, however, the crowd returned in an unfriendly mood and assembled before the house where the governor was staying. At first the governor told them to go home because the case of the arrested strike leaders was in the hands of judicial authorities and he could do nothing, but the workers refused and continued to demand the immediate release of their comrades. Bogdanovich persisted in his efforts to get the demonstrators to leave. Several times he entered the increasingly hostile crowd in an attempt to discuss matters face-to-face, though the workers were unwilling to approach Bogdanovich and preferred to yell at him from a distance. Angered by this, the governor called to one of the shouting factory hands: "If you want to talk with me, . . . come over here." When the worker refused, Bogdanovich then said, "Well, if you don't want to come to me, I'll go to you," and started to walk in the man's direction. The people made way for the governor but then closed in behind him while the local police, fearing an attack, pushed in and extricated the *nachal'nik gubernii* from the mob.[47]

---

43. Mandel'shtam, *1905*, p. 106.

44. Letter of D. E. Rynkevich to S. S. Manukhin, 11 February 1905, TsGIA, f. Min. iust., op. 105, 1904, d. 11059, p. 110.

45. Report of Kazem-Bek, ibid., pp. 14–15; protocol, ibid., p. 152. In his study of the military, W. C. Fuller notes that the report on the events in Zlatoust prepared for the Minister of War was inconclusive (*Civil-Military Conflict,* p. 91).

46. Mandel'shtam, *1905*, p. 106.

47. Kazem-Bek, TsGIA, f. Min. iust., op. 105, 1904, d. 11059, pp. 14–15.

At this point, Bogdanovich attempted to break the deadlock by asking the police to warn the protesters that if they did not disperse, troops might be ordered to fire. The workers refused to be cowed and stood their ground. Meanwhile, the procurator and the local chief of gendarmes tried to go to the prison, intending to take statements from the arrested strike leaders and then release them, but the crowd blocked their passage.[48] Again Bogdanovich admonished the demonstrators that if they did not break up he would allow the troops to use force. He was answered by shouts of anger and expressions of incredulity: "You have no right!" "You lie!"[49] Convinced that he had exhausted all peaceful remedies, the governor turned to the commander of the troops at the scene and asked for the use of arms. The soldiers did their duty according to law. Three warnings were given, but the large crowd apparently either could not hear or refused to believe. The troops opened fire, and when the shooting stopped, twenty-eight people lay dead at the scene, seventeen later succumbed from wounds received, and eighty-three suffered nonfatal injuries.[50]

What had failed? The governor's nerve? Perhaps, though Kazem-Bek's account has the *nachal'nik gubernii* displaying considerable physical courage. More central to the tragedy, however, was a failure of intellect and imagination. Bogdanovich had gone by the book. He had used most of the well-known remedies, but they proved inadequate. The militancy, even hostility of the workers did not let the governor accomplish his first duty, the restoration of order. Consequently, Bogdanovich never got the chance to move to the next stage of crisis management in which he could play a mediating role in the basic industrial dispute. Another governor—an Osorgin, an Urusov, or a Dzhunkovskii—might have been able to reason his way through the problem. But Bogdanovich apparently lacked the ability to improvise under pressure.

In the wake of the Zlatoust massacre, the MVD approved Bogdanovich's actions and kept him at his post, but the governor himself was profoundly depressed by what had transpired.[51] He would not suffer long. Less than two months later he was dead, assassinated by

48. Protocol, ibid., pp. 151–52. Mandel'shtam's account portrays the crowd as almost entirely peaceful and passive (*1905*, p. 109), but a Social-Democratic leaflet from the time implies that officials were indeed blocked from moving through the crowd (*Rabochee dvizhenie v Rossii v 1901–1904 gg*. p. 226).

49. Kazem-Bek, f. Min. iust., op. 105, 1904, d. 11059, p. 15.

50. Mandel'shtam, *1905*, p. 108.

51. Rynkevich to Manukhin, 15 October 1903, TsGIA, f. Min. iust., op. 105, 1904, d. 11059, p. 187.

Socialist Revolutionaries under the leadership of Grigorii Gershuni.[52] But something else killed Bogdanovich: the changing mood of the times which undercut lower-class respect for traditional authority and rendered established methods of control increasingly useless.

Within a month of the Zlatoust events, Kishinev, the capital of Bessarabia, exploded in vicious anti-Semitic rioting. The pogrom, which began on the afternoon of 6 April and lasted through the seventh, took at least forty-five lives, left scores severely injured, and was accompanied by uncounted rapes and heavy property damage.[53] The Kishinev tragedy ended a period of almost twenty years without major anti-Jewish outrages, and this example was soon followed in other parts of the empire. The Kishinev pogrom became the subject of considerable speculation. It was charged that the riots were engineered from St. Petersburg and were directed by the minister of internal affairs himself, V. K. Pleve. In May 1903 *The Times* of London published a letter that Pleve purportedly sent to Bessarabia's governor R. S. fon Raaben which warned that trouble was brewing but advised against using force in dealing with any anti-Semitic actions.[54] The letter was almost certainly a fabrication.[55] Yet, the legend of an anti-Jewish conspiracy at the highest levels has persisted,[56] and only recently has more careful and dispassionate research begun to discredit it.[57]

The facts on the Kishinev pogrom indicate that the local administration and especially the governor were primarily responsible for the disaster. Fon Raaben's behavior at the time of the crisis was clearly a dereliction of duty because he had been warned that anti-Semitic actions were being planned but took no steps to avert them.[58] When the riots broke out, the governor failed to go to the scene to get a firsthand impression of what was going on and instead he relied on subordinates, especially his chief of police, who were themselves unwilling or

---

52. Spiridovich, *Partiia sotsialistov revoliutsionerov*, p. 125.

53. Dubnow, *History of the Jews*, 3, p. 75.

54. The letter can be found in *Materialy dlia istorii antievreiskikh pogromov v Rossii* (2 vols.; Petrograd, 1919–1923), 1, pp. 223–24.

55. D. N. Liubimov, "Russkaia smuta nachala deviatisotykh godov, 1902–1906. Po vospominaniiam, lichnym zapiskam i dokumentam," pp. 59–61, BAR, Liubimov papers.

56. Dubnow, *History of the Jews*, 3, pp. 77–78; Louis Greenberg, *The Jews in Russia: The Struggle for Emancipation* (2 vols.; New Haven, 1944, 1951), 2, pp. 51–52.

57. Hans Rogger, "The Jewish Policy of Late Tsarism; A Reappraisal," *Wiener Library Bulletin* 25 (1971): 44–47; Judge, *Plehve*, pp. 93–104.

58. A. Pollan, procurator of the Odessa district court to the Ministry of Justice, 11 April 1903, *Materialy dlia istorii pogromov*, 1, p. 135.

unable to terminate the disturbances. Not until the middle of the second day did fon Raaben call on the army to suppress the rioters, but even then he used cumbersome written instructions instead of the swifter oral orders that would have been fully justified by the circumstances. The soldiers, too, apparently delayed, and only very late on 7 April did they apply sufficient force to restore order.[59]

There can be no excusing fon Raaben's failure to act more decisively during the pogrom, and his dismissal, though effected in a harsh and abrupt manner,[60] was something less than he deserved. Yet it should also be noted that fon Raaben's sins were primarily those of omission. His successor, S. D. Urusov, could find nothing to support the idea that the outgoing governor had desired or abetted the pogrom. Indeed, fon Raaben was an amiable gentleman of somewhat phlegmatic temper, ideally suited to the general character of the province entrusted to his care and was liked by Bessarabian society as well as the Jews.[61]

Moreover, Urusov's estimation is supported by the documents related to fon Raaben's conduct in office during the crisis. The telegram the governor sent to the MVD in the midst of the riots, his subsequent letters to the emperor and to Pleve, the statement he made to the Senate in 1905, show no sign of ill will toward Jews or any conscious avoidance of responsibility. Indeed, fon Raaben thought he was acting in accordance with accepted procedures, and he could understand neither the nature of his failure nor the cruel blow that had destroyed the work of a lifetime.[62]

Fon Raaben's confusion was, to a certain degree, justified, for his style of rule would have been quite sufficient a decade earlier. To be sure, the Bessarabian governor's incompetence in the Kishinev crisis exceeded that of Poltava's Bel'gard and Ufa's Bogdanovich, but like each of the other governors, fon Raaben was a victim of changing times. The governors in Poltava and Ufa were destroyed because they could not comprehend the shift in peasant and worker attitudes which rendered traditional approaches to lower class discontent inadequate. In a similar way, fon Raaben failed because he did not see that racial tensions, which were being fanned by an anti-Semitic press and encouraged by some central officials as a means of providing the masses with a nonrevolutionary outlet for their rage, could not be ignored or treated with liberal doses of gentleness, good humor, and tact. Fon

59. Ibid., pp. 136–38.
60. Urussov, p. 8.
61. Ibid., pp. 15–17.
62. *Materialy dlia istorii pogromov*, 1, pp. 130–31, 335, 337–46.

Raaben was undone because he did not understand how anti-Semitism was corrupting his subordinates in the police and made them unwilling to carry out the demands for the restoration of order he had made at the beginning of the pogrom.[63]

Taken together, the events of 1902 and 1903 marked the beginning of a new phase of Russian history. The time of relative quiet the empire had enjoyed since 1881 was clearly coming to an end. In the face of a rising wave of lower class hostility and resistance, governors in all parts of the country were finding that the old style of administration was not enough to maintain law, order, and civil peace. The great revolutionary storm that broke in 1905 would force the *nachal'niki gubernii* to react to events that were truly extraordinary and for which few of them had any preparation. The ensuing chaos would put the entire structure of provincial administration and the personal capacities of the governors themselves to a cruel test.

"If anything can go wrong, it will." Mr. Murphy's iron law of mishap governed the first Russian revolution.[64] And for the *nachal'niki gubernii*, the years from 1905 to 1907 seemed to produce a perverse gubernatorial corollary: "When everything that can go wrong has, you will be expected to fix it."

The list of the troubles that descended on the governors during the revolution was long indeed. Peasant disorders on an unprecedented scale, strengthened and deepened by wartime dislocation and major crop failure, swept the countryside. A lengthy series of strikes developed and culminated in the events of October 1905 which brought the urban areas of the empire to a virtual standstill. A "liberation movement" affecting mainly the educated classes turned "society" against authority at every level, converted the zemstvos into platforms for agitation, gave free reign to the radical tendencies of the "third element," and provided a congenial environment for the activities of militant revolutionaries and terrorists.

Under the impact of these forces, everything seemed to fall apart. At the local level, the land captains and the police were unable to provide adequate intelligence about impending disturbances or to check them once they started. The pattern of Poltava and Kharkov repeated itself on a national scale. The land captains proved to be out of touch with the inhabitants of their bailiwicks and cowardly in the face of peasant

63. Urussov, pp. 79–83.
64. Arthur Bloch, *Murphy's Law and Other Reasons Why Things Go Wrong!* (Los Angeles, 1982), p. 11.

violence. The police were too few and quickly overwhelmed by the extraordinary duties events imposed on them. In addition, things were made more difficult because the rural guard (*strazh*), authorized under the law of 1903, had not been established in most areas, and landlords, panicked by the growth of illegal peasant activities, were unceasing in their demands for police protection.[65]

In the gubernia capitals, administrative disarray was common as the dramatic events of the revolution heightened tensions and conflict between various agencies. Military commanders who had never been happy about being used for the maintenance of domestic order were now strained by the combination of war abroad, revolt at home, and mutiny in their own ranks. Undermanned and under pressure, they often balked when governors requested assistance.[66] At the same time, the *nachal'niki gubernii* found district procurators more than occasionally unhelpful. Even in the circumstances of peace, governors sometimes felt that the judiciary was overly concerned with legal niceties. Now, when quick action from the courts was vital for the suppression of disturbances, procurators appeared to drag their feet. In addition, many of them were unwilling to hold persons the governors regarded as politically dangerous in preventive detention, and so made it difficult to check the spread of pernicious agitation.[67]

And for a time, even the center failed to hold. As the intensity of the revolution grew, the governors had to work without consistent leadership because the signals from St. Petersburg were often contradictory. During the summer and fall of 1905, the central government made repeated concessions to an aroused public, yet at the same time it called on the local authorities to maintain order. Governors soon found, however, that they had insufficient means at their disposal and very little hope for additional support. Thus when Tula's M. M. Osorgin sent a desperate wire for additional troops to augment the already strained forces at his disposal, P. N. Durnovo, the minister of internal affairs, instructed the Department of Police: "Answer that nothing can be done."[68]

65. Manning, *Crisis*, p. 145 and passim.

66. Santoni, pp. 347ff.; Fuller, pp. 129–68. On revolt within the military, see John Bushnell, *Mutiny amid Repression: Russian Soldiers in the Revolution of 1905–1906* (Bloomington, Ind., 1985).

67. See, for example, Koshko, *Vospominaniia*, p. 50; the comments by Penza governor A. A. Khvostov and Poltava governor N. P. Urusov in *Krest'ianskoe dvizhenie v revoliutsii 1905 goda v dokumentakh*, ed. N. I. Karpov (Leningrad, 1926), pp. 178, 198–99. Hereafter this source will be cited: Karpov.

68. Osorgin's telegram dated 25 November 1905, Durnovo's instruction, the next

The failure of St. Petersburg to support and guide the governors during the revolutionary crisis was most dramatically demonstrated by the events surrounding the promulgation of the October Manifesto. This document, the most important governmental act since the emancipation, was issued without consultation with the governors who received neither advanced warnings nor supplemental explanations about the meaning of the decree.[69] Many governors learned of the manifesto establishing constitutional government from newspapers, wall posters, and student radicals. The government's abrupt change of policy caused the governors confusion, embarrassment, and even physical danger. Perm's governor A. P. Naumov was captured by a triumphant revolutionary mob and forced to march in a procession behind banners reading "Down with Autocracy!" Governor Palen of Vilna was humiliated at a public meeting and then shot at point-blank range. In Tomsk, Governor Azenchevskii was unprepared for the local conflict that the manifesto generated. He was unable to maintain order, and the result was a vicious riot.[70]

Governors' efforts to keep the peace during these turbulent times could bring them trouble. When soldiers guarding a railroad station fired into a crowd of demonstrators on 18 October, Minsk's governor P. G. Kurlov obtained the dubious distinction of being accused of both exceeding his powers and dereliction of duty. The governor, who had made elaborate preparations for maintaining order in the gubernia capital even before the promulgation of the tsar's manifesto, was now charged with bringing the army into the situation needlessly, encouraging it to use maximum force, and delegating too much authority to lesser police and military personnel. At the same time, for failing to go to the scene of the fateful confrontation between the troops and civilian demonstrators, Kurlov was condemned for not exercising his rightful powers.[71]

Indeed, Bibikov, the local procurator, not only brought charges against Kurlov, but also demanded that the governor quit the province

---

day. A. M. Pankratova et al., eds., *Revoliutsiia 1905–1907 gg. v. Rossii: Dokumenty i materialy* (Moscow, 1955–1963), in various volumes, variously titled, and in various parts. Volume cited here is *Vysshii pod'em revoliutsii 1905–1907 gg. (noiabr'–dekabr' 1905 goda)*, pt. 2, p. 211. Hereafter the collection will be cited: *Revoliutsiia 1905–1907 gg.*, followed by a shortened volume title.

69. Kurlov, *Konets*, pp. 31–33; report of Panteleev, in *Revoliutsiia 1905 i samoderzhavie*, ed. V. P. Semennikov (Moscow, 1928), p. 104.

70. Liubimov, "Russkaia smuta," pp. 326–31, BAR.

71. The accusation of the Vilna procurator against Kurlov is found in *Materialy k istorii russkoi kontr-revoliutsii* (SPb., 1908), pp. 299–304. The official charge of the Senate against Kurlov, ibid., pp. 326–27.

and turn administration over to the courts. This Kurlov refused to do, and shortly thereafter he received an abrupt summons to St. Petersburg, where he found near total confusion. Kurlov learned from the outgoing head of the MVD, A. G. Bulygin, that S. Iu. Vitte, the prime minister, had wanted him fired. But the new minister of internal affairs, P. N. Durnovo, who was unaware of Vitte's intentions, approved Kurlov's handling of the situation in Minsk and ordered him back to his post.[72] Still, the charges against the governor carried over into the following year. On 5 May 1906, the Senate found Kurlov's explanations satisfactory and dismissed the procurator's accusations.[73]

What happened to Kurlov was but an extreme example of the kind of pushing and pulling to which governors were subjected during the revolution of 1905–1907. All through this complicated period, the *nachal'niki gubernii* discovered that the traditional rule book had been thrown away and that in dealing with disorders the accustomed means and the normal ends were likely to satisfy neither the central government nor an aroused citizenry.

The story of how Vladimir's I. M. Leont'ev tried to cope with the 1905 strike in Ivanovo-Voznesensk provides a useful example of the way in which the revolution changed the situation for the governors. The strike, begun on 13 May, was a large one and involved workers from most of the major factories of the city. The workers were emboldened by their own solidarity, the growing mood of national discontent, and a barrage of radical propaganda. As a result, they showed less respect than usual for the governor's authority and were uncooperative when he sought to terminate the walkout. The factory management, too, was resistant to Leont'ev's attempts at mediation. Fearful of the aroused workers, the owners refused to come to Ivanovo to negotiate personally, and their absence made it difficult for the governor to pressure them into compromises. Perhaps expecting quick and vigorous government repression of the strike movement, management procrastinated and failed to make significant concessions until the workers engaged in serious violence. In addition, during the course of the confrontation, which continued through June, the factory owners regularly complained to St. Petersburg about the governor's lack of firmness.

While this was going on, Governor Leont'ev was frequently deprived of firm support for his efforts. Military force to maintain order

72. Kurlov, *Konets*, pp. 36–39.

73. Senate decision is reprinted in part in *Revoliutsionnoe dvizhenie 1905–1907 gg. v Belorusii* (Minsk, 1955), p. 383.

or to impress the workers was not readily available. Worst of all, the central authorities grew increasingly impatient with Leont'ev's efforts to exert control through the traditional means of persuasion, compromise, and delay. St. Petersburg often pressured the governor to take more effective actions.[74]

During the course of the strike, Governor Leont'ev consistently pursued the goal of ending the dispute without resort to arms. As a precautionary measure he asked for troops when the walkout began,[75] but he did not receive them at once, nor did he appear eager to use them. Arriving at Ivanovo on 14 May, he found the city calm and the workers peaceful. Despite urgings from the police chief to employ force against the strikers, the governor held firm to his intentions and was supported in this by the chief factory inspector.[76] Leont'ev addressed a crowd of some 10,000 workers and, given its peaceful character, allowed the demonstration to break up on its own.[77]

The governor returned to Vladimir a few days later, leaving a tense but quiet situation in the care of his second-in-command, I. N. Sazanov. But then matters worsened. The factory owners continued to refuse serious concessions, and the strikers' militancy increased. When the vice-governor used force to break up a crowd of workers and banned further demonstrations, sporadic outbursts of violence took place, and Leont'ev once more headed for Ivanovo.[78] On his arrival the governor found himself with few means to handle the situation. The workers and their employers were locked in conflict and neither side seemed willing to compromise. The use of force against the strikers appeared not only useless but also dangerous, for it might have provoked uncontrollable riots. In these circumstances, Leont'ev did his best to win the confidence of the workers by allowing them to hold peaceful meetings on the edge of the town.[79] But his chief hope lay in time. If the factory hands stayed on strike long enough, need would force them to submission.[80]

74. *Revoliutsiia 1905–1907 gg.: Revoliutsionnoe dvizhenie vesnoi i letom 1905 goda*, 1, pp. 403–65.

75. Telegram to the staff of the Moscow military district, 13 May 1905, ibid., p. 407.

76. See report of factory inspector V. F. Svirskii to the Manufacturing Department of the Ministry of Finance, 29 May 1905, ibid., pp. 432–33.

77. See Leont'ev's report to the MVD, 14 May 1905, ibid., pp. 409–10.

78. Telegram of Leont'ev to A. G. Bulygin, 23 May 1905, ibid., p. 422; Leont'ev to Bulygin, 24 May, ibid., p. 425; report of the procurator of the Vladimir district court to the procurator of the Moscow judicial district, ibid., pp. 433–34; Sazanov to Leont'ev, 3 June, ibid., 438–39.

79. Leont'ev's report to D. F. Trepov, 16 June 1905, ibid., pp. 450–51.

80. Telegram to A. G. Bulygin, 14 June, 1905, ibid., p. 450.

St. Petersburg officials did not look favorably on Leont'ev's cautious approach, however. "Negotiate less, and act more energetically," D. F. Trepov, the head of the Department of Police, scrawled on the governor's telegram of the fourteenth.[81] The governor defended the cause of patience, arguing that sterner measures would produce needless violence and claiming that the means at his disposal were limited. The military was less than entirely cooperative, and efforts of the administration, the procuracy, the factory inspectorate, and the gendarmes were poorly coordinated. On a personal level, Leont'ev complained that the strike was taking a heavy toll on his health and prevented him from attending to other important matters.[82]

Toward the end of June it appeared that Leont'ev's efforts to end the strike peacefully had been in vain. The workers' demands and hostility began to rise again, and the governor, driven to near despair, requested that the center dispatch a special agent to manage the crisis.[83] Then, on the twenty-fourth, a serious breakdown of order took place. When they learned that their rigid bosses still refused further concessions, gangs of outraged workers began vandalizing many of the factories.[84] The flash point that the governor had struggled so long to avoid had now been reached.

In the days that followed, Leont'ev came under heavy pressure from all sides. Disturbances continued in the streets, and the factory owners complained bitterly to Bulygin about the governor's lack of firmness.[85] Trepov wired from the capital that order had to be restored by any means and at whatever cost. "If you fail," Trepov demanded, "turn over authority to the military command. . . . I find further abuse and disruption impermissible."[86] The same day Leont'ev telegraphed the commander of the Moscow military district for more troops.[87] Yet, even as the crisis reached its height, fortune smiled. The united front of the Ivanovo factory owners collapsed and opened the way for further and more substantial concessions, while the resolve of the strikers finally gave way.[88] On the twenty-seventh the workers informed the chief factory inspector that they would end their walkout on the

81. Ibid.
82. Letter to Trepov, 16 June, ibid., p. 452.
83. Telegram to Trepov, 19 June, ibid., p. 453.
84. Report of the assistant chief of gendarmes in Vladimir to Trepov, 25 June, ibid., pp. 457–58.
85. Telegram dated 25 June, ibid., p. 458.
86. Wire dated 27 June 1905, ibid., p. 459.
87. Telegram dated 27 June, ibid.
88. Report of V. F. Svirskii, 27 June, ibid., pp. 460–63.

first of July.[89] Leont'ev's caution and patience appeared to have paid off.

On 5 July the governor dispatched a lengthy report to Trepov, justifying his policies and outlining in detail the problems he had faced. Expressing consternation at the criticism directed against his actions, Leont'ev claimed that he had terminated dangerous conflict without violence and, by so doing, had deprived antigovernment forces of grist for their propaganda mills.[90] But matters had not really been solved at Ivanovo-Voznesensk; indeed the circumstances of the summer of 1905 permitted no final resolution. The workers were willing to end the strike but announced that they were simply yielding to exhaustion and the threat of force. They further stated that they were returning to work only to rebuild their strength for another try and once again asserted their goals.[91] Given this mood, it is not surprising that sporadic strikes continued through the end of August.

Nor was the center satisfied with the outcome of events. Trepov never fully accepted Leont'ev's justifications and penned the following resolution on the governor's report of 5 July: "Of course it is undesirable to shoot; but to permit riot, theft, arson, and violence is still more undesirable, and called forth my well-grounded disapproval of the governor's indecisive measures."[92]

The difficulties and pressures Leont'ev faced in Ivanovo-Voznesensk show how the revolution of 1905 made it hard for the *nachal'niki gubernii* to employ the traditional means of persuasion, compromise, and limited force in coping with lower class disturbances. Other governors who continued to try this approach often obtained disappointing results. During his brief tenure as Samara's governor in the spring of 1906, I. L. Blok made repeated trips to mutinous villages and attempted to restore order without using severe repression. Sometimes he was successful, but on at least one occasion he found himself in a tight spot. Arriving at a village unaccompanied by troops, Blok sought to bring the peasants into submission using only words and his personal authority, but within a few minutes he noticed that something was very wrong. The faces in the crowd were universally hostile and, as he spoke, the peasants moved closer, menacingly.

89. Workers' declaration to Svirskii, ibid., p. 460.
90. Leont'ev to Trepov, ibid., pp. 463–65.
91. Workers' declaration, ibid., p. 460.
92. Resolution of Trepov dated 5 July, ibid., p. 465. For a detailed account of the events in Ivanovo-Voznesensk which gives more information on the workers and the actions of radical groups, see the article by William G. Gard, "The Party and the Proletariat in Ivanovo-Voznesensk, 1905," *Russian History* 2 (1975): 101–23.

Blok was neither a coward nor a fool. Wisdom dictated a quick departure, and he cut short his speech. Outwardly calm but inwardly shaken, he strode toward his carriage, but the crowd was reluctant to let him pass. " 'Make way for a Russian governor!' " Blok shouted, and the peasant ranks grudgingly opened. A great jeer and flying clods of mud followed the governor as his coach pulled away.[93]

The rapid breakdown of order and established relations, the sudden evaporation of lower-class respect for constituted authority left the governors confused and unable to explain why it had happened. This was particularly true in regard to the mass peasant uprising. When the MVD queried the *nachal'niki gubernii* on this point toward the end of 1905, the overwhelming majority stated that revolutionary propaganda was the main cause of rural disturbances.[94] Up to a point, this view was certainly valid, but the governors' failure to ascribe similar importance to the economic problems of the countryside betokened a reluctance to abandon their long-standing view of the peasants as naive children, easily misled by wily outside agitators.[95] The governors' analysis also suggests that at least some of them were loath to bring the full weight of repression to bear on the peasants and preferred instead to concentrate on revolutionaries and socialist propagandists.[96]

The high point of both the revolution and the government's efforts to suppress it came in the months following the October Manifesto, a period that coincided with the tenure of P. N. Durnovo as minister of internal affairs. Under Durnovo's leadership, the government's repressive activities were systematically developed and increasingly coordinated. For local officials, and especially the governors, Durnovo's ministry meant a greater demand for firmness and the expectation that all means would be employed in the defense of the regime.[97]

The foundations for Durnovo's repressive policies were the 1881 statute on increased and maximum security and the 1892 regulations on the introduction and application of martial law. In the minister's mind, these measures, if properly utilized, gave local authorities sufficient powers to deal the revolution a decisive blow. Consequently, from the end of October 1905 through the early part of March 1906, Durnovo steadily expanded the number of areas declared to be in

93. Koshko, *Vospominaniia*, p. 72.
94. Report of P. N. Durnovo, Minister of Internal Affairs, to Nicholas II, 29 January 1906, Karpov, p. 94.
95. Ibid., pp. 95–96.
96. Ibid., pp. 96–97.
97. The best discussion of government policies in this period is Wayne Santoni's dissertation, "P. N. Durnovo as Minister of Internal Affairs in the Witte Cabinet."

"exceptional situations" or under military rule.[98] In the states of heightened security under the law of 1881, the governors usually retained positions of command, though there were instances when a special plenipotentiary (General Panteleev in Chernigov) took control.[99] Under martial law, of course, soldiers were in charge while governors and other civilian authorities assumed supporting roles. Exceptional situations were usually introduced into specific regions by decree from St. Petersburg, though the center might be acting in response to a gubernatorial request. On 29 November, however, an imperial *ukaz* permitted governors-general, governors, and the chief administrators of major cities to decree states of increased or maximum security on their own authority if necessary to cope with a threatened railroad, post, or telegraph strike.[100]

Durnovo's faith in the efficacy of extraordinary methods was probably excessive, for as Count Ignat'ev, the tsar's special envoy in Kherson noted, exceptional states, even martial law, produced the desired results only when there were sufficient local forces to make them work.[101] And for much of Durnovo's tenure, such force was not consistently available. Beyond this, governors and other constituted authorities had to be willing to make full use of the powers granted them. Considerable evidence suggests that the *nachal'niki gubernii* abandoned more traditional approaches to peasant and working-class disorders only with considerable reluctance. Not surprisingly, then, we find that during Durnovo's ministry the central authorities bombarded the governors with circulars urging decisive, even ruthless, steps and sharply criticized them if they failed to act. The MVD ordered the *nachal'niki gubernii* to disarm peasants and workers, suppress local soviets, break up strikes, and arrest revolutionary agitators. Above all it demanded that the governors check every manifestation of rural rebellion by any means.

Yet, these commands from the center seem to have had only limited success in stimulating governors and other local authorities. On 23 December 1905, for example, Durnovo sent a circular to the *nachal'niki gubernii* and the heads of the provincial gendarmes voicing his anger and disappointment. The minister complained that many governors had failed to employ their full powers and had limited themselves "to narrow bureaucratic functions [*uzko-vedomstvennoi kompetentsii*]."

98. See Santoni, pp. 201–6, for a convenient list of areas and dates.
99. Ibid., pp. 197–98.
100. This decree is published in *Revoliutsiia 1905–1907 gg.: Vysshii pod'em*, 1, p. 145.
101. Ignat'ev's report is dated 18 June 1905, in Karpov, pp. 219–20.

Instead of actively suppressing the rebellion, they watched passively as it destroyed the foundations of the state. Durnovo called on the governors to mend their ways and to see that other gubernia officials also carried out their duties.[102] Durnovo's frustration also helps explain why other, more specific orders to the governors took on such an extreme, almost bloodthirsty character: "order them to act in the most decisive way, stopping at nothing"; "adopt a more decisive style of action and use arms against mutinous gatherings without any leniency"; "take measures to end the criminal activity of agitators and arrest them without regard to rank"; "using the most severe measures, bring these rebels and robbers to order, . . . employ arms at the least refusal to obey legal authority."[103] Finally, on 10 January 1906, Durnovo sent the governors a general order that called on them to punish all "outrages" by peasants "without mercy," and to destroy, if necessary, individual homes and whole villages.[104]

The tone of Durnovo's circulars to the governors gives the strong impression that the minister held the *nachal'niki gubernii* responsible for the shortcomings of local administration in the struggle with the revolution. And in part, Durnovo was right. During the course of 1905 and 1906, a number of governors proved incapable of providing the kind of leadership expected of an imperial viceroy. Poltava's governor N. P. Urusov and Kazan's P. F. Khomutov suffered nervous collapse under the strain. Governors D. D. Sverbeev of Kurland and D. I. Zasiadko of Samara were either unable or unwilling to make effective use of available force. And a few governors practically went over to the revolutionary side, notably I. V. Kholshchevnikov of the Zabaikal region and V. A. Starosel'skii of Kutais province in the Caucasus.[105]

102. TsGIA, f. Kants. MVD, op. 3, d. 107, "Tsirkuliary po MVD za 1905 g.," pp. 182–83.

103. Quotations from the following telegrams: To Vladimir governor Leont'ev, 12 December 1905, *Revoliutsiia 1905–1907 gg: Vysshii pod'em*, 2, p. 22; to Governor A. A. Lodyzhenskii of Vologda, 17 December, ibid., p. 269; to Moscow governor Dzhunkovskii, 30 December, ibid., 1, p. 837; to K. P. Frederiks, governor of Nizhni-Novgorod, 2 January 1906, ibid., 2, p. 159.

104. Ibid., 1, p. 170.

105. On N. P. Urusov, see E. M. Brofel'dt, "Vospominaniia: Poltava," p. 6, BAR, Brofel'dt papers; on Khuomutov, N. A. Mel'nikov, "19 let na zemskoi sluzhby," p. 120, BAR, Mel'nikov papers; on Sverbeev see the report of E. A. Vatatsi titled "Zapiska po delu o narodnykh volneniiakh v kurliandskoi gubernii v 1905 god," TsGIA, f. DOD op. 46, 1905, d. 175, "O bezporiadkakh v kurliandskoi gubernii," pp. 2–17; on Zasiadko, N. N. Speranskii, "Krest'ianskoe dvizhenie v samarskoi gubernii v gody pervoi revoliutsii," in *1905 god v samarskom krae*, ed. N. N. Speranskii (Samara, 1925), pp. 541–42; on Kholshchevnikov, Santoni, pp. 316–17; on Starosel'skii, see the governor's own writings "Krest'ianskoe dvizhenie v kutaisskoi gubernii," *Byloe* (September 1906): 229–41 and "'Dni svobody' v kutaisskoi gubernii," *Byloe* (November 1906): 278–306.

Such dereliction of duty was clearly an aberration, however. If governors wavered, they did so not out of cowardice or misguided principle but because they were inhibited by the weakness and lack of cohesion in gubernia institutions and the absence of sufficient military force. Central authorities, Durnovo included, understood this, and they worked strenuously to strengthen the provincial police, to goad the procurators into action, and improve communications between military commanders and local officials. In the latter effort, especially, the government was successful because as more troops became available and their use systematized, the forces of order gained the upper hand.[106]

But 1905 saw more than an administrative and military crisis. It witnessed the breakdown of a style of rule. If governors could not meet the demands the center imposed on them, this was largely the result of the fact that the accustomed patterns of provincial government were badly suited to the circumstances of a revolution. Despite their image as satraps and their reputation for arbitrariness, governors in the late nineteenth century ruled their gubernias more by persuasion and compromise than by compulsion. This was true for both the educated classes and the common people, so that when the troubles came, governors found that they were psychologically ill prepared to carry out the kind of ruthless suppression ultimately required of them. And it was not only the vigorous use of force against workers and peasants that the governors found unpalatable. The public antipathy that resulted from their repressive activities was also hard to endure. Governors were accustomed to a measure of popularity, and when they saw respect for their office and the support of local society evaporate, they were seized by despair. I. L. Blok, a competent governor and a decent man, must have expressed the feelings of many of his colleagues when he complained to co-workers in Samara: "You risk your life, you wear out your nerves maintaining order so that people can live like human beings, and what do you get? Not only is there no support. . . , but you also encounter condemnation at every step. You go about the city and catch hate-filled glances as if you were some kind of monster, a drinker of human blood. . . ."[107]

Moments after he uttered these words, Blok was dead, decapitated by a bomb that a Socialist Revolutionary terrorist had flung into his carriage. The macabre funeral that followed—Blok lying in an open casket, his mangled body somehow stuffed into a dress uniform, a

---

106. See Santoni, chaps. 9 and 12.
107. Koshko, *Vospominaniia*, p. 83.

large ball of batting taking the place of his missing head—was a perfect and terrible symbol of the governorship *in extremis*.[108]

Yet in the end, the line held. Governors who could not stand the pressure resigned or were removed from office, and new men who could do the job were found. Some governors, of course, responded magnificently to the crisis, at least from the government's point of view. Of these, P. A. Stolypin of Saratov was the most famous. His combination of personal courage and administrative competence and his willingness to use the most ruthless measures helped him suppress agrarian disturbances. At the same time he displayed political skill and reformist vision. He organized provincial moderates to oppose the revolution, and even in the midst of the struggle with sedition proposed significant changes in the empire's agrarian structure.[109] Stolypin's performance earned him condemnation in many quarters, but before the revolution was over, he had emerged as the empire's new "strong man."

By mid-1906 the revolution was clearly on the wane, though another year of difficult times lay ahead. On 15 September, P. A. Stolypin, now prime minister and head of the MVD, issued a circular to the governors establishing guidelines for continued efforts against the rebellion. This lengthy document called on the *nachal'niki gubernii* to take the most decisive measures against agitators, radical organizations, terrorists, and all manifestations of resistance to authority. Governors were urged to be real leaders and "to provide their subordinates and the population with an example of civil courage, to lift their spirits, and to take on themselves the responsibility for the terrible consequences of the success of the revolutionary movement."[110] Despite its demands for extraordinary exertions, the circular also contained signs of a return to more normal times. It cautioned governors about the excessive and unnecessary use of arms in dealing with peasant discontent and urged them to employ more traditional approaches. Governors were also supposed to be alert to situations wherein peasant disturbances were prompted by undue pressures on the part of landowners or their agents. In such cases, *nachal'niki gubernii* ought to assume a mediating role and use their influence to bring the landlords to a more reasonable position. Negotiation was stressed, though de-

---

108. Ibid., pp. 87–88.

109. Mary S. Bock, "Stolypin in Saratov," *Russian Review* 12 (July 1953): 187–93; report of General Trepov, in *Revoliutsiia 1905 goda i samoderzhavie*, pp. 99–103; report of Stolypin, 11 January 1906, in Karpov, pp. 161–62.

110. *Krasnyi arkhiv* 32 (1929): 182.

cisive force was always to be used if more moderate means failed.[111]

Further normalization took place in the years that followed, but the *nachal'niki gubernii* could never return completely to the methods they had used in handling lower class disturbances prior to 1905. On the whole, the governors who ruled in the postrevolutionary period appear to have been less involved in dealings with peasants and workers than their predecessors in the 1890s. This difference can be explained in part by the growing importance of other, intermediary institutions such as the factory inspectorate, trade unions and radical parties in the industrial centers, and the land reform agencies in the rural areas. Yet, the effacement of the governors also reflects the fact that despite the restoration of order, the events of 1905–1907 created a gulf between the state administration and the lower classes which was difficult to bridge. Increasingly, the old style of personal, "patriarchal" rule had become inadequate to the task.

111. Ibid., pp. 163–68.

— 10 —

Conclusions

Toward the end of February 1917, the telegraph wires that usually carried a high volume of official communications from Petrograd to the provinces fell unexpectedly silent. In Nizhni-Novgorod, Governor Aleksei Fedorovich Girs, accustomed to a steady stream of ministerial directives, became alarmed. On 1 March, the governor's concern increased as confused accounts of the revolutionary events in the capital began to reach the Volga city. In these disquieting circumstances, Girs tried to go about his regular schedule. He attended the traditional memorial service in honor of the martyred Tsar Liberator, but the cathedral, normally full on such an occasion, was virtually deserted.[1]

At 9:00 A.M. on the second, the police chief arrived to make his daily report. The news was ominous. During the previous evening, the leaders of the main elected institutions of the province had formed a "committee of public safety." Moreover, a deputation of workers had appeared before the newly established body and demanded the governor's arrest and incarceration. The committee had agreed to the arrest, but at the suggestion of the mayor decided to place Girs under guard at his official residence. Two hours later, General Pliutsinskii, the commander of the city garrison, now in the service of the revolution, appeared to tell Girs formally of the decision taken by the new "authorities." The general ordered the governor's office sealed, forbade

---

1. "Iz dnevnika L. A. Girs. Nizhnii-Novgorod, 1917," pp. 14–18, BAR, Girs family papers.

him to receive officials, and disconnected his telephone. Pliutsinskii posted a small detachment of soldiers to keep watch on the *"nachal'nik gubernii."*

All of this was highly discomfiting to Girs, but by the afternoon events had taken a more threatening turn. In a nearby park, a large crowd of angry citizens gathered. For a while, they vented their hatred on the physical symbols of tsarist power, but soon Girs heard voices shouting: "Give us the governor, he has drunk our blood long enough!" Then, in what seemed an instant, a noisy mob invaded the governor's mansion, and the stairway of the three-story building was suddenly filled with the vocal representatives of the people.

In this tense and explosive situation, the governor's wife, Liubov' Aleksandrovna, moved with determined swiftness. The shouting raised by the intruders had summoned her from the upstairs lazaretto where she had been tending some seriously wounded soldiers. Still wearing her nurse's uniform, she pushed her way down the staircase and ordered the crowd to be quiet lest they disturb the sick. Entering the first-floor reception hall, she saw her husband approach some of the demonstrators.

"You want the governor," he called, "here I am."

"Take him!" roared the crowd.

As Girs put on his coat to follow, Liubov' Aleksandrovna reached his side. "I'm coming with you," she said firmly.

"No. Stay here. Don't leave our daughter," Aleksei Fedorovich replied.

"Don't say that," his wife returned. "I'm going with you."

Liubov' Aleksandrovna's steadfastness may have saved the governor's life. Her decision to join her husband aroused the admiration of one of the soldiers in the mob.

"You have no need to go," he cautioned.

"Are you married?" the *gubernatorsha* asked.

"Married," came the reply.

"Your wife would go with you at such a moment. Don't stop me . . . ."

Just then, Moiseev, an officer, stepped from the crowd, and asked Mme Girs again if she wanted to accompany the governor. When she replied that she did, he acceded to her wishes.

"Go," he said. "I'll take responsibility for your safety."

Moiseev ordered some of the soldiers present to form a cordon around the Girses, and protected by this "guard of honor," the governor and his wife moved out of the kremlin into the even larger throng

Governor's house in Nizhni-Novgorod. Courtesy of TsGIA.

gathered on the streets beyond. Their goal was the relative security of the building occupied by the city duma.[2]

The mood of the crowd now was not friendly, however, and the guard quickly realized that they would have to gain the confidence of the demonstrators if Girs and his wife were to pass through unharmed. Turning to Liubov' Aleksandrovna, Moiseev asked: "Would you be terribly insulted if we lifted . . . your husband up?"[3] She consented, and the soldiers raised Girs to the point where he was visible to the people. The crowd burst into a shout of triumph. Moiseev, himself a member of one of the socialist parties, then addressed the demonstrators. His words were revolutionary, but his aim was to calm, not to inflame the mob. "We have arrested the governor," he concluded, "victory is ours!"[4]

After this, the danger passed. En route to the city duma the governor endured only one unpleasant moment when a worker, his face contorted with rage, pushed into the circle of Girs's protectors and tore the epaulets from his uniform. At the duma, the governor and his wife were met by an agitated mayor, a member of the executive board, and several citizens. Together they ascended to the third floor of the building by the familiar stairway used on so many formal occasions. But how strange the circumstances were this time! "At official ceremonies in the past, they had received us with honor," Girs wrote later. "Now we came like state criminals."[5]

The events of the February revolution took the *nachal'niki gubernii* by surprise. Just nine months earlier, the minister of internal affairs, B. V. Shtiurmer, had summoned sixteen governors from the central Russian provinces to a conference in Petrograd. There they had discussed "all sides of life in the empire and the needs of the time." The *nachal'niki gubernii* did not paint a rosy picture at that meeting: conflict with the zemstvos had diminished, but it still existed; a strike movement among the factory workers was growing and taking on an increasingly political cast; and the peasants, though for the moment economically satisfied, expected a large-scale transfer of state and private land into their possession. At war's end, this question was undoubtedly going to become increasingly touchy, and maintaining order

2. A. F. Girs, "Pravitel'stvo i obshchestvennost'," pp. 39–43, BAR, Girs family papers.

3. "Iz dnevnika L. A. Girs," pp. 44–45.

4. A. F. Girs, "Pravitel'stvo i obshchestvennost'," p. 43.

5. Ibid., p. 44.

would be difficult. Finally, many of the land captains had been called to the front, and police ranks, filled because of wartime draft exemptions, were bound to be depleted once hostilities ended.

The governors also noted a radicalization of the nation's politics. Left-wing forces were making steady gains in the urban areas, and the elections for the Fifth State Duma threatened to produce a sharp decline in the fortunes of conservative and progovernment parties. Yet in the face of these difficulties, the governors appeared if not sanguine, then at least undismayed. The records of the conference leave the distinct impression that although the *nachal'niki gubernii* saw serious problems ahead, they were confident that solutions could be found.[6]

Now, the collapse of autocracy had come with shattering speed. Across the empire, the scene that took place in Nizhni was repeated with minor variations as a burst of popular indignation swept away the tsar's viceroys.[7] On 5 March the new minister of internal affairs, G. N. L'vov, sent out a circular that removed the governors' and vice-governors' and empowered the chairmen of the provincial zemstvo executive boards, acting as "gubernia commissars," to assume their duties. Over two-hundred years of gubernatorial rule had come to an end.[8]

As things turned out, 1917 was surprisingly kind to the Russian governors because their overthrow came during the relatively good-humored early phase of the revolution. Some governors suffered abuse, and Tver's fon Biunting was beaten to death, but most were well treated by their victorious opponents.[9] Riazan's Governor Kisel'-Zagorianskii was taken from his official mansion to the comfortable confinement of a hotel room, where he whiled away the hours rereading *Madame Bovary* and *Penguin Island* and dined on food prepared

6. "Soveshchanie gubernatorov v 1916 godu," *Krasnyi arkhiv* 33 (1929): 146, 151, 153, 157–58, 164–65, 168–69.

7. For an excellent description of the overthrow of the old regime in Saratov, see Donald J. Raleigh, *Revolution on the Volga: 1917 in Saratov* (Ithaca, N.Y., 1986), pp. 75–85.

8. The decree is published in English in Robert P. Browder and Alexander F. Kerensky, eds., *The Russian Provisional Government 1917: Documents* (3 vols.; Stanford, Calif., 1961), 1, p. 243. As printed in this collection, the decree states that the removal of the governors was to be "temporary." William G. Rosenberg argues that the removal was intended to be permanent (*Liberals in the Russian Revolution: The Constitutional Democratic Party, 1917–1921* [Princeton, N.J., 1974], p. 59, n.24). According to D. N. Liubimov, the author of this order was S. D. Urusov ("Russkaia smuta," pp. 34–35, BAR, Liubimov papers).

9. See for example, F. G. Popov, *Letopis' revoliutsionnykh sobytii v samarskoi gubernii, 1902–1917* (Kuibyshev, 1969), pp. 428–36.

by some of the leading ladies of the provincial capital.[10] Briefly incarcerated in the city prison, he was soon released. The former governor first journeyed to Petrograd, then returned to his Moscow estate, and finally made his way to exile in France. Other governors also found safety in the West: A. F. Girs, I. F. Koshko, D. N. Liubimov, M. M. Osorgin, P. P. Stremoukhov, to list a few.

Governors escaped not only with their lives but also with most of their dignity. Moreover, the events of February relieved them of the task of trying to maintain order during the developing revolution. Men who had been governors could cherish the notion that had the office been preserved, the outcome of things might have been different. P. P. Stremoukhov believed that when the Provisional Government dismissed the governors, it pulled the lynch pin out of the governmental structure, and D. N. Liubimov implied that this act may have opened the way for the revolutionary surge that culminated in the Bolshevik triumph.[11] Yet, it is virtually impossible to imagine the governors' being able to check the elemental storm that swept Russia in 1917. Their performance during 1905 had not been impressive when they had been backed by considerable force. In 1917 the kind of power the governors would have needed to maintain law and order simply did not exist. The former *nachal'niki gubernii* were lucky to have been on the sidelines from where they could observe, no doubt with a certain amount of *Schadenfreude,* the efforts of their successors, whose problems were all too familiar.[12]

The sudden dismissal of the governors in March of 1917 was appropriate to their status as the tsar's viceroys. As creatures of the emperor, the visible symbols of his rule in the provinces, it was natural that both the governors and the governorship should fall with the monarchy. Beyond this, their being cast aside was an expression of the desires of a significant portion of the Russian public. For more than a generation, the *nachal'niki gubernii* had been the *bête noire* of liberals and radicals. Seen as satraps who used and abused vast powers, they were considered barriers to real self-government and all attempts at legiti-

---

10. Kisel'-Zagorianskii, "Mémoires," pp. 223–24, BAR, Kisel'-Zagorianskii papers.

11. Stremoukhov, "Administrativnoe ustroistvo," sec. 1, p. 1. BAR, Kryzhanovskii papers; Liubimov, "Russkaia smuta," p. 35.

12. On the difficulties encountered by the gubernia commissars, see the document entitled "Obzor polozheniia Rossii za tri mesiatsa revoliutsii po dannym otdela snoshennii provintsii vremennogo komiteta gosudarstvennoi dumy," in Ia. Iakovlev, ed., "Mart–mai 1917 g.," *Krasnyi arkhiv* 15 (1920): 39–41.

mate civic activity. When Maksim Gor'kii sought to describe what he regarded as the arbitrary authoritarianism of Lev Tolstoi, he compared the object of his scorn to a provincial governor. It was an image calculated to produce a strong negative reaction in his readers.[13]

So firmly fixed was their unfavorable reputation among the liberal public, that even if governors did well, it did them no good. In 1913, I. Zhilkin, the writer of *Vestnik Evropy*'s "provincial survey," reported that two governors, Kostroma's P. P. Shilovskii and Saratov's P. P. Stremoukhov, were leaving their provinces amidst outpourings of local affection and good will. But the journalist was clearly unhappy having to report this kind of news, and lest his readers get the wrong impression, he added the following comment:

> One need not think, however, that these governors brought about something especially good in the provinces they are quitting. Their great virtue was chiefly that they gave a certain amount of space to the natural movement of local life without crushing it by the usual repression. And thus the population sighs thankfully, following with moist eyes the departing authorities.
>
> How sad and backward is the life of our provinces that there even governors can acquire enduring popularity.[14]

Nor was the criticism of the governors limited to liberal and radical publicists. Many of the masters of Russian belles lettres—M. E. Saltykov-Shchedrin, F. M. Dostoevskii, A. P. Chekhov, and L. N. Andreev—portrayed the governors' abuse of authority, their cruelty, and even more vividly, their incompetence and folly.[15] Scholars, too, added their voices by focusing on the excess of gubernatorial power. Such writers as I. A. Blinov, A. D. Gradovskii, V. M. Gessen, and N. I. Lazarevskii stressed the fact that the *nachal'niki gubernii* carried out two mutually incompatable functions: supervision (*nadzor*) of all gubernia institutions and active administration. This dual role put the governors beyond effective control because they were cast as both judges and jurors in their own cases.[16]

13. Rogger, *Russia*, p. 52.

14. *Vestnik Evropy* 48 (February 1913): 376–77.

15. Shchedrin's major work on the governors is *Pompaduri i pomadurshi*. An English-language edition, *The Pompadours*, trans. D. Magarshack (Ann Arbor, Mich., 1985), is now available. Dostoevskii presents a stunning portrait of a governor in *The Devils*; Chekhov gives us a description in his short story "Anna on the Neck." Andreev's complex but negative treatment is found in his work *Gubernator*.

16. Blinov, *Gubernatory*, esp. pp. 358–60; A. D. Gradovskii, "Reforma gubernatorskoi dolzhnosti," in *Sobranie sochinenii*, 9, pp. 563–95; V. M. Gessen, "Guber-

Government officials also produced their own critique of the governors. Although recognizing that the governors could and did misuse their authority and were often improperly subordinated to the center, official critics stressed the weakness of the governorship and the inability of the *nachal'niki gubernii* to impose their will and, with it, the policy of the government on the provinces. St. Petersburg bureaucrats sought a variety of ways to enhance the governors' power and to improve the institutions under their command.[17]

When the governors eventually passed under the inspection of the historians, their treatment did not significantly improve. The old criticisms continued to be voiced, and in addition to the familiar indictments of their malfeasance, incompetence, and the arbitrary abuse of power, governors were portrayed as a dark force operating within the imperial administration. The *nachal'niki gubernii* formed an effective conservative lobby that inspired the "counterreforms" of the 1890s and checked, by a combination of foot dragging and sabotage, the efforts of enlightened officials to modernize the institutional and agrarian structures of the empire.[18]

The reader of the preceding chapters has already encountered much that justifies the established picture of the governors; yet we ought to redraw at least some aspects of their image. Certainly there were many governors who were inadequate to the tasks entrusted to them. But if we take the gubernatorial corps as a whole, there are signs that point

nator kak organ nadzora," *Severnyi vestnik* (January 1898): 183–211; N. I. Lazarevskii, *Lektsii po russkomu gosudarstvennomu pravu* (2 vols.; St. Petersburg, 1910), 2, pp. 223–34.

17. The most comprehensive effort to study the reform of local administration is Korf's *Administrativnaia iustitsiia v Rossii,* esp. volume 1. An excellent work on the question in the period after 1900 is Neil Weissman's *Reform in Tsarist Russia: The State Bureaucracy and Local Government, 1900–1914* (New Brunswick, N.J., 1981). Other useful works on the question include, B. V. Anan'ich et al., *Krizis samoderzhaviia;* V. S. Diakin, *Samoderzhavie, burzhuaziia i dvorianstvo v 1907–1911 gg.* (Leningrad, 1978); Zaionchkovskii, *Rossiiskoe samoderzhavie,* L. G. Zakharova, *Zemskaia konterreforma* (Moscow, 1968); G. A. Hosking, *The Russian Constitutional Experiment: Government and Duma, 1907–1914* (Cambridge, 1973); E. Judge, *Pleve;* Heide Whelan, *Alexander III and the State Council: Bureaucracy and Counter-Reform in Late Tsarist Russia* (New Brunswick, N.J., 1981); G. Yaney, *The Urge to Mobilize.* Of considerable value is Stephen Sternheimer, "Administration and Political Development: An Inquiry into the Tsarist and Soviet Experience" (Ph.D diss., University of Chicago, 1974). Local reform is also discussed in the previously cited dissertations of James Mandel, Thomas Pearson, and Theodore Taranovski.

18. Zaionchkovskii, *Rossiiskoe samoderzhavie,* p. 208; H. Whelan, p. 132; S. Sternheimer, "Administering Development and Developing Administration: Organizational Conflict in Tsarist Bureaucracy," *Canadian-American Slavic Studies* 9 (Fall 1975): 290–91.

to growing skill and a real, albeit limited, professionalization. The selection patterns the MVD developed over the course of three decades brought into governorships men who understood both the theory and the practice of provincial politics and administration. Increasingly, they knew the peasant world and its problems as well.

Without question, most governors were conservatives who were devoted to the autocracy and served it according to their lights. They were not, however, a cohesive force resistant to all change. Nor were the governors united on the projects for the reform of provincial government that came from the offices of the MVD, though they usually supported measures that would rationalize and extend local bureaucratic structures.[19] Generalizations are again difficult on the question of agrarian reform. Some governors opposed it; others, perhaps a growing number, favored it or at the very least worked honestly for its implementation.[20]

Finally, our discussion of the governors' manner of rule suggests that they were far from being satraps. To be sure, the powers of the governors were enormous, but their duties exceeded the capacity of a single man. Moreover, in exercising their authority, governors had to work through overburdened and inefficient institutions and had to rely on subordinates who were incompetent, corrupt, and often unresponsive.

Gubernatorial control and direction of provincial affairs was made more difficult by the administrative and political pluralism that flourished in the gubernias. The field officials of the various central ministries were not fully subordinated to the governors' authority. They maintained direct ties with the bureaus in St. Petersburg, and their specialized spheres of activity were largely sealed off from the intervention of the *nachal'niki gubernii*. In theory, governors could give commands to these agencies; in practice, they seldom did. Moreover, any order a governor issued was likely to be of a strictly negative character—a call to cease a particular operation or practice. Yet a local ministerial field agent who strongly opposed such an order could appeal to his minister, often with good results for himself and trouble for the governor. As a consequence, *nachal'niki gubernii* usually moved cautiously.

19. See *Svod mnenii gg. gubernatorov po predlozheniiam ob ustroistve mestnogo upravleniia* (St. Petersburg, n.d.), and "Izvlechenie iz otzyvov gubernatorov po voprosu o preobrazovanii gubernskogo upravleniia," TsGIA, f. DOD, op. 194, 1903, d. 150, ch. 1, "Po gubernskoi reforme."

20. Yaney, *Urge,* pp. 289, 295–302. In 1912 the government issued a medal (*znak otlichiia*) for distinction in land settlement work. By 1913, thirty of the forty-three governors who had been in office for over a year (70 percent) had received the decoration.

Much the same was true about the governors' relations with local self-government. Although a great deal has been said about the governors' oppression of the zemstvos and urban dumas, the extent and nature of their actions have been distorted. For it is easy to forget, when encountering an act of gubernatorial *proizvol*, that the *nachal'niki gubernii* possessed few direct controls over self-government, especially the zemstvos. A governor could only block the actions of elected institutions temporarily, and zemstvo and duma leaders had the right to appeal many of his rulings. Conversely, the *nachal'nik gubernii* was unable to force these bodies to undertake measures they opposed. If he desired to achieve positive goals, he had to use persuasion, not command.

The many problems the governors faced at the local level were compounded by the absence of consistent direction and backing from the center. Prior to 1905 there was not even the pretense of a unified government in St. Petersburg; afterward there was only the pretense. Even the MVD itself did not pursue a consistent course because the rapid turnover of ministers from 1895 to 1917 made this impossible. As a consequence, governors were often unsure of support from the capital when provincial conflicts developed.

All these circumstances rendered the exercise of gubernatorial power inconsistent and uncertain. The many obstacles that inhibited their work caused some governors to lapse into passivity, whereas others ran roughshod over those who stood in their way. Most *nachal'niki gubernii*, however, avoided either extreme. Relying on their viceregal status, service tact, and the political skills acquired after long provincial service, they entered into a seemingly endless series of negotiations and compromises with subordinate officials, independent state agencies, institutions of self-government, workers' delegations, and peasant communes. What resulted was a highly personal and variable style of rule. It was possible for governors to be quite arbitrary and oppressive, though they themselves were open to all kind of pressures and even humiliations. Circumstance were such that in the last years of the old regime governors managed the provinces as much through achieved consensus as by decrees and acts of administrative fiat. Far from being satraps, they were often supplicants. Time and again they had to act as salesmen in situations in which influence was as important as authority, and real power was but an illusive dream.

By the beginning of the twentieth century, the Russian governorship was an archaic institution.[21] Despite the rapid changes taking place in

21. The Soviet scholar P. N. Zyrianov calls "archaism" (*arkhaichnost'*) the chief characteristic of prerevolutionary provincial administration. See his "Sotsial'naia struk-

Russian society, the *nachal'niki gubernii* continued to operate in a personal, viceregal manner suited to earlier times. They had little choice, for they lacked the means to do otherwise. Individual governors, it is true, might display considerable skill in affecting a more up-to-date political style, taking on some of the attributes of a modern ward heeler or glad-handing politician. But there were marked limits to this kind of adaptation, so that gubernatorial rule, though it might be quite effective, was, just as often, intrusive and arbitrary. Always, however, it rested on weak foundations.

The Russian government and the educated public recognized the problems associated with the governorship, but the institution remained unreformed. And this fact highlights a larger issue; namely, that in the waning years of the old regime, Russians could neither agree on a way to improve local government nor find a means of combining tolerable levels of bureaucratic management and societal participation in a decentralized setting.

The path to reforming Russian local administration was not an obscure one and had already been blazed, most notably in France. There, an essentially viceregal officer, the prefect, had been absorbed into a coherent bureaucratic system in the course of the nineteenth century. Assisted by subprefects and a variety of other subordinates, the prefect presided over an integrated administration and thereby had the means of both maintaining order and meeting local needs. Yet that official's independence and capacity for abuse were restrained by the authority of the minister of the interior, the existence of elected institutions and autonomous bodies, and the principle of legality.

Under the old regime, Russia was unable to follow in the direction Europe had taken because the persistence of autocracy always limited the expansion of the bureaucratic principle. Indeed, the tsars were distrustful of the ministerial system they had created and looked for ways to bypass or subvert it. The extradepartmental (*vnevedomstvennyi*) governorship was a means to that end, and for that reason emperors resisted the attempts of reformers to make the *nachal'niki gubernii* creatures of the MVD. The tsars understood that if the governors were to be transformed into prefects, they would be links in the chain of ministerial power. As viceroys—personal representatives of the sovereign—the governors helped keep the emperors from becom-

---

tura mestnogo upravleniia kapitalisticheskoi Rossii (1861–1914)," *Istoricheskie zapiski* 107 (1982): 289.

ing dependent on their ministers and gave the autocrat a direct connection to the provinces and the people.

The viceregal governorship also survived because provincial elites were distrustful of efforts by officials at the center to rationalize local administration. These elites particularly opposed a crucial aspect of proposed reforms; namely, the creation of a government officer at the uezd level who would correspond to the French subprefect. Such a development would, they feared, undercut the nobility's traditional leadership and dilute their power in a series of bureaucratic instances and "all-class" institutions. Gentry suspicions made it impossible for reformers to devise a formula for local governance that could have placed gubernatorial power on firmer administrative footing.

But the persistence of the viceregal governorship was not simply the result of the tsars' concern for their power or the failure of governmental and social elites to agree on the shape of reform. The vast size and diversity of the empire and the difficulty of guiding local administration from the capital made it necessary to grant provincial officials a significant degree of autonomy. Moreover, long tradition had accustomed local people to the presence of a figure who appeared, at least, to wield real power in a direct manner; someone who was able to ignore or set aside often incomprehensible regulations and the decisions of lesser authorities. After centuries of *namestniki, voevody,* and *gubernatory,* this was the way that most Russians expected, even wanted to be governed.

Desired or not, the viceregal style of provincial rule proved enduring. The governors were, to be sure, swept away by the revolution. The stormy years following 1917 saw an upsurge of localism that made life difficult for those who tried to represent the central government in the provinces.[22] But by the end of the 1920s, strong local authority had once again been established. A new figure, the party first secretary, emerged as the leading force in provincial administration. Like his predecessor, the *gubkom*—later *obkom*—secretary stood outside the strictly governmental hierarchy embodying the party principle just as the *nachal'nik gubernii* had personified the idea of autocracy. Like the governor, the party first secretary combined broad supervisory author-

22. For a discussion of this problem see A. I. Mikoian's account of his experiences in Nizhni-Novgorod in the early years of Soviet power (*V nachale dvadtsatykh* [Moscow, 1975], pp. 24–161), and the article by T. H. Rigby, "Early Provincial Cliques and the Rise of Stalin," *Soviet Studies* 33 (January 1981): 3–28.

ity with the work of active administration and, as a result, was not easily called to account by local people. As the democratic tide flowing from the revolution began to ebb, the party secretary would stand as "God and Tsar" in the region entrusted to his care.[23]

Obviously, it would be wrong to draw too exact a parallel between pre- and postrevolutionary provincial chiefs. In many ways the party secretaries were more powerful than their tsarist counterparts. The revolution had greatly simplified the social structure of the gubernias by eliminating some of the classes, groups, and institutions that had so often frustrated the governors. The assumption by the state of a dominant role in both industry and agriculture at the end of the 1920s gave to the *obkom* secretaries a field of activity and a range of authority that no governor ever possessed. In addition, the new regime created a more complete administrative hierarchy at the local level, and though it was plagued by many of the same problems of bureaucratic incompetence, corruption, and inefficiency as the prerevolutionary apparatus, it offered, over time at least, the prospect of more effective management and control.

Ultimately, central authority also loomed larger in the life of the provincial bosses than it had in the years before 1917, but it took time for Moscow to achieve effective control over local leaders. In the late 1920s and early 1930s, party first secretaries not only wielded great power in their regions but also enjoyed wide autonomy and protected themselves and their subordinates through a network of clientage and corruption. Some, like Smolensk's I. P. Rumiantsev, crudely aped the style of their imperial predecessors and were viewed by local people much in the way that governors had been.[24] In fact, firm central control over the provinces was not achieved until the end of the 1930s. Then Stalin used purge and terror to curb the power of local hierarchs. Almost to a man, the *obkom* secretaries who had held office in 1937 were removed and disappeared. Moscow replaced them with young, often inexperienced people who were, as a consequence, far more tractable than their predecessors.[25]

23. Merle Fainsod, *How Russia Is Ruled* (2d ed.; Cambridge, Mass., 1963), p. 225.

24. Merle Fainsod, *Smolensk under Soviet Rule* (Cambridge, Mass., 1958), pp. 60, 225–29, 396–405.

25. For a discussion of the role of the purges in the reshaping of Soviet provincial administration, see J. Arch Getty, "The 'Great Purges' Reconsidered: The Soviet Communist Party, 1933–1939" (Ph.D diss., Boston College, 1979), pp. 518–26. Getty's views on the Soviet terror are presented with greater reserve in his book *Origins of the Great Purges: The Soviet Communist Party Reconsidered, 1933–1938* (Cambridge, 1985).

The regional secretaries did not lose all their authority, of course. They continued to supervise local administration and to coordinate a variety of economic activities. Many modeled themselves on Stalin and ruled in a manner reminiscent of the supreme "boss." Yet these officers, though not simple cogs in a wheel, were, nevertheless, now part of an integrated governmental machine. Clearly, the chief figure on the provincial scene was no longer a viceroy, he was a prefect.[26]

The system of local administration established in the late 1930s has persisted, for the most part, down to the present. The party secretaries continue to be "prefects," subordinated managers and coordinators operating within and through a hierarchical administrative structure. Yet, with the passage of time certain elements of the old "viceregal" style of rule have made their appearance. The trials of war and reconstruction thrust unprecedented burdens on the party secretaries and placed a high premium on personal independence and initiative.[27] Moreover, the post-Stalin era has been marked by the growing "pluralism" of Soviet society, and this has magnified the party secretaries' role as mediators between a variety of interests.

The current Soviet prefect as depicted by Jerry Hough and others regularly engages in a process of bargaining with key elements on the provincial scene, much as their prececessors did.[28] Undoubtedly, the *obkom* secretary's ability to function is enhanced by his role as the party's chief representative and his position outside the state's administrative structure in the same way as the governor's viceregal and extradepartmental status aided him in his work. Like the governor, the *obkom* secretary possesses the power of command, but it is a power used sparingly. As in the past, authority in the provinces remains considerably fragmented, and much more is to be gained by striking a deal with an important local figure than by striking him down. Hough's general estimate of the conduct of local party secretaries underlines the degree of continuity with gubernatorial practice: "The nature of the party organ's work makes it quite impossible for local party officials to be unbending ideologues intent upon enforcing the

---

26. The term "Soviet prefect" is Jerry Hough's.

27. See the memoirs of two former obkom secretaries, Leonid Brezhnev, *Trilogy: Little Land, Rebirth, The Virgin Lands* (New York, 1980), pp. 105–230, and N. S. Patolichev, *Measures of Maturity: My Early Life*, trans. Y. S. Shirokov and Y. S. Sviridov (Oxford and New York, 1983), pp. 190–289.

28. Jerry Hough, *The Soviet Prefects: The Local Party Organs in Industrial Decision-Making* (Cambridge, Mass., 1969), pp. 120–24, 311–15. See also Joel C. Moses, *Regional Party Leadership and Policy Making in the USSR* (New York, 1974), pp. 154–55.

letter of central decrees. If party officials are to be successful, they must have a keen sense of how and when to bend the rules, and surely they create far fewer grievances if they learn to bargain out conflicts instead of relying on fiat."[29]

The large role that negotiation and compromise continue to play in Russian local administration heightens the importance of the party secretary's personality, as can be seen from Soviet belles-lettres and memoirs. Since World War II a number of works published in the USSR devote a good deal of space to the party secretaries. Such depictions should not be seen as entirely realistic descriptions of governmental practices, though they shed much light on the kind of qualities desired in a Soviet prefect. Special attention is paid to the secretary's personal attributes—forcefulness, energy, and devotion to duty. At the same time, these works show the secretary as a man possessed of considerable charm, who is accessible to the public, and demonstrates fatherly concern for the people of his district. Soviet literature does not accentuate the party secretary's function as mediator and negotiator, for this emphasis might suggest a kind of conflict that would not square with the official image of societal harmony and clear, firm party leadership. Yet, the party secretary is not portrayed as rigid or inflexible. He is down to earth and practical, not a windbag ideologue.[30]

Local administration in the USSR today differs greatly from provincial government under the old regime. But personality still determines much. Therefore it is not surprising that the idealized Soviet prefects found on the pages of contemporary socialist realist writings meet most of Karamzin's desiderata for governors: men able to check the abuses of minor officials, maintain justice, satisfy the peasants, encourage industry, and protect the interests of the state and nation. How many such people have been found to lead Soviet local government we cannot say. The tsarist experience suggests that despite some success in creating a pool of talent and regularizing the paths to high provincial office, there were always corrupt and abusive *nachal'niki gubernii*.

29. Jerry Hough and Merle Fainsod, *How the Soviet Union Is Governed* (Cambridge, Mass., 1979), p. 510.

30. Peter S. Bridges, "The Character of the Party Secretary in Postwar Soviet Novels" (M.A. thesis, Columbia University, 1955), especially pp. 60, 125–28, 132–33. A full-scale novelistic treatment of the oblast party secretary is in Vsevolod Kochetov, *Sekretar' obkoma* (Moscow, 1963). In the same vein is the section of Leonid Brezhnev's "memoirs" titled "Rebirth" (Brezhnev, *Trilogy*, pp. 105–230). See also T. H. Rigby, "How the Obkom Secretary Was Tempered," *Problems of Communism* 29 (March–April 1980): 57–63.

And it would appear that comparable efforts at professionalizing the Soviet prefects and far more comprehensive methods of control have not solved the problem in the USSR.[31] Russia is still looking for fifty good governors.

---

31. Rigby, "Soviet Regional Leadership: The Brezhnev Generation," *Slavic Review* 37 (March 1978): 13–22; Robert E. Blackwell, Jr., "Career Development in the Soviet Obkom Elite: A Conservative Trend," *Soviet Studies* 24 (July 1972): 24–40; idem, "The Soviet Political Elite: Alternative Recruitment Policies at the Obkom Level," *Comparative Politics* 6 (October 1973): 99–121; Peter Frank, "The CPSU Obkom First Secretary: A Profile," *British Journal of Political Science* 1 (1971): 173–90; Nick Lampert, "Law and Order in the USSR: The Case of Economic and Official Crime," *Soviet Studies* 36 (July 1984): 366–85; and Konstantin Simis, *USSR: The Corrupt Society* (New York, 1982), especially pp. 65–95.

GLOSSARY

duma	city council
dvorianstvo	nobility, gentry
gubernator	governor
gubernatorsha	governor's wife
guberniia	province, gubernia
gubernskoe po krest'ianskim delam prisutstvie, later *gubernskoe prisutstvie*	provincial committee on peasant affairs
gubernskoe po zemskim i gorodskim delam prisutstvie	provincial committee on zemstvo and urban affairs
gubernskoe pravlenie	provincial board
ispravnik	police chief
kazennaia palata	fiscal chamber
MVD	Ministry of Internal Affairs
nachal'nik gubernii	governor
obzor	survey
otchet	report
pravitel' kantseliarii	head of chancellery
predvoditel'	marshal
pristav	district officer
proizvol	arbitrariness, rule by fiat
reviziia	inspection
revizor	inspector
sovetnik	councilor
uezd	county, uezd
uprava	executive board

upravliaiushchii kazennoiu palatoiu	fiscal administrator
volnenie	disturbance, riot
volost'	canton, volost
zemskii nachal'nik	land captain

BIBLIOGRAPHY

ARCHIVAL SOURCES

(Materials are listed by collection. In the case of Soviet documents, the number of the *fond* is given in parentheses.)

Bakhmeteff Archive (BAR)—Columbia University

V. M. Andreevskii
E. M. Brofel'dt
A. F. and L. A. Girs
A. D. Golitsyn
V. V. Khoromanskii
N. N. Kisel'-Zagorianskii
I. F. Koshko and family
S. E. Kryzhanovskii
D. N. Liubimov
N. A. Mel'nikov
A. A. Spasskii-Odynets
K. K. Troitskii

Gosudarstvennyi Arkhiv Kalininskoi Oblasti (GAKO)

Kantseliariia tverskogo gubernatora (56)
Tverskoe gubernskoe pravlenie (466)

Gosudarstvennaia Biblioteka imeni V. I. Lenina. Otdel Rukopisei (GBL)

M. M. Osorgin (215)

Gosudarstvennaia Publichnaia Biblioteka imeni M. E. Saltykova-Shchedrina. Otdel Rukopisei (GPB)

I. Ia. Denman (78)
Reviziia A. A. Polovtsova (600)

Leningradskii Gosudarstvennyi Istoricheskii Arkhiv (LGIA)

Kantseliariia petrogradskogo gubernatora (253)
Petrogradskoe gubernskoe po zemskim i gorodskim delam prisutstvie (259)
Petrogradskoe gubernskoe pravlenie (254)

Tsentral'nyi Gosudarstvennyi Arkhiv Literatury i Iskusstva SSSR (TsGALI)

Sverbeevy (472)

Tsentral'nyi Gosudarstvennyi Arkhiv Oktiabr'skoi Revoliutsii (TsGAOR)

Departament Politsii (102)
V. F. Dzhunkovskii (826)
V. V. fon Val' (542)
Kollektsiia otdel'nykh dokumentov lichnogo proiskhozhdeniia (1463)
V. K. Pleve (586)

Tsentral'nyi Gosudarstvennyi Istoricheskii Arkhiv Moskvy (TsGIAM)

Kantseliariia moskovskogo gubernatora (17)
Moskovskoe gubernskoe po zemskim i gorodskim delam prisutstvie (65)
Moskovskoe gubernskoe prisutstvie (62)

Tsentral'nyi Gosudarstvennyi Istoricheskii Arkhiv SSSR (TsGIA)

A. V. Adlerberg (882)
N. A. Bezak (895)
Departament obshchikh del Ministerstva vnutrennikh del (1284)
V. V. fon Val' i Miasoedovy (916)
Gosudarstvennaia kantseliariia (1162)
Kantseliariia Ministra vnutrennikh del (1282)
Kantseliariia Ministra vnutrennikh del po delam dvorianstva (1283)
Khoziaistvennyi departament Ministerstva vnutrennikh del (1287)
Komitet Ministrov (1263)
Ministerstvo iustitsii (1405)
Ministerstvo torgovli i promyshlennosti (23)
N. P. Muratov (875)
Osobaia komissia dlia sostavleniia proektov mestnogo upravleniia, "Kakhanov-
    skaia komissiia" (1317)
K. K. Palen (1016)

Reviziia senatora I. I. Shamshina saratovskoi i samarskoi gubernii (1391)

G. G. Savich (1045)

Sipiaginy (721)

Tekhnichesko-stroitel'nyi komitet Ministerstva vnutrennikh del (1293)

S. A. i S. D. Tol' (1064)

N. A. Troinitskii (1065)

Tsentral'nyi statisticheskii komitet Ministerstva vnutrennikh del (1290)

Upravlenie zheleznykh dorog Ministerstva putei soobshcheniia (273)

Zemskii otdel Ministerstva vnutrennikh del (1291)

Zhurnaly departamentov Gosudarstvennogo soveta (1160)

ARTICLES, BOOKS, DISSERTATIONS

Abbot, Robert J. "Police Reform in Russia, 1858–1878." Ph.D. diss., Princeton University, 1971.

Adelman, Jonathan R. "The Development of the Soviet Party Apparat in the Civil War: Center, Localities, and Nationality Areas." *Russian History* 9 (1982): 86–110.

Adres-kalendar'. St. Petersburg, annual.

Aleksandrov, M. S. *Gosudarstvo, biurokratiia i absoliutizm v istorii Rossii.* St. Petersburg, 1910.

Al'manakh sovremennykh russkikh gosudarstvennykh deiatelei. St. Petersburg, 1897.

Amburger, Erik. *Geschichte der Behördenorganisation Russlands von Peter dem Grossen bis 1917.* Leiden, 1966.

Anan'ich, B. V., et al. *Krizis samoderzhaviia v Rossii, 1895–1917.* Leningrad, 1984.

Andreev, Leonid N. *Krasnyi smekh: Izbrannye rasskazy i povesti.* Minsk, 1981.

Andreevskii, I. *O namestnikakh, voevodakh i gubernatorakh.* St. Petersburg, 1864.

Armstrong, John A. "Old Regime Administrative Elites: Prelude to Modernization in France, Prussia and Russia." *International Review of Administrative Sciences* 38 (1972): 21–40.

——. "Old Regime Governors: Bureaucratic and Patrimonial Attitudes." *Comparative Studies in Society and History* 14 (1972): 2–29.

——. "Tsarist and Soviet Elite Administrators." *Slavic Review* 21 (March 1972): 1–28.

B., P. "Neobychainyi gubernator (Stranichka iz vospominanii)." *Na chuzhoi storone* 8 (1924): 159–65.

Baedeker, Karl. *Russia: A Handbook for Travelers (A facsimile of the original 1914 edition).* New York, 1971.

Becker, Seymour. *Nobility ~nd Privilege in Late Imperial Russia.* DeKalb, Ill., 1985.

Benford, Benjamin L. "Tsarist Nationalist Policy and the Baltic Germans: The Example of Prince S. V. Shakhovskoi, Governor of Estonia, 1885–1894." *Canadian Review of Studies in Nationalism* 2 (Spring 1975): 317–333.

Berendts, E. N. *O proshlom i nastoiashchem russkoi administratsii.* 2d ed. St. Petersburg, 1913.

Blackwell, Robert E., Jr. "Career Development in the Soviet Obkom Elite: A Conservative Trend." *Soviet Studies* 24 (July 1972): 24–40.

——. "The Soviet Political Elite: Alternative Recruitment Policies at the Obkom Level." *Comparative Politics* 6 (October 1973): 99–121.

Blinov, I. A. *Gubernatory. Istoriko-iuridicheskii ocherk.* St. Petersburg, 1905.

——. "Nadzor za deialtel'nosti gubernatorov (istoriko-iuridicheskii ocherk)." *Vestnik prava* 32 (September 1902): 37–77.

Bock, Mary Stolypin. "Stolypin in Saratov." *Russian Review* 12 (July 1953): 187–93.

Bogoslovskii, M. M. *Oblastnaia reforma Petra Velikogo: Provintsiia 1719–27 gg.* Moscow, 1902.

Bol'shov, V. V. "Materialy senatorskikh revizii 1880–1881 gg. kak istochnik po istorii mestnogo upravleniia Rossii." *Vestnik moskovskogo universiteta, seriia istorii* no. 4 (1976): 38–54.

Bonch-Bruevich, V. D. *Izbrannye sochineniia.* 3 vols. Moscow, 1959–63.

Bonnell, Victoria E. *Roots of Rebellion: Workers' Politics and Organizations in St. Petersburg and Moscow, 1900–1914.* Berkeley, 1983.

Brezhnev, L. I. *Trilogy: Little Land, Rebirth, The Virgin Lands.* New York, 1980. Originally pub. 1978.

Bridges, Peter S. "The Character of the Party Secretary in Postwar Soviet Novels." M.A. thesis, Columbia University, 1955.

Browder, Robert P., and Alexander F. Kerensky, eds. *The Russian Provisional Government: Documents.* 3 vols. Stanford, Calif., 1961.

Brower, Daniel R. "Labor Violence in Russia in the Later Nineteenth Century." *Slavic Review* 41 (Fall 1982): 417–31.

Bushnell, John. *Mutiny amid Repression: Russian Soldiers in the Revolution of 1905–1907.* Bloomington, Ind., 1985.

——. "The Tsarist Officer Corps. 1881–1914: Customs, Duties, Inefficiency." *American Historical Review* 86 (October 1981): 753–80.

Chapman, Brian. *The Prefects and Provincial France.* London, 1955.

Chicherin, B. I. *Oblastnye uchrezhdeniia Rossii v XVII-m veke.* Moscow, 1856.

Christian, David. "The Supervisory Function in Russian and Soviet History." *Slavic Review* 41 (Spring 1982): 73–90.

Daniels, Robert V. "The Secretariat and the Local Organizations of the Russian Communist Party, 1921–1923." *American Slavic and East European Review* 16 (March 1957): 32–49.

De Madariaga, Isabel. *Russia in the Age of Catherine the Great.* New Haven, 1981.

Diakin, V. S. *Samoderzhavie, burzhuaziia i dvorianstvo v 1907–1911 gg.* Leningrad, 1978.

——. "Stolypin i dvorianstvo." *Problemy krest'ianskogo zemledeliia i vnutrennei politiki Rossii. Dookiabr'skoi period.* Leningrad, 1972.

Diatlova, N. P. "Otchety gubernatorov kak istorichesii istochnik." *Problemy arkhivovedeniia i istochnikovedeniia.* Leningrad, 1964.

Drezen, A. K., ed. *Tsarizm v bor'be s revoliutsiei 1905–1907 gg: Sbornik dokumentov.* Moscow, 1936.

Driagin, N. "K voprosu o diskretsionnoi vlasti gubernatorov." *Pravo* (May 20, 1901): 1065–68.

Dubnov, S. M. *History of the Jews in Russia and Poland.* 3 vols. Philadelphia, 1918.

Edelman, Robert. *Gentry Politics on the Eve of the Russian Revolution: The Nationalist Party, 1907–1917.* New Brunswick, N.J., 1980.

Efremova, N. N. *Ministerstvo iustitsii rossiiskoi imperii, 1802–1917 gg.* Moscow, 1983.

Elistratov, A. I. *Osnovye nachala administrativnogo prava.* Moscow, 1914.

Emmons, Terence. *The Formation of Political Parties and the First National Elections in Russia.* Cambridge, Mass., and London, 1983.

——. and Wayne Vucinich, eds. *The Zemstvo in Russia: An Experiment in Local Self-Government.* Cambridge, London, New York, 1982.

Engel'gardt, A. P. *Chernozemnaia Rossiia: Ocherk ekonomicheskogo polozheniia kraia.* Saratov, 1902.

——. *A Russian Province of the North.* Translated by Henry Cooke. Westminster, 1899. Originally pub. 1898.

Eroshkin, N. P. *Istoriia gosudarstvennykh uchrezhdenii dorevoliutsionnoi Rossii.* 2d ed. Moscow, 1968.

Fadeev, A. M. *Vospominaniia, 1790–1867.* 2 vols. Odessa, 1897.

Fainsod, Merle. *How Russia Is Ruled.* 2d ed. Cambridge, Mass., 1963.

——. *Smolensk under Soviet Rule.* Cambridge, Mass., 1958.

Frank, Peter. "The CPSU Obkom First Secretary: A Profile." *British Journal of Political Science* 1 (1971): 173–90.

Fried, Robert. *The Italian Prefects: A Study in Administrative Politics.* New Haven and London, 1963.

Frieden, Nancy M. *Russian Physicians in an Era of Reform and Revolution, 1856–1905.* Princeton, N.J., 1981.

Fuller, William C., Jr. *Civil-Military Conflict in Imperial Russia, 1881–1914.* Princeton, N.J., 1985.

Gantvoort, John G. "Relations between Government and Zemstvos under Valuev and Timashev, 1864–1876." Ph.D. diss., University of Illinois, 1971.

Gard, William. "The Party and the Proletariat in Ivanovo-Voznesensk, 1905." *Russian History* 2, pt. 2 (1975): 101–23.

Gessen, V. M. *Voprosy mestnogo upravleniia.* St. Petersburg, 1904.

Getty, John Arch. "The 'Great Purges' Reconsidered: The Soviet Communist Party, 1933–1939." Ph.D. diss., Boston College, 1979.

——. *Origins of the Great Purges: The Soviet Communist Party Reconsidered, 1933–1938.* Cambridge, 1985.

Gogel, S. K. "Gubernskie prisutstviia smeshannogo sostava, kak organy administrativnoi iustitsii na mestakh." *Vestnik prava* 36 (1906): 393–466.

Gosudarstvennyi sovet: Pechatnye materialy, 1896–1906. 180 vols. St. Petersburg, 1896–1906.

Got'e, Iu. V. *Istoriia oblastnogo upravleniia v Rossii ot Petra I do Ekateriny II.* 2 vols. Moscow, 1913–1941.

Grabbe, Paul. *Windows on the River Neva.* New York, 1977.

Gradovskii, A. D. *Sobranie sochineniia.* 9 vols. St. Petersburg, 1899–1904.

Greenberg, Louis. *The Jews in Russia: The Struggle for Emancipation.* 2 vols. New Haven, 1944, 1951.

"Gubernator dobrogo starogo vremeni. Vospominaniia starozhila." *Russkaia starina* 131 no. 7 (1907): 188–96.

Gurko, V. I. *Features and Figures of the Past: Government and Opinion in the Reign of Nicholas II.* Stanford, Calif. 1939.

Haimson, Leopold H., ed. *The Politics of Rural Russia, 1905–1914.* Bloomington, 1979.

Hamburg, Gary M. *The Politics of the Russian Nobility, 1881–1905.* New Brunswick, N.J., 1984.

——. "Portrait of an Elite: Russian Marshals of the Nobility, 1861–1917." *Slavic Review* 40, (Winter 1981): 585–602.

Hamm, Michael F. "Khar'kov's Progressive Duma, 1910–1914: A Study in Russian Municipal Reform." *Slavic Review* 40 (Spring 1981): 17–36.

Hanchett, Walter. "Tsarist Statutory Regulation of Municipal Government in the Nineteenth Century." In Michael F. Hamm, ed. *The City in Russian History.* Lexington, Ky, 1976.

Hosking, Geoffery A. *The Russian Constitutional Experiment: Government and Duma, 1907–1914.* Cambridge, 1973.

Hough, Jerry F. "The Bureaucratic Model and the Nature of the Soviet System." *Journal of Comparative Public Administration* 5 (August 1973): 134–68.

——. "The Soviet Concept of the Relationship between the Lower Party Organs and the State Administration." *Slavic Review* 24 (June 1965): 215–40.

——. *The Soviet Prefects: The Local Party Organs in Industrial Decision-Making.* Cambridge, Mass., 1969.

—— and Merle Fainsod. *How the Soviet Union Is Governed.* Cambridge, Mass., 1979.

Hutton, Lester T. "The Reform of City Government in Russia, 1860–1870." Ph.D. diss. University of Illinois, 1972.

Iakovlev, Ia., ed. "Mart–mai 1917 g.." *Krasnyi arkhiv* 15 (1920): 30–60.

Ikonnikov, N. *N d R, La Noblesse de Russie.* 2d ed. 51 vols. Paris, 1957–1966.

Iordanskii, N. M. "Sekretnye Tsirkuliary (Iz arkhiva zemskogo nachal'nika)." *Golos minuvshego* 4 (May–June 1916): 181–88.

Istoricheskie dannye ob obrazovanii gubernii, oblastei, gradonachal'stv i drugikh chastei vnutrennogo upravleniia imperii, s ukazaniem vysshikh chinov etogo upravleniia v khronologicheskim poriadke po 1 noiabria 1902. St. Petersburg, 1902.

Ivanovskii, V. "Obshchie nachala v ustroistve gubernshkikh vlastei." *Zhurnal iuridicheskogo obshchestva pri imperatorskoi s-peterburgskoi universitete* 26 (January 1896): 47–94.

——. *Uchebnik administrativnogo prava. (Politseiskoe pravo. Pravo vnutrennogo upravleniia).* Kazan, 1907.

"Izvlechenie iz otcheta pomoshchika upravliaiushego zemskim otdelom Ministerstva vnutrennikh del, deistvitel'nogo statskogo sovetnika Stefanovicha, o revizii kaluzhskogo gubernskogo prisutstviia i nekotorykh krest'ianskikh uchrezhdenii kaluzhskoi gubernii." *Izvestiia zemskogo otdela* (1907) no. 10: 425–51.

Jacob, Herbert. *German Administration since Bismarck: Central Authority versus Local Autonomy.* New Haven, 1963.

Jones, Robert E. *The Emancipation of the Russian Nobility, 1762–1785.* Princeton, N.J., 1973.

——. *Provincial Development in Russia: Catherine II and Jacob Sievers.* New Brunswick, N.J., 1984.

Judge, Edward H. *Plehve: Repression and Reform in Imperial Russia, 1902–1904.* Syracuse, N.Y., 1983.

Karamzin, N. M. *Memoir on Ancient and Modern Russia.* Translated by Richard Pipes. Cambridge, Mass. 1959. Originally pub. 1861.

Karnovich, E. *Russkie chinovniki v byloe i nastoiashchee vremia.* St. Petersburg, 1897.

Karpov, N., ed. *Krest'ianskoe dvizhenie v revoliutsii 1905 goda v dokumentakh.* Leningrad, 1926.

Khitrovo, L. "Gubernator-original, 1861–63 (Stranichka iz vospominanii)." *Vestnik Evropy* 49 (December 1914): 221–37.

Khizhniakov, V. M. *Vospominaniia zemskogo deiatelia.* Petrograd, 1916.

Khoromanskii, V. M., ed. *Stoletie tipografii saratovskogo gubernskogo pravleniia.* Saratov, 1895.

"K istorii agrarnoi reformy Stolypina." *Krasnyi arkhiv* 17 (1926): 81–90.

Kizevetter, A. A. *Mestnoe samoupravlenie v Rossii, IX–XIX st.: Istoricheskii ocherk.* Moscow, 1910.

Klochkov, M. V. *Ocherki pravitel'stvennoi deiatel'nosti vremeni Pavla I.* Petrograd, 1916.

Kochetov, V. *Sekretar' obkoma.* Moscow, 1963.

Korelin, A. P. *Dvorianstvo v poreformennoi Rossii, 1861–1904.* Moscow, 1979.

Korf, S. A. *Administrativnaia iustitsiia v Rossii.* 2 vols. St. Petersburg, 1910.

——. "Ocherk istoricheskogo razvitiia gubernatorskoi dolzhnosti v Rossii." *Vestnik prava* 31 (November 1901): 130–48.

Korkunov, N. M. *Russkoe gosudarstvennoe pravo.* 4th ed. 2 vols. St. Petersburg, 1901.

Koshko, I. F. *Vospominaniia gubernatora (1905–1914 g.). Novgorod, Samara, Penza.* Petrograd, 1916.

Kosich, A. I. *Tsirkuliary, ukazaniia i rechi g. nachal'nika saratovskoi gubernii General-Leitenanta A. I. Kosicha, 1887–1891 g.* Saratov, 1891.

Krest'ianskoe dvizhenie 1902 g. (Materialy po istorii krest'ianskikh dvizhenii v Rossii, vypusk 3.) Moscow, 1923.

Krest'ianskoe dvizhenie v Rossii. Iiun' 1907–iiul' 1914. Edited by A. V. Shapkarin. Moscow and Leningrad, 1966.

Krest'ianskoe dvizhenie v Rossii v gody pervoi mirovoi voiny, iiul' 1914 g–fevral' 1917 g. Edited by A. M. Anfimov. Moscow and Leningrad, 1965.

Krest'ianskoe dvizhenie v Rossii v 1870–1880 gg. Edited by P. A. Zaionchkovskii. Moscow, 1968.

Krest'ianskoe dvizhenie v Rossii v 1881–1889 gg. Edited by A. V. Nifontov and B. V. Zlatoustovskii. Moscow, 1960.

Krest'ianskoe dvizhenie v Rossii v 1890–1900 gg. Edited by A. V. Shapkarin. Moscow, 1959.

Kryzhanovskii, S. E. *Vospominaniia.* Berlin, n.d.

Kucherov, Samuel. *Courts, Lawyers and Trials under the Last Three Tsars.* New York, 1953.

Kuprin, A. I. "Ten' Napoleona." In *Sobranie sochinenii*. 9 vols. Moscow, 1973, 7: 420–27.

Kurenkov, A. N. "Dnevnik samarskogo gubernatora A. D. Sverbeeva." *Istochnikovedenie i istoriografiia. Spetsial'nye istoricheskie distsipliny. Sbornik statei*. Moscow, 1980.

Kurlov, P. G. *Konets russkogo tsarizma: Vospominaniia byvshego komandira korpusa zhandarmov*. Petrograd and Moscow, 1923.

Kuzmin-Karavaev, V. D. *Zemstvo i derevnia, 1898–1903*. St. Petersburg, 1904.

Lampert, Nick. "Law and Order in the USSR: The Case of Economic and Official Crime." *Soviet Studies* 36 (July 1984): 366–85.

Lazarevskii, N. I. *Lektsii po russkomu gosudarstvennomu pravu*. 2d ed. 2 vols. St. Petersburg, 1910.

LeDonne, John P. "Catherine's Governors and Governors-General, 1763–1796." *Cahiers du Monde Russe et Sovietique* 20 (January–March 1979): 15–42.

——. "The Evolution of the Governor's Office, 1727–64." *Canadian-American Slavic Studies* 12 (1978): 86–115.

——. "From Gubernia to Oblast: Soviet Territorial-Administrative Reform, 1917–1923." Ph.D. diss., Columbia University, 1962.

——. *Ruling Russia: Politics and Administration in the Age of Absolutism*. Princeton, N.J. 1984.

Lesnitskaia, V. "Vospominaniia o Burkharine." *Russkaia starina* 158 (April 1914): 128–38.

Letopis' revoliutsionnogo dvizheniia v Rossii za 1902 g. Saratov, 1924.

Levin, Alfred. *The Second Duma: A Study of the Social-Democratic Party and the Russian Constitutional Experiment*. 2d ed. Hamden, Conn., 1966.

"Libava ili Murman? Iz arkhiva S. Iu. Vitte." *Proshloe i nastoiashchee*, vyp. 1 (1924), pp. 26–39.

Liberman, A. A. "Sostav instituta zemskikh nachal'nikov." *Voprosy istorii* (August 1976): 201–4.

Lieven, Dominic C. B. "The Russian Civil Service under Nicholas II: Variations on the Bureaucratic Theme." *Jahrbücher für Geschichte Osteuropas* 29 (1981): 336–403.

——. "Russian Senior Officialdom under Nicholas II: Careers and Mentalities." *Jahrbücher für Geschichte Osteuropas* 32 (1984): 199–223.

Lindenmeyr, Adele. "Public Poor Relief and Private Charity in Late Imperial Russia." Ph.D. Diss., Princeton University, 1980.

Litvak, B. G. *Ocherki istochnikovedeniia massovoi dokumentatsii XIX–nachala XX v*. Moscow, 1979.

Liubimov, L. D. *Na chuzhbine*. Moscow, 1963.

Lopukhin, A. A. *Nastoiashchee i budushchee russkoi politsii*. Moscow, 1907.

Macey, David A. J. "The Peasantry, the Agrarian Problem, and the Revolution of 1905–1907." *Columbia Essays in International Affairs*. Vol. 7, *The Dean's Papers*. Edited by A. W. Cordier. New York and London, 1972.

Mamadyshskii, N. "Zemstvo v arkhangel'skoi gubernii." *Vestnik Evropy* 41 (January 1910): 298–308.

Mandel, James I. "Paternalistic Authority in the Russian Countryside, 1856–1906." Ph.D. diss., Columbia University, 1978.

Mandel'shtam, M. L. *1905 god v politicheskikh protsessakh: Zapiski zashchitnika*. Moscow, 1931.

Manning, Roberta T. *The Crisis of the Old Order in Russia: Gentry and Government*. Princeton, N.J., 1982

Martynov, A. P. *Moia sluzhba v otdel'nom korpuse zhandarmov: Vospominaniia*. Stanford, Calif., 1972.

Materialy dlia istorii antievreiskikh pogromov v Rossii. 2 vols. Petrograd, 1919–1923.

Materialy k istorii russkoi kontr-revoliutsii. St. Petersburg, 1908.

Materialy po vysochaishe utverzhdennoi osoboi komissii dlia sostavleniia proektov mestnogo upravleniia[MVUOK]. 10 vols. St. Petersburg, n.d.

Mikoian, A. I. *V nachale dvadtsatykh*. Moscow, 1975.

Miliukov. P., et al. *History of Russia*. Translated by Charles Lam Markmann. 3 vols. New York, 1968.

Ministerstvo vnutrennikh del. Departament politsii. *Sbornik sekretnykh tsirkuliarov obrashchennykh nachal'nikam gubernskikh zhandarmskikh upravlenii, gubernatoram i pr. v techenie 1902–1907 gg.* n.p., n.d.

Mitiaev, K. G. *Istoriia organizatsii deloproizvodstva v SSSR*. Moscow, 1959.

Morgan, Glen G. *Soviet Administrative Legality: The Role of the Attorney General's Office*. Stanford, Calif. 1962.

Moses, Joel C. *Regional Party Leadership and Policy Making in the USSR*. New York, 1974.

——. "Regionalism in Soviet Politics: Continuity as a Source of Change, 1953–1982." *Soviet Studies* 37 (April 1985): 184–211.

Mosse, W. E. "Russian Provincial Governors at the End of the Nineteenth Century." *The Historical Journal* 27 (1984): 225–39.

Nardova, V. A. *Gorodskoe samoupravlenie v Rossii v 60-kh–90-kh godov XIX v. Pravitel'stvennaia politika*. Leningrad, 1984.

Novitskii, V. D. *Iz vospominanii zhandarma*. Leningrad, 1929.

Obolenskii, D. D. "Iz vospominanii kniazia D. D. Obolenskogo o N. M. Baranove." *Russkii arkhiv* 39 (October 1901): 258–64.

Obshchii obzor deiatel'nosti Ministerstva vnutrennikh del za tsarstvovaniia Imperatora Aleksandra III. St. Petersburg, 1901.

Obukhov, B. P. *Russkii administrator noveishei shkoly: Zapiska pskovskogo gubernatora B. Obukhova i otvet na nee*. Berlin, 1868.

Obzor trudov vysochaishe uchrezhdennoi pod predsedatel'stvom stats-sekretaria Kakhanova Osoboi Komissii. Edited by M. V. Islavin. 2 vols. St. Petersburg, 1908.

Ocherki istorii SSSR, period feodalizma: Rossiia vo vtoroi chetverti XVIII v. Moscow, 1957.

Ocherki istorii SSSR, period feodalizma; Rossiia vo vtoroi polovine XVIII v. Moscow, 1956.

Ocherki istorii SSSR, period feodalizama: Rossii v pervoi chetverti XVIII v., preobrazovaniia Petra I. Moscow, 1954.

Ol'mniniskii, M. S. *Shchedrinskii slovar'*. Moscow, 1937.

Orlovsky, Daniel T. *The Limits of Reform: The Ministry of Internal Affairs in Imperial Russia, 1802–1881*. Cambridge, Mass., 1981.

Orzhekhovskii, I. V. *Iz istorii vnutrennei politiki samoderzhaviia v 60–70-kh godakh XIX veka: Lektsii po spetskursu*. Gor'kii, 1974.

Otchety po deloproizvodstvu Gosudarstvennogo soveta. 1869–1907. St. Petersburg, 1870–1908.

Paina, E. S. "Senatorskie revizii i ikh arkhivnye materialy (XIX–nachalo XX v.)." *Nekotorye voprosy istoricheskikh dokumentov XIX–nachala XX v.* Leningrad, 1967.

Pamiatnaia knizhka imperatorskogo uchilishcha pravovedeniia. K stoletiiu so dnia ego osnovaniia, 1835–1935. Paris, 1935.

Pankratova, A. M. and L. M. Ivanov, eds. *Rabochee dvizhenie v Rossii v XIX veke: Sbornik dokumentov i materialov*. 4 vols. Moscow, 1950–63.

Pankratova, A. M., et al., eds. *Revoliutsiia 1905–1907 gg. v Rossii: Dokumenty i Materialy*. Moscow, 1955–63.

Patolichev, N. S. *Measures of Maturity: My Early Life*. Translated by Y. S. Shirokov and Y. S. Sviridov. Oxford and New York, 1983. Originally pub. 1977.

Pearson, Thomas S. "Ministerial Conflict and Local Self-government Reform in Russia, 1877–1890" Ph.D. diss., University of North Carolina, 1977

——. "The Origins of Alexander III's Land Captains: A Reinterpretation." *Slavic Review* 40 (Fall 1981): 384–403.

Pershin, P. N. *Agrarnaia revoliutsiia v Rossii: Istoriko-ekonomicheskoe issledovanie*. 2 vols. Moscow, 1966.

Petrunkevich, I. I. "Iz zapisok obshchestvennogo deiatelia." *Arkhiv russkoi revoliutsii* 21. Berlin, 1934.

Pintner, Walter M. "The Russian Higher Civil Service on the Eve of the 'Great Reforms,'" *Journal of Social History* 8 (Spring 1975): 55–68.

——. "The Social Characteristics of the Early Nineteenth Century Russian Bureaucracy." *Slavic Review* 29 (September 1970): 429–43.

Pintner, Walter M. and Don K. Rowney, eds. *Russian Officialdom: The Bureaucratization of Russian Society from the Seventeenth to the Twentieth Century*. Chapel Hill, N.C., 1980.

Pipes, Richard. *Russia under the Old Regime*. New York, 1974.

Pirumova, N. M. *Zemskaia intelligentsia i ee rol' v obshchestvennoi bor'be do nachala XX v.* Moscow, 1986.

——. *Zemskoe liberal'noe dvizhenie. Sotsial'nye korni i evoliutsiia do nachale XX veka*. Moscow, 1977.

Pokrovskii, M. N., ed. *1905. Istoriia revoliutsionnogo dvizheniia v otdel'nikh ocherkakh*. Vol. 1. Moscow, 1926.

Polievktov, M. *Nikolai I: Biografiia i obzor tsarstvovaniia*. Moscow, 1918.

Polnoe sobranie zakonov Rossiiskoi imperii. 1st, 2d, and 3d series. St. Petersburg, 1830–1911.

Popov, F. G. *Letopis' revoliutsionnykh sobytii v samarskoi gubernii, 1902–1917*. Kuibyshev, 1969.

Poulsen, Thomas M. "The Provinces of Russia: Changing Patterns in the Regional Allocation of Authority, 1708–1962." Ph.D. diss. University of Wisconsin, 1963.

Rabochee dvizhenie na iartsevskoi fabrike v 1880–1917 godakh: Sbornik dokumentov i materialov. Smolensk, 1956.

Rabochee dvizhenie v Rossii v 1901–1904 gg.: Sbornik dokumentov. Leningrad, 1975.

Raeff, Marc. "The Bureaucratic Phenomena of Imperial Russia, 1700–1905." *American Historical Review* 84 (April 1979): 399–411.

———. *Michael Speransky, Statesman of Imperial Russia, 1772–1839.* The Hague, 1957.

———. "The Russian Autocracy and Its Officials." *Harvard Slavic Studies* 4 (1957): 77–92.

———. *Understanding Imperial Russia: State and Society in the Old Regime.* Translated by Arthur Goldhammer. New York, 1984. Originally pub. 1982.

Raleigh, Donald J. *Revolution on the Volga: Saratov in 1917.* Ithaca, N.Y., 1986.

Rawson, Donald. "The Death Penalty in Late Tsarist Russia: An Investigation of Judicial Procedures." *Russian History* 9 (Spring 1984): 29–52.

"Reviziia gubernskikh prisutstvii: chernigovskogo, poltavskogo, tambovskogo i saratovskogo (Izvlechenie iz otcheta upravliaiushchego zemskim otdelom d.s.s. Litvinova)." *Izvestiia zemskogo otdela* (1908), no. 4: 240–43; no. 5: 276–81; no. 6: 306–12; no. 7–8: 349–54.

"Reviziia gubernskogo prisutstviia i nekotorykh krest'ianskikh uchrezhdenii novogrodskoi gubernii (Izvlecheniia iz otcheta st. sov. Kupreianova)." *Izvestiia zemskogo otdela* (1908), no. 3: 185–92.

Rigby, T. H. "Early Provincial Cliques and the Rise of Stalin." *Soviet Studies* 33 (January 1981): 3–28.

———. "How the Obkom Secretary Was Tempered." *Problems of Communism* 29 (March–April 1980): 57–63.

———. "The Soviet Regional Leadership: The Brezhnev Generation." *Slavic Review* 37 (March 1978): 1–24.

Robbins, Richard G., Jr. "Choosing the Russian Governors: The Professionalization of the Gubernatorial Corps." *Slavonic and East European Review* 58 (October 1980): 541–60.

———. *Famine in Russia, 1891–1892: The Imperial Government Responds to a Crisis.* New York and London, 1975.

———. "Russia's Famine Relief Law of June 12, 1900: A Reform Aborted." *Canadian American Slavic Studies* 10 (Spring 1976): 25–37.

Rogger, Hans. "The Jewish Policy of Late Tsarism: A Reappraisal." *Wiener Library Bulletin* 25 (1971): 42–51.

———. *Russia in the Age of Modernization and Revolution, 1881–1917.* London and New York, 1983.

———. "Russian Ministers and the Jewish Question, 1881–1917." *California Slavic Studies* 8 Berkeley, Calif., 1975: 15–75.

Rosenberg, William G. *Liberals in the Russian Revolution: The Constitutional Democratic Party, 1917–1921.* Princeton, N.J., 1974.

Rowney, Don K. "Higher Civil Servants in the Russian Ministry of Internal Affairs: Some Demographic and Career Characteristics, 1905–1906." *Slavic Review* 31 (March 1972): 101–10.

———. "The Study of the Imperial Ministry of Internal Affairs in the Light of Organizational Theory." *The Behavioral Revolution and Communist Studies.* Edited by Roger E. Kanet. New York, 1971.

Rubakin, N. "Mnogo li v Rossii chinovnikov? (Iz etiudov o chistoi publike)." *Vestnik Evropy* 45 (January 1910): 111–34.

Rukovodstvo k nagliadnomu izucheniiu administrativnogo techeniia bumag v Rossii. Moscow, 1858.

S., S. "Viatskoe zemstvo." *Vestnik Evropy* 15 (October 1880): 838–77.

Santoni, Wayne D. "P. N. Durnovo as Minister of Internal Affairs in the Witte Cabinet: A Study in Suppression." Ph.D. diss., University of Kansas, 1968.

Sbornik tsirkuliarov nachal'nika saratovskoi gubernii. Saratov, 1875.

Sbornik tsirkuliarov nizhegorodskogo gubernatora po gubernskomu pristutstviiu, a takzhe i samogo gubernskogo prisutstviia za vremia s 1890 po 1 ianvaria 1914. Nizhnii-Novgorod, 1914.

Semennikov, V. P., ed. *Revoliutsiia 1905 i samoderzhavie.* Moscow, 1928.

Shakhovskoi, S. V. *Iz arkhiva kniazia S. V. Shakhovskogo. Materialy dlia istorii nedavnogo proshlogo pribaltiiskoi okrainy (1884–1894 gg.).* 3 vols. St. Petersburg, 1909–1910.

Shenshin, V. *Sbornik tsirkuliarov po administrativnoi chasti lifliandskoi gubernii za 1888–1895 goda.* Riga, 1896.

Shepelev, L. V. "Izuchenie deloproizvodstvennykh dokumentov XIX nachala XX v.." *Vspomogatel'nye istoricheskie distsipliny.* Vol. 1. Leningrad, 1968.

———. *Otemennye istoriei: Chiny, zvaniia i tituly v rossiiskoi imperii.* Leningrad, 1977.

Shipov, D. N. *Vospominaniia i dumy o perezhitom.* Moscow, 1918.

Shreider, G. *Nashi gorodskie obshchestvennye upravleniia.* St. Petersburg, 1902.

Shubin-Pozdeev, N. *Nastol'naia kniga dlia uezdnykh predvoditelei dvorianstva.* 2 vols. St. Petersburg, 1902.

Sinel'nikov, N. P. "Zapiski senatora N. P. Sinel'nikova." *Istoricheskii vestnik* 59 (1895): 39–75; 380–97; 721–36; 60 (1895): 45–57; 373–87; 693–711; 61 (1895): 27–46.

Skal'kovskii, K. A. *Nashi gosudarstvennye i obshchestvennye deiateli.* St. Petersburg, 1891.

Skripitsyn, V. A. *Saratovskie gubernskie vedomosti: Chast' neofitsial'naia, 1888–1894.* Saratov, 1895.

———. *Voistinu chelovek. Iz vospominanii ob Aleksandre Platonoviche Engel'gardt.* St. Petersburg, 1903.

Sletov, P. S. "Vospominanii o N.P. Sinel'nikove." *Istoricheskii vestnik* 51 (1895): 231–37.

Sliozberg, G. B. *Dorevoliutsionnoi stroi Rossii.* Paris, 1933.

Sokolov, K. "Ocherk istorii i sovermennogo znacheniia general-gubernatora." *Vestnik prava* 33 (September 1903): 110–179; (October 1903): 39–75.

Solov'ev, Iu. B. *Samoderzhavie i dvorianstvo v kontse XIX veka.* Leningrad, 1973.

Speranskii, N. N., ed. *1905 god v samarskom krae.* Samara, 1925.

Spiridovich, A. I. *Partiia sotsialistov revoliutsionerov i ee predshestvenniki, 1886–1916.* 2d ed. Petrograd, 1918.

———. *Zapiski zhandarma.* 2d ed. Khar'kov, 1928.

Spisok grazhdanskim chinam pervykh chetrekh klassov. St. Petersburg, 1842–1916.

Spisok litsam, sluzhashchim po vedomstvu Ministerstva vnutrennikh del. St. Petersburg, 1860–1914.

Spisok vysshikh chinov tsentral'nykh i gubernskikh uchrezhdenii Ministerstva vnutrennikh del, namestnichestva na dal'nem vostoke i oblastei, nakhodia-shchikhsia v vedenii Voennogo ministerstva. St. Petersburg, 1904–1916.

Starosel'skii, V. A. "'Dni svobody' v kutaisskoi gubernii." *Byloe* 2 (July 1907): 278–306.

———. "Krest'ianskoe dvizhenie v kutaisskoi gubernii." *Byloe* 1 (September 1906): 229–41; (November 1906): 262–77.

Starr, S. Frederick. *Decentralization and Self-Government in Russia, 1830–1870.* Princeton, N.J., 1972.

Sternheimer, Stephen. "Administering Development and Developing Administration: Organizational Conflict in Tsarist Bureaucracy, 1906–1914." *Canadian-American Slavic Studies* 9 (Fall 1975): 277–301.

———. "Administration and Political Development: An Inquiry into the Tsarist and Soviet Experience." Ph.D. diss. University of Chicago, 1974.

Stoletie viatskoi gubernii: Sbornik materialov k istorii viatskogo kraia. Viatka, 1880.

Strakhovskii, I. M. "Gubernskoe ustroistvo." *Zhurnal ministerstva iustitsii* 19 (September 1913): 28–92; (October 1913): 70–120; (November 1913): 122–71.

———. *Zapiska turgaiskogo gubernatora I. M. Strakhovskogo o preobrazovanii upravleniia turgaiskoi oblasti.* Orenburg, 1901.

Stremoukhov, P. D. "Iz vospominanii o grafe P. A. Valueve." *Russkaia starina* 116 no. 11 (1903): 273–93.

———. "Nizhegorodskii gubernator A. N. Murav'ev (Iz vospominanii)." *Russkaia starina* 106 no. 5 (1901): 349–61.

Stremoukhov, P. P. "Moia bor'ba s episkomom Germogenom i Iliodorom." *Arkhiv russkoi revoliutsii* 16 (1925): 5–48.

Svod vysochaishikh otmetok po vsepoddanneishim otchetam general-gubernatorov, gubernatorov, voennykh gubernatorov i gradonachal'nikov za 1881–1902. 20 vols. St. Petersburg, 1882–1904.

Svod zakonov Rossiiskoi imperii. Vol. 2. St. Petersburg, 1857, 1876. 1892.

Taranovski, Theodore. "The Politics of Counter-Reform: Autocracy and Bureaucracy in the Reign of Alexander III, 1881–1894." Ph.D. diss., Harvard University, 1976.

Taylor, Jackson, Jr. "Dmitri Andreevich Tolstoi and the Ministry of the Interior, 1882–1889." Ph.D. diss., New York University, 1970.

Thurston, Robert W. "Urban Problems and Local Government in Late Imperial Russia: Moscow, 1906–1914." Ph.D. diss., University of Michigan, 1980.

Timberlake, Charles, ed. *Essays on Russian Liberalism.* Columbia, Mo., 1972.

Trubetskoi, P. P. *Pamiatnaia kniga dlia uezdnogo predvoditelia dvorianstva.* Odessa, 1887.

Umanets, S. I. *Vospominaniia o kniaze S. V. Shakhovskom i baltiiskie ocherki.* St. Petersburg, 1899.

Urussov, [Urusov] S. D. *Memoirs of a Russian Governor.* Translated by Herman Rosenthal. London and New York, 1908. Originally pub. 1907.

Ushakov, I. F. *Kol'skaia zemlia: Ocherki istorii murmanskoi oblasti v dooktiabr'skii period.* Murmansk, 1972.

Usilenie gubernatorskoi vlasti. Edited by P. B. Struve. Paris, 1906.

Veselovskii, B. B. *Istoriia zemstva za sorok let.* 4 vols. St. Petersburg, 1909–1911.

Viktor Antonovich Artsimovich—Vospominaniia—karakteristika. St. Petersburg, 1904.

Walkin, Jacob. *The Rise of Democracy in Pre-Revolutionary Russia: Political and Social Institutions under the Last Three Czars,* New York, 1963.

Weissman, Neil B. *Reform in Tsarist Russia: The State Bureaucracy and Local Government.* New Brunswick, N.J., 1981.

——. "Regular Police in Tsarist Russia, 1900–1914." *Russian Review* 44 (1985): 45–68.

Whelan, Heide. *Alexander III and the State Council: Bureaucracy and Counter-Reform in Late Imperial Russia.* New Brunswick, N.J., 1982.

Wortman, Richard S. *The Development of a Russian Legal Consciousness.* Chicago, 1976.

Yaney, George L. "Bureaucracy as Culture: A Comment." *Slavic Review* 41 (Spring 1982): 104–11.

——. *The Systematization of Russian Government: Social Evolution in the Domestic Administration of Imperial Russia, 1711–1905.* Urbana, Ill., 1973.

——. *The Urge to Mobilize: Agrarian Reform in Russia, 1861–1930.* Urbana, Ill., 1982.

The Years 1881–1894 in Russia: A Memorandum Found in the Papers of N. Kh. Bunge. A Translation and a Commentary. Translated and edited by George E. Snow. Philadelphia, 1981.

Zaionchkovskii, P. A. "Gubernskaia administratisiia nakanune krymskoi voiny." *Voprosy istorii,* September 1975, pp. 33–51.

——. *Krizis samoderzhaviia na rubezhe 1870–1880-kh godov.* Moscow, 1964.

——. *Pravitel'stvennyi apparat samoderzhavnoi Rossii v XIX v.* Moscow, 1978.

——. *Rossiiskoe samoderzhavie v kontse XIX stoletiia.* Moscow, 1970.

——. *Samoderzhavie i russkaia armiia na rubezhe XIX–XX stoletii.* Moscow, 1973.

Zakharova, L. G. *Zemskaia konterreforma 1890 g.* Moscow, 1968.

"Zapiski V. M. Zhemchuzhnikova: Iz posmertnikh bumag." *Vestnik Evropy* 34 (February 1899): 634–64.

Zhilkin, I. V. "Provintsial'noe obozrenie." *Vestnik Evropy* 48 (January 1913): 371–79; (February 1913): 365–77; (June 1913): 335–43; (July 1913): 370–78; 49 (March 1914): 356–63.

Zhurnaly Vysochaishe uchrezhdennoi osoboi kommisii dlia sostavleniia proektov mestnogo upravleniia. St. Petersburg, 1881–1885.

[Zinov'ev, N. A.] *Kurskoe zemstvo: Otchet po revizii proizvedennoi v 1904 godu senatorom N. A. Zinov'evym.* 2 vols. St. Petersburg, 1906.

——. *Otchet po revizii t.s. Zinov'eva zemskikh uchrezhdenii moskovskoi gubernii.* 3 vols. St. Petersburg, 1904.

——. *Otchet po revizii zemskikh uchrezhdenii viatskoi gubernii.* 3 vols. St. Petersburg, 1905.

Zuckerman, Frederic Scott. "The Russian Political Police at Home and Abroad (1880–1917): Its Struture, Functions, and Methods and Its Struggle with the Organized Opposition." Ph.D. diss., New York University, 1973.

Zyrianov, P. N. "Sotsial'naia struktura mestnogo upravleniia kapitalisticheskoi Rossii (1861–1914 gg.)." *Istoricheskie zapiski* 107 (1982): 226–302.

INDEX

Library of Congress Cataloging-in-Publication Data

Robbins, Richard G., 1939–
  The Tsar's viceroys.

  Bibliography: p.
  Includes index.
  1. Local government—Soviet Union—History.   2. Soviet Union—
Governors—History.   3. Soviet Union—Politics and government—1894–
1917.   I. Title.
JS6063.R6   1987   320.8'0947   87-47700
ISBN 0-8014-2046-6 (alk. paper)